CARDINAL CUSHING
OF BOSTON

RICHARD CARDINAL CUSHING

CARDINAL CUSHING

OF BOSTON

by

John Henry Cutler

HAWTHORN BOOKS, INC.   PUBLISHERS   NEW YORK

For Rob, Dave, Meg, Gail, and Rick

CARDINAL CUSHING OF BOSTON

ACKNOWLEDGMENTS

ALTHOUGH millions of words have been written about Richard Cardinal Cushing in newspapers, magazines, and books, much of the untold story of his life exists in the recollections of friends, colleagues, clergymen of almost every faith, politicians, and statesmen. Most of the new anecdotes which illumine the personality of the prelate came from them.

During my research in southern Ireland in the spring of 1968 I received complete cooperation from Peter Kilroy and Walter Mahon-Smith, editors of *The Catholic Standard*, and from the editors of the leading newspapers in Dublin, who also gave me full access to their files on Cushing. I had pleasant and rewarding interviews with President Eamon de Valera; Lord Mayor Colum Kilcullen, of Waterford; former Lord Mayor Sean McCarthy, of Cork; his successor, Lord Mayor Pearse Wyse; as well as with the Very Reverend Michael Canon Hurley, P. P. Richard Rice, and James Fouhy, all of Glanworth. I received information from the Reverend John O'Shea, Whitechurch, County Cork; the Reverend Matthew Sheehan, of St. Colman's Seminary in Cork; the Mother Abbess of Collettine, P. C. Monastery, Ballsbridge, Dublin; Joseph Murphy, of the *Irish Echo*; and Mrs. John (Kitty) Tobin, the last Dahill descendant in the vicinity of Ballyduff, who shed light on Cardinal Cushing's mother. Gearoid F. O'Clerigh, who in 1968 was the Irish Consul General in Boston, was most cooperative.

Genealogical data came from Yvette Adams, George Henefield, Goddard Light (former president of the Rye Historical Society), and Attorney Daniel E. Kelly, all of Rye, New York. Mr. Kelly handled the legal affairs of the "Cushion" branch of the family for almost half a century. Mrs. Geraldine Zuccaro and Mrs. Dorothy Bruce, both of Portchester, New York, provided further information on the cardinal's forebears.

Some of the information in this book came from extended interviews with the late mayors James Michael Curley, of Boston, and William O'Dwyer, of New York; the late Senator Michael Ward; and John Murtagh, former Chief Magistrate of New York. Thanks to the continuing cooperation of former Mayor John B. Hynes, of Boston, I interviewed many principals in the Cushing story, including Judge Francis X. Morrissey; Richard J. Condon, head of the St. Vincent de Paul Society; Senator George Kenneally; Maurice Donahue, president of the Massachusetts Senate; and Francis Kelly, former Attorney General and Lieutenant Governor of the Commonwealth. I wish also to thank Frank Buxton, former editor of the Boston *Herald;* Milton E. Lord, former director of the Boston Public Library; his successor, Philip McNiff; associate director John J. Connolly; assistant director Francis X. Moloney; and other librarians, including Joseph B. O'Neil, James A. Monahan, and Max Anapolle, who uncovered information that might otherwise have escaped my notice.

For anecdotes and items of human interest I thank Maeve Brennan, Judge Joseph Collins, the late Edwin O'Connor, Harold Kaese, "Bud" Collins, Clement Norton, Professor Warren McIsaac, Nathan M. Pusey, Frankland W. L. Miles, Jr., Krister Stendahl, William Duncliffe, and Lester Zwick and John Murphy, of the *Record-American,* plus those wonderful librarians in the "morgue"; Alison Arnold, John H. Fenton, Rocco Paoletta, and the librarian at the Boston *Herald Traveler;* Daisy Weichel, Arch MacDonald, Paul Benzaquin, William Hahn, and especially Marjorie Mills, who set up many appointments that proved fruitful, including one with Mrs. Vincent (Marie) Green, who was in close touch with the cardinal during the sixteen years she served as president of The League of Catholic Women.

Although space does not permit mention of everyone who contributed to this book, I want to single out the Reverend Dr. James T. Murphy, whose family knew the Cushings early in the century in South Boston, and Mrs. Frank Courtney, Mrs. Maurice Brodie, Mrs. John J. Canty, and Robert Heffernan, who supplied material for the early chapters. I also thank Ruth Wakefield, Gerald Kilcullen, Teresa S. Fitzpatrick, Laura White, Paul Maguire, Lawrence Stone, Sidney Rabb, Mary Kelleher, Joseph DeMambro, Ralph Tedeschi, Frank Christian, George Putnam, Joseph Lund, Charles F. Eaton, Jr., James Kelso, Roger Babb, John Murdock, Richard Lamere, Leo Motley, David Mittell, James Dickson, Torrey Capo, James Carroll, Stanley Blinstrub, Joseph Dever, Pierce Robinson, Alan Fox, Mrs. J. Hindon Hyde, Winona Strachan, and the Reverends Joseph Fichte, Francis Cloherty, and A. Alan

Travers. Of all the religious I interviewed, none gave a clearer insight into the warmth and humanity of Cardinal Cushing than did Sister Irenea, C.D.P., and Sister Angela Marie, of Albertus Magnus College, Connecticut. Station WEEI permitted me to listen to both the taped and untaped Howard Nelson Show on which the cardinal spoke at length, and station WNAC-TV gave me a private showing of a documentary film on Cushing. Another private showing at the Boston Public Library of the elevation of Cushing to the cardinalate made me feel I was witnessing the proceedings.

Finally, I thank my son, David, who researched the files of *The New York Times,* and my mother-in-law, Cid Ricketts Sumner, who took so many kinks out of the first draft.

Those that remain belong solely to me.

J. H. C.
Duxbury, Massachusetts
December, 1969

CONTENTS

A section of photographs appears on pages 143 to 160.

It is a great disgrace to religion, to imagine that it is an enemy to mirth and cheerfulness, and a severe exacter of pensive looks and solemn faces.

Sir Walter Scott

chapter one

ORIGINS OF A "SOUTHIE"

GLANWORTH, where a parliament for all Ireland once sat, is a village in the rolling hills of southern Ireland about thirty miles northeast of the city of Cork and five miles from the busy marketplace of Fermoy. Along with its ancient landmarks and historic ruins, it has a Marist shrine on the site of the "Cushion" homestead.* The tiny thatched stone cottage has long since crumbled away, but the spot is not forgotten.

Late in August 1953, after a wearisome drive along winding dusty roads, Archbishop Richard James Cushing of Boston visited Glanworth for the first time.[1] The villagers of the flag-draped community, in full regalia and with pipes playing, paraded a hundred yards up a knoll to a hill overlooking a lush green valley. Here Archbishop Cushing knelt in silent prayer at a temporary altar near the stone monument that marked the birthplace of his father. Its inscription reads: "Here dwelt Patrick Cushing, father of Most Reverend Dr. Richard J. Cushing, Archbishop of Boston."

A detachment of Irish army reserves with fixed bayonets was drawn up as the archbishop approached the nearby Holy Cross Church. The band played "The Star-Spangled Banner," and the troops presented arms. Bishop James Roche and Canon Michael J. Hurley, pastor of the church, greeted the prelate, who, after the benediction, gave Canon Hurley a check for ten thousand dollars to build pews in memory of his father. The archbishop told the congregation that he knew little about his father other than that he had "emigrated to America, worked hard as a blacksmith, and thought

---

* The branch of the family that emigrated to Rye, New York, spelled the family name "Cushion." The Boston family used the "Cushing" spelling; Cardinal Cushing has no idea why.

I

only of his children. That is why I am here today." He told the villagers to stay in Ireland and stop dreaming about greener pastures. "A different situation prevailed when my parents emigrated. There was a famine here then."

Oral tradition often takes the place of vital statistics in the villages of southern Ireland. From the scanty evidence available, it appears that in the 1850s the first Cushings moved from Newmarket, County Cork, to Glanworth. According to evidence given to the editors of *The Catholic Standard* by patriarchs of Glanworth, the first Cushings (Cushions) were "workers with Canon Alwart, a Protestant vicar at the Glebe, Glanworth. James, a convert from England, who had a brother, John Cushion, a tailor in England, married and had four children, one of whom was Patrick, the cardinal's father. The only daughter was Nora, known as Nan, who married Thomas Morrissey, and died in Glanworth." According to Richard Rice, who remembers Patrick Cushing well, the Morrissey ancestral home was "at the top of the village," and it was drafty. "As much smoke used to come out the door as went up the chimney," Rice recalls.[2]

The other sons of James Cushion were Richard and John, both of whom went to America. Richard settled in Rye, New York, where he was a blacksmith. John, a tailor who had learned his trade in England from his uncle (John Cushion), had worked at his specialty in Glanworth until his children grew up. After coming to America, where he was unhappy, he returned to Glanworth to spend a few years with the Richard Rice family. After that he came back to Boston, where he died.

There was one forge at the end of the Cushion homestead in Glanworth, and there James Cushion and his sons, Richard and Patrick, made nails by hand until machine-made products ruined the business. When Richard Cushion invited his brother Patrick to join him in Rye, Pat jumped at the opportunity.

In 1879, the young nail-maker left Glanworth with all his belongings in a cart of the kind natives of Ireland call "ass carts." The night before was one to remember, with the merrymaking, tearful farewells, and priestly blessing, typical of the emigration story of the time. As late as 1958, David Gibbons, a friend and neighbor of the Cushions, who in 1879 was a schoolboy, remembered seeing Pat drive down an "unkept" road to the desolate Ballyhooley railway station on his way to Cobh, where an emigrant ship was waiting in the beautiful harbor cupped in a natural amphitheater.[3] Cobh was then the principal port of call for transatlantic liners.

As the ship slowly headed out to open sea, Pat looked back on the soaring spire of majestic St. Colman's Cathedral. From the deck he caught his last glimpse of Erin. There must have been tears in his eyes as he left that harbor of tragic memory for hundreds of thousands of earlier Irish emigrants who, in the years of the potato famine, from 1845 until 1855, paid the twenty-dollar fare to cross the Atlantic in "coffin" ships. In one year, more than thirty thousand of the hundred thousand Irish passengers died during the six-week voyage.

Familiar with horses and donkeys in the homeland, many Irish immigrants in America became blacksmiths, as well as hostlers, stablers, and coachmen, and the colleens became the charwomen and domestics considered so gauche by the Yankees, who called them "girls fresh out of the bogs." They told of one who always came downstairs backward because stairs had been unknown in her Irish home, where she had always used a ladder.

After a two-year apprenticeship to a blacksmith in rural Rye, Pat was ready to answer a want ad in a Boston newspaper for a similar job in South Boston. In 1849, a Bostonian considered it "something of a sensation" to see an Irishman in South Boston, but by 1871, that section was filling up with alien illiterates from Ireland.

Boston, originally a narrow peninsula, was surrounded by water or marshland except at Roxbury Neck, and even there, in heavy storms, the overflow made the city an island until early Irish immigrants filled in sections. They leveled the hills and, to create more living room, narrowed rivers and filled in canals, tidal inlets, and marshlands. Some of Boston's present streets were once canals, and much of modern Boston was submerged or was wasteland at high tide until the latter part of the nineteenth century.

By the time of the Civil War, Boston was still confined to the original peninsula, with only two outlying areas: East Boston, as Noddle's Island was coming to be known, and South Boston, a peninsula that curved a protective arm into Boston Harbor. According to a local historian, "Boston, proudest of all the cities of a proud old Commonwealth, has no prouder section than that known as South Boston, a hilly peninsula thrust out into the beautiful harbor like the arm of a combatant on guard." [4]

South Boston, Erin-oriented from the landing of the first Irishmen and soon to become the heartland of Irish democracy in America, had been planned as a fashionable suburb, with wide roadways designed for carriage traffic, and lanes for mews.[5] Its waterfront, however, attracted industry and provided jobs as longshoremen, stevedores, and teamsters for newly arrived Irishmen, some of whom also found work in the area's factories and machine shops that processed raw materials brought in by ships. Elsewhere in Boston, other once elegant residential neighborhoods were also declining.

The earliest immigrants, who came to Boston because it was the terminal of the Cunard Line packet ships, were the outcasts, "the base of the social pyramid," [6] prompting one historian to call them "the worst-treated white minority that has ever existed." [7] They were the muckers—the dig-and-toss blacklegs of the pick-and-shovel pool of cheap labor who built sewers, water systems, and housing. William Shannon mentions an Irishman's thoughts after reading of an immigrant's death by drowning in 1836: "How often do we see such paragraphs in the paper as an Irishman drowned . . . crushed by a beam . . . suffocated in a pit . . . blown to atoms by a steam engine—ten, twenty Irishmen buried alive by the sinking of a bank." [8] The hapless, unskilled, illiterate laborers wore themselves out lifting, hauling, digging ditches, carrying the hod, or driving garbage wagons in all weather from dawn to dusk. Many of them died in their late thirties or early forties. Emerson, in a letter to Thoreau, mentioned his surprise at learning that local Irish laborers worked a fifteen-hour day for fifty cents, adding: "Theodore Parker observed in Boston in 1846 that he rarely saw a 'gray-haired Irishman,' inferring that they all died young." [9]

In the 1850s, Irish laborers could not earn enough to raise a family, and matters got no better in ensuing years. "During the first-year depression of the Civil War," writes Francis Russell, "the newcomers in their Paddyvilles and Mick Alleys starved." He noted that construction bosses from all over America hired Irishmen. "The Paddies went as contract laborers in coaches with sealed doors, the curtains nailed across the windows. Along the Erie Canal and the new railroad lines they died like flies." [10]

During the Civil War, jerry-builders threw up two- and three-decker tenements for Irish laborers as South Boston became a community of workingmen who earned from nine to twelve dollars a week. Some families, like the parents of United States House Speaker

John W. McCormack, couldn't afford $1.25 a week for rent. The family stove was fueled with stray lumps of coal picked up in the railroad yards, and the McCormack children often had to go to a community center for a "pauper's basket" of dried fish, a bag of potatoes, and occasionally a few onions. Conditions were especially wretched for large Irish families. In the desolation that followed when the head of a house died in the prime of life, his sons, at the age of twelve, thirteen, or fourteen, were forced to quit school and work up to fourteen hours a day hauling freight, carrying the hod, or doing other menial work. To keep the family fed, clothed, and housed, wives had to earn supplementary income. It was a time of heartbreak, as Oscar Handlin suggests: "In Ireland they had occupied a clearly defined and important position in the cottiers' economy. That place being gone, they went off to serve at the table of strangers and to bring home the bitter bread of banishment." [11]

In 1882, soon after Patrick Cushing had settled in South Boston, "a Puck cartoon derided an Irish ditchdigger laying city sewer pipe while others ineptly carried hods, tamped stones and troweled bricks as their womenfolk took in washing." [12] This dismal economic picture lasted through most of Pat's life, although he provided his family with comforts lacking in many neighboring Irish Catholic families. Some of the luckier and more enterprising Irishmen in South Boston found jobs as butchers, soap or leather salesmen, bartenders, grocers, and blacksmiths. Meanwhile, thanks to their church and the intolerance of the entrenched Yankee * Protestants, they were welded into a unit by their fanatic loyalty to one another. "If God came down to South Boston and ran for office against a fellow born in the district, He'd be licked," a saying went. Cushing would often mention this loyalty.

By the end of the century, South Boston was still overwhelmingly Irish Catholic and politically Democratic. Unlike other immigrant-dominated districts, such as East Boston and the North and West Ends, "Southie" was a relatively settled community. In the other sec-

---

* According to William V. Shannon, the term "Yankee" includes not only descendants of the original colonists but also those who emigrated to the city from farms and small towns of New England during the nineteenth century and the Protestant immigrants from Nova Scotia and other parts of eastern Canada. The term "Brahmins" refers to Yankee aristocrats. Swamp Yankees are white Anglo-Saxon Protestants who have money or professional prestige but not "blue blood."

tions succeeding waves of immigration replaced one another; as the Italians moved in, the Irish moved out. "New immigrants," including Slavs, Poles, Jews, Portuguese, and French, later supplanted the Italians, but South Boston remained an Irish Catholic citadel for almost half a century. Thus, many of those who were born and reared there during the last decade of the nineteenth century and the first decade of the twentieth were second or third generation Irish Americans.[13]

Patrick Cushing's schooling in hardship in Ireland steeled him for the grim existence in South Boston. "My father perfected his trade as a blacksmith," Cardinal Cushing recalled, "and in the days of horse-cars in Boston he worked for the old Boston Elevated. So did his brother Richard.* Pat Cushing had shod horses in the blacksmith shop in Rye, but in South Boston he was primarily a wheelwright, working in the long narrow pits in a block-sized car barn near his home. He spent most of his eleven-hour day, seven-day week, bent over white-hot wheels at an open forge of the trolley car repair pit in the division five car barn of the Boston Elevated Railway. On Sundays the boss gave him an hour off to attend church. His salary was seventeen dollars a week—more than motormen and streetcar conductors received. His children called him "Pa." Easygoing, serene, and affable, Pat was reticent and shy. His son, Richard, ascribes his "silences" to a work load that left him all but numb with exhaustion.

South Boston Irishmen, like others in the city, worked, suffered, prayed, and raised large families while sending home for "greenhorn" relatives, ever mindful of the continuing scorn in which they would be held. Pat Cushing's relatives were coming, the dates of their arrival,

---

* This statement differs from that of Daniel E. Kelly, an attorney in Rye, New York, who for many years handled the legal affairs of the Cushion family. In a letter dated September 16, 1968, Kelly, then eighty-seven, wrote: "My information is that Richard (Senior), brother of Patrick, remained in Rye and never journeyed to Boston. The Cushion blacksmith shop here in Rye was run by him during his lifetime. The old shop remained an eyesore for a number of years and gradually so deteriorated that it was razed as a public hazard in 1958, but the Cushion house still stands on a bluff overlooking the Post Road. Richard Senior had six children: Mary Jane, Rebecca V., Annie R., John, James and Richard, and none of them ever married. The last member of the Cushion family was Annie, at whose funeral Cardinal Cushing officiated." Richard Senior apparently died in Rye city limits before 1904, since the City Clerk's office has no record previous to that date. After his death his sons James and John ran the blacksmith shop.

hazy. It would be a tedious exercise in futility to set down an account of the ebb and flow of Cushings in Boston. According to a weekly newspaper published in Ireland, "The question is often asked in Glanworth, 'How many years is Johnny Cushing in America?' Johnny, a brother of Patrick, left some years later. One old lady, when seeking the old age pension, gave her age by saying she was born the night that Johnny Cushing left for America." [14] According to Canon Hurley, John's ten children came to America in pairs, and several of them died prematurely.[15]

Among new immigrants were the Dahills from the townland of Toornageeha, two miles north of Ballyduff village on the banks of the Glounagad stream in County Waterford. In the late 1880s, Mary Dahill, Cardinal Cushing's mother, left Cobh as a steerage passenger on the Cunarder *Pavonia*. The eldest of six children—three boys and three girls—she took a job as a cook in the home of a Yankee judge. Although she earned only two dollars a week, she sent money to Ireland to "bring out" the remaining Dahills. They settled in a tenement near South Boston's waterfront, which, at low tide, according to Speaker McCormack, who was born and raised in "Good Old Southie," consisted of "stinking mudflats."

Mary Dahill's mother was a regular communicant of nearby Saint Eulalia's Church. Her two sisters worked as domestics or in local factories and shops, and her brothers—James, Thomas, and John—became day laborers.

Mary Dahill had switched jobs by the time she met a blacksmith's helper named Patrick Cushing, a bachelor, who ate at Mrs. Ness's boarding house at the corner of K Street and Broadway. Mary prepared meals for Mrs. Ness, and Pat found them delicious. She was impressed by his courtesy and humility and was flattered when he praised her cooking.

As early as 1866, there were two Roman Catholic parishes in South Boston: Saints Peter and Paul and the newly created Gate of Heaven Church. After their marriage in the latter church in 1890, Mary and Patrick moved into a cold-water flat in a boxy, wooden three-decker on East Third Street, a few minutes' walk from the car barn where Pat worked. Living conditions were primitive. "If there was any toilet at all," Cardinal Cushing recalled, "it was in the cellar.* For a bath

---

* Once, while showing a group around the cardinal's residence, Cushing gestured toward the elegant surroundings. "What do I need with a joint like this? In South Boston we had an outhouse."

you went to a public bathhouse; for a swim, to the beach right down the street."

Their first child, Elizabeth, was born in 1892 and was followed by Mary Jane, Richard James (named for his Uncle Richard), Anna, and John. One child, Rebecca, died in infancy. By the time Anna was born in 1899, the family had moved to larger quarters at 44 O Street.

On August 25, 1895, Mary and Patrick put on their best clothes and watched in Gate of Heaven Church while the Reverend Thomas Brannan baptized their first son. Here Richard would later receive his first Communion and the sacrament of Confirmation.

After two daughters, Pat was delighted to have a son and heir. By this time, according to his fellow workers, America, except for Ireland, was the greatest country to be born in, and South Boston the best community in the nation. With its intermingling of rich and poor, "Southie" was a friendly, tightly knit community with the neighborliness of a small town. It was a pleasant district, with a sandy beach that terminated in a pier at one end and an island promontory commanding a view of Boston Harbor at the other. There were open fields across from the tenements. The Headhouse at City Point, a short walk from the Cushing home, was opened to the public in 1896. The Headhouse, which would be another pleasure spot for young Cushing and his friends, was a picturesque building that resembled a medieval German municipal council house. On both sides of it were long flights of steps leading to a promenade platform that flanked the building and led directly to an iron pier. Beneath and between these platforms were bathing accommodations for five hundred persons. No other Paddyville of the era had so many diversions.

Although living conditions for Irish Catholics were still poor, they had improved by the turn of the century. More and more became policemen and firemen, and soon there would be Irish Catholic school teachers as the Irish assumed political control.

Pat and Mary Cushing were glad the road would be smoother for their children than it had been for them. A wheelwright at the car barn told Pat that if young Dick did not prove strong enough to become a blacksmith, he could, with his father's influence, get a job as motorman or conductor on one of the new electric trolleys, which were replacing horsecars at the end of the century. In the opinion of blacksmiths and wheelwrights, who prided themselves on their trade, running a trolley would give a man professional standing far above that of a horsecar driver.

Pat, in his quiet way, nodded, but in his heart he knew that the best thing he could give his children was a good education. America was one place where an educated man could get ahead. After all, Archbishop John Joseph Williams, who had come to America early in the century when his Halifax-bound ship was blown off course, was the son of a Tipperary blacksmith. It was a comforting thought for Patrick and Mary. Their son might even set his sights higher and become a priest. They had reason to think so. South Boston produced more nuns and priests than any other community in the nation. Cardinal Cushing would one day say that his home town was "a veritable nursery for priests." It was also a nursery for politicians. As a South Boston barkeep summed it up years later: "The Irish and the Catholics, you know what they done. They dug their ditch and their kids went into politics. That's the only way they survive."

They went into politics—or they became priests.

chapter two

THE HARD WAY

I<small>N</small> 1950 Cardinal Cushing recalled the days of his youth: "I was born and brought up in a tenement district. We were ordinary people, poor, but comfortable. I loved my neighbors because they were neighborly. When, as a boy, I was sick or lonely, they took care of me. South Boston folks are still a laboring people, born and brought up in an area which has contributed greatly to America's way of life. The people . . . have a tremendous love for one another, and a tremendous interest in one another. Protestant, Catholic, and Jewish, they are all wonderful folks who work together." [1] He preferred the community to Ireland. After an early trip to the old country when he was an archbishop, the prelate again spoke of his boyhood: "They were good years. There is nothing so beautiful over there as my South Boston."

The Cushing children grew up in a climate of good humor, warmth, patient understanding, and family loyalty. Mary and Pat had brought from Ireland the deep, comforting belief in Catholicism typical of refugees, and this they imparted to their children. While the Cushing home lacked luxuries, it was a solid household in which hard work and love for one's fellow man was stressed. In the *Pilot,* the archdiocesan newspaper, Cardinal Cushing wrote: "The family is the unit of society, the kindergarten where we learn to live as children of God. Here fathers and mothers devoted to their vocation bring up children to shoulder their own independent lives." Friends and neighbors considered the Cushings worthy members of the community, and Richard, who got his height from his blue-eyed, dark-haired mother, and his arm and shoulder strength from his sturdy father, who was of medium height, was a devoted son.

Like the home, the church was a focal point of community life. Religion, Cushing has said, "was as much a part of the family as eating or breathing. It was never talked about much. It was a simple fact of life." [2] The Cushings said the rosary together every night, and Father

Cushing never sat down to a meal at the kitchen table without saying grace. When Richard was ten, his mother asked at the breakfast table whether he had said his prayers.

"No, Mama. I forgot."

"What are you, a heathen?" [3]

Except for the family Bible and a few books, there was no library. The children depended on their schools and the public library for their reading. They were a closely knit family who enjoyed being together, especially on Christmas, when the children emptied their stockings.

"Youth has its own schedule," Archbishop Cushing recalled, "and visiting grandparents, granduncles, grandaunts can be a bore, let's face it. Yet how often a grown man finds satisfaction in the evenings he gave to that generation, recalling how much comfort his visits afforded." Considering the limited opportunity for adult recreation early in the century, it is easy to understand the pleasure the old folks got from such visits.

"We did everything the hard way," Cushing recalled. "My parents seemed to take no recreation at all. Life was simply a daily grind. There was no piano, no conveniences." [4] There was little time for Pat Cushing to play his home-made flute. On his way home from work, he might stop in a pub, the poor man's club, for a beer, but generally he enjoyed staying at home with his family. "We were happiest at sundown, during the pleasant seaside evenings of spring and summer and fall," the cardinal remembered. "We would be sitting on the front steps at O Street. We were relaxed and trying to console one another. We talked about the weather and everything under the sun." [5]

In the evening, when friends or relatives dropped in for a glass of beer or a cup of tea, the group might play whist, hearts, or casino, while the children played dominoes or checkers, or they might sit in the parlor chatting. On Saturday nights the neighborhood often resounded with music for a jig, reel, or hornpipe, but Lucius Beebe was not speaking of the Cushing household when he wrote that South Boston was one of the "shabby but joyous and at times riotous outposts of the Old Sod." [6] The Cushings did not even have a Graphophone.

One imported custom was "waking the dead." There was a time in Ireland when wakes were far merrier than weddings, but the traditional custom had virtually died in Ireland. "There's no fun in dying any more," an oldtimer recently complained in Connemara, where traces of old style wakes linger.[7] In South Boston, wakes were at times boisterous, full of good humor and heavy drinking, but for the most part they were somber occasions. Neighbors and relatives, usually bringing food, came to console the surviving members of bereaved families, kneeling in prayer by the corpse, which was laid out in the parlor. There were always bowls of tobacco for the men's clay pipes. After lighting up, they gathered in the kitchen to talk and drink while the women keened in the parlor and "the guttering candles cast flickering shadows on the waxen features of the corpse," writes John Fenton.[8] At least one member of the family would sit up through two nights with the body of the departed, and the parish priest always came to lead the mourners in the rosary. "No matter what sort of a life the departed might have led, he was a saint until after the funeral mass on the third morning. One of the stories that is still told in South Boston is of the gang foreman who said to the widow of one of his ditch-diggers, 'Pat was a good shoveler; not a fancy shoveler, mind you, but a good shoveler.' " [9]

Irish politicians collected votes at wakes. During Cushing's childhood, John F. (Honey Fitz) Fitzgerald, who daily scanned death notices in the Boston *Globe*, rarely missed a wake, where he demonstrated his thespian gift of easy tears. Honey Fitz and other colorful politicians staged many such shows, which impressed an adolescent Dick Cushing in days when lamplighters came around to light gaslights at night and extinguish them in the morning.

Life moved faster than it did in the Old Sod, where a donkey cart might stop for a few minutes to let a dozen cattle cross a dirt road. Swaying trolleys went up and down Broadway, and delivery carts and horse-drawn wagons lurched and clattered through streets littered with horse droppings, added to by the horses that pulled the street sweepers and watering carts.

Hucksters shouted their wares, and the driver of a junk wagon, snapping the reins on his horse's haunches, yodeled between his "Giddaps": "Any rags today?" The sleepy-eyed banana peddler, pushing a cart laden with fruit and vegetables all the way from the wholesale market district in the North End, was less communicative than the white-frocked, straw-hatted driver of the James H. White Company butcher wagon, who often exchanged greetings with Mother Mary Cushing. Every morning after sweeping the sidewalk in front of her house, she walked to the grocery store to buy the staples—bread, meat, potatoes, cabbages, and (when they were in season), fresh peas

—and pickles and baked beans and brown bread for Saturday's supper. Along with tipcart peddlers and the jingle of wagons jouncing over the pavement were hawkers who sold ice as well as bags of coal or coke and bundles of kindling. Boys in the neighborhood followed the coal wagons, hoping they would drop a few lumps. When pickings were scarce during the winter, they threw snowballs at the drivers, who, falling for the bait, in their wrath would heave lumps of coal at them.

It was a picturesque world of guttural chants intermingled with the nostalgic music ground out by the hurdy-gurdy man with his performing monkey who doffed his cap after picking up coins thrown out of tenement windows. Young Dick and his friends on a hot summer day caught chips of ice flying out from under the iceman's pick, but it was more of a treat when the horse-drawn Boston Molasses Company tank truck with its dangling rubber hose drove into the neighborhood. The boys would rush into whoever's house was nearest for a hunk of bread and stick it into the hose until it was saturated with molasses. This was more fun than hanging around street corners with thirty or forty friends until the cops, wearing tall gray helmets, and fingering their billies suggestively, ordered them to move on. Sometimes the gang strolled over to Fort Point Canal to watch Irish stevedores unload sugar and molasses from Puerto Rican ships, for there were refineries along South Boston's waterfront.

Mother Cushing soon became adjusted to her new environment, where everyone dressed so differently than in Ireland. There were times when she longed for the sight of the women of Cork in their traditional hooded cloaks, but she enjoyed her shopping tours at Falvey's,* the popular department store, and at Cassidy's. After he became cardinal, Cushing wrote to a milliner who had congratulated him: "I well recall the store in South Boston and I well remember my beloved mother speaking of 'Cassidy's' in referring to the famous milliner. In memory of old times, I am sending you the enclosed spiritual bouquet witnessing to a mass I will celebrate for you." [10]

The home was the center of activity. Here Mother Cushing, who did the family washing, ironing, mending, and cooking, was also the disciplinarian, stern enough on occasion to use a razor strap. She called her older son Richard unless she was annoyed with him; then

* The Falvey Brothers Company Building was at the corner of West Broadway and F Street.

it was Richard James—a warning to brace for a scolding, if not a strapping. Once, when his sister Elizabeth found him weeping because he felt he had been unfairly punished, she sent him into the kitchen to reason with their mother. He asked whether he was the "best boy in Boston."

"No," she said, "you are the worst boy in Boston." When he kept repeating the question, she smiled. "All right, Richard, you are the best boy in Boston."

"Well," Elizabeth said on hearing he had become a prince of the church, "he's certainly the best boy in Boston now." [11]

"My parents directed the children more by example than words," Cushing said. One boyhood experiment, however, might have rated a birching had Mother Cushing heard about it. One night Dick and his friend Maurice Brodie slipped into the woods on the Falvey estate to sample a cigar. After a few puffs, Brodie, turning green, handed the cigar to his friend. "Tastes great," he said between coughs. It was Dick's turn to gag when he tried a few drags. Boys of the era also sampled cigarets made of dried leaves, corn silk, or sweet ferns, or they were daring enough to try a cubeb or Sweet Caporal.

Dick worked hard from his earliest years. In those days lads as young as five or six ran errands or sold newspapers, as Dick did on street corners in South Boston and around South Station. Some of the poorer boys had little home-made pushcarts and went around collecting empty whisky bottles and rags and, occasionally, lead pipe out of vacant houses, which they sold to the "junky." Or they might forage in the railroad yards for stray lumps of coal to fuel the kitchen stove. Boys in South Boston and the South End could also go junking for iron and brass scraps dumped from industrial plants behind the wharves. These by-products, depending on haggling skill, could be sold for nickels, dimes, and occasionally quarters to "junkies" who made periodic visits. Father Mortimer Twomey, who knew this and was fond of Richard, saw him walking down Broadway one day.

"Young man," he shouted from across the street, "what did you do with the lead pipe in the rectory cellar?" The pastor smiled as onlookers tittered at the youngster's embarrassment.[12]

Household chores included washing, drying, and putting away the dishes, scrubbing woodwork and floors, sifting ashes, and lugging scuttles of coal and firewood up flights of creaky stairs. Richard gathered driftwood near Castle Island and chopped it up for the stove. His maternal grandmother, who lived with the family, was a kind lady who wore a bonnet, shawl, and copious underskirts. She gave her grandson pennies for bringing her pitchers of salt water. She soaked herself in this water, thinking it a cure for her rheumatism. In his spare time, Dick also did chores for Father Twomey, who assured him that "work never killed anyone."

Father Cushing, whose wisdom and common sense were unusual (like his wife, he had had only two or three years of formal instruction), knew the value of education.

"What schooling my parents received," the cardinal recalled, "was hit-or-miss from 'hedge schoolmasters,' who hid with them in the bushes." These itinerant tutors functioned at a time in Ireland when it was considered a crime to teach the Irish to read or write. "Classes," usually held in a cottage or beside hedgerows, gave only a rudimentary knowledge of reading, writing, and arithmetic and occasionally of the classics.

While living at O Street in the City Point section, Dick entered the Pope School at C and Fifth Streets.* He later attended the Lincoln School and the Oliver Hazard Perry School at City Point. One grade-school teacher remembered him as "a bright boy, one who would go places." Miss Mary Dee, who also taught him in the primary grades, said when she learned of his elevation to archbishop: "Richard was a fine little fellow, quiet and studious. When others in the room were raising high jinks, as they often did, I can remember him sitting there, reading his book and paying no attention to the noise and confusion around him. He never gave me the least bit of trouble." [13]

Monsignor George Casey, who became pastor of St. Brigid's Church in Lexington, Massachusetts, was one of Cushing's boyhood friends. "Dick was always smart," he recalls. "When a question was asked, he'd be on his feet with his hand in the air while the rest of us were still thinking about it, and I remember him reciting The Gettysburg Address from memory." [14] One of his teachers, Miss Agnes E. Barry, recalled his oratorical talent at class exercises on Columbus Day and Lincoln's Birthday.

Monsignor Casey remembers when teachers at the Perry School at City Point took Catholic students for the long walk to Gate of Heaven Church. "We kids from the Point felt like the Pilgrims going through Indian territory." The youngsters, he adds, didn't feel safe when they

---

* It is now the home of the South Boston Council 78, Knights of Columbus. The Lincoln School is now the site of the South Boston Library.

entered the church. "Going down the center aisle . . . we used to get jostled and tripped, and then stood a pretty good chance of getting a cuff on the ear from Father O'Brien or Father Brennan for creating a disorder." [15] Father Twomey more than once threw a breviary at a Sunday-school student who got out of line. Monsignor Casey's memory goes back to a St. Patrick's Day entertainment in St. Michael's Hall when a "teacher's pet" came on stage to sing, only to be pelted with ripe fruit and vegetables. "In the uproar we City Pointers scrambled out of there quick and ran down Fourth Street so fast we almost landed in Pleasure Bay before pulling up." [16]

Skipping the seventh grade, Richard found himself in the same eighth-grade class as his sister Mary Jane, called "Dolly" because she was petite. While doing their homework, he might affectionately call her a blockhead for failing to keep up with him.[17] Richard was still in grade school when a former South Boston friend invited him to spend a week in Medford, a city north of Boston. After a few days, Mother Cushing and Dolly brought him home, they missed him so much.

At graduation exercises at the Oliver Hazard Perry Grammar School in June 1908, Richard was one of three boys in short pants. The others wore trousers. His class photograph shows him smiling in a white starched shirt and knickerbockers with 124 classmates. In the same picture, his friend George Casey, who had been hit by a stone a few days before, sports a shiner. Waiting on a warm summer day to have their graduation picture taken, the class grew fidgety. The girls especially, in their high-buttoned shoes and dainty ruffled dresses, were jostling one another while moving into position. The teacher admonished one of the squirming boys. "Richard Cushing, step to the right. Alice Ware's hair ribbons are blocking your face. If you're not in the picture, how are your classmates going to remember you?" [18] None of the graduates of that grammar school class of 1908, a literary critic wrote more than sixty years later, "has ever had to rely on that picture to find out who Cardinal Cushing is." [19]

In September 1908, Richard entered South Boston High School, which sits on top of Dorchester Heights where George Washington's batteries fired on British warships in the harbor. "Toward the end of the first year," he said in 1964, "I knew I was in trouble. I quit. I was absent too many times." [20] According to one account, "the day he was named archbishop, a teacher at South Boston High School recalled that the new prelate had been a chronic truant. The principal, finding the record in the file, tore it up and dropped the pieces into the wastebasket." "I've had enough of this place," Richard said as he cleaned out his locker.[21]

On a television show in 1964, the cardinal was thinking of this crucial year when he counted among mistakes he had made "the fact that, like the average youngster in my day, I never took school too seriously. I thought life was a bowl of cherries. . . . I . . . admit all this because the average youngster today is making the same mistakes . . . and as a result he is having a hard time in school." He went on to say that if he had his life to live over, "I certainly would dedicate myself more fully to the scholarship opportunities that I neglected." [22]

At this time, Richard, remembered by neighbors as "just an ordinary boy," was blue-eyed, freckled, gangling, with a shock of unruly dark hair that fell from both sides of a center part. Not until he had entered high school did he train it to a side parting. According to a newspaper account, "He was a student, but no scholar; athletic, but not an athlete; pious, but capable of returning from boyhood fisticuffs for a dab of iodine and a dab of discipline." Later, Cushing put it another way: "I identified myself with the other young lads in South Boston and mixed up in all their joys and actions. In those days, the boys were tough and they were strong. I was as rough as any of them, and they were pretty rough." From the earliest days of immigration, there had been a rivalry between the sons of Galway, who settled in Roxbury, and the "Corkies," whose stronghold was South Boston. The South End, which separated the two districts, was often a battleground.*

Long before Richard Cushing was born, there was a floating bathhouse at the Dover Street Bridge, leading from Albany Street in the South End toward South Boston. Here the sons and daughters of immigrants learned to swim. The Dover Street Bathhouse in the South End was the first public bathhouse in the United States. Here, for two cents, you got a towel, soap, and a shower. Dick Cushing and his friends swam under the lumber wharves in the old South Bay section or went skin-diving off the oil wharf at the foot of P Street in South Boston or slipped into bathing suits to romp on the beach at City Point, pausing

---

* In *I'd Do It Again,* Curley tells of "gang fights, especially with 'toughies from Southie,' or with other 'wise guys' who came around, sometimes armed with rocks and slingshots."

now and then to scale flat stones through the surf. The most popular spot was the Headhouse, with its bathing facilities, bandstand, and boardwalk. From its iron pier, the boys could dive, fish, or relax on summer nights, with a southwest breeze rippling over the bay, listening to a barbershop quartet at the Headhouse sing old favorites. Another nostalgic sound was the "long-drawn wail of steamship whistles," [23] and a familiar sight was sidewheelers passing Gastle Island on their way to Maine. Wishing they were aboard, the boys used to wave at the passengers.

In the summer, the boys played scrub baseball on the sandlots near Andrew Square, sometimes using an old golf ball with string wrapped around it until it was the size of a baseball and fastened with black tape. They played handball at L Street or, against the car barn walls and at night under the flickering light of a gas lamp, played kick the bar, peggy, or duck-on-the-rock. In winter, when Marine Park was flooded for skating, they played shinny hockey or coasted down neighborhood hills on double-runners, taking time out for an occasional snowball fight. In 1907, when Dick Cushing was twelve, his young sister Anna was bruised while coasting down Third Street. He took her to nearby Carney Hospital, but refused to enter.

"You go in by yourself, Anna," he said. "I'm waiting right here." [24]

One annual thrill was crawling under the tent at the old Andrew Square Circus. It was always a lark to hook a ride on the rear of a trolley. Neighbors were glad Halloween came only once a year. The boys delighted in stirring up their wrath by putting tin cans against the front door, ringing the bell, then scampering off into the night as the cans went clattering down the wooden steps. Perhaps Cardinal Cushing was thinking of this mischief when he said: "Now I ring bells and everyone runs." [25] It was difficult, however, to get into any real trouble, according to a neighbor of the Cushings. "In South Boston we lived too near churches and police stations." [26]

At a time when there was little extra money for luxuries, it was always a treat when Patrick and Mary took the children on a holiday afternoon to the zoo at Franklin Park in Dorchester or to the amusement park at Norumbega Park in Auburndale, a more distant suburb. The climax of the day might be a "college ice," banana split, candied apple, or ice-cream soda. The Cushing children particularly enjoyed riding in an open trolley to the seashore crescent between Castle Island and the Headhouse and seeing the nickelodeon show at City Point. One of Cushing's boyhood friends remembers walking to downtown

Boston to go window-shopping. One vendor sold statuettes: "Little Jesus" for a nickel, "Big Jesus" for a dime. He had a quaint sales pitch: "For Christ's sake, buy one." Cushing's boyhood friend also recalls the disdain in which young Catholics held Protestant churches. "When we went by a Protestant church in Southie, we stepped off the curbstone and walked in the street until we passed the church."*

Catholic churches were vibrant centers for the children, especially when there was an outing, minstrel show, or other neighborhood entertainment. The Cushings, like most Irish Catholic families in South Boston, were wrapped up in church activities.

----

* Children in some Catholic families got along amicably with their non-Catholic neighbors.

chapter three

TWO ROADWAYS

WHEN GOVERNOR Al Smith was asked whether he was an active church member as a boy, he said: "Of course, what else was there to do?" Young Richard Cushing could have said the same thing. For him, the church, along with his home, was a center of social as well as religious life. "We seemed to know only two roadways in life," he remembers, "the one that led from home to church and the other that led from the church back to the home." [1]

Parishes were primary social centers in South Boston during the nineteenth century and the first decades of the twentieth. Irish Catholic congregations were bound by linguistic as well as ethnic and religious enthusiasm. In America, "the Irish became more Irish and Catholic than in Ireland," writes Lawrence Fuchs. "It was their way of defense against the harshness and hostility of the cities and the strangeness of America's ways." [2]

In the absolute monarchy of a Catholic parish, the pastor reigned as king. He could run his domain any way he wished as long as his ledger balanced. In the South Boston ghetto, the church was the church of the poor, and the priests, close to the parishioners, gave them courage, hope, and a sense of belonging. The pastor, usually the best educated person in the community, was the leader around whom the often frustrated and bewildered parishioners gathered for personal advice as well as for social, economic, and political direction. In lieu of a psychiatrist's couch, the confessional box sufficed.

In 1900, St. Eulalia's Church had opened as a chapel and mission of the Gate of Heaven Church. Eight years later, it received full standing as a separate church and parish. When the church burned in 1933, it was rebuilt as Saint Brigid's Church. Its first pastor, the Reverend Mortimer F. Twomey, was "a priest from the top of his head to the soles of his feet," according to a contemporary journalist. [3] Whether he leaned back, resting his elbows on the altar, or raised a clenched fist, he cast a spell of delight on the faithful Irish of City Point, and his booming voice was as familiar as the foghorns in Boston Harbor. He was one of the bombastic messiahs of a memorable era that included the Reverend Arcturus Zodiac Conrad, pastor of the Park Street Congregational Church in Boston, which was known as "Brimstone Corner," partly because of his scorching sermons and partly from a legend that gunpowder had been stored in the church basement during the War of 1812.

Twomey was at his best when thundering against such tools of the devil as rollercoasters and merry-go-rounds, which he kept out of the South Boston parks. When Twomey blasted venal sin, he made it sound like a felony. As would Cushing later, he could move an audience from tears to laughter, from remorse to enthusiasm in a matter of seconds, but he was most impressive when giving the devil his due. As a youngster, Dick Cushing learned to respect his glare.

While in Sunday school, Dick became an unofficial part of the parish organization. "I wasn't a pious lad. I was not much for being around the church save to do manual work. I mowed lawns, stoked fires, shoveled snow, swept and mopped floors, opened the church in the morning and locked it up at night." He also helped Twomey run picnics, lawn parties, and other fund-raising affairs. "St. Eulalia's was always yelling for money," he said when he got the reputation of being an effective fund-raiser, "Maybe that's where I got the idea."

At the age of fourteen Richard became assistant janitor. One day, while repairing the church roof, he fell and broke an arm. Another time he received a tongue-lashing for using outdoor paint on the interior. "You've ruined the rectory," Father Twomey said. "You had several gallons of paint in the cellar. Why did you pick the wrong one?" [4]

Recreation became organized for the first time in 1908, when the Reverend Jeremiah F. Driscoll, a curate, became spiritual director of the new boys' club. "One of the boys." Father Driscoll played baseball with his charges and was, in general, as much a participant as an adviser. When Father Twomey added a parish school complete with recreational facilities in the basement, including bowling alleys and a pool room, teenagers and others could shoot pool for a nickel a rack and bowl for a dime a string. The night managers were Richard Cushing and Maurice Brodie, two of the trio known as "the three musketeers." * Cushing and Brodie as part-time entrepreneurs made ice

---

* The third musketeer was George Casey's brother, Daniel, who became judge of the West Roxbury court.

cream in the cellar of their homes. The venture failed when customers detected bits of egg shell in their product. The boys, noting that the recipe called for an egg, had dropped one into the mixture, shell and all.[5]

On the night shift, the young managers occasionally had to evict cut-ups, sometimes by the scruff of the neck. Richard hired and supervised pinboys in the bowling alleys, which were open until eleven. He collected cash, paid for maintenance, and, after the alleys closed, swept, steel-wooled, and waxed them. It was usually past midnight when he crawled into bed. He and Brodie were each paid three dollars a week. "Just before Christmas," Brodie recalled in 1958, "Father Twomey called Dick and me into his office. 'You have been two fine boys,' he said. 'You have performed outstanding work, and your honesty must be recognized. I wish to reward you." Each of the sealed envelopes he handed them contained a crisp one-dollar bill.[6]

After he had become archbishop, Cushing told Brassil Fitzgerald, a boyhood friend: "What's that line of Shakespeare about the uses of adversity being sweet? When I was a lad in Southie, Father Mortimer Twomey quoted it to me one night in the parish hall where I used to work evenings tending the pool table. A great priest, Father Twomey, scholar and poet and man of God. I myself was but one of the many vocations he encouraged. 'Sweet are the uses of adversity.' " [7]

After dropping out of South Boston High School, Richard had planned to go to work. "But a cousin of my father, the Right Reverend Monsignor Richard B. Cushion, a classmate of Patrick Cardinal Hayes at Manhattan College, sent me to Boston College High School. In those days they called it the 'refuge for sinners.' " * Soon after school opened in September, Richard learned that students who had attended parochial schools had advantages in a school staffed by Jesuits. For one thing, they had been taught to be altar boys.

"We had to assist the priest at mass," Richard recalled, "and finally it came to my turn. Well, I had never served in my life, but I thought I did pretty well. At the end of the mass, while the priest was taking off his vestments, he would mention mistakes you had made. In his criticism of me, he was blunt: 'Young man, I am not going to ask you

---

* The high school was originally housed in the same building as Boston College on James Street in the South End, once known as "the most beautiful slum in the world." Boston College High School was then part of Boston College.

if you ever served a mass before. I'll just ask you if you have ever *seen* a mass.' " [8] Richard soon caught on, however, and joined Maurice Brodie and George Casey as a regular acolyte at St. Eulalia's.

On Homecoming Day at Boston College in 1959, Cardinal Cushing was thinking of his sophomore year in high school when he said: "I am an encouragement to the average student. I was an uncouth lad, nonstudious. I found it hard-going, not only in studies, but in deportment, too." Students kept after school for misbehavior were said to be "put in the jug." [9] Cushing admitted he had compiled the "best jug record" in the sophomore class. He was too modest to add that by the end of the year he received honorable mention on the list of academic prize-winners.

He was becoming more studious. He frequented the South Boston Public Library and recorded tidbits that caught his interest in a "commonplace book." "It is a good practice to read with pen in hand, marking what is liked or doubted," he recalled years later. "It rivets attention and enables one to see what progress one makes with his own mind."

Monsignor Cushion, a cousin of Richard's father, paid the $63-a-year tuition, but there were other expenses, including books, carfare and lunch. Fortunately, Richard had become accustomed to working during school vacations and after school since his freshman year at South Boston High School, when he earned a few dollars a week as a timekeeper at Commonwealth Pier, not far from his home. One afternoon his father dropped by to see how he was getting on. "Just as he arrived, a bell diver emerged from the water, and my father smiled. 'If I had known you could do that,' he said, 'I myself would have walked all the way over from Ireland.' " [10] At other times, to earn money for high school and college, Richard worked in various capacities for Walworth Manufacturing Company on East First Street, a few steps from his home, and for the Boston Elevated Railway in the Maintenance of Way Department. As a rodman, he worked with hammar and anvil alongside his father and also as a waterboy for a crew laying tracks for the Boston Elevated. In his junior year in high school, when he became interested in debating and public speaking, his forsenic skill was not confined to Boston College High School. "I used to make speeches for various causes and was well paid for them," he said. His grades suffered as a result of his extracurricular activities and moonlighting, and when he was a junior in high school (at the age of sixteen), he became discouraged, partly because of low grades

in his midyear examinations, partly because he was worried about his
family's finances.

After the midyear examinations, the prefect of studies sent for Patrick Cushing and asked him to come in for an interview. It had to be
an evening appointment, for the street lights were on when Pat left
for work and were burning again before he came home. "Ten hours
he worked, seven days a week, a big man and gentle," Cushing recalled,
"A good provider, the neighbors said. And so said Father Twomey." [11]

That night in the kitchen, Pat turned to Mary after reading the
letter from the prefect: "Never mind the stew, Mary; we'd best get
started. Comb your hair and put your rubbers on, Richard, it's beginning to snow."

In the rectory, the prefect questioned the wisdom of keeping Richard in school. Forty years later, Cushing vividly remembered the
scene: "Big and straight in his chair, my father listened, his best hat
in his lap, firmly held in both hands. Only once, and quietly, he spoke
in my defense. 'It could be, Father, he's been working too hard,
weekends and evenings, for Father Twomey.' "

According to his sister Elizabeth, Richard was in high school when
he first mentioned his ambition to be a priest. He was a cardinal when
asked about this. "What do you mean? I always wanted to be a priest."
Father Twomey had first planted the seed in his mind, and the Jesuits
at Boston College High School had influenced him toward the Society
of Jesus. And it was the ambition of many Irish Catholic parents of
the era to have a priest in the family. There were times when Richard
himself was convinced that he had a genuine vocation. He had been
steered continually toward the priesthood until the prefect in high
school implied it was a hope never to be realized.

Cushing never forgot the "cold wet dark of the car stop, and the
rain that was snow in the oncoming lights of our southbound car."
His father and he rode home in gloomy silence until Richard deject-
edly said: "They can have their diploma. I'll get a job and help at
home." Standing next to his father on the crowded trolley, Richard
could hear only three words of his comment, spoken "between two
clangs of the motorman's bell." But he would always remember them.

"Carry on, son." Patrick did not speak again until they got off the
streetcar at City Point. Then this immigrant, whom his children often
remembered as being inarticulate, took his son by the arm: "Do the
best you can. 'Tis all God asks. He'll do the rest." [12]

Had "Pa" Cushing been less understanding, his son never would have finished high school, and instead of becoming a priest, he might have turned into a politician.

"Politics," John W. McCormack once said, "was the natural thing for anyone born in South Boston." It was the easiest way to escape the treadmill of poverty. "The only place for an Irishman in Boston was in the church or in politics," Cushing said when he was cardinal. "As far as banking was concerned, the 'Irish need not apply.' " * There was a saying that "The Lodges own the banks, but the Irish control the votes." According to another saying, "The Irish landed on Monday and voted on Tuesday," thanks to the firm political control of Irish Catholic padrones. The immigrants and the sons of immigrants sought careers in sports, the church, or politics—professions that required little capital and did not depend on pedigree. In the politics of young Richard's era, it was an asset to be an Irish immigrant because of South Boston's Irish Catholic solidarity. And politics was the only profession for which no training was necessary.

By the time he was in high school, Cushing was well schooled in Boston's murderous brand of politics. South Boston rallies provided a show no circus could match. Richard was fifteen when the whine of "Sweet Adeline" came to South Boston one night just before eleven o'clock during a bitter mayoral battle between John F. Fitzgerald, the warbler, and the patrician James Jackson Storrow. Honey Fitz, who had endeared himself to immigrants and their sons when he built the City Point Aquarium and the Franklin Park Zoo, topped that evening's hoopla by singing "Sweet Adeline" from the roof of a hack. His opponent, meanwhile, was being driven out of the district by a howling mob of two hundred men and boys swinging torches and throwing chunks of ice. One piece hit Storrow in the arm. Politics was rough in "Southie," as it was in its legendary tavern: "What was a man with a paper skull doing in Garrity's saloon in the first place?"

Politics was even rougher when James Michael Curley moved into South Boston with his goon squads. In a day when political rallies following torchlight parades gave street-corner crowds something to cheer about, Curley put on a show that, writes Francis Russell, "was a combination of vaudeville, Chautauqua, and the prize ring. No one, his opponents realized too late, could equal him as a showman; no

---

* During a tour of South Africa, the late Robert Kennedy told a student audience: "My father left Boston . . . because of the signs on the wall that said 'No Irish Need Apply.' "

one could talk him down." [13] Cushing and his chums used to see friends and neighbors crowd into Bethesda Hall and other battlegrounds in South Boston. Partisans would wait for hours to see in action such colorful candidates as Fitzgerald and Curley, two Irish folk heroes, who sometimes bought a cartload of apples and distributed them to the crowd as they spoke from a wagon in front of Walworth's gate or at a street corner. The cruising of their motorcades through South Boston during frenzied campaigns was a sideshow; the main event took place in the halls of the peninsula.

In 1912 in Flood Square in South Boston, Cushing spoke for Curley from the tailgate of a wagon when the Roxbury candidate was running against William McNary, the pride of South Boston. Economic necessity prevailed over loyalty in this instance. As usual, political rallies were wild and disorderly, as voters knocked one another down while police swinging clubs tripped over brawlers. In his autobiography, Curley tells how McNary was threatened with bodily harm at a ward meeting in his home town. As "the boys closed in, he jumped up and grabbed the chandelier. The brothers took hold of his swinging legs and hauled, while Bill clung on. . . . They tugged away until the chandelier came out by the roots." [14]

Richard Cushing did not have to walk far to see rough-and-tumble street-corner rallies, and later in life he often alluded to his experiences as an orator who made long, rambling, and often humorous speeches. "Originally, I wanted to be a politician. I used to make money speaking for politicians from the back of wagons. I spoke for Jim Curley. I spoke for the suffragettes and the anti-suffragettes—anyone who would pay me." The outdoor speechifying, he added, accounted for his later loud style of speaking indoors. Once, after hearing a playback of a radio talk he gave, he said: "What this archdiocese needs is voice training, starting from the top." The first time he addressed the League of Catholic Women (when he was auxiliary bishop) at the Somerset Hotel, the microphone went dead. "You and I are the only persons who can talk loud enough to be heard without a mike," he said to the president, Mrs. Vincent (Marie) Green.

Oldtimers remember Dick Cushing speaking from Gerald Kearney's truck and from a peddler's wagon at street-corner rallies advertised in posters. Windham ("Ambie") Heffernan played the piano, while George ("Mutt") Dennis * and Frank ("Jeff") Mayne sang. After

---

* Gertrude Dennis, widow of George Dennis, became the second wife of James Michael Curley.

the entertainment, Dick Cushing, the tailgate orator, plumped for his friend Daniel Casey, who was elected to Congress when he was twenty years old. This quartet appeared at several rallies during the campaign.

In a television interview with Ed Murrow on "Person to Person" on Good Friday night in 1954, Cushing said Father Twomey had told him he wasn't suited to politics. "I think the country lost a poor politician," he added. "I hope the church found a worthy servant." There is a more colorful, if apocryphal, account of this encounter.

One day Father Twomey saw his sixteen-year-old acolyte delivering a speech for a congressman for reelection. The tall, burly Twomey pushed through the crowd, reached up, grabbed Cushing's legs, and yanked. Then he grabbed him by the scruff of the neck, aimed a kick at the stern, and bellowed, "You'll either be a priest or a politician. Make up your mind!"

Both in Boston College High School and at Boston College, Cushing had difficulty in making up his mind.

Reminiscing about his student days, the cardinal said: "When I worked—when I studied—I was able to hold my own. But when I didn't work hard, I fell far below average. I can't think of any subject in which I particularly excelled."

During his last three semesters in high school, he continued to do odd jobs at St. Eulalia's, but he gave up moonlighting when his father warned that he was doing the work of an adult. A bowling alley, Pat said, was no place for a teen-ager! "There are rough and tough customers that go in there."

Although he might have made the varsity baseball team as a second-baseman,* his interests lay elsewhere. In his junior year, when he was on a committee promoting a play, *Sebastian,* tickets were moving slowly until he urged an assembly to "get behind your school and schoolmates." In his senior year, he was the best speaker in the Bapst Debating Society and was chosen in the class of 1913 as one of three orators at graduation exercises. His theme was "The Press as an Intellectual Force." He won the Edward J. Campbell Medal for scholastic excellence and second prize for academic achievement in Latin and Greek. Although he had trouble with algebra and trigonometry,† he received honorable mention in plane and solid geometry. Years after

---

* One childhood ambition was to become a professional baseball player.
† "To get a passing mark in these subjects, I practically memorized the problems," he said.

he graduated from high school, an instructor remembered being impressed by Richard's quiet seriousness: "He accomplished things without fanfare. He was not among the top of his class in early years, but he climbed there by dint of serious application. He attracted crowds around him. He had a retentive memory and a puckish sense of humor. His humor was semi-serious, and would catch you unawares." [15]

After graduating from Boston College High School, he was slated to enroll in the Jesuit novitiate at St. Andrew-on-Hudson, New York. "I changed my mind the night before I was to leave," he told a friend. "I never went. Why, I don't know, but I never went." Two friends chosen for the novitiate were disappointed when he didn't board the train for New York.

Richard earned money for college in the summer of 1913 as a streetcar conductor for the Boston Street Railway Company. As an alumnus of the Boston Elevated he would later march with the company's employees in their annual procession and attend their memorial mass. On each trolley were a motorman and a fare collector. By pulling a rope, the conductor would ring up a fare to register on a meter at the end of the streetcar. The fares were five cents with transfer privileges, and there was no charge for children. Cushing collected fares on a trolley that made the Broadway run around City Point. "That's where I got this awful voice," he quipped, "yelling 'A Street, B Street, C Street.' "

In September he enrolled at Boston College.

chapter four

THE VINEYARD OF
THE LORD

IRISH-YANKEE rivalry polarized around Harvard University and the Jesuit colleges (Boston College and Holy Cross) early in the century. As late as 1908, it was unusual for Boston Irish boys to go to Harvard, as Joseph P. Kennedy did. College-bound Irish Catholics almost always went to a Jesuit institution, and the few who enrolled at Harvard commuted by streetcar. Professor Julian Coolidge called them "untouchables." Even in the 1920s and 1930s, exclusive clubs like The Fly and the Gas House listed no Irishmen. "The only ones seen around those sanctuaries," writes Joe McCarthy, "were the boys who delivered the ice and the White Rock." [1]

A 1922 news story began: "The Irish, not the Jews, present the real problem at Harvard. The new plan of class selection will cut down the number of Irish as well as Jews." [2] This statement was made by a Harvard man who resented the criticism directed against the university because of the announcement that fewer Jews would be admitted.

This was the year of President A. Lawrence Lowell's *numerus clausus* proposal. Worried because the number of Jews at Harvard had risen from seven per cent to more than twenty-one per cent since the turn of the century, Lowell proposed a quota to maintain ethnic balance. President Emeritus Charles W. Eliot opposed it, as did most of the Overseers.

The newspaper noted that, although no religious line would be drawn, "those who are of Irish descent will be limited." The reason was not social. "The Jew is opposed socially," a student said, "but the real objection to the Irish student comes in athletics. Groton men, or fellows from . . . prep schools whose fathers went to Harvard, should be the team leaders always. The Irish, in common schools,

secure athletic training and if they make the teams they assert themselves and usually a coach wants them elected captain."

The Boston Irish considered Harvard heretical. Their resentment
could—subconsciously at least—be traced to a conviction that Harvard
College offered a superior education. For more than two hundred
years Harvard had dominated the local education scene, and, as one
writer puts it, "The weight of this history, these great names, and
these awesome institutions was oppressive to the Boston Irish. It could
not help producing in them a massive inferiority complex." [3]

Boston College had been founded in the South End in 1864 in an
era of bigotry and intolerance, and although over the years it helped
dispel prejudice, the Jesuit institution suffered from the same narrow-
ness that had prompted the Boston *Herald* to refer to the supposedly
low intelligence of Irish immigrants, while Harvard Professor William
B. Munro lauded the superior "political ingenuity of the Anglo-Saxon."
Recognizing the dislike of Irish Catholics for Harvard, John Gunther
writes: "Harvard is the great rival of the archbishopric for intellectual
control of the community. 'I don't know why Harvard should dominate the city, but it does,' one famous prelate sighed not long ago."
Gunther adds that "the Irish say that Harvard 'discriminates against
them.' " [4]

Tempers flared at the end of the last century when Harvard University dropped the name of Boston College from the list of institutions
whose graduates could be admitted to Harvard Law School. Dr.
Charles W. Eliot, president of Harvard, said in 1898: "We found . . .
that graduates of Boston College . . . would not be admitted even to
the Junior class of Harvard College." In the following year in *The
Atlantic Monthly* he charged that the curriculum of Jesuit colleges
had "remained almost unchanged for four hundred years," with "some
trifling concessions made to natural science." Dr. Eliot mollified
some critics when he supported David I. Walsh in the gubernatorial
campaign in 1913, even though Walsh ran against such proper Bostonians as Charles Sumner Bird and Augustus Peabody Gardner. "I
cast my ballot . . . for Mr. Walsh," Eliot said. "The fact that he is a
Roman Catholic should not interfere with my ballot." Walsh, the
first Catholic to be elected governor of Massachusetts, gave the hierarchy a lift, and it was further pleased when Eliot added: "Indeed,
today, this puritanical state is said to be Roman Catholic . . . What a
marvelous change from the days of our Puritan and Pilgrim forefa-

thers! This religious transformation . . . is the greatest transformation of Puritan Massachusetts and New England." [5]

In their feeling of oppression, Irish Catholics put Harvard in the category of the hated English. Congressman James A. Gallivan of South Boston, a Harvard-educated politician who was always attuned to his Irish Catholic audiences, was lauded in 1921 when he introduced a bill into Congress to deport Admiral William S. Sims to Canada as "an undesirable alien" because he said Ireland could not be trusted during World War I.

Conflicting goals of Catholic and nonsectarian institutions brought Cushing into the dialogue. He refuted the charge that the church segregates Catholic children from the rest of the community in a separate school system that censors their cultural diet. He debated Dr. James Bryant Conant, president of Harvard University, on this issue. Early in his career Cushing took a dim view of Harvard.

The Reverend Thomas I. Gasson, S.J., who became president of Boston College in 1907, wanted to separate the college from its high school to give it room to expand into a university. William Cardinal O'Connell, mindful of the seven hills of Rome, had long dreamed of moving Catholic institutions out of Boston's "catacombs" to hilltops in a more fashionable section of the city. He realized part of his dream in 1909, when a new Boston College with Gothic towers, soaring spires, and mullioned windows rose on a beautiful plateau overlooking twin reservoirs in the elegant Chestnut Hill section, once the site of Amos A. Lawrence's farm. The building program later included the nearby St. John's Seminary, a new chancery, and an episcopal residence that looks like a small palace, St. Elizabeth's Hospital, and several other Catholic institutions.

Dick Cushing was not in the first group of young men wearing derbies and carrying "Boston bags" who took a streetcar to the college on Lake Street on March 28, 1913, the day the new Boston College opened to greet seventy-one students. The first complete collegiate year in the new building began on September 17 of that year, with a record enrollment of almost four hundred students in the freshman class, including Cushing. It was an hour trip from his new address at 910 Broadway in South Boston.

Cushing and two classmates staged the freshman "Smoker," which *The Stylus,* the college magazine, called the "final frolic" of the first semester. Guests of honor were the 1913 football team, and the speaker was E. Mark Sullivan, former assistant district attorney of the United States.

Classmates remember Dick Cushing as being "vigorous, energetic, full of life, facile of tongue, good company and humorous. He looked pretty husky and no one ever pushed him around." A class photograph shows him lantern-jawed, with straight-up, brush-up hair. George Casey, a sophomore in the class of 1916, remembers him as "retiring, undistinguished; nothing like he is now." [6]

In college, Cushing earned two dollars an hour tutoring students in Latin and Greek and worked part-time in Jim Doherty's drugstore at the corner of Broadway and O Street, dishing out ice cream, delivering prescriptions, and sweeping the floor. Father Twomey dropped in for a soda now and then to check on his progress. Cushing remembers hiding behind the counter to keep the priest waiting as long as he dared. One night, when Dick and a friend were keeping an all-night vigil at St. Eulalia's, which was then across the street from the drugstore, they slipped into the pharmacy to have some coffee. Later that night, Cushing's friend asked whether it would be all right to smoke in the rear of the church.

"If we smoke here," Dick said, "we'll smoke in the hereafter."

In the little leisure time he had, Cushing studied and did research at the South Boston Library. His diversion came on Sundays. Maurice Brodie recalled that after the nine o'clock mass at St. Eulalia's, he, George Casey, and Dick often walked to Castle Island. "That's about the only recreation Dick had. The rest of the gang used to save up for a couple days' vacation in Maine every summer. Dick never could seem to get enough money together, and he never made the trip, but he'd be at Castle Island to wave his handkerchief at us as the boat, the *City of Bangor,* sailed out of the harbor." [7]

Occasionally Cushing joined a friend, John McNamara, in a cruise around the island in the *Anita,* when there was gas in the tank of the day boat. Otherwise, they drifted around the harbor, with fishing lines draped over the side. On one expedition with Daniel Golden (later pastor of St. Monica's Church in South Boston), Cushing helped haul aboard forty fish. In early spring he used to help McNamara scrape and paint the boat before launching it at the South Boston Yacht Club.

In his sophomore year, Richard was elected vice-president of his class. "He was alert in class and made good recitations," a student remembered. "Once, when Father John S. Keating, a professor of

Greek, criticized a student for giving a wrong answer, Cushing nudged him when he sat down. 'Forget it,' he said. 'Tomorrow is another day.' " Cushing used to tease classmates who lived in the suburbs, asking them how things were "in the sticks."

Richard found college mathematics difficult, but before the end of his sophomore year, he had won several medals for scholarship, including one in debating. As a member of the Marquette Debating Society, he upheld the affirmative in one contest: "Resolved: That Japan was justified in its claims on Germany." He was on a committee that held a dance in Horticultural Hall in Boston in November. That same month he stumped for his friend, Daniel Casey, then a Boston College junior, in his successful bid for the state legislature.

At the end of his freshman year, Cushing had again entertained the idea of enrolling in the Jesuit novitiate but after much soul-searching decided against it: "I had been observing young men from the parish going away to the Society," he explained, "to the Benedictines at St. Anselm's up in New Hampshire, and to the Oblates. These seemed to be the more popular vocations which Father Twomey developed in many of us, as the instruments of God. Twice, at the moment of decision, I think I sensed that I was cut out more for the active life and not the teaching apostolate, which is the major concern of the American Jesuits. I just didn't think I was the academic type." He added that the Jesuits were lucky he didn't join them, "because if I had, they would have lost their best benefactor."

In his sophomore year he made up his mind. According to one familiar story,[8] he was on a trolley on his way to college one morning when he met a cousin, John P. Kenneally, a night school law student who was a daytime adjuster for an insurance association. Kenneally suggested a transfer to law school, adding that there was a good future for claim adjusters.

Richard shook his head. "Not for me. I'm going to be a priest."

"A priest? What do you want to do that for? What do you get? Three square meals a day, a place to sleep, and a lot of hard work, no doubt, and you can't even get married."

Richard, who had never shown any particular interest in girls, shrugged. "I know all that, but that's what I've always wanted to be, ever since I was a kid."

Cushing, an observer noted, "had to overcome an aversion to scholarship and a zeal for political speechifying to become a priest." There was a joyous scene in the Cushing parlor when Richard told his family of his decision. At the time Elizabeth was twenty-two; Dolly, twenty-one; Anne, fifteen; and John, eleven. The kitchen was the center of family activity, but when company came the family sat in the parlor. The girls, who had to be in by dark, entertained at home. Mother Cushing taught them to sew and cook.

On May 7, 1915, a German submarine sank the *Lusitania,* with a loss of 1198 lives, and the nation recoiled from the shock. Like many other young men, Richard enlisted in the United States Army. After spending a few weeks at a training camp in New York he was discharged because of an asthmatic condition that was to plague him throughout the rest of his life.

In September 1915, with a strong letter of recommendation from Father Twomey, he enrolled at St. John's Seminary, a two-minute walk downhill from Boston College. There was a note in *Sub Turri,* the college yearbook, under "History of the Class of 1917": "Many of our men, finding that their calling was not toward the conquering world, entered an institution near at hand to labor in the vineyard of the Lord."

Until 1911, when William Henry O'Connell succeeded John Williams as archbishop of Boston, Sulpician priests from Paris had staffed St. John's Seminary, built in 1884 by Archbishop Williams. Since 1911, Boston clergy, trained at the seminary or in Rome, have done the teaching.

The Romanesque chapel on a wooded site bordering Commonwealth Avenue and Lake Street is the heart of seminary life. The main building is the turreted Theology House built of puddingstone quarried on the seminary grounds. In 1915 its north or front wing was enlarged, and a library, lecture halls, and more student rooms were added. Another part of the complex was the Philosophy House, where Cushing first lived. Crowning a hill near the Commonwealth Avenue side, it was capped by a white tower in traditional New England style.

The schedule at Philosophy House ran from 5:50 in the morning until 9:50 at night. In between were practices of piety, meditation, mass, spiritual reading, and examination of conscience, along with classes, study periods, special lectures, and cultural programs. On Thursday afternoons, student foursomes took long walks.

"As we walked," a classmate recalled, "Dick would be examining the scenery on all sides, missing nothing. He was full of semi-sophisticated quips about what he saw—the most amusing of companions." [9]

Richard was particularly impressed by the rector, the Right Reverend John B. Peterson, who taught philosophy, and Dr. Louis P. Kelleher, a professor of dogmatic theology. Later Cushing named both men bishops: Peterson as the ordinary of the diocese of Manchester, New Hampshire, and Kelleher as auxiliary bishop of Boston. Cushing was "lector" (reader) in Dr. Kelleher's theology class. After he read from the Epistles of St. Paul, the professor interpolated.

When Cardinal O'Connell lectured on the career of Pope Leo XIII, a prize was offered for a formal essay that best evaluated the series of talks. Cushing won it. By this time he was advanced enough to spend occasional recreation periods helping other students, especially around examination time. Considered a plugger, he drove himself so hard that he was warned by classmates to slow down. By the end of his second year at the seminary, he made the honors list and maintained this record. He was one of three top seminarians chosen by Cardinal O'Connell to continue his education at the North American College in Rome. His father was puzzled when Richard asked permission to study abroad.

"What are you asking me for? You will be home tomorrow night, won't you?" [10]

Patrick and Mary came to St. John's on visitor's Sunday, and Richard spent Easter and Christmas vacations with his family.

When the rector mentioned the danger of German U-boats, Richard nodded. "I don't care one way or the other, Monsignor. If you want me to go, I'll go. Ships are still going back and forth." [11]

"Yes, and they're still going up and down." Monsignor Peterson canceled the trip, rather than risk the lives of the three seminarians.

In 1917, at the end of the philosophy period, Cardinal O'Connell officiated at the tonsure ceremony, and after a vacation from June 24 to July 23, Cushing did some farm work, raising crops for the war effort, as did other students after the United States declared war on April 6. "When I was at St. John's," he recalled in 1967, "we hoed potatoes and slept on cots. Now they have wall-to-wall carpeting and television. It's like living in a plush motel." [12]

During summer vacations, seminarians served as counselors at boys' camps or worked for contractors or the State Department of Public Works, mowing median strips of lawn or shoveling loam on state borders of state highways. One summer Richard earned money as a rodman under maintenance chief Thomas Sullivan, later police commissioner of Boston and a close friend. Cushing also had pleasant memories of summer days at St. John's villa on Lake Winnepesaukee, New Hampshire. But there were grimmer intervals. During the influenza epidemic the seminary was turned into a hospital for about three weeks as army trucks and other vehicles were pressed into service to transport the dead. Cushing remembers the stacks of coffins piled outside Cassidy's Funeral Home in South Boston. By 1918, the shortage of priests had become so acute that ten seminarians at St. John's were ordained ahead of schedule.

There was the traditional griping about the quality of food served at the seminary, although nobody complained about the shortage of muffins at breakfast. "I think I ate six thousand," Cushing recalled. His duties as student master of ceremonies were to train younger seminarians "all the way up from altar boys to the priesthood." From these contacts, he knew which students had mothers who sent food back in the laundry basket. "When I thought they had received some from home, I'd go around and get something to eat from them." [13]

A former kitchen helper remembered his appetite and her doubt about his ever becoming a priest. "He was full of the devil. He used to turn on the radio, pick up his cassock, and start dancing, he did. He was always fooling around and he liked my fried bread. That, he did. He'd come around for it, between meals, and I'd give it to him, too." She mentioned a sullen cook, who was hard on the students. Cushing once turned on him. " 'Riley,' he said, 'when I'm ordained, I'm going to get a gun and come back for you.' " "Oh, he was full of it, that one!" the kitchen assistant said.[14]

One day when he left the seminary grounds without permission, Richard ran into Monsignor Peterson in downtown Boston. Summoned to the rector's office that evening, he looked directly at Peterson. "I can't tell you why I was down town, but I take full responsibility for my action. I accept the entire blame."

The rector arose and extended his hand. "You're a man." That ended it.

At St. John's Seminary, the Mission Academia was a student organization with goals similar to those of the Society of the Propagation of the Faith (known to seminarians as "Proppy"). Fascinated by missionary reports read at the monthly meetings, Cushing was encouraged to soak up the history, geography, and folklore of pagan lands. According to the secretary's report, he gave "an interesting and instructive lecture which, together with its humor, furnished the members with a half hour of real enjoyment and profit."

A classmate remembered Cushing as the best fund-raiser for "Proppy." "He was marvelous. He'd get a nickel here, a dime there, and a quarter from someone else. Then when we all thought he was satisfied, he'd pop up with a new scheme to bring in a few pennies more." He broke all records in collecting funds, the first step toward his goal as bishop of the missions.

In 1919 he had been elected secretary of Mission Academia, and in his final year at the seminary he was elected president in a close contest. In that capacity, Cushing, whose longest previous trip had been to the Cape Cod Canal, went to St. Louis to give the main address on the ideals and techniques of missiology at a convention of the Students Mission Crusade, with which Mission Academia was affiliated. His theme echoed a verse from Ecclesiasticus, which he was one day to adopt as his archepiscopal motto: "They many know Thee, as we also have known Thee, that there is no God beside Thee, O Lord!"

In August 1920, Cushing addressed the Washington convention of the Catholic Students Mission Crusade.

Cushing was still president when the Academia celebrated its twentieth anniversary in 1921. At this time Monsignor Peterson noted: "The two most important factors in increasing the zeal and the piety of the students have been obedience to the decrees of Pius X on daily Communion and the work of the Academia." The *Pilot* had a comment: "Much of the great success of the Propagation for the Society of the Faith in this diocese is due . . . to the knowledge and love of the missions that burns in the breasts of the priests who were once members of the Academia."

In his final (diaconate) year at St. John's, Cushing was named second prefect, which meant that he was the second best scholar in his class. After six years of study, he presented himself for ordination to Cardinal O'Connell on May 26, 1921, in the Cathedral of the Holy Cross. He was serene and happy, even though Monsignor Peterson told him just before the ceremony: "You'll have a hard life, because you're original, and no one can control your thinking. But be yourself." [15] The rector gave him a piece of advice he put into practice:

"Take your priesthood seriously, but never yourself." Cushing recalled these words many years later, when he told a congregation: "I have always tried to be a manly man and a priestly priest."

After a reception in the Cushing apartment on Broadway following the ordination ceremony, six boyhood friends gathered in the South Boston home of Maurice Brodie, who recalled in 1958: "All his pals gave him a party at my house—just close friends—and we presented him with a purse. It didn't amount to much, because none of us had much." When Daniel Casey handed Cushing a purse containing six five-dollar gold pieces, his words were prophetic: "Dick, here is a token of our esteem. Next time we meet, it will be to celebrate your getting the Red Hat." [16]

On the following Sunday, Father Cushing said his first mass at St. Eulalia's Church in the presence of his family, grandmother, aunts, and other relatives, including Dahill cousins. Mother Cushing, her dearest wish fulfilled, wept quietly at the sight of her son officiating. Father Twomey, who was beside him on the altar, recalled Richard's experiences at Boston College High School, Boston College, and at the seminary and warmly praised his parents for encouraging him. Richard himself had a feeling of fulfillment. "To be a priest is the greatest call one could receive from Almighty God," he said as a cardinal. "When I was ordained in 1921 at the age of twenty-four, I was not much of a success as an assistant in local parishes. I had three different assignments within three weeks, so I came to the conclusion that I was hopeless as a curate or that the pastors didn't like me."

Since 1912, Cardinal O'Connell had sent priests from the seminary to the South Shore of Boston, where churches were overburdened by Catholics on vacation during the summer. While awaiting a regular assignment, Father Cushing served for two weeks at the Church of St. Ann in Cohasset: "I heard my first confessions there. I said my first masses there,* and the first baby I baptized, I baptized there." When he met this infant years later, the child was a deaf mute. "From that time on I took an interest in handicapped children," he said.

He next served as curate at St. Patrick's Church, a large, red-brick Gothic structure at the intersection of Dudley and Hampden Streets in Roxbury, Massachusetts. The parish included a girls' school and convent, along with the rectory. Under the new curate's prodding, its St. Patrick's Mission Club became an effective branch of "Proppy."

---

* Except for the mass at St. Eulalia's on the day of his ordination.

During his brief tenure, Father Cushing often said mass at St. Joseph's Home for the Aged, staffed by the Little Sisters of the Poor. The home was never so happy as when Father Cushing came. The old folks loved him because he was the only priest whom "even deaf people could hear . . . they could hear me down at the Dudley Street elevated station."

Young Father Cushing was like Bishop Jean Louis de Cheverus, * a French Roman Catholic who had fled to the United States during the French Revolution and later was consecrated as the first Roman Catholic bishop of Boston (1810). Cheverus, then a priest, said to Bishop John Carroll: "Send me where you think I am the most wanted, without making yourself anxious about the means of supporting me. I am willing to work with my hands, if need be and I believe I have the strength to do so." Father Cushing felt the same way. He learned quickly that he was never intended to be a neighborhood padre, hearing confessions, running bazaars, and becoming a bingo caller.

"I'm sorry to say I lasted only two weeks at St. Patrick's," he told one audience. "The pastor didn't like me. So I went to St. Benedict's Church in East Somerville, a suburb on the other side of the city. I did a little better there." He paused. "I lasted *four* [17] weeks. About two and one-half months after ordination, I had been in three parishes. So I said to myself, 'Either I'm queer or these pastors are!' I came to the conclusion that I was hopeless as a curate."

A few days after leaving St. Benedict's he took "heaven by storm." [18]

---

* William Ellery Channing, known as the "Apostle of Unitarianism," organized the American Unitarian Society in 1825. He and his friend Bishop Cheverus may have been America's first true ecumenicists. When Channing died in 1842, a Roman Catholic bell tolled for his funeral procession. In 1799, when Cheverus undertook to build what was to become the Cathedral of the Holy Cross on Franklin Street in downtown Boston, Unitarians were heavy contributors, and Charles Bulfinch, a non-Catholic, drew up the plans. In 1969 Cushing recalled it was Unitarian divines who were often the protectors and counsellors of the first Catholics to come to Boston.

chapter five

HIDDEN YEARS

WILLIAM CARDINAL O'Connell's parents, potato-famine refugees from Ireland, had come to Lowell, Massachusetts, where both worked at looms in textile mills. Cold, austere, stern, and urbane, Cardinal O'Connell could have been mistaken for a frosty Renaissance prelate, especially since he favored ceremonial robes and spoke fluent Italian. He was an esthete who played the organ, composed hymns,* and collected works of art. His prestige enabled him to mix easily with Boston Brahmins. Considered a power in the state legislature, where he was known as "Number One," he made the cardinal's residence in Brighton the counterpart of Cardinal Spellman's New York City chancery, which was called "the powerhouse." The Boston prelate was less reverently called "Big Bill," "Crimson Willie," and "Gangplank Bill," the last because he was so often photographed boarding a ship. "Every year as the New England blizzards began to descend," writes John H. Fenton, "the old cardinal would embark for Nassau in the Bahamas to his winter residence—because, it was sometimes remarked behind the hand, he could not bear to see his poor parishioners shiver in the cold." [1]

One morning Father Cushing, who did not have a formal appointment, rang the bell at the cardinal's office. "I thought I'd taken heaven by storm, Your Eminence," he said when the cardinal confronted him. "He almost threw me out," Cushing recalled. "I didn't get to heaven but I got the storm."

The cardinal led him in and motioned toward a chair, waiting for him to speak.

"Your Eminence, I couldn't be in worse trouble than I am now . . . I've been in three parishes . . . and I've come to the conclusion

---

* One of the prelate's compositions, "Hymn to the Holy Name," was played by the U.S. Marine Band outside St. Matthew's Cathedral at the funeral of President John F. Kennedy.

that I don't belong here. I'll never be happy in any one of the parishes. The work is not for me." When the prelate said he was scheduled to attend Catholic University, the young priest told him he would never be happy in a teaching assignment that would follow courses at the university. "I think I made a mistake. I should have followed the Jesuit persuasion, because I want missionary work." [2]

The cardinal, shifting his ample frame in his chair, leaned forward. "Well, what do you want?"

"I'd like to go to China or Africa, or join the Marist fathers in the Solomons. Anywhere. I'm big and strong."

The cardinal could say amen to that. Father Cushing was six feet tall and weighed about two hundred pounds. "I was very husky in those days and was athletically inclined," Cushing recalled. "I looked something like Gene Tunney, the heavyweight champion, and the cardinal, who could never remember my name, called me 'Tunney' pronouncing it 'Tooney.'" Cushing may not have known that the cardinal also referred to him as "the Irish Swede."

Father Cushing's interest in foreign missions had been kindled by his association at St. Patrick's Church in Roxbury with the Reverend James A. Walsh, the pastor whom he would later call "the greatest missionary that America has ever given the church." Thus it was while the idea of going to mission fields was still haunting him that he had gone to see Cardinal O'Connell, convincing him that he would be more effective working among pagan souls than by fulfilling his duties in routine parish work in Boston.

"The cardinal did not give his opinion on the matter just then," Cushing said in a speech in Ireland in 1959,[3] "but a few weeks later I was appointed to do propaganda work for the Propagation of the Faith in Boston. A year or so later, I was recalled by the Bishop, who evidently thought I was 'a dangerous man to have on the road,' and I was assigned as assistant director of the Propagation . . . for the archdiocese under Monsignor Joseph McGlinchey." He began this work in 1922.

Founded in Lyons, France, in 1892, the society had given financial aid to Bishop Benedict Fenwick and his successors in Boston. In 1845 grants had ceased because the society had expanded sufficiently to contribute to its headquarters. Then, because of the heavy influx of Irish immigrants, Bishop Fitzpatrick requested a further subsidy, although parish branches of the organization continued to donate to the headquarters in France.

In 1903, Archbishop Williams named Father Walsh the first Boston director of the society. The original office was in a room that shared the second floor with Mrs. Farrell's Laundry in a wooden frame building * near Holy Cross Cathedral. Father Walsh called his cubicle "the rookery." When he resigned in 1911 to found the Maryknoll Missioners, Father McGlinchey succeeded him. By 1922, the society annually collected about four thousand dollars for missions. The first assignment of Father Cushing, who would make that figure seem puny, was to encourage vocations, collect money, and interest Catholics in aiding missions.

For years, Cardinal O'Connell had dreamed of architectural changes in the archdiocese. The South End, once an affluent residential neighborhood with broad, tree-lined streets and attractive parks, had deteriorated, giving way to the most elegant rectangle in the Back Bay, which, before it was filled in beginning in 1857, had been a rat-infested marsh. Holy Cross Cathedral, once considered the stateliest church between Baltimore and Montreal, remained an architectural triumph in a section that become shabbier each year. An ugly elevated railway, with its deafening clatter of commuter trains roaring past the cathedral, drowned out sermons and interrupted devotions. A section that once boasted rows of brick mansions slipped into a wasteland of run-down rooming houses, dingy saloons, and hole-in-the-wall shops. The South End became an urban wilderness, the skid row of Boston.

Diocesan offices once located in houses on Union Park Street were no longer easily accessible to residents of outlying districts.

When Father Cushing became McGlinchey's assistant, his office and living quarters were in the old chancery building, an ornate Back Bay mansion on Granby Street just off Commonwealth Avenue near the Charles River. This Diocesan House had been the home of Cardinal O'Connell until he moved to Rawson Road in nearby Brookline.[4] The cardinal insisted that Father Cushing come to the office every day, even on hot summer days when there were no visitors and little to do. "A chancery official and I used to go down into the basement, drink beer, and throw rocks at the big rats that came in from the Charles River," Cushing told students at a retreat at St. John's Seminary in 1960.[5]

In 1927, the cardinal built the handsome episcopal residence on the grounds of St. John's Seminary, and his Brookline home became the

---

* At 62 Union Park Street.

St. Francis Friary and Retreat House. Two years later he built a
chancery near his residence in Brighton. Another ambition was to
locate in one building diocesan offices that were scattered around the
South End. In the mid-1930s, Cardinal O'Connell opened the new
diocesan office at 49 Franklin Street in downtown Boston. Father
Cushing moved into an office on the third floor after spending thirteen
years at the Back Bay headquarters. The cardinal, who daily visited
his chancery office on the third floor of the Diocesan House in the
Back Bay, used to say he could hear Cushing from the downtown
office on Franklin Street.

"The cardinal considered me the noisiest man he ever had in his
office," Cushing recalled, "but it didn't bother me." He liked the story
about O'Connell's comment after hearing Father Cushing give a sermon: "Rags, bones, bottles." Cushing was still a priest when the cardinal criticized him for preaching too loudly into the public address
system at the cathedral. O'Connell sent a cleric to tell Cushing to turn
down the microphone. "He hasn't got it on," the priest said on his return. Cushing enjoyed that story, too. "I didn't know there *was* a
sound system," he said, smiling. Years later, when, as a cardinal, Cushing spoke at a Boston College assembly, a listener had to leave early to
keep an appointment. When he finally hailed a taxi a block away, he
said, the Cushing baritone was still clear.

Cardinal Cushing remembered his superior as "a good boss who
never bothered me," and in relaxed moments he amused friends with
accounts of the days he spent with O'Connell in the Diocesan House
on Granby Street. "Somehow or other, Cardinal O'Connell liked me.
He was always very kind to me. He was the best boss I ever had. I
found him a great man to work for, because when he assigned you to a
job, he let you do it. He wouldn't be looking over your shoulder all
the time—not even on a job involving millions of dollars a year." [6]

During one of the cardinal's winter vacations in Nassau, Father
Cushing looked after his residence on Rawson Road. "Tooney, I'm
going away for a rest," the prelate said. "I'm taking all my official
family with me, and you will be here alone. I want you to take good
care of Moro, and remember, Tooney, above all things, that dog means
more to me than you do."

The cardinal's huge black poodle was royally treated during his
owner's absence, even though Cushing is not especially fond of dogs.
He tells of the trouble he had with the Irish cook.

"I feared her more than I did the cardinal. She would come up in the morning and wouldn't ask what you would like to eat. She simply set down a plate loaded with eggs, bacon, baloney, and sausages and glared. 'Eat it!' " The moment she left the room, Cushing would give the sausages and baloney to the dog, who expired two days before the cardinal returned. Father Cushing figured he would finally be "shipped off to the foreign missions."

"I have very sad news," he told his superior. "Moro died." He saw the stunned look on the cardinal's face. "He must have pined away for his master." Actually, he thought, Moro had probably succumbed to the rich diet.

Another time, while staying at the Brookline residence during the absence of the prelate, Father Cushing was plagued by rats "as big as cats, and you could hear them coming down the stairs—patter, patter. I spent a good deal of my time throwing rocks at them." [7]

Cushing has often said that his happiest days were spent as a simple priest with the Society for the Propagation of the Faith. This was literally a labor of love, and it continued until he became archbishop and no longer had much time for personal missionary zeal. Every Sunday he went to a different church to speak at every mass. That meant he gave as many as seven sermons during the morning, with perhaps a final appeal for the poor and for foreign missionaries at an afternoon benediction. He preached three or four times in every parish in the archdiocese and elsewhere during those twenty "hidden years." He gained a reputation not only as a remarkable administrator and fund-raiser, but also for his organizing techniques and his platform and pulpit manner, which brought unprecedented results. "Long before he became archbishop, people came from miles to hear Cushing," Joseph Dinneen wrote in 1951, "and gave generously when he asked for money. Sales managers studied his technique and sent their staffs to do likewise." [8] Merchandisers of group insurance plans and Red Cross and Red Feather agency speakers also studied his platform delivery. Cushing could give them no particular clue to his methods.

Audiences knew him as a nimble-witted and entertaining raconteur, adept at switching their moods. He was an imposing as well as an amusing pulpiteer. A stranger, after hearing him speak, congratulated him. "I was convinced, Father, as I listened to you tonight, that you must be one of the famous Cushings of Boston."

"No, sir, I am one of the Cushings of South Boston."

Another time, after introducing a canon from a Roman university, Cushing told an audience: "I am a canon from South Boston." When

Hugh Frazier, the British author, visited Cushing years later at the cardinal's residence, the prelate asked whether he knew any Cushings in England, where the name was common.

"No." Frazier said. "But when I return to England I'll be able to say that I have met the most distinguished Cushing in the United States."

Cushing was at his best when dramatizing faraway projects, and this helped him become known as the bishop of the missions. In 1928, he formed two clubs to spread the knowledge of missions into every Catholic home in his jurisdiction: the Sen Fu * Society for Women, which was limited to missionary work in China, and the Father Jim Hennessey Club for men.

Father James Hennessey, a curate at Holy Cross Cathedral who lived at the rectory, was fascinated by stories visiting missionaries told about their pioneer work in tropical outposts where a yard of mosquito netting was a luxury. He recognized the pressing need of priests in foreign missions. Why couldn't American priests volunteer for the work, he asked Cushing. "I am ready to be the first. I'd go to the diocese of the next bishop who pops in to see the cardinal, no matter where he comes from."

The first was the Most Reverend Thomas Wade, S.M., vicar apostolic of the mission area South Pacific. Bishop Wade, who called Father Cushing "the most selfless man I ever met and certainly the most generous," died in 1969 after a fantastic career. Bishop Wade, who had been taken prisoner by the Japanese after the invasion of Bougainville, escaped to the hills, where he arranged for the rescue of nuns and others by a submarine, which took them to New Caledonia. In his eulogy in 1969 of Bishop Wade's accomplishments and adventures while hiding out with his religious co-workers and parishioners in the hills of the islands, Cardinal Cushing said: "Anyone who tries to tell his story in simple human terms will find it incomprehensible." [9] American Marines called him "the Fighting Bishop of the Solomon Islands." After World War II, Cushing sent one hundred thousand dollars to the people of these islands.

In 1936 Father Hennessey wrote to Cushing from the then comparatively unknown North Solomon Islands: "Is it lonely? I have not found it so. Nobody likes company . . . better than I, but being alone for a change is not unpleasant. I often think of home and join in the

---

* Sen Fu means "Heavenly Father" in Chinese.

spirit the nightly gathering at the cathedral, and see you all, but not in a lonely way." [10]

Cushing was also the best friend of missionary nuns. His devotion to nuns was well known, and of all the sisters, his favorite was the founder of the Franciscan Missionary Sisters for Africa, Mother M. Kevin, who was called "a little bit of Irish impudence concealed but not hidden behind a Franciscan habit." [11] Mother Kevin was in Cushing's thoughts when, in one of his visits to the Medical Missionaries of Mary in Drogheda, Ireland, he spoke in the tiny oratory: "I love nuns. I have a great love for the missionary sisters and it is time that someone in the Catholic Church in a high position made that statement."

"Mama Kevina," as African natives knew her, called Cushing "my best living friend, the one who has helped us most throughout the years." At Father Cushing's suggestion she came to Boston in 1929 to get funds for her work. With her were Sisters Camilla, Annunciata, and Xavier, whose story Cushing told in a pamphlet, "The Three Bostonians." In 1929, Mother Kevin found Cushing "a fine, ardent, enthusiastic, and very handsome young priest, full of life and zest, and still full of the love of God and of souls."

Born in Ireland, she was one of six nuns sent in the early 1900s to Uganda, Africa. In 1923 she accepted the first applicants as Little Sisters of St. Francis and a novitiate was established three years later at Nkonkonjery, Africa. In 1928 she went to Europe to found a novitiate for the Missions in Yorkshire, England. The following year she came to Boston to get money for Holmes Hall, which housed the novitiate. Father Cushing asked how much money she needed.

"Oh, about fifty thousand dollars."

He asked how she expected to raise it, and she smiled. "You, Father, will do that for me."

Through his personal introductions of Mother Kevin to the Catholic Daughters of America and other groups, and his own efforts, she collected the money within two years. Apart from the fifty thousand dollars, Father Cushing asked what her most immediate need was.

"Well, it is on my mind, for I don't like debts," she said. "We bought a piano for the novitiate sisters so they could learn music so essential for Africa, and I have not paid for it yet. It cost five hundred dollars."

"Well," Father Cushing said, "curiously enough a benefactor came to my office today and handed me five hundred dollars for the first needy missionary, so here you are."

In 1935 Sister Kevin established a foundation at Mount Oliver, Dundalk, Ireland, to receive Irish postulants. In 1956 the motherhouse of the congregation Mother Kevin founded was transferred from Uganda to Mount Oliver, and the novitiate at Holmes Hall was also relocated there. In an address given at Mount Oliver Convent in 1959, Cardinal Cushing said of Mother Kevin: "She was the first missionary I had ever met to penetrate Equatorial Africa. . . . In 1953, I invited her to found a novitiate in Boston, giving her a site opposite St. John's Seminary. . . . Mother Annunciata was the first superior. . . . Mother Kevin was the greatest missionary of them all. . . . She spent herself, wore herself out, for God." A few hours before she died at the age of eighty-three in the convent in Brighton, she was speaking to a group about the needs of the missions. Cushing, at the request of Africans, had her laid to rest at Nkonkonjery, the motherhouse of the Little Sisters of St. Francis, and in her memory built a new convent on the old site in Brighton at a cost of five hundred thousand dollars. "Here," he said, "I hope many American and Canadian girls will enter and follow in the footsteps of Mother Kevin."

In 1955, when Mother Kevin received the O.B.E. in the Queen of England's birthday honors list, in recognition of her fifty years of outstanding work in Africa, the ceremony was held in the British Embassy in Washington, D.C., where the British ambassador, Sir Roger Makins, bestowed the insignia in the presence of Archbishop Cushing and the Irish ambassador.[12]

During his years with the society, Cushing was at his desk fifty-two weeks a year, never taking a formal vacation. He might take time off to go with his brother John to a Red Sox baseball game at Fenway Park or drop in to visit his family, but for the most part it was a steady grind. And it was a sad day in 1924 when Father Cushing said the funeral mass for his father, who had died of pneumonia.

At his office on Franklin Street his lunch was often a sandwich and a glass of milk or ginger ale, unless he brewed tea in the kitchenette. He ate supper from a tray in his study, often interrupted by the telephone, which he answered himself, usually identifying himself as "Father Cushing." If called to the telephone while dictating or if interrupted while in conference, he would return five or ten minutes later to repeat the last phrase before continuing. According to one reporter,[13] "he dictated hundreds of letters a week, wrote and edited scores of leaflets, pamphlets and brochures," and for years filled four columns in the *Pilot* with comments, quotations from letters sent by foreign missionaries, and appeals for funds.

After a full day at the office, Father Cushing was available evenings. To his office on Franklin Street, as to his first office on Granby Street, came missionaries from all parts of the world, knowing they would be cordially received by Cushing of Boston, whose benefactions were widely known by the early 1940s. They outlined projects and told their needs. The number of missionaries who came sometimes gave the impression that the United Nations was in session. Father Cushing was on duty even while in the cathedral rectory, where he lived with Monsignor Francis Spellman, who was six years older. Spellman, who had been ordained in Rome in 1916, was at this time assistant chancellor of the archdiocese.

One night Bishop Turquetil of the Oblate Missions among Eskimos, motioned toward the pounding radiators. "I never appreciated coal until I went to the Far North," he said. "Some coal up there costs $125 a ton."

"That got me out of my chair in a hurry," Father Cushing told an audience when he was pleading the cause of the Alaskan Oblates.[14] The force of his oratory was a powerful aid to the mission field, as he eloquently told of sacrifices made by men and women who forsook comfort to go to remote corners of the globe where their efforts were hampered by the indifference of ignorant pagans. "The aid and encouragement afforded by the Society to these missioners according to their own testimony in many cases weighed the balance from bare subsistence to vigorous growth," the *Pilot* reported in 1954, in a review of Cushing's missionary work.

Most of what was left of Father Cushing's salary after he paid for basic expenses and donated to missions went to buy shoes or clothing for the needy. Any gifts received passed quickly through his hands. Mother Mary, after giving him ten dollars, learned that he had handed the money to the wife of an alcoholic. "A benefactor gave Father Cushing a new overcoat, feeling that the vintage coat being worn by the priest could not have passed examination by the St. Vincent de Paul Society," a reporter wrote. "But the new coat was shortly on the shoulders of a visiting missioner." [15] A South Boston synonym for overcoat crept into Father Cushing's speech one night when he went to an American Legion meeting in Concord, Massachusetts. He handed the coat to an usher: "Hold onto this bennie. It's the last one I own."

His personal poverty is no myth. In keeping with a promise made when he was a young priest, he has accumulated no estate. This is one reason people have given to him unstintingly from the time he was a priest. He never keeps for himself anything that is given to him. By the second day after Christmas he has sent all his gifts to orphanages, hospitals, or homes for the poor or aged. "I can't use this," he may say, handing a present to a startled stranger. On the eve of his departure for the North American College anniversary reunion in October 1959, he found a new black hat and a new leather briefcase in the old-fashioned bureau of his bedroom. He gave these and three shirts to a visiting missionary. "Take whatever I give you," he said, "because I'll only give it away anyhow." On the return trip he pointed to a wrapped package on the rack of the jet plane. "Bishop Cornelius Lucey gave me that," he told a sister sitting beside him. "I don't know what's in it, but you can have it." In the package were eight choice Waterford goblets. The same nun has a silver platter hanging on her wall in a shadow box, a gift to Cushing from President Manuel Prado of Peru.

When he gave Madeline McMahon, one of his secretaries, a box of candy, he told her it was supposed to be a delicacy. She nodded. "Thank you very much. I know they're delicious. It was I who bought them for you." Another time she gave him two sport shirts to take on a fishing trip. A few weeks later John Cushing brought the shirts to the secretary and asked her to give them to the cardinal: "Someone gave them to me, but I don't remember who."

"I can tell you," she said, "because I bought them for your brother —and if he didn't keep them the first time, I guess he won't keep them now, either."

Soon after he became archbishop, Cushing won a pony at a fair. He named it Fanny and turned it over to Father Bruno Hagspiel, who kept it at Miramar in Duxbury, Massachusetts, headquarters for the Society of the Divine Word. One hot afternoon soon after, Cushing was sitting on his throne in Holy Cross Cathedral listening to a tedious homily by a long-winded visiting bishop. One of the two attendants flanking him was Father Hagspiel. Patting back a yawn, Cushing leaned toward him. "How's Fanny?" he asked. Choking with laughter, Father Hagspiel rose, made an obeisance, and walked to the sanctuary so that he could laugh without causing a commotion.

In the 1930s, Father Cushing was well known on South End streets.

Students at Cathedral High School exchanged greetings with him as he walked from the rectory to his office on Franklin Street. "How's everything, boys?" he usually said. "Give it all you have."

One morning a little girl was fretting at the prospect of being late for school. Father Cushing hoisted her over the fence, and she almost landed on a nun on the other side. She had a pat excuse for the scolding she got.

"Well, you see, Sister, Father Cushing pushed me up from the other side." [16]

In the bleakness of a dawn blizzard, Father Cushing was walking down Arlington Street across from Boston's Public Garden when he saw two nuns heading for mass at a church a half mile away. To make things easier for them, for the following eight years he climbed to the chapel of their headquarters on Arlington Street to say mass.[17]

He was on call around the clock. Once he was summoned to a nearby department store to give last rites to a man who had suffered a heart attack. Kneeling beside him, the priest asked: "Do you believe in the Father, Son, and the Holy Ghost?"

The man turned to the nurse. "Here I am dying, and he's asking me riddles." [18]

When children trailed their favorite padre down South End streets, they knew he would stop at a store to buy them candy bars or licorice stems. Panhandlers from skid row followed him, pleading for handouts. Crossing the parking lot behind the cathedral, he saw a dirty-faced urchin wandering around. Reaching into his pocket for some change, Father Cushing came up with only a religious medal, having given all his coins away. After borrowing a quarter from an aide to give the boy, he took his name and address and, discovering that he came from a destitute family, arranged to give them help.

One morning, after he had given his last dime, he found himself in front of a subway booth without carfare. The coin-changer extended credit to the following morning.[19] The man who later raised millions of dollars for charity was often pauper poor. He likes to repeat the words of Pope Pius X: "I was born poor; I have lived poor; and I shall die poor." He told one assembly that he began his priesthood as a penniless man. "In this capacity I intend to die. I do not owe a cent and do not have a cent." His net worth when he became archbishop was the cash value of a two-thousand-dollar insurance policy, which he took out to spare relatives the cost of his burial. Anyone who thought he was "loaded," he said, should read his will. An aide agrees. "When he dies, we'll throw out his toothbrush and thus dispose of his estate."

During the hidden years, the simple priest was not too proud to climb tenement stairs in Roxbury and the South End to collect bundles of clothes for the needy. Individuals, as well as organizations, dropped money in the till. He was amused when a housewife came into his office to put a contribution on his desk.

"Here's a dollar for them 'leapers,' " she said, referring to a leper colony to which Father Cushing had sent carpeting purchased wholesale from a rug dealer who had grown up with him in South Boston. Later, as bishop, he renovated St. Teresa's Convent in Bedford, Massachusetts, where American novitiates of the Society of Mary (Marists) are trained. He felt rewarded when these nuns volunteered to staff a leper colony on Jamaica, British West Indies.

Cushing ran raffles to ransom black babies in pagan lands and encouraged parochial schools to raise money for this purpose. In every class, boys vied with girls to see which group could bring in the most pennies, nickels, and dimes to the sister's desk. One girl, whose father was a grocer, tilted the balance in the girls' favor by dropping $2.80 on the desk, whereupon a lad handed the nun the thirty-five cents his mother had given him that morning to buy hamburger for supper. The only reward the students expected was the privilege of choosing Christian names for their adopted infants.

One afternoon two little girls with mission money from a parochial school waited for Father Cushing in the anteroom. When he saw them eyeing the bear rug apprehensively, he simulated a growl. As the girls fled in panic, he called them back. "Hey, don't run off without giving me the money." [20]

Cushing learned that he could often get repeat donations by sending thank you notes to contributors. An apocryphal story has him thanking the owner of the Kasanof bread company for a large donation: "I will remember you in my prayers."

"As long as you are going to do that," Kasanof responded, "would it be too much to ask you to change the Lord's Prayer slightly so it will read: 'And give us this day our Kasanof's bread?' "

Among his fund-raising groups was the St. Patrick's Mission in Roxbury, the Teresian Guild of St. Ann's in Neponset, the Mission Circle of the Boston Elevated Railway, the State Public Works Mission Circle, and the Hotel Statler Mission Group. He kept expanding the list.

His organizational genius was beginning to show.

chapter six

BISHOP OF THE
MISSIONS

FATHER CUSHING attended a Boston College assembly in 1936 when Cardinal Eugenio Pacelli, then papal secretary of state, sat on the platform with Cardinal O'Connell. Pacelli arose to address the students.

"I give you one day off," he said, exercising an ancient prerogative. When the cheering died, he said, "I give you two days off." The worried rector became even more concerned when Pacelli, raising three fingers, said, "I give you three days off." At this point, the rector dismissed the students and escorted the two cardinals off the platform.

Later Cushing occasionally exercised his privilege of giving students time off. He bypassed it once because a Jesuit professor complained: "I lose a century when there's a day out of class." Knowing Cushing's propensity for giving informal vacations, school administrators scheduled his speeches with that thought in mind.

Three years after meeting Cardinal Pacelli, Cushing received a brief from him appointing him a domestic prelate with the rank of the right reverend monsignor. By this time the Italian prelate had become Pope Pius XII. Cushing's new rank entitled him to wear the violet cassock or soutane and mantelletta, a silk or woolen sleeveless vestment reaching to the knees. Cushing, after casually adding red piping to his soutane, looked around at his office staff. "That takes care of that," he said, returning to work. He told a friend: "The only reason I'm getting ahead with the cardinal is that I'm bringing in money."

Monsignor Cushing continued to visit diocesan churches, begging for money in his long, rambling, sometimes slangy, and usually humorous speeches spiced with earthiness. He spoke in a flat, nasal monotone, occasionally with a "shanty town" inflection or a South

Boston locution such as he might use in a conversation with an old friend, who would say, "It's nice to see you." Cushing might respond, "The same to yourself." Cardinal O'Connell likened his voice to Father Coughlin's, which could carry to the last row in the largest hall, but Cushing could more aptly have been compared to Al Smith, of whom it was said, when he was speaker of the assembly, that he did not need a gavel, because he had a gavel in his throat. A former baseball reporter assigned to the religious beat compared Cushing to the loquacious Casey Stengel. He was, nevertheless, a powerful speaker who ranked with leading orators of his era. There was substance, as well as conviction, in his talks. When Governor Leverett Saltonstall of Massachusetts was praised for a Thanksgiving Day proclamation, he told the press that Archbishop Cushing had drafted his speech.

His gravelly voice and gestures were occasionally mimicked behind his back, as happened one afternoon when he came to speak for the missions at a benediction at St. William's Church in Dorchester. While he had lunch with the pastor, two acolytes who were to assist him noticed his red cape and biretta in the sanctuary. One slipped into the flowing cape and pulled the biretta down over his ears, strutting around sprinkling holy water. Noticing the look of horror on the face of the other altar boy, he slowly wheeled.

"That outfit looks very good on you," Monsignor Cushing said as he donned his violet robes. He did not comment on the acolyte's nasal delivery.

By this time, Cushing was one of the most popular clergymen in the state. "Thousands remember him in their clubrooms talking baseball after a speech," John Fenton wrote, "or standing in a kitchen at gatherings of women, complimenting the cook. Elderly Irish women who once called him Father were at the same time likely to look upon him as a son."

Two months after notifying Cushing that he had been made a monsignor, Cardinal O'Connell had another announcement: "I have received word . . . from the Papal Secretary of State that the Holy Father, at my request, has named the Right Reverend Richard J. Cushing as Auxiliary Bishop of Boston." For Cushing it was priest to monsignor to bishop in eight weeks.

Cardinal O'Connell, eighty years old and with failing eyesight, recognized Cushing as a tireless worker eminently qualified to succeed Bishop Francis Spellman who, in turn, had succeeded Patrick Cardinal

Hayes as archbishop of New York. Spellman was surprised when O'Connell chose Cushing. "I asked the cardinal to appoint Louis Kelleher as my successor in Newton Center and he said he would." [1]

"Whether he (O'Connell) wanted me or not," Cushing said years later, "I don't know. I think he had others in mind, although he was always very good to me, like a father."

Mother Mary Cushing, then eighty-one, was overjoyed at the honor that had come to her forty-four-year-old son. "I always knew you'd be a bishop," she said. Much less enthusiastic was the prelate. The new office, he felt, would handicap a simple priest who visited jails and mingled with the poorest of the poor in slums.

"I just don't want this thing, Your Eminence," he said. "It just doesn't appeal to me. I'm perfectly happy where I am. There must be a number of priests who want to be bishops." The cardinal told him to think it over. Two days later Cushing was more determined than ever. "It doesn't appeal to me, and the only way I'll take it is if Your Eminence makes it a command."

"You take it!"

"So I took it," Cushing recalled years later. When Irish visitors visited him in 1964, he told them: "When they made me a bishop twenty-five years ago, I didn't want it at all, but I couldn't get out of it."

A grinning South Boston police officer congratulated him. "You've come a long way Dickie boy, since I used to boot you one on Broadway." [2]

At the consecration of June 20, 1940, four thousand persons turned out, some of them forced to stand outside Holy Cross Cathedral. Cushing's immediate family and relatives filled the front pews. Archbishop Spellman watched from the sanctuary as Cardinal O'Connell celebrated one mass at the main altar, while Cushing sang another at a side altar. The co-consecrators were Cushing's old rector, Bishop Peterson, and Bishop Thomas A. Emmet, S.J., of Jamaica, British West Indies.

After most of the congregation had left, the new bishop came forward and, visibly moved, looked straight at his family and friends. "Please don't forget the missions." Then he walked to the altar rail to give his first blessing to his mother, who was weeping softly.

Ten weeks later, while Bishop Cushing was giving a sermon at a special mass opening the academic year at Boston College, word came of his mother's death. He was too upset to officiate at her requiem mass. Afterward, having seen the governor, mayor, and other prominent civic and political leaders at the ceremony, he told an aide: "Mother Mary would never have believed it." [3]

As auxiliary bishop, he became the cardinal's action man. He also succeeded Spellman as pastor of Sacred Heart Parish in Newton, an affluent suburb outside Boston. As the continuing director of the Society for the Propagation of the Faith, he bolstered Boston's position as a leader in fund-raising for missions. Foreign missionaries and military chaplains who visited him at the rectory recounted the horrors of night bombing and the hardships in concentration camps during World War II. Father Hennessey went down with a Japanese prisoner-of-war ship in the waters north of Luzon. Word kept coming back of the capture and imprisonment of missionaries. One returned missioner told Bishop Cushing of the bayoneting in the South Pacific of Father Arthur C. Duhamel, S.M., of Methuen, Massachusetts. On April 21, 1943, Cushing told this story to eleven separate congregations at Mission Church in Roxbury and by the end of the day collected fifteen thousand dollars for missionaries in the Solomons. In Methuen in 1944, he dedicated a memorial to that town's first gold star missionary, calling him "a genuine double for Christ, his divine model, for like his master, he gave all, even life itself."

A Chinese bishop who had escaped from the Japanese during their advance in the South Pacific, and a chaplain on furlough, told Sacred Heart students what their contributions had done for destitute children in the Far East. They were all the more inclined to donate when Bishop Cushing read them a navy commander's letter to his son written just before he was shot down in the Pacific after sinking a Japanese cruiser.

While American forces in their advance rescued priests and nuns, Bishop Cushing gave money to rebuild missions. In 1943 he set the goal at fifty thousand dollars and raised twice that sum in his tireless rounds of preaching. When American troops in the Solomons learned of the project, men of all faiths sent large contributions through their chaplains. Many servicemen first heard of the "Boston Bishop of the Missions" from native islanders, and American GI's landing on the outposts of Oceania had only to say they were from Boston to be greeted as brothers. A familiar question was, "You know Faddah Cushin'?" According to Monsignor Francis Lally, "Many a life was saved due to the natives' warm response to the assurance by the GI that he 'came from Father Cushing's place in America.' " [4] Just after the war, a visiting missionary told Father Hagspiel that in every remote outpost he had visited, he heard of donations made by Cushing when he was a priest, monsignor, or bishop.

"I don't know a fourth of the church's cardinals," Cushing recalled in 1964. "But I know all the poor missionaries with long beards." [5]

In a leaflet, "What Our Fighting Men on Guadalcanal Think of Catholic Missions," Cushing published a letter from an army chaplain who gave actual comments of servicemen and the amounts they contributed. This leaflet brought in more donations for the "resurrection" of the Solomons. Bishop Cushing sent silver rosaries to departing servicemen and personally exchanged letters with thousands of young people in the armed forces.* He saved the shredded garments worn by the first missionary victim of the invaders of Guadalcanal, keeping them in a receptacle on which he had inscribed: "Lest I Forget." †

American marines who cleared the Japanese from the Gilbert Islands found only three white women there—American nuns at the Sacred Heart Mission. The leathernecks replaced their candles with electric lights, gave them a radio, and installed a kerosene refrigerator. Cushing was even more generous. Through missionaries, he gave the islanders motorboats and motorcycles—novelties among tropical waterways and jungle trails. He also sent field altars to chaplains, along with much needed supplies. His name was remembered long after World War II.

When Franklin D. Roosevelt, Jr., on a mission for President Kennedy, stopped in Bukoba, Tanganyika, Africa, where Laurian Cardinal Rugambwa was addressing a gathering, he was unable to push through the crowd to pay respects to the prelate until a companion shouted: "Cardinal Cushing, Cardinal Cushing, Cushing of Boston!" Then a path opened and the cardinal, tracing the voice, came to the Americans. Through Roosevelt, he sent warm regards to Cardinal Cushing and President Kennedy.

In January 1943, Cardinal Spellman, military vicar of the American armed forces, landed at Logan Airport, ending a thirty-two day, 28,000-mile trip. He arrived just in time to assist Bishop Cushing in

---

* During the Korean War, Archbishop Cushing said mass in military hospitals, visited camps, and set up a Catholic Servicemen's Bureau. He also sent GI's Christmas cards and gifts.

† U.S. marines kept the belt of the first marine killed, writing under it, "Lest We Forget."

dedicating our Lady of the Airways Chapel. A few weeks later Spellman was again in Boston to confer with Cushing about a visit to Generalissimo Chiang Kai-shek, Lieutenant General Eisenhower, and Major General George Patton, Jr. "We had a fine talk," Spellman said, "and as usual, he approved of me and my acts." [6]

Nine years later, Spellman again conferred with Cushing after visiting chaplains and troops in Korea.[7] In his eulogy of Cardinal Spellman at a memorial mass at the cathedral in December 1967, Cushing said in part: "He would be pleased to be remembered . . . not so much as he appeared on occasions of honor or at great ecclesiastical functions, but rather on those gray hillsides of Korea and the green jungles of Vietnam, when he offered mass before dawn for the young soldiers of America." Spellman performed similar functions during World War II, contributing as much to GI morale as did Cushing.

During the five years Bishop Cushing lived at the rectory of Sacred Heart Parish, nuns could look out the window to see him playing catch with pupils. He kept parents informed of their children's progress. To one parent who was worrying about her children, he said there was no cause for concern. "Boys will be boys," he wrote, recalling his own boyhood. During these years he carried a heavy load. "I went to the Propagation office every morning at eight and came back every night at eight."

As pastor of the large parish, he went out of his way to assist the Little Sisters of the Poor, who staffed the parochial school. No detail escaped his attention. He checked report cards, judged speaking contests, staged plays, and chaperoned dances. He ran lawn parties, took seniors on excursions, heard confessions, visited prisons and charitable institutions, directed fund drives, officiated at requiem masses for the war dead, and maintained a heavy speaking schedule. When asked to give a talk, he checked his appointment book and invariably obliged if he had free time.

"He barely leaves himself time to hurry from one place to the next," one of his curators said. Late for a Communion breakfast, he said the woman who picked him up wore such a large hat it blew out of the car window and he had to walk back to pick it up.[8] Priding himself on being punctual, he was surprised one evening to find nobody in a banquet room at the Statler Hilton, where he was scheduled to speak. It was the wrong hotel. For once, when he arrived at the Sheraton Hotel, he was late.

Since time was important, he bridled at any unnecessary delay. Once at Sacred Heart Church, when he was officiating at a marriage, he waited for the wedding music to begin and the bride to come down the aisle. She and her attendants were waiting for the music, and the organist, apparently, was waiting for the procession to start. As minutes dragged on, Cushing impatiently barked to a curate: "I'll give that bride another minute. If she doesn't get down here by then, someone else can marry her." It was a sight to see the curate flying down the nave, waving on the bride and her attendants.

Between whirlwind visits to every church in the diocese to audit parish accounts and ordain priests, he was always on call, always willing to do favors. The greater the need, the more eager he was to help. "He is impartial," a nun said, "but if he favors any particular group, they are the needy and those in sorrow. He never has refused to help anyone whose need is honest." [9] Once, when a Protestant minister came to borrow some folding chairs, Bishop Cushing told him that if he could find a few men to do the unloading, "I think I can find a truck to deliver them . . . tonight." [10]

His thoughtfulness did not pass unnoticed. "It's amazing how he can remember people," a woman who had met him briefly said. Months later she attended a ceremony at his church in Newton. On the church steps, Cushing warmly greeted her. "Not only that, he talked on the very subject we had spoken of on the first occasion. For him, it was as though we had met only the day before." [11] Another woman, whom he had confirmed at a low mass, attended a more formal Confirmation ceremony ten months later. Bishop Cushing extended his ring for her to kiss, "You're getting the trimmings now that you missed the first time," he said.

He usually confirmed children in the presence of their parents, and before administering the sacrament, he would pace up and down the nave, asking questions from the catechism. By posing simple questions and glossing over blunders, he quickly set at ease candidates who, in their panic, gave the wrong answer.

"Who made the world?" he asked Michael Cronin, son of Joseph Cronin, then manager of the Boston Red Sox and later president of the American League.

"God made the world."

"Who made the Red Sox?" Bishop Cushing asked.

"Tom Yawkey."

Cushing waited for the tittering to end. "You certainly know your catechism," he said.

On his confirmation tours he stressed the need for more priests, nuns, and brothers who would be useful at home as well as on missionary outposts in every corner of the globe. Most of them, he realized, would have to be recruited from young men and women in high school or at the beginning of college careers. When he asked one group of confirmation candidates whether any of them wanted to become priests or nuns, a baby in the audience embarrassed his mother by squalling.

"That's wonderful," Cushing said, "And I'm sure that some day you'll make a fine priest, too." [12]

Another duty was to ordain priests. Once, after consecrating six Marist priests at Holy Cross Cathedral, he startled them in the sacristy by kneeling to ask their blessing, just as they had earlier prostrated themselves before him.

The frantic pace undermined his health, often leaving him drawn and exhausted. Once, while dictating to a stenographer, he pitched forward and slumped onto his desk. He would have fainted had he not rested for a few minutes on a sofa. "It's nothing," he told his worried stenographer. "If you'll just put a cold cloth on my forehead I'll be all right." [13]

In his autobiography, Bishop William Lawrence cited the importance of a sense of humor in a bishop. Compassion was important, too, "for the pathetic, tragic, and commonplace enter one's life almost every hour." It might be a mother seeking advice about a wayward son, a widow worried about a mortgage being foreclosed, or a released convict looking for a job. Bishop Cushing had all these problems and many more.

The very names of charitable organizations in the slums of the South End and Roxbury suggested heartbreak and despair. In the former, once planned as a pleasant residential area, were St. Joseph's Home for Sick and Destitute Servant Girls and the Penitent Females' Refuge and Bethesda Society, which established a home "for the reformation of abandoned women." Other institutions in the area were the Home for Aged and Indigent Men, the Boston Female Asylum, and the Children's Friend Society. The names of the institutions changed, but the wretchedness remained. During his priestly career Cushing did more than any other churchman for the poor and needy.[14]

He might spend a day visiting the Boston City Hospital in the morning, kneeling at the bedside of a dispirited patient to say the rosary with him, then spend an hour or two at the House of the Good

Shepherd in Roxbury, home for wayward women and girls. Bishop Cushing, who hated sin, loved sinners and did all he could to ease their anxieties and tensions. At the House of the Good Shepherd he added courses in shorthand, typewriting, and hairdressing so the women could find work when released. He bought a beauty shop and sent all its equipment to the institution and installed three juke boxes, which he called nickelodeons.[15] He built new quarters for the Sisters Magdalens, a branch of the Good Shepherd Community composed of penitents who, rather than leave the home after getting a new outlook, preferred to assist the Sisters of the Good Shepherd. Cushing also founded the Good Shepherd Guild.

"Pure religion," said Chatfield, "may generally be measured by the cheerfulness of its professors, and superstition by the gloom of its victims." Wherever he went, Cushing touched the friendless and forlorn with the warm glow of his lightheartedness. One afternoon he met on the church steps a parishioner who was ninety-eight years old.

"You won't forget me, Father, will you? You won't forget me?"

"How could I forget you?" Bishop Cushing put his arm around her shoulder. "I'm your boyfriend."

His informality delighted faculty and students at Sacred Heart School, where he let pupils select recordings for the juke box in the recreation room. One day, when a blare of music disturbed her class, a sister sent a girl to turn off the din. The culprit was Bishop Cushing. The teacher asked what he was playing.

"Well, Sister, it wasn't Bach." [16]

At parish socials Cushing passed around refreshments and mixed with youngsters, lifting them onto Ferris wheels and pausing occasionally to take a colored photograph or to permit a student to snap his picture. Again, he would pose with them so that a professional photographer could take their picture. He made sure that every child in the group received a memento of the occasion, knowing it would be treasured. At one Confirmation ceremony a lad trailing him was trying to line up a shot. Cushing turned, picked out a spot where the light was suitable, and asked the boy how he should pose.

"He's only a little shaver now, but he'll remember this day when he grows up." [17]

Another time he tied on an apron made for him by a girl at St. Pauletta's in Stoughton, Massachusetts. He knew the child would be thrilled when he told her he wore her apron on television.

One morning Bishop Cushing delayed his departure from a parish while a boy whom he had just confirmed raced home for a camera. On another Confirmation visit a lad brought his camera into the sacristy while Cushing was slipping into his ermine cape. "Whom do you represent, the *Pilot?*" Cushing asked. When the boy did not answer, he said, "Maybe he's from the *South Boston Gazette.*" [18] His aim always was to put youngsters at ease.

Parents, as well as children, liked his informality, even while he was administering Confirmation. "Let's wait for the photographer," he often said, pausing during a ceremony to make things easier for the press. "Okay, boys, we'll call the show off for a minute so you can take pictures." Personally shunning publicity, he nevertheless knew what it meant to families involved.

He lightened burdens wherever he could. "I am not a Catholic," a girl wrote from the Peabody Home for Crippled Children, "but I asked my minister if I could write you, and he said I could. What I want to know is when you are coming again to give us another movie show?" [19] On one visit to this institution, Cushing—by this time a cardinal—brought along Jimmy Durante, who greeted every child and did a brief impromptu skit for the group.

"When I done dat show for dem retarded kids," Durante said, "one of dem comes up to me when I was leavin' and hands me a quarter. 'Here,' he says, 'go buy yourself something; you give us a good show.' " [20]

Bishop Cushing lost none of his informality in the presence of proper Bostonians. One night in 1943 when he addressed the Charitable Irish Society in Boston, guests at the head table were Senator Robert A. Taft, of Ohio, and Governor Leverett Saltonstall, of Massachusetts. Bishop Cushing hoisted the microphone.

"Taft," he intoned. There was a long pause. "Saltonstall." The hotel auditorium was silent. "Cushing." He spread out his hands in a familiar gesture. "What a ticket!" [21] The applause was deafening.

By this time, almost everyone in New England realized that the prelate's vision went beyond the limits of his archdiocese to the needs of the whole world. No diocese, he said, was fully mature until it sent missionaries to plant the seeds of faith in other lands. The clergy and laity under him combined to support his vast programs in religious, educational, and social action fields, helping to implement his episcopal motto: "That they may know Thee" (*Ut cognoscant Te*).

His willingness to serve people of all faiths was quietly demonstrated on the afternoon of October 12, 1942, when several hundred American servicemen crowded into the parish church in Ayer, Massachusetts, to attend a mass celebrated by Cushing. Gerald M. Kilcullen of Jamaica, New York, vividly remembered the occasion a quarter of a century later:

"Several features of the celebration were remarkable. The saying of mass in the late afternoon was, in that pre–Vatican II period, unusual. Some of those present said it was an important first in this respect. A memorable feature was its spontaneity. Word got around soon after lunch that anyone wishing to attend mass would be excused from the usual military formations at Fort Devens. There was incredulity. Mass in afternoon as an excuse from Retreat? Then came a motley assortment of jeeps, trucks, staff cars, and weapon-carriers to transport the uniformed men to the church just a few yards outside the main gate of Fort Devens.

"More than a trace of ecumenicism was visible during this part of the proceedings, with officers, regardless of their religious affiliations, cordially inviting Catholic soldiers to join in. Most of the ranking officers of the small Devens world attended the mass, and no one laughed when the pastor, a Friar Lawrence type, complete with a wispy halo of white hair encircling a neat expanse of scalp, interrupted the concluding prayers to leap onto the Communion rail and bellow an invitation to all uniformed men to a big dinner at the nearby USO. This was Father Hasenfull, a convert from Lutheranism. Bishop Cushing was the after-dinner speaker, and was loudly applauded by the 1,200 men present." [22]

Gregarious though he appeared, Bishop Cushing knew moments of loneliness, especially on festive occasions. At Thanksgiving, Christmas, and Easter, when he would have enjoyed being with his own family, he sent his three curates home for family reunions, and he handled their routine work at church, visiting the ill, hearing confessions, greeting visitors, and answering the telephone. Before a light supper in his study, he might read a newspaper while listening to recordings ranging from an Irish hornpipe to Beethoven's Ninth Symphony, and there was always a heap of correspondence to handle. Alfred C. Wasilauskas, his chauffer and general assistant, helped answer letters, operated the movie projector, set up tables and chairs at parish functions, and was always on call for an errand. Cushing had a buzzer installed when he moved into the cardinal's residence so he could reach Wasilauskas or his wife Genevieve at any time of day or night. One day in 1943 Bishop Cushing was asked to preside at a parochial school competition at Boston College. The committee, learning at the last minute that he was bringing a guest, put an extra chair on the reviewing stand. Not until Cushing's car drove past the gate was the guest's identity known. Sitting beside the prelate was little Ann Wasilauskas, the chauffeur's daughter.

Cushing's responsibilities were at times awesome. They became more so early in 1944 when Cardinal O'Connell's health declined. During his last illness, Cushing went to see him every night on his way home from the office in town. After suffering a cerebral hemorrhage, O'Connell took another turn for the worse, developing bronchial pneumonia. A biographer writes: "During his last days he clasped firmly in his hands the crucifix that had been his as a seminarian in Rome; blessing with the crucifix the nephews and nieces, the priests of his household [and] Bishop Cushing who led them in the recitation of the rosary. But they never heard again the strong, melodious voice." [23]

The cardinal's death late in April was a personal sorrow for Bishop Cushing, who was at his bedside. Later Cushing said, "He was a brilliant man, and he was always good to me. Nobody really understood him. I saw him at his best and at his worst. Toward his death he was very lonely. He died in the room I sleep in." [24] Another time Cushing said: "I feel that if he could have stayed in the background and have stayed out of controversial subjects, he could have been the greatest churchman of his time." When Congressman Joseph O'Connell called his death an irreparable loss to the church, Archbishop Amleto Giovanni Cicognani said: "No question about it. Your uncle did a great deal of good for the Church, but the Church most go on." [25]

On April 28, the cardinal, who had guided the spiritual destinies of more than a million Catholics, was laid to rest in a fieldstone crypt in a chapel he had built near his residence. The simple service contrasted sharply with the Old World pageantry in a city that had never before witnessed a funeral of a prince of the church. The five-day requiem ended with the greatest mass demonstration of devotion ever seen in New England. In Holy Cross Cathedral, twenty-five hundred persons attended a three-hour service, while ten thousand others stood outside to listen through an amplifying system. Archbishop Cicognani celebrated the pontifical requiem mass from the throne the cardinal had occupied for thirty-seven years.

In his eulogy, Bishop Cushing said: "Behold a great priest. He whose mortal remains lie here before the altar . . . could ask for no more satisfying recognition. That was his ambition; that was his triumph—to be a great priest." Cushing noted that the cardinal had combined "a genuine love of his priests and people with a detachment which kept him from the softening consolation of their friendships; but he paid the price for this magnificent service to God and country with a lonely life and no less lonely death." Cushing, who himself soon discovered that power and responsibility bring loneliness, once said, "I have no close friends."

During the long service in the cathedral, Cardinal O'Connell lay in state before the altar, his red galero at the foot of his bier until it was hung from the vaulted ceiling of the church. The prelate had maintained his prestige to the very end. When a large Boston insurance company neglected to put its American flag at half mast on the day he died, it was so swamped with telephone calls that, as a belated mark of respect, it remained closed on the day of the cardinal's funeral.[26]

Six monsignori, serving as archdiocesan consulters, chose Bishop Cushing to administer the archdiocese pending papal appointment of O'Connell's successor.

Although Cushing had never been out of the United States, save for a brief trip to Bermuda, and was not personally acquainted with Vatican prelates, his achievements in the missionary field were well known to Pope Pius XII, who called him "the unparalleled auxiliary." Cushing had served O'Connell well as an executive and administrator. One writer called him "a talented, spirited junior whom the cardinal never could quite dominate or do without. Both had remarkably comparable backgrounds, but were cast in different molds." [27]

There was no certainty that Cushing would be named the sixth ordinary and third archbishop of Boston. But on September 28, 1944, official word came from Pope Pius XII that Cushing, at the age of forty-nine, was the new archbishop of Boston. Spellman had been the heir apparent until the death of Patrick Cardinal Hayes changed the picture.

The Boston *Herald,* like all Boston newspapers, hailed the appointment: "The know-it-all gossipers had named a dozen men as successors to Cardinal O'Connell, but Bishop Cushing was hardly mentioned." One clergyman had reported a coolness between Cushing and Spellman. "The difference was to a large degree temperamental

—the difference between a roughie [Cushing] and a smoothie. The smoothie thought he could tell the roughie what to do—and he couldn't." Cushing dismissed the report as "ridiculous." He told one audience: "Spellman got me this job! Pius XII himself told me this."

Editorial writers agreed that the new archbishop loved human beings as human beings, and especially those at the extremes—the young and the ailing old. A nun gave one of the most telling assessments of the prelate: "All his life this priest would know how to lift others out of the gloom that chills the lonely soul. He would . . . understand the suffering that comes from loneliness, because he would voluntarily choose the solitary path . . . to dedicate himself completely to his life task of helping others." [28] The Right Reverend Henry Knox Sherrill, episcopal bishop of Boston, spoke for clergymen of all faiths: "I am delighted at hearing of Bishop Cushing's appointment to head the Boston archdiocese. He is a friend of mine and I am sure his ministry will grow with the opportunity that now is his." Missionaries in the leper colony of Father Damien fame on the island of Molokai congratulated him, as did the Negro seminarians at Bay St. Louis, Mississippi.

Cushing's appointment was unusual in one respect. Few archbishops are native to their archdiocese. It would have been more normal to have brought into Boston an archbishop who had had broad administrative experience. Cushing knew this: "I never had anything to do with the running of the diocese," he said. "I was always on the outside, never involved in internal affairs." He received the news of his elevation "with feelings of profound humility and reverential gratitude," adding that he did not deserve "the recognition that has come to me. . . . I accepted it only because I felt that it was a tribute to the priests of the archdiocese." [29]

The tall, rugged prelate, who looked like a well-trained athlete, was the youngest archbishop in the world when Archbishop Cicognani, apostolic delegate to the United States, installed him on November 8 as shepherd of the second largest Catholic see in the nation. Ranking prelates in richly colored mantles and white and gold vestments, along with a record number of several hundred priests, abbots, and nuns, crowded Holy Cross Cathedral. Hundreds of persons who were unable to get into the church stood in the bitter cold to hear the ceremonies over a public address system.

Cushing wet his lips as he glanced at the wide-brimmed, round-domed galero suspended high above him from the rafters over the altar, conscious of the weight of responsibility he was inheriting from his predecessor. Monsignor Jeremiah Minihan, chancellor of the archdiocese, read the decree of appointment and installation. Bishop Francis P. Keough of Providence, Rhode Island, said in his sermon: "Rarely in the history of our country has the elevation of a prelate to such a high office been more sincerely and universally welcomed than in the case of this archbishop." Dignitaries on hand were senators David I. Walsh and Sinclair Weeks, Governor Leverett Saltonstall, and Mayor Maurice J. Tobin, of Boston.

After the ceremony, the new archbishop was host at a luncheon at the Copley Plaza Hotel to a thousand priests of the archdiocese. At the same time, three thousand other priests, brothers, and nuns seated themselves in their respective institutions as his "guests." In a brief address, Archbishop Cushing said the principal problems facing the church were intellectual skepticism and moral indifference. "Skeptics," he said, "do not attack Christianity, they ignore it. How shall we meet them? By every possible means whereby individual souls can be reclaimed to the truth." Later at a press conference he added: "I was born in Boston, I was bred in Boston, I love Boston. I'm for everything that will promote Boston's welfare. I'm against every 'anti'."

By this time, Cushing had earned the love, respect, and complete good will of every clergyman and layman of his own creed and of many Bostonians of every other creed. Casual, congenial, and unfailingly forthright, he was nevertheless a man of great dignity, and his common sense and good humor were well known. Soon after his elevation he went to the State House to be sworn in as corporation sole of the Boston see. Although this is an ecclesiastical position, the candidate must be installed in a civil ceremony. When a group of stenographers knelt to kiss his ring, he smiled: "My name is Cushing." He could be even more informal among friends. When he showed his episcopal ring to Kate Mann, an old friend, he said, "I got this at a bargain."

It was not easy to follow Cardinal O'Connell on the stage. During his tenure, the Boston see had moved from the status of mission to a position of permanence and strength, especially during his thirty-two years as cardinal. Few middle-aged persons could not remember when O'Connell had not been head of the archdiocese. Cushing rose from monsignor to archbishop in less than five years—scarcely a moment as the church measures time.[30]

chapter seven

GETTING THE HANDOUTS

ARCHBISHOP CUSHING was the second high-ranking prelate to live in the sixty-four-room stone mansion on Commonwealth Avenue at Lake Street. Under Cardinal O'Connell, the episcopal residence had been cold and formal, and few Bostonians had ever seen its lavish interior. One room was in Italian Renaissance style; another was baroque; the dining room was late Victorian. In his love of splendor, the cardinal had filled the little palace with oriental rugs, marble chests, carved oak furniture, a Cuban mahogany clock with Westminster chimes, and oil paintings in massive frames.

Under the new archbishop, the residence became a vibrant center of charity, hospitality, and human traffic. "Everybody has a key to this joint," Cushing quipped.

"When he moves in," the Boston *Post* observed, "he will probably carry all his worldly possessions in two traveling bags. For the new occupant of the big Italian-style house is by nature a man of humility and simple tastes, little interested in material things."

Stripping the residence of its luxurious furnishings, he auctioned off art treasures, antiques, and carved wooden pieces, using the proceeds to finance the education of priests at St. John's Seminary. He turned the third floor into a dormitory for students whose education he financed at Harvard University and the Massachusetts Institute of Technology, where they took special courses unavailable at Catholic colleges.

He drained the swimming pool to make room for drawing boards, blueprints, files, mimeograph machines, and the voluminous literature sent him.[1] He dismissed the cardinal's valet and replaced his retinue of servants with four nuns (later the number was increased) to do the cooking, cleaning, and housekeeping. After the students vacated the premises, the nuns moved up a flight. Cushing quickly dispensed with a listed telephone number. "I don't mind it so much in the daytime," he said of the frequent calls, "but I found out the hard way how a fireman feels when pulled out of bed at three in the morning." [2]

He replaced three limousines with a sedan and hired Wasilauskas as chauffeur. Cushing told John Gunther "with great pride that his chauffeur, Lithuanian born, had married an Italian girl." [3] Genevieve Wasilauskas continued to work as the prelate's stenographer. When her husband died in 1958, her son succeeded him. A Chrysler equipped with a telephone and siren was one gift to him. One hot summer afternoon the sisters at Sacred Heart High School in Kingston, Massachusetts, became alarmed when the sound of a siren kept coming closer. In their wooded area they fear forest fires. They were relieved when Archbishop Cushing drove up in the Chrysler accompanied by five youngsters wearing firemen's helmets.

Archbishop Cushing found it difficult to keep only one automobile. In 1954, the Packard motor corporation gave him a ten-thousand-dollar, custom-built, air-conditioned, bullet-proof Packard sedan. President Eisenhower and Cardinal Spellman received the same gifts. The Cadillacs Cushing rides in today are gifts from Peter Fuller, who owns a large automobile agency.

When feeling well, Cushing was as accessible as the humblest curate and often answered the front door himself, just as he picked up the telephone receiver in his study. There were days, however, when his infirmities put him in a sour mood. "You'd better not come today," one of his secretaries might say when someone asked for an appointment. She would, however, be more likely to say, "This would be a good day to see him." [4]   Visitors are often startled by his comments as he leads them around the residence. "What do you think of the joint?" he may ask. He may ask a guest like Liberace, who visited him in 1954, to sit down at the piano.

When Lawrence Stone was ushered into the chancery, he heard Cushing's voice drift down the elevator shaft. "Bring him up, I don't have to put my biretta on for him." The prelate was wearing a T-shirt and trousers when Stone walked into his bedroom. "How's your mother?" Cushing asked. After they chatted awhile, he said, "You're the first person I've seen today who didn't want anything."

Cushing does not have to stand on dignity. Told that his new rank called for knowledge of more than one language, he listened for a few weeks to French and Italian recordings on a linguaphone before setting them aside. "Cush, be yourself," he said.

Once he became archbishop, it was almost impossible to keep up

with him. Even an attempt to list his accomplishments in chronologi-
cal order would end in confusion, for he had so many projects going
at the same time in various stages of development that a biographer
would quickly run into a series of overlaps. He arose at six to say
mass in his private chapel, then set a driving pace that often continued until midnight, and he throve on this heavy schedule. "Unless
you build your life around some form of congenial work, you cannot
live a full life," he said. "All I've done is work, work, work," he said
at another time. "For thirty-eight years [since ordination] I've lived
for nothing but Christ. . . . And all there is ahead of me is more
work." He said in a sermon: "There is something wrong with a
joyless view of work. It is not merely an activity to produce external
commodities; it was intended by Divine Providence to become a
means of personal development. We should not have to work just to
live; that is slavery. We should love to work; that is freedom."

In his study, chancery office, at the altar, or in his endless public
appearances, he carried a load that would be burdensome for four or
five ordinary men. As archbishop, he was the ultimate executive who
supervised the activities of hospitals and schools, institutions for the
needy and handicapped, guilds and societies, and bureaus of every
description. Included in holdings were rehabilitation centers, oratories,
seminaries, chapels, convents, rectories, monasteries, and guidance centers for the wayward. His immediate domain in 1944 encompassed
almost twenty-five hundred square miles and well over a million persons scattered from New Hampshire south to Plymouth and west to
Worcester. He directed the activities of more than seven thousand
priests, nuns, and brothers, as well as laymen. By 1967, his archdiocese
included fourteen thousand priests and six thousand nuns.

He launched a massive building program because of the lack of
facilities and the poor condition of existing buildings. "No one," he
said on his tenth anniversary as archbishop, "was more astonished
than I by the magnitude of the construction problems which were
lurking . . . waiting for me to pull out the chair behind my desk."
He rushed from one end of the archdiocese to another, checking
architectural drawings, laying cornerstones, and dedicating buildings,
while somehow finding time to officiate at weddings, funerals, and
commencements.

For graduation exercises at Cathedral High School in 1945, the
sister superior made elaborate plans for greeting the archbishop. She
was cautioning her charges to look and act their best when the prelate,

arriving before schedule, hurried into the auditorium, gathered up his robes, and hopped onto the stage.

"Good afternoon, boys and girls," he said. "I seem to have arrived early." When the sister apologized for the students' appearance, he grinned. "Sister, I don't care if they are dressed in bathing suits."

Over the years he renovated and enlarged the Cathedral of the Holy Cross and built more workers' chapels at railroad terminals, Boston's fish pier, and at busy centers in hotel and shopping districts, including St. Anthony's Shrine in downtown Boston, where mass is celebrated daily. He also built chapels in suburban shopping centers. He established the Paulist Information Center on the slope of Beacon Hill to aid in the conversion of non-Catholics and installed brown-robed Capuchins in a shrine in downtown Boston. He continually invited communities and orders of priests, nuns, and brothers to establish or expand foundations in the see, particularly those engaged in social and missionary work. Among them were black-hooded Benedictines, Ursuline nuns, Salesian fathers, and white-cowled Dominican fathers. In a talk to the Society for the Propagation of the Faith he said in 1946: "We must bend our shoulders not merely to the superhuman task of rebuilding our American missions in the Far East, but also to the task of helping salvage Asian and African missions."

The Society of African Missions was one of the first missionary orders to settle in the archdiocese. It trains future apostles in mission fields of Africa. The Irish-founded Columban fathers opened a minor seminary in 1945, and that same year the La Salette fathers instituted a seminary to train missionaries for work in Asia. The Xaverian Mission Fathers' Seminary—the first in America—trains men for China and the Far East missions.

"My principal chore, in cooperation with them," Cushing explained, "was to build and raise money—all for the universal church." The bishop of the missions, who would later be known as the cardinal of charity, sponsored more institutions to help the needy than any other churchman in history. In the South End's skid row section he opened the St. Francis Refuge, which fed over seven hundred men daily —the old, poor, and derelict. Turkey dinners are served on Thanksgiving and Christmas, when gifts are distributed. No one is refused, no questions are asked, no payment is accepted. "A year ago while in Boston," an anonymous correspondent wrote, "I was broke and hungry. St. Francis Refuge fed me. Please accept this little gift for St. Francis being so good to me."

Cushing forgot nobody. "Charity," he said, "springs from the love of God, and it must not be confused with generosity. It is love of our neighbors. Piety is a manly virtue and a strong one." At one meeting of a society whose chief aim was relief of the poor the treasurer happily announced a tidy cash balance.

"Are there no more poor?" Cushing asked. He suggested that on his next visit he would expect to see the treasury empty and the funds in the hands of the poor.

He remembered the friendless and the forgotten. In July 1945, he went to Fort Devens to confirm German prisoners of war. Willy Vellen of Aachen, Germany, wrote him on his elevation to cardinal: "I didn't forget, Your Eminence, all thirteen years long, because you have given us a great courage and a powerful hope as a Catholic priest and bishop during the hard life in our imprisonment after the Second World War." [5]

Cardinal Cushing likes the Gaelic proverb: "If the best man's faults were written on his forehead, it would make him pull his hat over his eyes." He unfailingly helped sinners, keeping a promise made when he became a bishop: "I put forth my hand in friendship to everyone in this community, and I shall never withdraw it."

From the time he became archbishop, he visited the State Reformatory for Women in Framingham to offer spiritual consolation to errant women, just as he had been doing at the House of the Good Shepherd. He chose the pitiful and outcast as those most worthy of his personal word of courage and comfort.

During Christmas holidays he found time to console prison inmates. On New Year's Day in 1945, in an unprecedented ceremony, he confirmed eleven inmates of Charlestown State Prison, a grim, granite dungeon a century old. There was a dramatic scene in the auditorium at the top of the rotunda on Christmas Eve, 1946, when six hundred men dressed in shapeless gray uniforms assembled to hear Cushing. The gallery was lined with prison officers, alert for any disorder. On the platform was a temporary altar, with lighted candles, poinsettias, and gleaming altar lilies. At one side, a choir of convicts sang carols and hymns. Archbishop Cushing, who had come to confirm inmates, spoke from a makeshift platform. He told his "dear friends" that life was like a baseball game: "We may make errors in the early innings, but the thing that really counts is the score when the game ends. We all make mistakes. Forget the errors of the past and start the ball game all over." Glazed eyes brightened as he continued. "Your hearts and souls are just as precious in the eyes of God as my own or any man's. . . . Speak to God in your own language. He will understand you."

During the devotions, a convict jumped up and accused the parole board of unfair treatment. Patiently hearing him out, Cushing said he would investigate the matter. During that session, Monsignor Joseph A. Robinson, the prison chaplain, presented twenty-one candidates for confirmation. They filed up to kneel before the mitred prelate in his flowing white and gold cape.

Suddenly there were gasps from the onlookers—clergy, prison officials, and inmates. Two of the candidates filing up the steps of the platform were manacled, each handcuffed to flanking prison guards, who knelt with them. Both were convicted murderers who returned to the death house after the ceremony. It was an unforgettable moment as Cushing told his hushed audience behind stone walls of St. Dismas, the repentant thief who "stole heaven" and was canonized on a cross by Christ on Calvary, who said to him: "This day you shall be with me in Paradise."

A few weeks later Cushing confirmed three inmates of the Massachusetts Reformatory at West Concord.[6] His concern for prisoners continued after he became cardinal. Early in 1963 he wrote to one of his generous friends: "I was at the Suffolk County Jail last Friday with the Dominican Sisters of Bethany visiting prisoners and speaking to them. I talked to them for about an hour and asked if they had any needs. They said they would like to have two television sets. Please send them without delay. Charge them to me, if you will. I would send you a check immediately, but I am *broke*."

In December 1948, Cushing founded the Guild of Our Lady of Ransom, dedicated to the rehabilitation of inmates of Massachusetts prisons, or parolees, and of inmates released after completing their sentences. The idea had taken shape during the poignant scene on Christmas Eve two years before. The guild aided hundreds of inmates. One volunteer worker had seven parolees, all convicted and sentenced to long terms for serious crimes. Six got back on the track. Cushing, who invited released convicts to visit him at his residence, gave the same moral support to female inmates.

The guild meets twice a year. In the spring a Holy Hour at St.

Clement's Shrine in the Back Bay precedes a coffee hour at the Hotel Bostonian across the street. Breakfast served at the Harvard Club in the fall follows a Communion mass at the same shrine. In October 1954, Cushing in his Communion breakfast talk said no malefactor should be despised by Christians, regardless of how heinous his offense, sin-steeped his soul, or repellent his personality. "We may be the instruments that will bring redemptive grace as well as earthly happiness to an otherwise abandoned and rejected soul." At the session the toastmaster presented the archbishop with a kneeling bench made by inmates of Charlestown State Prison.[7]

In 1945 he had illustrated his belief in redemption by telling the story of Bobby Stapa, who, by the time he was thirteen, was the best-known stowaway in the nation, having been hauled out of ocean liner holds four times during one six-month span. After the Children's Court of Queens County sent him to the New York Merchant School and Seaman's Institute, Bobby rose to the rank of captain in the United States Merchant Marine.[8]

Cushing may have thought of Bobby that year when he bought two handsome buildings in the Fenway section of Boston for a Catholic Boys' Guidance Center, complete with sleeping quarters and recreational facilities. The aim was to give wayward boys a wholesome outlook. "Never," commented the *Pilot,* "has there been a greater need for this unique type of activity (the most modern methods of social service combined with emphasis on the spiritual) which presents a well-defined program of assistance to boys in trouble." Cushing also set up a Catholic Girls' Guidance Center in Jamaica Plain and raised four million dollars for the Madonna School for Girls to house the Good Shepherd Sisters and the troubled girls in their care. In 1945 he pioneered a Juvenile Chaplaincy program for Catholic priests who function as a liaison between court and parish. He gave financial aid to the Catholic Charitable Bureau, the state's largest private child caring agency, with departments for unwed mothers, problem children, refugees, and displaced persons, as well as placing children in foster homes, arranging for their adoption, and operating settlement houses and a camp program for the underprivileged, it cooperated with the St. Vincent de Paul Society. The archbishop not only established centers for boys and girls in trouble with the law, but visited them often, as he did patients in mental asylums.

He has an unmatched love for mentally or physically handicapped children. He quotes the slogan of the New York City Police Athletic

League: "A man never stands so straight as when he stoops to help a child." Monuments of his devotion to helpless children are St. Coletta's School, Nazareth, and the Joseph P. Kennedy, Jr., Memorial Hospital.

At St. Coletta's, a homelike residence and school for children once considered social outcasts, mentally retarded boys and girls are encouraged to develop according to their potential. In 1947, at the invitation of Cushing, the Sisters of Saint Francis of Assisi from Jefferson, Wisconsin, came to staff the new school—the answer to the prayers of scores of parents who, in their despair, wondered what they could do with their handicapped children.

Under the supervision of Sister Shawn, the "forever children," as Cushing sometimes calls them, take parts in shows on stage and television, as well as in operettas. The prelate has often served as master of ceremonies for their song and drama festivals given at the school or at the archdiocesan Donnelly Memorial Theatre in the Back Bay, another Cushing project. Here, after one performance, he welcomed a lad sent to the stage to present him with a check for St. Coletta's. The youngster pulled away when the archbishop reached for the check, and although this was not part of the act, it brought down the house.

"They're brighter than we think," Cushing said of his exceptional children. "Once I asked a group, 'Why are you here?' One lad popped up with, 'Because we're not all there.' You should hear those children give the responses in a dialogue mass. They answer in Latin better than the so-called normal children, but, of course, although it is beautiful to see, they don't understand what they are saying." [9]

Cushing has tragic, as well as amusing, stories to tell about the "least of the brethren," still another term he has for his favorite children. There was Stevie Smith, a Jewish boy with a serious brain injury. After medical science had done all it could for him at Kennedy Memorial Hospital, Cushing sent him to St. Coletta's, where there were more than three hundred children in residence—mongoloid, spastic children, and boys and girls with brain injuries.

Just before Christmas, the nuns took the children into the woods behind the school to collect pine cones and seasonal greens. Although Cushing had cautioned the sisters never to let the lad out of their sight, he wandered from his group and fell by a creek. Next day Cushing hired a helicopter to search for him. The pilot saw the shoes, and there was poor Stevie. Late the night before, as if he were going to bed, he had taken off his shoes and stockings and lain down in the cold.

"Well," the prelate said, "I buried Stevie. And I went to the synagogue and to the grave and I participated in his burial service." The grieving archbishop was misty-eyed as he walked from the grave with the boy's parents.[10]

In a magazine article written years later,[11] Cushing said: "My dear children of God, I know when you laugh and I know when you cry, because I have a whole family of exceptional children myself." By "exceptional," he explained, he meant children who were mentally or physically handicapped. "I call them 'exceptional' . . . not because they are very beautiful or brilliant, but because they give me an exceptional opportunity of showing my love for the Christ Child by loving them."

Cushing has special ways of raising money for the school to augment donations received from Joseph P. Kennedy and other philanthropists. Couples pay a hundred dollars to attend the "Springtime at St. Coletta's Festival" in May, when a donor receives a "Friends of St. Coletta Award." The affair is ecumenical. In 1968 a rabbi, a Baptist minister, and a Catholic priest participated in a brotherhood service before the dinner. At a private Christmas party for the school's benefit, more than a hundred donors were moved when several exceptional children arrived unexpectedly to sing carols.

On the school grounds, Cushing built a replica of the Portiuncula Chapel in Assisi, where St. Francis is buried, importing the stone from Assisi. Cushing, who is a member of the First Order of St. Francis, will be buried beneath the sanctuary floor in the cowled, terracotta habit of a Franciscan friar. Explaining that he does not live as ascetically as a Franciscan monk, he does keep the letter and spirit of the order. "St. Francis to me is the most perfect human reproduction of Christ. He loved everyone. That's what the world needs today, a love of man for man." [12]

Cushing, who considers death another step on a long journey, recalls that Pope John XXIII said when told he was dying: "My bags are all packed."[13] Cushing is ready at any time to render an account of his stewardship. "When my time comes, I hope the Blessed Mother takes me fifteen minutes before the devil knows I've gone." [14] He was thinking of the Gaelic blessing that ends: "May the wind be ever at your back and may you all be a long time in heaven before the devil knows you're gone." Another time Cushing explained why he wanted to be buried near "those kids . . . they are the ones who will really pray for you. Cardinal O'Connell has a tomb right here on the place [near the cardinal's residence], but I have never seen anyone praying for him."

Another favorite project is Nazareth, a multi-million-dollar complex that replaced the Home for Catholic Children in the South End. It accommodates three hundred fifty boys and girls, including orphans or temporarily homeless children of every faith. "It will not be an orphan asylum," Cushing explained, "but more like a private school for any poor child. This school will be the most expensive and intensive project in eastern Massachusetts."

Almost two thousand persons attended a garden party in Scituate in the summer of 1952 on Cushing's fifty-seventh birthday. Proceeds from the auction sale, plus donations, came to twenty-five thousand dollars —all earmarked for the construction of Nazareth. Cushing told the gathering that half of his mail "came from poor mothers asking help in buying clothes for their children so they can return to school." The Nazareth New Child Care Center would, he said, also have a staff of women to take over households in emergencies and would offer bus service to pick up children for whom eight or ten hours of daily care are necessary. Facilities would include a chapel, school, and ten cottages.

The toastmaster at a 1953 banquet attended by almost a thousand persons gave Cushing a check for one hundred twenty-five thousand dollars toward the construction. "As you know," Cushing said, "every bishop has a coat of arms. Mine should include a wolf." His wolf at the door, he went on, "has always been a spur to achievement, a warning against sloth and 'taking it easy.' " He said his howling wolf reminded him how much work there was to do "for my neighbor, for the underprivileged, and for God."

A non-Catholic had the speech printed and sent it to friends, noting that the archbishop had "won the affection and admiration not only of his own people, but of Protestant and Jew, for his spirit of service, his broad understanding, his friendly way. That night, at the Bradford Hotel, he gave an address that is a gold mine of inspiration for all of us."

In his *Pilot* columns, Cushing often dramatized his appeal for funds. One theme was "A Marine Comes Home." He told of young Tommy and his two sisters who were sent to Nazareth when their mother was hospitalized. Tommy joined the marines, always returning to Nazareth when on furlough. "On one leave," Cushing wrote, "his car skidded over an embankment into a river. Tommy drowned. His body . . . was brought home. All the children, sisters and employees at Nazareth welcomed him with tears of love."

In June 1945, the archbishop cut into his schedule to take thirty boys and girls from refuges like Nazareth to the Ringling Brothers and Barnum and Bailey Circus at the Boston Garden. It was the first time he had been to a circus since he crawled under the tents at the old Andrew Square circus in South Boston. Cushing had the king of clowns bring his trained pigs to the children seated down front. The youngsters, thrilled to be in a world of popcorn, crackerjacks, and cotton candy, squealed with delight. Cushing had trouble keeping his straw hat on as a four-year-old girl clung tightly to one hand while an excited Negro girl two years older kept flinging herself into his arms.

Archbishop Cushing's vast building program spawned anecdotes. According to one wag, a surgeon who removed his kidney found four cornerstones. Another story has Cushing trying to enter the gate of heaven. When St. Peter couldn't find his name, he turned to go. "Just a minute," St. Peter said. "I was looking for your name under churchmen, but it's listed under realtors."

While archbishop, Cushing launched an extensive hospital program. By 1959 eight general and five special hospitals were accommodating 186,000 patients a year.* Carney Hospital in South Boston was about to fold when Cushing, heading a drive to "Save the Carney," transferred it to a handsome new eight-million-dollar plant in Dorchester. To St. Elizabeth's Hospital, which had been founded by a few Franciscan nuns in 1858 in a little South End house (the hospital was later moved to Brighton) he added the Archbishop Cushing Pavilion at a cost exceeding two million dollars and a nurses' home that cost eight hundred thousand dollars. In Methuen he built Bon Secours Hospital, which houses a psychiatric unit, and in 1946 dedicated a chapel at Convent Secours, a community of nursing nuns introduced into Boston for the first time. These nuns drive cars so they can visit the sick. Along with other hospitals built in the archdiocese, are a convalescent home maintained by the Hospitaller Brothers of St. John of God and a rest home run by the Grey Nuns.

---

* By 1967, Cushing's hospitals were accommodating three hundred thousand patients a year.

Several other orders operate hospitals in the diocese, including the Franciscan Missionaries of Mary.

Cushing completed payment for each building so that it could inaugurate its service debt-free. On the Searles Estate in Methuen he erected a seminary for the Basilian Salvatorian Order of Monks, and he turned the Gralyn Hotel in the Back Bay into a guild for women.

Special schools include branches of the Catholic Guild for the Blind, which issues *Listen*, a newspaper, and the Marian Rehabilitation Center for physically impaired children. The Cardinal Cushing Educational Clinic treats those with reading deficiencies. One Cushing-sponsored institution is the Catholic Guild for the Deaf, staffed by Sisters of St. Joseph, who bring the shy and dispirited back to a happier social life. Cushing's special school system also includes schools of nursing and institutes for delayed vocations and secretarial training. Several units of the Catholic Charitable Bureau of Boston train students in crafts, trades, and hobbies.

After making the Guild for the Blind the largest in the nation, Cushing opened St. Paul's Rehabilitation Center to aid the newly blinded. On one visit he amused the residents by trying to walk blindfolded with a seeing-eye dog. A mere visit was never enough when cheer was needed. At a home for old ladies he sampled a pie baked by one of them, despite his ulcers. His breezy, homespun manner delighted the aged poor at three St. Joseph manors he regularly visited in the Back Bay, Roxbury, and Brockton. In one "appearance" in 1945, he donned a baker's apron, festive with red ribbons, and served the old folks, giving them mulligatawny soup for an appetizer.[15]

"Soup's on," he shouted. "Come and get it."

He laughed when a recluse thanked him afterward:

"Mere words, however grouped, cannot convey to you the gladness, the real jubilation which your visits to our home occasion. Just to see you, hear your voice, and watch your stereotyped smile."

Cushing broke in as the old man's voice trailed off. "How about that one? My stereotyped smile!"

"God bless him," an old woman said. "Ain't he the one, though!" She nodded approvingly as he stooped to spoon-feed a frail companion.

Even a blizzard did not keep him from a rocky ride in a jeep to a scheduled visit to the Home for the Aged in Foxboro, run by the Little Sisters of the Poor. The residents told him that during the summer they cultivated a plot variously known as "Cushing Park" and "The Bishop's Garden."

A friend intended no disrespect when he called the prelate "the clown prince of compassion," for he could don a mask for any occasion, even when he knew he was being "corny." He spent long hours in hospitals because he knew his presence was a tonic for patients. "My dear," he says to a bed-ridden octogenarian, "you look better than I do." Sisters in charge of elderly patients are themselves cheered when he brings smiles of hope to wrinkled faces by telling them to keep going, keep smiling, keep living. "You'll be dead long enough." It is his way of restoring dignity and self-respect to those who have lost a zest for living.

A list of projects the archbishop reorganized or established would read like several columns in the yellow pages of a metropolitan telephone directory. He built a nursing school and several centers for visiting nurses and renovated the Catholic Men's Club (formerly the Soldiers and Sailors Club), staffing it with Hospitaller Brothers. Here any man could find refuge. High school students interested in joining the priesthood could attend St. Botolph's Guild and take instruction from visiting missionaries as well as from regular priests. Cushing created an office of Director of Vocations and made St. John's Seminary the largest in the country. His expansion program while he was archbishop would have been even more impressive had it not been for a number of antireligious laws passed by certain towns in Massachusetts.

In 1931 the town of Weston, Massachusetts, decreed that religious teaching by private or sectarian schools or a college was prohibited. It passed this law a few years after the establishment of Regis College, a Jesuit institution for girls. In 1945 Dover, Massachusetts, adopted the same bylaw, when the Dominicans tried to establish a chapel and priory there to train students. After a two-year legal battle, Attorney General Francis E. Kelly, a close friend of Cushing, succeeded in having the law nullified, and the Supreme Court upheld the decision. Weston also removed its 1931 bylaw.

Two days after the Supreme Court's decision (1951) in favor of Kelly's action against the Dover law, the Reverend Harold Ockenga of the Park Street Congregational Church publicized a communication to the attorney general in which he asked three questions: Did Massachusetts have the right to lease the Bradley W. Palmer estate in Topsfield to the House of the Good Shepherd? Would the property soon be sold or given to Archbishop Cushing? What were the terms of the gift?

Kelly gave a decisive answer. The House of the Good Shepherd was a nonsectarian institution, and the sisters in charge of girls sent there by the Commonwealth wanted the Palmer mansion only as a vacation home.[16]

Cushing named some of the high schools he built after his predecessors. One central school was named for Bishop Fenwick, another for Archbishop Williams. He also built the Pope John XXIII High School in Everett. The more he built, the more places he had to visit and give commencement addresses to. On "sports night" in 1958 at Archbishop Williams, he told an assembly that athletes often asked for divine guidance before an event. "Signs in sports are the signs of the cross," he said. "Athletes of all ranges make signs of the cross at crucial times, and in many different ways. A Jimmy Piersall draws a cross on the ground with his bat at the plate." He told of a Catholic Youth Organization boxer, all dressed up in new boots and purple trunks, fighting a rival church member who wore worn-out sneakers and bathing trunks. The latter sat stolidly on a stool as his dapper opponent kept blessing himself while waiting for the gong.

"Will that help him win?" the chaplain was asked.

"Sure," he said. "If he can fight." [17]

That year Cushing announced that a new three-million-dollar school under construction in Brockton would be named the Cardinal Spellman Central High School—appropriate, since Spellman was a native of Whitman, a town adjacent to Brockton. Cushing dedicated the school in 1958 as part of the sesquicentennial celebration of the Boston archdiocese. Spellman, who as a newsboy had sold the Brockton *Enterprise,* was so pleased with the honor that he donated a hundred thousand dollars toward the auditorium provided it be named the Cardinal Cushing Auditorium so that "thus we shall be closely associated in memory as we have been in life for nearly four decades of priesthood." [18]

Archbishop Cushing enlivened the dedication ceremonies. A girl watching the ground-breaking for Roncalli Hall at Boston College, shook her head in wonder.

"Doesn't the cardinal flip that dirt real good!" Cushing smiled when he heard the story. "Well, you tell the young lady I've had a lot of experience flipping dirt. Don't forget, I'm from South Boston." [19]

Cushing is an honorary member of the Street Railwaymen's Union in recognition of summer vacation days when he hefted a pick and shovel for the Boston Elevated Railway.

He and Father Michael Walsh, S.J., president of Boston College, were wielding ceremonial shovels for the construction of the Boston College School of Nursing, which the archbishop donated to his alma mater. At the end of the program he hopped into the cab of a steam shovel and operated the levers like a professional. Even during such busy occasions he finds time for kindness. Soon after he became cardinal, he was dedicating a new dormitory at Boston College when an Ethiopian student, who was to live in the dormitory, was introduced to him. Learning that Boston College students had paid for his passage and dormitory fees, Cushing said, "Well, you better put in a bid for an overcoat, young man. You'll need one around here." He saw that the student got the coat. The encounter was unique for the lad, who said at graduation exercises that the meeting with Cardinal Cushing was the highlight of his stay in America.[20]

Among institutions built in Massachusetts by Cushing were Merrimack, Stonehill, and Cardinal Cushing colleges. In his far-reaching program he gave special attention to racial minorities. He gave Negroes in Roxbury their own church, St. Richard's, and for Chinese-Americans he brought the Maryknoll Sisters to Boston to set up an instructional center for Chinese parishioners in Chinatown in Boston's downtown retail district.

His energy and administrative skill astounded parishioners accustomed to the snail-like growth of the archdiocese under Cardinal O'Connell. They could see that there was no end to his vision as he modernized plants, facilities, and operations in his sprawling diocese.

He even revitalized the *Pilot,* the oldest Catholic newspaper in the United States. It had long been O'Connell's personal mouthpiece, and nothing he disliked could be printed. Cushing took the journal from under wraps and made its editor, John Sexton, editor in fact as well as name. Within six years its circulation quadrupled to eighty thousand. Archbishop Cushing himself was one of the paper's best columnists, as he kept subscribers informed of the growth of the archdiocese, which under his administration became the second largest in the nation, exceeded only by the Chicago see. Eventually, as ordinary of the see, the prelate would personally supervise more than thirty magazines edited by teachers, missionaries, social workers, and labor and student groups in and around Boston.

By the time Cushing became cardinal, the Boston see had almost

2,700 priests, as compared to 1,292 in 1944, and 400 parishes as against 325. Hospitals had increased to twelve, and there were seven Catholic colleges or universities as compared to three when Cushing became archbishop. The Catholic population in that time had jumped from 1,113,075 to 1,482,677.

As cardinal, Cushing would become even more of a "tireless fund-raiser out of the mold of brick-and-mortar prelates," as *Time* put it.[21] By 1967, he would be responsible for more than three hundred million dollars worth of construction, including three hundred elementary and high schools, and eighty-six new parishes.

His financial skill put him in the same class as David Rockefeller as he called in all surplus funds from his parishes and established his own banking system. He also set up an insurance plan for archdiocesan property that saved his parishes ten million dollars in twenty years. He kept architects, contractors, and suppliers prosperous, and he supervised every detail. "You have the job of installing the public address system in the Pope John XXIII Seminary in Westwood," he told one executive. "Send the bills to me and keep them within reason. Confer with the general contractor, John Scully, with regard to it. I have cleared everything with the architects." The same firm installed linguistic laboratories at Fenwick High School, Archbishop Williams High School, St. Joseph Academy, and many other schools. "I should be on the payroll," Cushing quipped.

No combination of twenty American bishops had ever raised as much money for domestic and foreign missions as had Cushing, and as a builder he has had no peer in ecclesiastical history. His extensive programs are partly financed by money from the "mighty mites" or average Catholics. Flowing into the till are donations in weekly envelopes, proceeds from raffles, smokers, bazaars, lawn fetes, parish reunions, schools, and theatrical entertainments, along with sports spectacles. This is enough for parish needs, but because of Cushing's dedication to the universal church, his largesse goes far beyond the confines of his archdiocese. Actually, his see received only about half of the money he raised.

Cushing is a generous contributor to the Vatican and has donated millions of dollars to build and renovate churches and missions in foreign lands and to aid many causes during his administration as archbishop and cardinal. Modest examples are the two hundred thousand dollars he gave to renovate the Church of the Holy Spirit in Pope John's home town of Bergamo; two hundred twenty-two thousand dollars to build a cathedral for Laurian Cardinal Rugambwa of Tanganyika, Africa, and a million dollars to Fu-Jen University in Formosa. Cushing also sent many missionaries abroad. His massive efforts made Boston the largest single contributor of missionaries among all the sees in the United States.

Cushing became known as a last-resort donor. A missionary from Huei province, China, who needed funds for an asylum for abandoned waifs, had sought money in vain through Europe and in several American cities. After visiting Cushing, he left Boston with the funds.

When Father Edward Conway, S.J., launched the Peace Research Center in 1961, he faced a funding problem. "I went to see one of my great favorites, Cardinal Cushing," he said at a testimonial dinner in Washington, D.C. "I don't know how I had the nerve; I went up to Boston, said I needed five thousand dollars. This was on a Saturday. Cardinal Cushing said, 'I can't give it to you now. My accountant isn't here. Can I send it to you Monday?' Then he asked me if I had cab fare!"

In her autobiography, Helen Hayes tells of taking a priest who conducted an orphanage in Mexico to see Cardinal Cushing at a time when the orphanage desperately needed funds. "The cardinal answered the door himself, in a red cassock and a purple rage. . . . His Eminence was in high dudgeon about something." The prelate took them into his study, where he listened to the actress's appeal.

"His Scowling Eminence was scornful. 'You can't do this kind of thing alone. This kind of work should be in the hands of the Dominicans.' "

After a long lecture, Cushing agreed to give Father William Wassen ten thousand dollars. Miss Hayes lost her raptured look when he added: "Yes, I'll make it ten thousand if *anyone* wishes to match it."

"We were a tableau, we three," the actress writes. "Father Wassen basking in the cardinal's gruff charity; I, with God's will, being forced to share it; and His Eminence ready to bring the wrath of God down on me if I didn't." [22]

Another time, a collector for the United Fund in Boston, hoping to get ten thousand dollars from the prelate, said he would have been pleased to receive half that amount.

"I'm glad you came to see me," Cushing said. "If you hadn't, I would have gone to you." He handed the visitor an envelope containing a check for twenty-five thousand dollars.

A donor of this magnitude needs a broad umbrella for his overall operations, and no "beggar" pleading for money was ever much more successful day in and day out. A reporter, arriving late for a Cushing appearance, went to the platform to ask for a copy of his speech. "Do you have a handout, Your Eminence?"

"I don't give handouts, young man," Cushing said. "I get them."

He got them and he gave them, and the more he gave, the more he was called upon to give. "I've come to the conclusion," he said repeatedly after assuming control of the archdiocese, "that everybody thinks I own Fort Knox, the United States Treasury, and the Rockefeller and Kennedy Foundations. I want to tell you that I don't own any of them."

He won't divulge all the sources of his enormous income from gifts, which for a time averaged over thirty-five thousand dollars a day. "No one knows anything about it," he told a reporter, "and I am not going to tell you. But when the day comes when I can no longer gather money to help people who need it, especially people dedicated to the poor and the service of God, I will be ready to pass on."

chapter eight

MASTER FINANCIER

IT HAS BEEN SUGGESTED that Richard Cushing would make an admirable Secretary of the Treasury. He would perhaps be more effective as head of the Internal Revenue Service, for he is a compulsive collector of money. At a church service he has been known to pick up a long-handled wicker basket and angle it into the pew rows. He has ended hundreds of speeches by saying, "And now we'll take up a collection." Viewing audiences of women, he has more than once said: "Some of you ladies are single, and I'd like to remind you that if, in the course of events, you meet a millionaire, I wish you would introduce him to me." [1]

His fame as a fund-raiser was so well known by the time he moved to the episcopal residence in Brighton that he received one letter addressed simply to "Come On Wealth Avenue." Apocryphal anecdotes attest his financial acumen. When a girl swallowed a quarter and every effort failed to dislodge it from her windpipe, someone suggested summoning Cushing instead of a physician: "He'll get that coin, if anyone can." Another story has him sent to Hades by mistake. An embarrassed St. Peter, bidding for his release, was told that the matter would have to rest until Cushing had completed his current goal. "He is nearing his quota of raising enough money to air-condition hell."

By 1964, when he had completed most of his expansion program, he could tell a group of Radcliffe students: "I can't sing and I'm too old to dance. I'm no scholar, but I'm pretty good at collecting money. That's my job. I have to help people who cannot help themselves." [2] This story is not apocryphal.

The warm responses to Cushing's charity appeals are the envy and despair of professional fund-raisers. His sources of revenue when he was a bishop were a mere ripple compared to a tidal wave when he took over the actual administration of the see. He set up Catholic guilds and organizations in scores of industries, crafts, and public services. Cushing has organized guilds of wash women, post office employees, school teachers, plant men, State Street brokers, employee groups in police and fire departments, the Gillette Razor Blade Company, Boston Edison and other utility corporations, and the beverages industry, including soft drinks and "hard." The Caritas Guild (licensed beverage industry), as does the Catholic telephone operators' guild, donates up to sixty thousand dollars a year to the prelate's charities. A typical source of revenue was the cylindrical cardboard coin containers placed in Greater Boston barrooms. Cushing had first to clear with the State Alcoholic Beverages Commission, the bartenders' and teamsters' unions, and with police and local licensing officials. Although the venture was lucrative, he dropped it when secular containers for the Jimmy Fund and cerebral-palsy drives began to appear.

Physicians in St. Luke's Guild and dentists in St. Appollonia's not only raise money for the diocese but also minister to the poor without charge. There is St. Michael's Guild for communication workers, St. Agatha's for nurses, St. Ives' for lawyers, St. Francis de Sales' for journalists, and St. Joseph's for general workers. All money raised from guilds goes into the Archbishop's Charity Fund (later the Cardinal's Charity Fund), and Cushing determines how it is spent. His stream-lined techniques are similar to Red Cross and Red Feather Agency pledge cards, each of which represents a promise to pay specified amounts at intervals throughout the year. This method is especially effective at large, convivial conventions. At an international meeting of the Knights of Columbus held one year in Swampscott on the north shore of Boston, Cushing persuaded each Knight to pledge a small amount every month for two years. The total approximated a million dollars.

From the beginning of his episcopate to his later years, Cushing has been swamped by contributions primarily because of the charitable uses to which he put them. Even his table-hopping at large gatherings paid off, as guests stuffed five- and ten-dollar bills into the long cuffs of his cassock. It would take pages merely to list organizations that donate year after year. Money comes from the Chatterbox Club, of which he was chaplain, the annual Policeman's Ball, newspaper circulation directors, and employees of the Metropolitan Boston Transit Authority.

At Camp Drum, New York, one summer, National Guardsmen gave Cushing, their chaplain, a check for three thousand dollars. Cushing wore unmarked field fatigues when he went to Camp Drum to check on his chaplains and usually disappeared to "a remote area of a mock battleground where there are no reporters." [3]

In one brief period, Cushing received the proceeds of a professional football game between the Boston Patriots and the Houston Oilers, a golf match played between Arnold Palmer and the late Tony Lema when he was British Open champion, and an annual Irish Field Day held in Brookline. Every year he receives the proceeds of a similar field day held in New York. In the fall of 1960, Joe Kennedy paid all expenses for a benefit game at Manning Bowl in Lynn between the New York Giants and the Philadelphia Eagles. After the game, the "winning" football was presented to Cushing, who promptly gave it away to a lad. When Paul Dever was governor of the Commonwealth, he used to get substantial donations from fellow members of the Engineers' Club to present to Cushing. Some of the donors were non-Catholics.

When Mount Alvernia Academy in Chestnut Hill wanted to modernize its kitchen, the archbishop raised the money by staging a sports night. The magnets were Joe Cronin, manager of the Boston Red Sox; his super-star, Ted Williams; and other popular players. To make it easier for the caterer, Cushing permitted Catholics to eat meat, although the affair was held on a Friday night.

No American churchman has ever received as much free publicity as Cushing, and although he would shun the spotlight if he could, he knows the value of its fund-raising potential. One reporter, who said he considered the prelate a saint, went up to the platform after Cushing spoke to get his autograph. "I got the autograph, all right," he said, "but he also handed me a press release. That brought me out of my trance."

It is always publicity for a cause, however, and the press unfailingly cooperates. When Mrs. Edward (Joan) Kennedy displayed her talent as a fashion model at a Cardinal Cushing benefit, showing clothing designed by Oleg Cassini, the Boston *Globe* ran a large front-page photograph of her wearing a dazzling white evening gown. "Among all the lovely Boston models," the paper reported, "the blond, slender Mrs. Edward Kennedy won first prize with the women."

Women vie for opportunities to aid Cushing projects. During the early days of the famed Toll House in Whitman, when the seating capacity was limited, a Catholic guild gave a luncheon for a Cushing charity. Mrs. Kenneth Wakefield, then the hostess-owner, recalled the affair: "Many tickets were sold in advance, and extra seats were added in case they might be needed. However, many ladies arrived early and took the seats which the committee should have reserved for those who had already paid. At the hour luncheon was to be served there were more than a hundred ladies with no place to seat them! I told the committee that if those who were already placed would dine and not linger we could have a second seating. This worked out beautifully, and resulted in a double profit for the archbishop, who was present, and so pleased that I received from him a leather-bound copy of *Readings from the New Testament* accompanied by his usual warm words of appreciation. His expressions of thanks for the slightest service make one eager to help him more."

Non-Catholic children, as well as those in parochial schools, swell the treasury. A penny-a-month club raised two thousand dollars for Cushing charities on radio station WEEI, Boston. But the prelate is no Micawber waiting for something to happen. He seizes the moment. Early in the 1950s, when he was installing a new abbot at St. Anselm's College in Manchester, New Hampshire, the archbishop sat beside a wealthy industrialist. Before the luncheon was over, he persuaded him to "pick up the tab," as he put it. Cushing's loyal supporters are equally brash. When Patrick McDonough, a member of the governor's council, ran a fund-raising party for Cushing at the Boston Club, the owner handed him a bill for eleven hundred dollars. McDonough returned it.

"This is your contribution to the Cushing Fund," he said.

"If I had known that," the proprietor smiled, "I'd have put on an even bigger splash, and made the party much more deductible in taxes." [4]

Entertainers as well as politicians have been strong boosters of the prelate. Jimmy Durante never fails to call at the cardinal's residence when he comes to Boston and gladly plays the piano for the nuns at Cushing's request. And he always leaves a thousand-dollar-check before departing.

One of Cushing's ventures is the Chapel of Don Bosco in the hotel and bus terminal area of Boston. The chapel, which caters primarily to bellboys, bus and taxi drivers, and traveling salesmen, has two side altars. Durante donated one. Jacqueline Cochran, the author-aviatrix-politician, financed the other.

Jimmy Durante, like dozens of other stars, has often donated his talent in the name of Cushing charities at a South Boston nightclub known as Blinstrub's Village. By 1952 it accommodated eight hundred fifty patrons and later became the largest and most popular nightlife center in New England, until it was destroyed by fire in 1968. No other restaurant anywhere has ever raised so much money for charity. Cushing held so many charitable functions there that Blinstrub's Village became known as "The Boston Vatican." Cushing himself has been called "Blinstrub's singing waiter" because of the annual Thanksgiving parties for the aged he sponsors in the role of chief entertainer. During all the years the owner, Stanley Blinstrub, the son of a Polish nobleman, has never charged the prelate a penny for the turkey fiestas given for as many as fifteen hundred persons.

After the nightclub had burned down, Cushing explained why he was heading a campaign to raise a hundred thousand dollars to help Blinstrub rebuild. "My heart goes out to this man, who has helped everybody: Protestants, Catholics and Jews. . . . He ran the cleanest, the most attractive nightclub in the city, and would never let anyone go on his program unless I approved so that no one who went to Blinstrub's would ever be shocked." It has been said that Blinstrub's would book only acts "that a priest taking his mother out for dinner could see and hear."

Cushing guests at the annual Thanksgiving parties ranged in age from the sixties to over a hundred. They came from the city, surrounding towns, nursing homes, lonely furnished rooms, and senior citizen clubs. Typical was the party he gave in 1954 for three hundred women. He paid for their round-trip in taxis and gave each a crisp two-dollar bill as she left. Bagpipes, drums, a bull fiddle, and a bassoon provided music for the elderly, among whom were the blind, lame, and deaf.

"The archbishop is going to be a saint when God calls him," one said. Another smiled. "I'd say he is a saint right now."

Cushing pulled two women to their feet. "Let's have a fling," he said, tapping out a jig. He sang in a barbershop quartet, carved the turkey, and moved around with a word of cheer for everyone. He gave a similar performance at Blinstrub's a few months later, when he invited retarded children, as well as the aged and ailing. *Life* magazine noted that his "beaked face" was "wreathed in conviviality."

At a later Thanksgiving celebration, jubilant old ladies again toasted him. "Archbishop," one said, "you're real dynamite." Another sang, "He's our cardinal forevermore. There's no doubt he'll wear that hat like it's never been worn before." One guest at this fete (in 1959) was Bishop Cornelius Lucey of Cork. "Nothing like this ever happened in the Old World, not even in Ireland," he said. "Never have my eyes witnessed anything to equal this. 'Tis a wonderful thought to remember people who have no one to go to on a day like this."

At this party, Cushing met a Charles Cushing. "He is one of the Cushings who came over on the *Mayflower*," the prelate told reporters. "My folks walked over."

For Cushing the fund-raiser, Blinstrub's was a Klondike. Stanley Blinstrub's generosity rubbed off on such entertainers as Arthur Godfrey, Patti Page, Sammy Davis, Jr., Nat King Cole, and others who became Cushing fans. The money he normally would have paid Blinstrub for Thanksgiving parties went to aid the afflicted, old and young.

The Boston Vatican staged dozens of charity events for Cushing and was often oversold when a big star was scheduled to appear. Cushing sent blocks of tickets to hospitals and charitable institutions and encouraged his clergy to promote charity affairs. For one benefit performance a priest sold twenty-three hundred tickets at a time when accommodations were limited to seventeen hundred. "He prayed for rain," Blinstrub said, "and he got his wish. Nevertheless, my place was filled almost to capacity." In a blizzard, singer Connie Francis entertained fourteen hundred persons to swell the prelate's treasury.

Some of Cushing's biggest benefits were staged at the Boston Garden. Singer Dennis Day attracted over fifteen thousand persons to his first show and came back for the next three years. Others who raised money for the charity fund were Bob Hope, Ted Mack and his Original Major Bowes Amateur Hour, Perry Como, Jerry Colonna, and Fred Waring and his Pennsylvanians. Cushing often shared the stage with them and stole the spotlight. There seemed to be no end to the cornucopia. Annually Monsignor Ralph Gallagher staged the city's biggest horse show to raise money for Cushing's charities, and more revenue flowed in from dozens of sports promoters.

His "Old Jewelry for Charity" campaign, one of many miscellaneous drives, drew a typical comment from a donor who sent in two valuable watches: "Although my folks were Orthodox Jews, they were liberal in their religious thinking. I have followed the same practice throughout my life. I know you will make good use of the jewelry." One gift was a ninety-seven-year-old timepiece given him on his Bar Mitzvah.

In thanking him, Cushing said it would be used in accordance with the appeal he wrote in his *Pilot* column. "There is no need of telling you of my cordial affiliation with all Jews, Orthodox and otherwise. I have a sister who was married to a Jewish lad, and they lived most happily for thirty-five years until his death. He was a great example to me, and in all honesty a girl could never have had a more devoted husband." Cushing went to his funeral, sat in a synagogue with his hat on, and accompanied relatives to the cemetery. After the services, he gave grieving relatives three hundred dollars to contribute to Jewish charities.

Cushing told the donor of the night he took a taxi after giving a speech at the Statler Hotel. "It was raining. I got into the taxi and told the Jewish cabbie where I was going. As I got out of the cab, he asked whether I was the archbishop. I said I was.

" 'Well,' he said, 'you're the best rabbi in Boston.' He was a smart fellow. He got a five-dollar tip for that one." [5]

Cushing translated the jewelry into charity, including valuable items left him by the first Mrs. James Michael Curley when she died. Years later he received donations that had nothing to do with his "Old Jewelry for Charity" drive. South American government officials presented him with precious jewels worth a king's ransom in appreciation of his efforts in behalf of Latin Americans. Cushing put the gifts to good use.

In the late 1940s and early 1950s he organized an old license plant and scrap metal campaign, along with an "Archdiocesan Waste Paper Drive." At the bidding of their priests, parishioners baled old newspapers and magazines and left them on the sidewalk for collection. The *Pilot* explained that the drive would not only swell the Cushing Charity Fund but would also replenish stockpiles at New England paper mills.

Members of the Catholic Youth Organization hauled the bales to freight yards in borrowed trucks. Meanwhile, junkmen complained, and non-Catholics objected to the trucks, which disrupted the Sunday calm, although the drives gave them a chance to clear out their cellars and attics. The net profit in one eighteen-month period was over two hundred eight thousand dollars.

Money came from unexpected sources. When the archbishop confirmed the grandchildren of Protestant governor Alvan T. Fuller in the Brighton chapel, the latter picked up a check his son Peter had made out to Cushing. The governor, who had just completed a pleasant tour of the grounds with the archbishop, pulled out a pen and changed the figure from a hundred dollars to a hundred thousand dollars to be used for any charity Cushing wished. "And every year thereafter," Cushing recalled, "he would invite me to lunch, and at the side of my plate he would put an envelope. He would say nothing about it; in the envelope was a hundred thousand dollars. And there was no publicity on it, none at all." [6]

Alvan Fuller continued this practice until he died. His wife, the former Grace Davenport, was a devout Roman Catholic, and every time her husband donated to a Protestant cause, she matched the amount and sent it to Cushing. A few days before she died at her summer home in New Hampshire, Archbishop Cushing drove up to celebrate a special mass. "I got there just in time," he told a reporter. More than most prelates, Cushing believes in the efficacy of prayer, considering it "thunder in reverse," as it has been called.

Along with the Kennedys, there have been generous individual donors. Louis Perini, contractor and owner of the Boston and Milwaukee Braves National League Baseball Team, who was the inspiration for the Jimmy Fund, was one of the top donors to the Don Orione Home for Elderly Italians in East Boston. Among his known contributions to Cushing projects was $1,118,000 he gave at a kickoff dinner for St. Anselm's College's four-million-dollar building development program.[7] Another heavy contributor was Joseph Sullivan, brother-in-law of Monsignor Thomas Reynolds, rector of Holy Cross Cathedral.

"I used to drop in to visit Father Cushing a lot when he was with the Propagation of the Faith," Sullivan recalled. It was Cushing's turn to aid Sullivan later when the latter chaired a hospital drive to which the prelate donated one hundred thousand dollars. On dedication day, Cushing and Sullivan, arriving early, asked where the archbishop could don his vestments.

"Although the hospital had three elevators," Sullivan said, "the sister had us climb three flights of stairs. Both his eminence and I were then sixty-three years of age. Sister escorted us to a men's room." [8]

Cushing is a master of the parlay when it comes to raising funds. Learning that Sullivan printed pari-mutuel tickets and racing programs for horse and dog tracks all over the country, he wangled an introduction to one of his wealthy clients, the late Louis Smith, who, with his wife Lutza, operated Rockingham Park for horse and harness racing in Salem, New Hampshire. For years "Uncle Lou" and Lutza ran a benefit barbecue on a Sunday at Rockingham Park for the nonsectarian Crippled Children's Fund. No horses ran on that day, and all expenses were paid by the Smiths. Top entertainers who volunteered their services brought the net profit from this yearly single benefit to about fifty thousand dollars.

The Smiths also gave annual parties at Kennedy Memorial Hospital on the day they handed Cushing a donation. Once in accepting seventy thousand dollars, Cushing told the handicapped children: "This money is raised by Lutza Smith, and in my entire lifetime, I never, never have met a more dedicated or more generous Jewish lady, or of any other faith, for that matter." On a Valentine Day's visit, Cushing told the children more about the Smiths, for whom a new wing of the hospital was named. "Children, can any of you count to a million?" He paused. "Well, in the past seventeen years, Aunt Lutza and Uncle Lou Smith, your great, great friends have given more than a million dollars to maintain this place. It helps all the kids of poor parents who never could afford to pay to use an institution of this type."

Cushing's thank-you notes, not to mention his appeals for funds, alone make him the most prolific correspondent in American church history, and his letters are rarely perfunctory. He somehow finds time in a jammed schedule to keep in touch with hundreds of friends. Even his letters of introduction reflect his thoughtfulness. When the Smiths went to Dublin, Cushing asked an editor of *The Catholic Standard* to squire them around: "He and I are trustees of Boston City Hospital. He sponsors Ford Fall Forum, where leaders of the pluralistic society of the United States have an opportunity to express their views on controversial subjects. Please make them as comfortable as possible." The editor obliged by taking the Smiths to see the Irish Sweeps Derby in the Midlands. In appreciation for the efforts of *The Catholic Standard* in behalf of the church in Ireland, Cardinal Cushing in 1965 sent the editors a check for five thousand dollars. He never forgets a friend, nor does he ever let a friend forget him. When it comes to ferreting out possible sources of revenue, Cushing is like a beagle on a scent.

In the fall of 1955 he saw a squib in a Boston newspaper about a friend who had just been elected president of the National Electronic Distributors Association in Columbus, Ohio. One sentence caught his eye: "Total sales of association members is expected to reach $750,000,000 this year."

"I saw the enclosed in Friday night's paper," he wrote the executive. "Is there any chance of getting some of that $750,000,000 for the

Archbishop Cushing Charity Fund, the Community Chest, for the Catholic charities, and other institutions of the archdiocese? Keep healthy, happy, humorous and holy, and all things else will be added unto you."

Cushing, never afraid to make the bold move, persuades his affluent friends to tap their affluent friends. Early in 1960, he sent a select list of donors "a copy of a letter I propose to send to a few people to increase our annual charity collections. Anything you can do for me with regard to contacting prospective donors will be appreciated. The difficulty is, I don't at the moment have a good list of prospective donors to whom I could send this letter." Cushing's unspoken slogan is, "Do unto the rich as Harvard does unto the rich, but do it first."

Profits from ticket sales to charity functions might suffice for lesser churchmen, but not for Cushing. Dozens of times he has told associates: "If we are going to make any money on this dinner we will have to do it through prizes." In July 1962, he reminded certain donors of "the birthday party that the telephone girls are giving me on August 23. Since tickets are only five dollars apiece, I don't think I will make much on a ticket. However, they are going to have a drawing after the dinner at a dollar a ticket. I promised them the following prizes."

In recent years demands on his charity have kept pace with contributions. "I never needed your help any more than I do now," he told regular donors in the spring of 1963. "I have the greatest projects ahead of me. When they are finished, I also expect to be finished."

Fund-raising for Cushing is arduous and time-consuming, yet represents only a fraction of his overall program once he became the chief spokesman for the church of New England.

chapter nine

DEFENDER OF THE FAITH

ARCHBISHOP CUSHING was drawn into religious controversies in the 1940s and 1950s, despite his promise to refrain from "all argument with our non-Catholic neighbors and from all purely defensive talks about Catholicism." Charges made by certain critics, however, were too provocative to be ignored. The most persistent gadfly was Paul Blanshard, a Unitarian lawyer who in 1947 wrote a series of articles in *The Nation* attacking Roman Catholic views on medicine, sex, and education.

Blanshard's central thesis was that the Catholic Church was a wealthy, powerful monolith bent on destroying the American way of life. In 1949, he wrote the first of five books published over the course of eleven years, challenging Catholics to prove their loyalty to concepts of American freedom. His first book, *American Freedom and Catholic Power,* charged that Rome and Moscow had something in common in the struggle for men's minds, and while he repudiated the bigotry of the Know-Nothings and the American Protestant Association, he struck a responsive chord among Protestants. For years he was sponsored by such groups as Protestants and Other Americans United for Separation of Church and State, a group that Archbishop Cushing labeled a "refined form of the Ku Klux Klan." Dr. Louis D. Newton, chairman of the executive committee, countered: "It is just another instance of resorting to abuse when you have no argument."

It was nonetheless a fact that Blanshard's wild charges of an alleged Catholic conspiracy recalled the excesses of nineteenth-century alarmists who said the nation was in danger of being taken over by "Papists." These charges lay dormant during the first quarter of the twentieth century, when few talked about a Catholic conspiracy. "Catholics fought bravely in World War I, were national heroes in the boxing ring, on the football field and the baseball diamond," writes Lawrence Fuchs.[1] "It was hard to believe that Knute Rockne and his team at Notre Dame were conspiring to anything more subversive than a victory over Army." But for Blanshard, the Pope was a reactionary bent on conquest. Blanshard hammered away on this theme so often that Catholics finally attacked him as a bigot. Al Smith spoke for millions of Catholics when he threw up his hands and said: "Will someone tell me what the hell a papal encyclical is?"

Blanshard, while not questioning the loyalty of Catholics, criticized their leaders, whose policies, in his opinion, conflicted with American tradition. In his category of leaders were Spellman and Cushing, as well as the Pope. Citing Cardinal Spellman as the church's political leader, he said no American face was more familiar to readers of New York newspapers in 1947 and 1948. "Archbishop Cushing received comparable treatment in the Boston press. Publicity worth millions of dollars in revenue and good will is given to the Catholic hierarchy every week by the newspapers and magazines of the country, all glamorous and respectful, with never a critical tone."[2] He was suspicious of every large Catholic turnout.

In June 1945, thirty thousand members of the Holy Name Society and other Catholic men gathered in Fenway Park. "We are banded together to revive a world that almost died by its own hand," Cushing told them during a ceremony that commemorated the 3,912 dead of the archdiocese. As servicemen standing before an immense altar formed a cross, the assembly said the rosary. In heavy rain Cushing crossed the field to bless wounded servicemen and shake the hand of each. "These are the real heroes," he said, "men who dare to become saints." He told the meeting that the "only union which we Catholics seek in America and in the world is that for which the President of the United States pleaded in his recent letter to the Holy Father: 'I desire to do everything in my power to support and to contribute to a concert of all the forces striving for a moral world.' "[3]

In September 1945, forty-five thousand young people filled Boston College Alumni Field, when Catholic Youth Organization members from 325 churches observed a holy hour.[4] The following June, forty thousand men crowded into Braves Field, not far from Fenway Park, for an archdiocesan holy hour at which armed forces chaplains of the diocese received citations from Cushing. For Blanshard this was another sinister fact of Catholic solidarity. Prelates from all over the world attended a national convention of the Confraternity of Christian Doctrine held at Boston Garden four months later, when Cushing recommended the canonization of Pope Pius X. Pope Piux XII addressed the congress by radio from Castel Gandolfo.

In 1947, Archbishop Cushing himself led one hundred thirty thousand Catholics in a Holy Name Society parade, the largest religious turnout ever seen in Boston. He did not look like an arch conspirator as he walked along, pausing now and then to put his biretta on the head of a child whom he picked up and carried for a few yards. He slapped friends on the back, and when spectators tried to kiss his ring, said: "No adults. Just the children." He solemnly selected a peanut from a bag offered by a four-year-old boy, while asking bystanders the score of the Yankee-Brooklyn World Series game. The Brooklyn contingent with whom he was marching cheered when he said, on hearing that Brooklyn won the game, "Well, I guess we pulled Brooklyn through today, all right."

"Where is your top hat?" he asked a monsignor whom he passed.

"I gave it back to the undertaker," the cleric said.

This was as conspiratorial a remark as was made during the parade. Cushing did not appear to be a fascist leading storm troopers. Blanshard, however, showed a paranoid interest in the event. He estimated that this "greatest religious demonstration in the history of New England" would have stretched forty miles if all units were lined up behind each other. The procession, which included eighteen hundred uniformed New York City policemen and eight hundred firemen, took eight hours to pass the reviewing stand. Temporary mayor John B. Hynes, who was on the stand during that time, chuckled when Archbishop Cushing came up the steps to greet senators Leverett Saltonstall and Henry Cabot Lodge, and Governor Robert Bradford, all Yankee Protestants. "The Holy Namers think you three fellows have become Catholic converts," Cushing said.

Dr. Harold J. Ockenga, pastor of the Park Street Church, which had been newsworthy during the ministry of the Reverend Arcturus Zodiac Conrad, brought the church back into the spotlight in 1948 when, in a sermon, he compared a parade of eighty thousand CYO members to marches of children in Germany under Hitler and in Italy under Mussolini. More than a million spectators had lined Boston streets to see this parade, with its colorful floats picturing a variety of religious scenes. The parade had been publicized as "the Hub's greatest demonstration of faith in God and country." In the line of march was Archbishop Cushing, who handed a bouquet a nun had given him to a four-year-old drum majorette. He was almost mobbed by youngsters. The parade was that innocent.

The *Pilot* ridiculed Dr. Ockenga's charges, made from "one of Boston's most venerable pulpits," implying that the procession posed a threat to the future of mankind. Dr. Ockenga, the editorialist said, "was reminded by the bands and the marching feet of the sights he had seen in Italy and Germany and he wondered if what happened there was now appearing here. There are some . . . who don't know a child's step from a goose step, nor a parade from a rehearsal for war. Or perhaps there are some who, unable to trust their own motives, refuse to trust the motives of others."

In 1949, President Harry Truman, who generally visited Cushing when he came to Boston, appointed General Mark Clark United States ambassador to the Vatican. This act, said Ockenga, was "the culmination of a long process of political aggression on the part of the Roman Catholic Church. This should be the opening gun in the greatest battle for the American principle of separation of church and state this nation has ever seen."

Cushing soon thereafter addressed more than five thousand delegates to a national convention of the Holy Name Society in Boston, warning that a new bigotry was rampant. "I speak for perhaps twenty-five million Catholics who live . . . completely confident of the perfect harmony between their duties as Catholics and their duties as Americans." Another time he quoted Al Smith: "The Catholics of the country can stand bigotry. The Jews can stand it. But the United States cannot stand it. It is aimed at every clean concept on which the American pattern of life is founded."

When Paul Blanshard stepped up his attacks, Cushing asked what American Catholics had ever done that their loyalty should be questioned. "Have we ever taken up arms against our government? Have we ever plotted for its overthrow?" He pointed out that in the 1950s Catholics exercised less influence on the thought and legislation of the country "than some of the weaker of the Protestant sects, though we number almost half of the active membership of all the churches combined. Catholic religious power is therefore great, but it is false and vicious to talk of Catholic political power."

In 1947, Cushing clashed with seven Protestant clergymen who, after visiting Yugoslavia, said Catholics, including the jailed Archbishop Stepinac,* enjoyed freedom of worship. Cushing, calling them "innocents abroad," blasted their stand in his talk to the Knights of Columbus at their sixty-fifth national convention in Boston: "Seven hand-picked American Protestant clergymen have signed an infamous, monstrous document when they testified that Catholics enjoyed freedom of worship in Yugoslavia. . . . It is with pain and regret that I denounce these men and the campaign of misrepresentation and malice." Cushing decried the wave of anti-Catholicism and anticlericalism spreading in America, encouraged by such groups as these ministers who were trying "to sell to the American people the Red Fascist line with regard to what is happening to religion in Eastern Europe." By this time Cushing was outraged by the jailings, tortures, and confiscations of the clergy.

One of the seven ministers, the Reverend Emory Bucke, editor of *Zion's Herald,* said that in the course of compiling their report, his group had conferred with the head of a Catholic theological school in Zagreb, a Serbian Orthodox seminary in Belgrade, and a Jewish rabbi. The report found no restriction of religion under the Tito regime. The right to worship, he continued, "was in no way curbed by government policy." Dr. Guy Shipler, editor of the *Churchman,* an unofficial Episcopal magazine, called Stepinac a "quisling collaborator with Hitler," adding that the Catholic hierarchy wanted no such revelations reported. The Catholic Church could avoid criticism by becoming "only a church and not a political state. Every decent Protestant respects the constitutional rights of . . . Catholics, but increasing numbers are determined to fight the type of political clericalism which has been so disastrous to other countries." [5]

The Boston *Herald,* read mostly by Protestants, backed Cushing: "His anxieties bring us back to our previously expressed concern for that segment of the Protestant clergy which seems all too willing to be taken in by Soviet semantics. They are the Henry Wallaces of the Protestant Church." [6]

In 1949, with the jailing of Stepinac in mind, Cushing had said it was easy "to imprison a cardinal or an archbishop . . . but it is im-

---

* Stepinac was released in 1951, elevated to cardinal in 1952, and died in 1960.

possible to stifle hundreds of millions of the faithful in all the countries of the world." [7] Cushing contrasted the passionate beliefs of communists with the West's lukewarm talk about democracy and freedom, which was "not on the sublime level of ideas which inflame. . . . It has lost its Christian heart. It has lost its Catholic soul. It has lost its 'guts.' "

In various speeches, Cushing said the United States was probably the only nation that tolerated "and at times blesses the parlor pinks, the fellow travelers, and out-and-out communists who thrive in our midst." He repeatedly advocated teaching that communism is evil. "We must teach it . . . as we teach the evil of sin in the moral order, or cancer in the physical order." He further said that America was full of Soviet intelligence agents. "Every time they send a ballet team or a hockey team . . . you will find some communist intelligence officers, a fancy word for spies." He mentioned young spies who had infiltrated seminaries to study for the priesthood or ministry.

In 1953, Archbishop Cushing charged that Harvard, Boston University, and Northeastern University had too many professors who were destroying the faith and Americanism of Catholic students. "It is American education which has supplied communism in the past with its opportunity." Observing that religion was being attacked just as viciously in America as it was in Europe, he said: "While there are no atheists in foxholes, there are atheists in the comfortable chairs of secular universities teaching pagan doctrines in the name of science." He saw no reason for Catholic students to attend these institutions "when they can get an education at a Catholic institution."

Cushing's animus against communism stemmed from a conviction that in a world that was becoming more secularized, Catholicism was the strongest bulwark against it. He argued that Rome and Moscow were poles apart, and there was evidence to support the theory in the Soviet Union itself. Stalin had Pope Pius XII in mind when he asked, with the same sarcasm Napoleon had used: "How many divisions has he?" As early as 1946 the Pope, in reference to the continuing battle between the church and atheistic communism, told a Sicilian bishop: "It is not impossible that one day the Pope may be hanged on the gallows in St. Peter's Square." Insiders recognized Cushing's aim. When J. Edgar Hoover in 1948 gave the prelate a copy of his book *Masters of Deceit,* he autographed it "To Archbishop Cushing whose magnificent fight against atheistic communism has inspired the writing of this book."

Cushing was one of the church leaders an ex-priest * had in mind when he said they "made a saint of Franco without pausing to hear the other side. They supported the insanity of McCarthyism despite the protests of more balanced men." In his defense of both men, Cushing thought of them as fighters against the foes of religion, without pausing to evaluate them otherwise.

Other Catholic spokesmen took the same tack. Judge John Swift, supreme knight of the Knights of Columbus, lauded Franco at the same time he attacked the United Nations Organization for considering Boston as a possible home: "UNO," Swift said, "has banished the very name of God from its deliberations. All the world knows that the godless Russia has torn the Atlantic Charter to shreds and enslaved millions of our fellow Catholics." On the other hand, Swift praised Franco for "his consistent, courageous, unwavering, and triumphant opposition to the communist revolutionaries whose crimes against civilization and whose unspeakable atrocities on innocent women and children stand unparalleled even among the . . . atrocities of World War II." Judge Swift reflected the views of many Boston Catholics who were even more isolationist than Colonel Robert McCormick, publisher of the Chicago *Tribune*. This parochial isolationism explains the tolerance in Boston of Curleyism, Coughlinism, and America Firstism.

The dread of communism, along with the residual resentment of some Irish Catholics against long years of persecution by Yankee Protestants, largely explained why Catholics supported Senator Joseph McCarthy, who achieved international notoriety overnight following a Lincoln Day address he had given in Wheeling, West Virginia, in 1950, when he held up a sheaf of paper which, he said, bore the names of 205 persons in the State Department who were communists. The televised Army-McCarthy debate made him one of the best-known personalities in the nation. He rose to power by skillfully exploiting the disillusionment of many Americans in the wake of expanding communist power after World War II. The senator was especially popular with Midwestern Republican Protestants, "many of whose parents and grandparents had zealously believed the Maria Monk fraud † and had joined theAPA and KKK. For them, communists had

* Father James Kavanaugh, author of *A Modern Priest Looks at His Outdated Church* (1967).

† *The Awful Disclosures of Maria Monk* was a hoax written by a professional writer. Maria, who died in prison after being arrested for picking the pockets

replaced Catholics as the preeminent threat to the so-called 'American way of life.' " [8]

McCarthy's most rabid followers, however, lived in the poor Irish neighborhoods of New York, Chicago, and Boston, where anticommunism, patriotism, and Catholicism were equated. Lawrence Fuchs makes an illuminating observation: "Catholics, particularly Irish Catholics, behaved as if they were more American than anyone else. After all, the greatest threat to American freedom was now communism, not Catholicism. . . . In the cold war against 'godless, monolithic communism,' both the international religion of Catholicism and the culture-religion of Americanism seemed threatened." [9]

Thus McCarthy, the only Irish Catholic Republican ever elected to the United States Senate in the Midwest, became a hero when he identified militant, parochial Catholicism with opposition to the nation's principal external threat. McCarthy was all the more popular because he gave the impression that Protestants were mainly the subversives, as Thomas Murphy, the prosecutor of Alger Hiss in two trials, noted: "I can't even recall one Irish name among the many thousands called before the House Committee on Un-American Activities."

It was comforting to Irish Catholics to see that the senator's targets were the very WASPs who had treated them so shabbily. McCarthy tarred the Protestant clergy with the same brush, charging that they posed the most serious communist threat to America, thereby supporting some of Archbishop Cushing's charges. Some of the senator's staunchest disciples could be found in the Ancient Order of Hibernians and Holy Name societies. In 1954, the senator was the featured speaker at a Communion breakfast attended by six thousand Catholic members of the New York City police force. Monsignor Joseph Mc-Caffrey, retiring chaplain of the force, introduced him as "one who has devoted time and talent and his life to the exposure and uprooting of communists." Cardinal Spellman, who attended the breakfast, applauded McCarthy and shook hands with him.

Bishop Bernard J. Sheil, of Chicago, who was idolized in that city

---

of a man in a brothel, said her Mother Superior had ordered her to "obey the priests in all things," including living "in the practice of criminal intercourse with them." Children born of these unions were baptized and immediately strangled, the story went. Nuns who balked were murdered and buried in the convent basement. A secret corridor led to the priestly quarters, where nightly orgies were held. Maria, according to her mother, had never been in a convent, but had lived in an asylum for delinquents before escaping.

as well as by Catholics in New York and Boston, considered the senator a symbol of smear and distortion. The church, said Sheil, took no position in matters of public controversy, but it did take a stand on calumny, unfounded charges, and calculated deceit. They are "not justified by any cause—least of all by the cause of anticommunism which should unite rather than divide all of us in these difficult times." [10]

Senator Ralph Flanders, a Vermont Republican, while agreeing that Cardinal Spellman had congratulated the senator at the breakfast, lauded Sheil's denunciation of McCarthy's tactics, adding that the prober had "driven a blundering axe deep in the heart of his own church."

This drew a comment from Archbishop Cushing, who, homeward-bound on the *Queen Mary* in 1953, told reporters that the senator was in no way dividing the church. "Americans, as a people, like to argue. The televised hearings offer a good diversion, and the people are enjoying it. They are being educated." The issue, he said, depended on one's attitude toward communism: "If you look upon it as one of the greatest evils that has attempted to undermine Western civilization, naturally you do everything you can to save our way of life from the inroads of this evil. . . . I sympathize with anybody interested in keeping communism in all its phases and forms from uprooting our traditions and our wonderful opportunity of assuming the leadership through the world that is the only hope of oppressed people."

Cushing spoke at a time when McCarthy, fading from the scene, was about to be censured by the United States Senate. In his television show ("See It Now") on March 9, 1954, Ed Murrow unleashed a devastating attack on the senator. The archbishop was scheduled to appear on another Murrow show, "Person to Person," which was seen Friday nights in over eight million homes. The format was for Murrow to visit celebrities in their homes by means of a camera. Among those he had interviewed were Eleanor Roosevelt, Senator and Mrs. John F. Kennedy, and movie stars such as Marilyn Monroe and Elizabeth Taylor.

A week after the McCarthy broadcast, Cushing was one of two scheduled guests for "Person to Person." "It was generally believed that Cushing and much of his diocese supported the senator's investigations," Fred Friendly of Columbia Broadcasting Company wrote, "and Ed decided that he owed the archbishop a phone call." [11]

After telling the prelate that he would understand, because of his recent broadcast, his diffidence about appearing on the program, Murrow offered to postpone the interview for a few months or indefinitely.

"Mr. Murrow, you and I have a long-standing engagement; I expect to keep it." It was the first time television cameras were used in the cardinal's residence. Cushing told Murrow, in answer to a question, that news photographers often came. "I'm their best customer." He became a priest, he said, "because I wanted to give my life to a cause —the cause of personal sanctity for myself and others." Another time he said: "Being a priest gives you so much opportunity for doing good for the little people who get kicked around, the consolation of making little people happy." He told Murrow that he once had thought of going into politics. "But one day my good pastor called me in and told me, 'You're not fit for politics.' I think the country lost a poor politician. I hope the church found a worthy servant."

Even as late as 1957, when Senator McCarthy died, many Catholics felt they had lost a great champion.

Three other controversies enmeshed the archbishop in the 1950s. In 1952, the Paulist Fathers were scheduled to celebrate a public mass on Boston Common at noon on the day before Christmas, to be followed by a vesper service conducted by the Very Reverend Edwin J. Etten, dean of the Episcopal Church of St. Paul. Dr. Ockenga protested, calling it a "violation of our nonsectarian religious traditions." He asked all citizens of Boston to protest vocally and by letters to newspapers and the city fathers.

"I defend anyone's right to preach on the Common," he said, "but it should not be identified with a civic function. We Bible Protestants believe mass is idolatrous in that the Roman Catholics teach that bread and wine become the blood of Christ through the blessing of the priest."

In a letter of protest to Mayor Hynes, Dr. Ockenga also objected to "that monstrosity" that had been placed on Boston Common opposite the side entrance of the Park Street Church. Hynes politely explained that the eight-foot statue represented St. Francis of Assisi cowled in his brown Franciscan habit and refused to ban the religious exercise. Archbishop Cushing said during the celebration of the mass that it "would be strange, indeed, if the holy sacrifice of the mass, which is so welcome on the battlefields were not welcome within the peaceful precincts of the Common."

The Boston Public Library was another area to witness a conflict between Protestants and Roman Catholics, whose interests were represented by the Boston *Post*. Archbishop Cushing, following a precedent set by Cardinal O'Connell, did not stoke the fires of the controversy, but he did the job he was supposed to do when Mayor Hynes named him a trustee of the library. He cooled off John Fox, the publisher of the *Post*.

In the 1930s, the only Catholic on the board of trustees of the Boston Public Library was Cardinal O'Connell, who had been appointed by Mayor Curley. The prelate, who sometimes strolled along the Charles River esplanade not far from the library dropped in one afternoon to see Director Milton E. Lord. "I suppose people thought I'd fill the library with prayer books and lives of saints when I joined the board," he smiled. According to Lord, the cardinal's main complaint was that the trustees talked more about sewers and roofs than books. Catholicism was never an issue as far as the library's policy was concerned while two Catholic prelates—O'Connell and Cushing—were on the board.

Roman Catholics appointed later included Patrick McDonald, a steel executive; Judge Frank Donahue, of the Superior Court; and Monsignor Robert H. Lord, a former Harvard history professor who, as a convert, had lived in a monastery before he was ordained a priest. In 1952 the busiest man in Boston—Archbishop Cushing—succeeded Monsignor Lord, who said he was too busy to continue serving on the board. The other members at the time were McDonald, Donahue, Sidney Rabb (a leader of the Jewish community), and Frank Buxton (the brilliant former editor of the Boston *Herald*). Buxton and Rabb were impressed by Cushing's objectivity.

Buxton, who used to sit directly across the table at the trustee meetings, which normally lasted about two hours, remembers a discussion during which Cushing said: "There's something wrong with this board. We should increase its number from five to seven. You have me, a representative of the Catholic Church. You should add a rabbi and an Episcopalian churchman." Rabb said Cushing never threw his weight around. "His concern was for people. Frequently, in the midst of a weighty consideration, he would change the subject to ask, for example: 'What about the women who wash the floors in the library? What are we doing for the people who work here?' "

Cushing could, however, sound off when necessary. The matter of building a branch library in South Boston brought him into conflict with William Foley, a sometimes hotly eloquent member of the Boston City Council. Cushing thought the library should be built on the site of an abandoned school, for since the city already owned the property, it would be no tax burden. Foley favored a site owned by a friend—one which the trustees finally voted to buy, since it was in a business district, and thus more accessible to the public.

As the discussion grew heated, Cushing blasted Foley, winding up a stinging rebuke with a query. "What did *you* ever do for the people of South Boston?" Frank Buxton recalled the incident in 1969: "I never knew the archbishop to lose his temper while he was on the board, except on the day when he laid into Billy Foley. Incidentally, he did not have a harsh, rasping voice in our library discussions. His voice was emphatic, but not at all unpleasant. He discussed issues easily and well and almost always voted with the majority. He missed few meetings, even when his health was very poor."

After the stormy session, a chastened Foley walked out into the lobby of the library with the associate director, John Connolly. "Are all your meetings as wild as this one?" he asked, grinning.

Buxton further recalled that the archbishop had no obsessions about improper books. "I don't remember that he ever questioned the judgment of the various persons who selected books for the library." Cushing, who had no truck with book-banning, was amused by some of his experiences while serving as a trustee. At a meeting of the Catholic Library Association a nun asked him whether the library should shelve such possibly risqué publications as *Life* magazine. The real test of the prelate's objectivity came late in September 1952 when the Boston Sunday *Post* disputed Milton Lord's statement that communist and Soviet books were not openly displayed in the library but were kept available for study and research.

"The Boston Public Library is promoting communist literature in a large-scale lobby display urging people to read basic books on communism," the *Post* charged, adding that under a sign reading "Be a Better Citizen, Person, Parent," there was a copy of Karl Marx's *Communist Manifesto*. "Any reader, young or old, can have the Collected Works of Lenin completely revised in 1942 with the alterations of the Marxist line dictated by Stalin," the story continued.

Judge Donahue said that since he had been on the board he had vainly tried to find out what books were bought by the library and who ordered them. He wanted to know who was responsible for buying the books on communism. Before a hearing of the Boston City Council, Milton Lord said he had no way of determining how many books on communism and Soviet propaganda were in the library, noting that a book selection committee made up of librarians was given a list of possible purchases.

When the *Post* maintained its attack, the Boston *Herald* defended the director, saying he had acted with courage and principle in refusing to remove from the shelves books and publications on Soviet propaganda. "In these tense times it is more important for us to be informed about our enemies than our friends," the *Herald* editorialized.

The *Post* countered that the *Herald,* in reaffirming its position that pro-Soviet literature should not be suppressed in public libraries, gave them the right to place poisonous literature on shelves open to anyone. John Fox, the contentious publisher-author of the blistering editorials, told his readers that Americans "when captured by the enemy are receiving the same treatment as our missionaries, priests, nuns and ministers, being chained by their necks, hands tied behind them, while they are paraded through the towns and cities of China, stoned and beaten by a populace aroused to a frenzy by our enemy."

During the newspaper duel, Judge Donahue and Patrick McDonald sided with the *Post,* while Sidney Rabb and Frank Buxton defended Lord, whom McDonald wanted fired. Since Cushing held the deciding vote, McDonald tried to swing him over during their private conversations in his plush Brookline apartment and while driving back and forth in his chauffeured limousine to trustee meetings. Snatches of conversation heard by McDonald's chauffeur were passed on to the head shipping clerk, with whom the chauffeur talked while waiting for his boss. The clerk was Francis P. Moran, führer of the New England Christian Front, a civil-service appointee.

"This isn't a parish library," Cushing was reported to have told McDonald in one exchange. "This is the public library of the city of Boston." He referred the matter of book displays to the scholarly Monsignor Edward Murray, who succeeded him as trustee, but took no action himself. He left the administration of the library to its competent director.

While Cushing was on the board, twelve editions of an anonymous scandal sheet were published under the title "Report to the Board of Trustees by *The Library Mentor*." (Inmates of the Charlestown State Prison had earlier launched a periodical called *The Mentor*. Later, convicts at the Norfolk Prison Colony published it.) Francis P. Moran, as articulate as he was unpopular at the library, is believed to have been the chief author of this scurrilous sheet, whose chief target was Director Lord. Both Lord and Cushing were attacked in the January 17, 1958, issue of *The Library Mentor*.

"On January 3, 1958, an asinine panegyric appeared on the editorial page of the Boston *Herald*, entitled 'A Librarian's Battle Ribbons,' " the nameless scribe wrote. "It hailed the courage of Milton Edward Lord in maintaining the right and duty of the library to make available all materials covering both sides of any controversial question—in this case, communism. Mr. Lord did fight publicly for the principle involved but, not mentioned in the *Herald* editorial, he also issued a panicky order to the library employees to remove all pro-communist material from the shelves immediately, making it inaccessible to the public and, particularly, to the reporters of the Boston *Post*. Time has proved Lord's political acumen, since there is much reason to believe that it is due primarily to the archbishop's influence that Lord has not been fired within the past several years, and a competent administrator appointed. We do not thank His Excellency. Nor do we have any sympathy for his position in this matter. He has done such wonderful work in his religious field that it is heart-breaking to see him show such weakness in this, ignoring the welfare of the many for the benefit of a few." In another passage the scribe wrote: "Your Excellency, Archbishop Cushing, we hesitate to call you a hypocrite. Some of us are of your faith, but we are compelled to recognize your intelligence and thus find it difficult to reconcile your preachments with your lack of conscientious recognition of plain fact and of consequent action."

As an excerpt from the *Library Journal* shows, there was no hypocrisy or subterfuge in the trustees' position: "At the meeting of the trustees on the day following, two resolutions were brought to the floor. The first, adopted by a three-to-two vote (Cushing usually held the decisive vote), read in part: 'Material presenting all points of view concerning the problems and issues of our times, international, national and local, should be available to the public. The library authorities have no right to exercise censorship, that their individual or collective points of view shall prescribe what the public shall read and what shall be banned.

" 'The public must be afforded an opportunity in a great library to have facilities to learn both sides of any controversial question of importance.' " [12]

These entries, dated November 1, 1952, were prompted by the duel between the two Boston newspapers. During that controversy, Monsignor Lally, with Cushing's approval, praised Director Lord for his stand. Later, when Lord went to the cardinal's residence to thank Cushing, the prelate said, "What other action could I have taken?"

When Judge Donahue resigned in 1956, *The Library Mentor* noted in a burst of verse titled "Our Apology!":

> He fought for the library's overall needs,
> And inordinate greed and ambition abhorred—
> Then, because he was true to his creed, he walked out
> In disgust at the rest of your board.

The scribe, finally wearying of tilting with windmills, suspended publication of the *Mentor*. After Donahue resigned in 1956, Mayor Hynes discussed his successor with Milton Lord, and the name of Erwin Canham, editor of *The Christian Science Monitor,* came up. When Lord mentioned that Archbishop Cushing said he didn't think any more priests should be members of the board, Hynes said, "I wish he'd tell that to me." Before appointing Canham, Hynes checked out the appointment with "Lake Street." Cushing approved of the editor.

Cushing himself resigned from the board in 1958 in favor of Monsignor Edward Murray so that he could give more time to his assignment as a trustee of Boston City Hospital. "Shortly after he was appointed to the board of the hospital," Sidney Rabb said, "I asked him how he was able to accept such a time-consuming post with the demands on his time already far beyond the normal capacity of one man. His answer was typical: "I've heard so much about the problems of the poor at hospitals that I'm making the time.' " Behind Cushing's remark was a little story that illuminates his personality.

Before Mayor Hynes named the prelate to the hospital board, the chairman of the trustees, William H. Ellis, had gone to the cardinal's residence to ask for a blessing. When Cushing seemed diffident, apparently wondering why a Protestant (as he mistook Ellis to be) should want a blessing from a Catholic bishop, the board chairman said:

"Your Eminence, you don't understand. I've just come from Holy Communion right across the street here at St. Ignatius. I'm asking your blessing on my new work at the hospital."

Putting his arm around the visitor's shoulders, Cushing invited him into his study for a chat, and when Ellis later asked him to become a trustee, he agreed, spending all the time he could cheering up patients in the wards in his own special way.[13]

It was a time of overlapping controversies. Archbishop Cushing once more found himself in the middle during a religious dispute that rocked the Boston hierarchy in the late 1940s and early 1950s.

Harvard Catholics had established St. Benedict's Center in Cambridge in 1940 along the lines of the more independent Newman clubs for Catholic students in other universities. Under the direction of Father Leonard J. Feeney, S.J., the center became a full-dress academy, offering courses in Greek, church history, hagiography, literature, and philosophy. Known in Catholic circles as the American church's best light essayist and as a cheerful poet, the gray-haired eccentric priest charmed his students. They loved his impersonations of celebrities spouting nonsense. He was at his best when taking off on President Franklin Delano Roosevelt discussing the state of the church or Katharine Hepburn broadcasting a prizefight. After one hilarious class session, three students who took a taxi had the driver roaring with laughter as they told how Feeney conducted the class. "No charge," he said as they got out of the taxi. "For a show like that, I should pay you."

Feeney was a despot, however, when his judgment was questioned. When a woman criticized a statement, he pointed toward the door. "Out!" he shouted. The angered student picked up her books. "I'll go," she said, "but I'll take my candlesticks." [14]

In 1948, three Boston College instructors and a teacher at Boston College High School accused the Boston College president, the Very Reverend William L. Keleher, S.J., of heresy on three counts: he let students be taught that there might be salvation outside the Catholic church; that a person might be saved even though he did not hold that the church was supreme among churches; and that he might be saved without submission to the Pope.

Keleher told the press that the instructors were under contract to teach philosophy and physics. He had warned them to leave theology to competent teachers, but they continued to speak in and out of class on matters contrary to the teaching of the church—"ideas leading to bigotry and intolerance." Keleher found their erroneous doctrine intolerable. As a result, St. Benedict's Center lost its ecclesiastical standing, and Catholics were forbidden to attend. This also meant that Feeney could no longer preach or hear confessions.

Late in April 1949, Cushing decreed that Feeney could perform no other priestly functions, including saying mass and teaching religion. At about the same time, the Vatican unofficially said Cushing was a "very prudent" man who must have had reasons for his action. The Vatican ordered the four teachers and Feeney to submit and return to the church at the peril of their souls.

In happier times, Feeney had brought his yearly crop of converts to meet the archbishop. Even when Feeney first aired his heresy, Cushing, trying to put him back on the track, was extremely considerate, but Feeney remained obdurate.

"The reason I am silenced," he told the press, "is because I believe there is no salvation outside the Catholic Church and without personal submission to our Holy Father, and Archbishop Cushing believes there is, and Bishop Wright believes there is." Auxiliary Bishop John J. Wright of Boston (later named a cardinal by Pope Paul VI) was the popular chaplain of the League of Catholic Women who had served as secretary for both O'Connell and Cushing. There is a story about Cardinal O'Connell walking around the seminary grounds with Father (later monsignor) Walter Furlong.

"Such a pretty robin song!" the cardinal said. When Furlong told him it was a woodthrush, O'Connell gave him an icy stare. "Father Furlong," he said, "you may go."

A decade later Cardinal Cushing was walking with young Father Wright. Noticing the splashing in the bird bath, he turned to Wright. "Just what kind of bird is that?"

"I'm about the last priest in the archdiocese who could identify that bird for you," Wright said.

"Well, you must ask Father Furlong," Cushing said deadpan. "He'd know."

Wright—who, said Cushing, "was all over the place; I could never find him"—tried to straighten out Feeney, but, like Cushing, he received abuse instead of gratitude. In his defiance, the priest said the center had not been founded "by a decree of the archbishop and will not be dissolved by such a decree." He noted that Cushing had said nothing about closing the Center.

In September 1949, the *Pilot* published an official censure of Feeney by the Vatican, and an unofficial English translation detailed the doctrine of salvation, upholding Cushing and the Boston College Jesuits. The *Pilot* said Feeney had rejected an invitation to come to the cardinal's residence to hear the decision ahead of publication. Cushing spoke: "As the shepherd of the archdiocese . . . my heart goes out in love to Father Feeney and to those . . . misled by false ideas. It is my fervent hope that now, after the supreme authority of the church has spoken, Father Feeney and his followers will prove themselves loyal children of the church and of our Holy Father, Pope Pius XII." Feeney went to see Cushing a few days later, kissing his ring, and greeted him as "my father," adding, "I'm glad to see that I'm still your son." According to a spokesman at the center, Feeney told his superior: "In the name of the Blessed Virgin Mary, I accuse you of heresy." A month later, Feeney was dismissed from the Jesuits, and in 1951 the center lost its official approval from the state board of collegiate authority.

Feeney and his "tight-lipped followers" picketed the cardinal's residence, and the "contumacious Irishman," as Evelyn Waugh called the priest, heaped abuse on Cushing, calling him "The Archdiocesan Ragman," in reference to his newspaper drives. In a public demonstration he blasted the prelate for opening a Catholic chapel at Jewish Brandeis University and even accused him of improperly accepting an honorary degree from the Massachusetts Institute of Technology. When Feeney and his disciples chanted on his lawn, Cushing summoned Police Commissioner Thomas Sullivan. In his exasperation, when the "Slaves of the Immaculate Heart of Mary," as they called themselves, explained that they merely wanted to say the rosary, Sullivan turned to a sergeant.

"Pull them up! Arrest them! Get them out of here!" The demonstrators, on their knees, continued to recite the rosary while Sullivan told the sergeant to drag the lector off to the paddy wagon.

"Commissioner," the sergeant said, "this is one pinch you'll have to make yourself. It goes against my conscience to arrest people while they're saying their prayers." The demonstrators left quietly after saying the beads.

When Feeney and his "Slaves" wildly demonstrated on the Common, Mayor Hynes was asked to silence them. He refused, explaining that soap-box orators had a right to sound off there. "I heard so much about Feeney, I went to the Common one Sunday afternoon and hid behind a tree hoping he couldn't see me. When he did spot me, he mistook me for the Fire Commissioner, 'I see you, Mike Kelliher,' he yelled. 'Why don't you come out from behind that tree so everyone can see you.'" In another tirade, Feeney from his perch pointed to a grinning listener, who had booed him. "You, you hooknosed Jew, what have you to say?"

"Business is good," the spectator shouted. "How are things with you?"

Another heckler, arms folded and leaning against a tree, called the priest a liar. Pointing toward him, Feeney screamed that he was a pervert known as "Wacky Oscar."

To save the fanatics from injury by irate bystanders when they distributed inflammatory literature on the Common, the police loaded them in patrol wagons and transported them to safer ground. The Sunday spectacles attracted crowds who marveled at the way Feeney ranted, spurred on by frenetic disciples dressed like seminarians. The female zealots wore black nunlike garb. Every Sunday, in any kind of weather, the hymn-singing processionists waved their signs, and Cushing came in for as much abuse as Masons, Jews, and Protestants. Feeney, in a four-page leaflet published monthly, damned his targets in sick rhetoric, and his believers sold books written by him or themselves.

When they moved from Boston, they were man-handled by police in points as far removed as Indiana. In the fall of 1952 twenty-five students crashed the residence of Archbishop Cicognani, apostolic delegate to the United States, on Embassy Row, in Washington, D.C. After storming into his office, they were dragged off the premises by the police. In the summer of 1953 six fanatics were rushed off the Notre Dame campus after trying to incite a riot. "The first sign of your approaching damnation," one fanatic shouted, "is that Notre Dame has Protestants on its football team." Ten days later the same group was jailed in Chicago for trying to invade the office of Samuel Cardinal Stritch. Was Feeney still a priest? If so, they screamed, it was the cardinal's duty to see that newspapers stopped calling him an "ex-priest." It enraged him to be called "Mr. Feeney."

In 1955, the three co-chairmen of the Boston chapter of the National Association of Christians and Jews denounced Feeney and his followers: "It is disgraceful that such a group exists, and particularly that it should take such action in an effort to create hatred and misunderstanding among our people."

For Archbishop Cushing it was a rekindling of passions incited by Father Coughlin and the Christian Fronters in the 1930s and 1940s, much to the embarrassment of the Catholic hierarchy. The Boston *Observer* reported that Coughlin testified in 1936 before Internal Revenue Service agents that most of his income came from Boston supporters, and when he entered a team in the 1936 presidential election, he chose as running mate for Lemke, Thomas C. O'Brien, a Boston lawyer. Cushing was a bishop when George Cardinal Mundelein of Chicago said the Detroit priest was not speaking for the church. By then, after calling President Roosevelt a "great betrayer and liar," his influence began to wane, but he was still popular in Massachusetts circles. Cardinal O'Connell, however, called him a "hysterical demagogue" and warned priests against listening to his radiocasts. Archbishop Edward Mooney finally muzzled him when the Justice Department ruled that his broadcasts resembled Nazi propaganda. But the damage was done. Coughlin had already exploited the fears and resentments of hundreds of thousands of Catholics.

His Christian Front headquarters in Boston, arousing passions that were more political than religious, for years had pumped out vicious streams of slander against Jews, and the hierarchy was further shamed when Francis P. Moran, leader of the New England Christian Front, called President Roosevelt a "Jew" guilty of "treason," ranted about the "communist-riddled government of the United States," and charged that the White House sold military secrets to England and France." [15] He was merely echoing Coughlin's tirades.

A sign on Moran's office on Massachusetts Avenue in Boston read "Sociological Research." Stacked in cubicles were poison tracts written by subversives, including George Sylvester Viereck, a Nazi agent. Moran, while working in the shipping department of the Boston Public Library, was called "a calculating and cold-blooded propagandist of the Bund's Gerhard Kunze type." [16] He was an intimate friend of the Reverend Edward Lodge Curran, a fascist admirer of Father Coughlin.

Archbishop Cushing became directly involved in the anti-Semitic issue after an ugly outbreak of Jew-baiting in the spring of 1944 in Chelsea, Brookline, and Dorchester, where "Jewish boys and girls were set upon and severely beaten by 'patriotic' bums glowing with Coughlinite 'Christianity'." [17] The skirmishes, which at times bordered on riots, marred the image of the Catholic Church, whose priests dismissed the incidents as "kid stuff."

John Gunther, while noting that some normal youthful hooliganism was involved, writes: "A gang of a dozen alley rats would run into a pair of Jewish boys, and beat them up, or windows would be stoned at the Jewish home in Dorchester." [18] Three young hoodlums assaulted an aged Jew on a trolley, and eight others mauled two Harvard students. Boston newspapers hushed up the incidents until *PM*, the New York liberal newspaper, exposed the brutality. Although none of the Boston hierarchy was in any way connected with anti-Semitic activity, the clergy was scored for its passive role. In 1944 *The Atlantic Monthly* aired the issue: "There seems to be reason to doubt that the focusing of juvenile delinquents upon Jewish victims was part of the Front's work, and that the principal support of the Front in Boston has come from Irish-Americans."

Christian Fronters met in Hibernian Hall in Roxbury not far from the Jewish district to hear anti-Semitic speeches by rabble-rousers who quoted Viereck. The police finally closed Hibernian Hall (the FBI closed Moran's office in 1942). The "Lauriat Avenue gang" hounded Jews in Dorchester, and a roller-skating rink in that community was a meeting place for young hoodlums who formed gangs that vandalized Jewish neighborhoods, breaking the windows of one kosher butcher shop week after week, as well as assaulting Jews.

South Boston, to Cushing's embarrassment, was another hot-bed of anti-Semitism. There Father Curran spoke at the invitation of the South Boston Citizens' Association. Some of the worst riots were in South Boston. At the Evacuation Day parade there in 1944 a gang of young Irish Americans attacked the junior band of the Malden Post of the Veterans of Foreign Wars as they were boarding a streetcar, injuring several young Jews and smashing their instruments. During the melee the hoodlums shouted anti-Semitic obscenities. This is a section where Congressman John W. McCormack was vilified by his Catholic constituents for appointing a Jew to the United States Naval Academy. In one ward of his Twelfth District he is still known as "Rabbi John." What was behind the animosity?

"At the bottom," according to *The Atlantic Monthly*, "among the frustrated and the embittered, these feelings find their most direct expression; there the age-old desire for a scapegoat breaks out with a vengeance. The entrenched Yankees are invulnerable. But the Jew is relatively impotent and defenseless."

After World War II, Jewish community leaders became alarmed when returning Jewish GI's organized vigilante groups whose members wore helmets and carried billies. Sidney Rabb went to see Archbishop Cushing to ask for help. "Please stop it," he told the prelate. "We don't want anyone killed. Tell those Catholic gangs to disband." On the following Sunday at every mass the priests of the archdiocese passed along Cushing's message and the trouble abruptly stopped. Cushing, who will tolerate no religious prejudice among his clergy, at times suppressed anti-Semitism by ordering Priests to go into homes to talk directly to parents whose children were causing trouble. He made his position clear at meetings of the National Conference of Christians and Jews.

After the incidents, the archbishop was acutely aware of growing fears of anti-Semitism. In November 1948, he made a surprise visit to the Statler Hotel to speak to fifteen hundred delegates of the Union of American Hebrew Congregations: "No man," he said, "could have my faith concerning Christ without desiring to be more like Him and, therefore, seek, like Him, to help and befriend all men without exception—white, black, Gentile, Jew. Always remember that a Catholic bishop took time from a busy day to come here to tell you that. I can and do pledge the friendship of my people." Referring to the ignorant and malicious attitudes of some Christians toward Jews, he added: "I ask you not to believe these things; they are lies and they are uttered in order to delude us." The delegates gave him a standing ovation.

It was the first time a high ranking Catholic prelate had addressed a Jewish body, and it was a prelude to the later ecumenical trend inaugurated by Pope John XXIII.

John Gunther in his 1947 book observed that it would cause no comment in most American cities "if a rabbi and a priest were to be seen publicly together; in Boston, this event occurred at a recent book fair and it was considered not only a new development but a sensation." It was no sensation for Cushing, who from the outset of his career had embraced believers of all faiths. By the time he became archbishop he was more esteemed in Jewish and Protestant circles than by the "latter day snobs of his own religious persuasion." [19] It is accordingly understandable how upset he was when Father Feeney's militant anti-Semitism was so widely publicized in the early 1950s.*

---

* By 1957, the "Slaves" were living in a cluster of houses near the former St. Benedict's Center, which was in a back street off Harvard Square. When they were ousted for violating the building code, they moved to a site in Harvard, a town about twenty miles west of Cambridge. Here Feeney and some followers still live.

Yet, during all the years of the controversy, he refused to speak harshly of Feeney.

In 1964, however, in a talk before the Massachusetts Clerical Association, an organ of Episcopal clergymen at Trinity Church in Boston, he said Christians should recognize differences in dogma without quarreling over them. "We are told there is no salvation outside the Church! Nonsense! Nobody can tell me that Christ died on Calvary for any select group." Then, with a sly twinkle, he added: "As the fellow says, 'It's great to live with saints in heaven, but it's hell on earth!' "

Although it was hard to fault Cushing's judicial handling of the Feeney affair, Paul Blanshard charged that even if Feeney was a fanatic, his view "was far more honest and accurate than the liberal make-believe adopted by Archbishop Cushing." [20] Blanshard said the Vatican stood by Cushing for the sake of appearances. His fanatical belief that canon law was a fundamental motivation of the Catholic hierarchy in no way applied to Cushing, who scored what one reform-minded layman called "Chancery Catholicism." [21] A Jesuit professor at Holy Cross College noted that Cushing "has no tolerance for any kind of legalism in the church."

The archbishop was caught in another emotional issue when Marjorie McCoy Doherty, a Catholic who had a child by a Protestant intern, gave the infant to a Jewish couple, Mr. and Mrs. Melvin B. Ellis of Brookline. They paid five hundred dollars and a $157 hospital fee for the infant. When Miss Doherty learned that her baby had been placed in a Jewish home, she tried to transfer her to the Charitable Catholic Bureau until a Catholic home could be found, but the Ellises refused to surrender custody. Court actions dragged on for six years. The couple were arrested in Miami by a Massachusetts state trooper in 1957, but Governor Leroy Collins denied a petition of extradition for trial. The Ellises returned later with Hildy, as the child was named.

In 1955, the *Pilot* had reported that the case was back in the news, "and despite court orders, Catholic Hildy McCoy is being held captive by the Jewish couple." Monsignor Francis Lally,* the brilliant editor of the newspaper, told his readers that some local papers had exploited

---

* Lally succeeded Bishop Wright as spiritual director of the League of Catholic Women, served on the executive board of the National Council of Christians and Jews and on the national committee for UNESCO. Mayor Hynes named him to the Boston Redevelopment Authority, of which he became chairman.

"the cheap emotional angles, and weep through their various editions. They have already begun by reprinting the brazenly partisan visit of a New York sob sister to the Ellis hideout."

A bill was proposed in the legislature to permit a mother to give her child for adoption to persons of another faith. The *Pilot* argued that such a law would encourage a revival of "the black and gray markets with all the bargaining in babies which the legislature made possible in the present law."

Cushing, admitting that a word from him was overdue, blasted the attacks made on the commonwealth and Miss McCoy in a few national illustrated magazines and in "the inevitable anti-Catholic magazines. . . . I have read that Hildy's mother has been 'pressured' by that omnipresent pressure force, 'the Roman Catholic Church,' in making her valiant stand. I welcome this chance to give the lie to that familiar line of attack." He said Miss McCoy had paid a high price to alert girls in trouble to the dangers threatening their security if they become webbed in the black market, warning them to turn to trustworthy agencies which could protect them "against individual doctors, lawyers, or others not sharing the regard for conscience and for the common good which, fortunately, characterizes the overwhelming majority of Massachusetts professional men, social workers, and jurists."

In another controversy, Cushing tangled with Dr. James Bryant Conant, president of Harvard University. In 1952 the prelate defended parochial schools in rebuttal to an address given by Conant to the American Association of School Administrators in Boston. Arguing that independent schools operated for religious reasons had resulted in divisive attitudes and stratification in the American community, Conant said public schools should be improved, encouraged, and attended by all social and religious groups. The association responded by passing a resolution opposing public support for private schools.

Cushing interpreted Conant's remarks to mean that all who believe in the American principle should not debate tax support or scholastic standards but should take the position that the independent school is an offense against democracy, a violation of the American principle. "Independent schools like the parochial school, we are told, offend against democracy because they bring what Dr. Conant calls 'a divisive attitude' into American society and they do so because they are not state monopoly schools."

The archbishop was amazed that Conant would make such charges "while making not so much as a passing reference to the past three hundred years of educational history in Massachusetts, with its *numerus clausus* in colleges, its admissions restrictions of a completely nonacademic character, and its ingrained caste system." If religious schools were inconsistent with American democracy, how did it happen that Catholic nuns had for long been teaching colored children?

Cushing focused on Conant's charge that private high schools operated along religious lines endanger "the American principle of a single public school system for all youth." Why should such a basic concept apply only to primary and elementary schools? he asked. "Can it be that President Conant intends to recommend that his own university and like universities be turned over to the commonwealth . . . or to the federal government so that they become 'citizens' colleges, to be operated in accordance with this newly found 'American' principle of a single public school system for all youth?"

Cushing thought Conant would protest that such regimentation, when applied to a university, would be fascism—"and in this he would be quite right. It is strict totalitarianism—'everything in the state, nothing outside the state'—which is why fascism of every stripe opposed private and parochial schools and always demands a single state school system without independent competition, challenge, or rival of any kind."

Cushing's views on federal aid to parochial schools were clear as early as 1946, when he said he would refuse such aid because it would compromise the freedom of the church in its teaching. "Once you have religion tied up with a state, religion is going to come out in second place," he said in one speech. "We have to live within the letter and spirit of the Constitution. Once a state or government starts financing church schools or a church system of education, the next step is a controlled system."

There were times, however, when he questioned the interpretation of the Constitution, and when he marveled at the incongruity of recommendations of the Civil Liberties Union.

In the spring of 1948, the United States Supreme Court made a decision in the McCallum case that seemed to slam the door against any direct federal aid to Catholic schools. It decided one narrow question: Can local American school boards use public classrooms for "released time" religious classes? The answer was no by eight to one: "The First Amendment has erected a wall between church and state which must be kept high and impregnable." The only Catholic jurist on the Supreme Court, Frank Murphy, united with his fellows in this interpretation.

"I am at a loss to understand how the Catholic member of the Supreme Court could go along with that opinion," Cushing commented.

He was at more of a loss to understand how the Civil Liberties Union could ask whether the American principle of the separation of church and state was not violated by the singing of Christmas carols in classrooms. Where would this kind of thinking lead us? he asked. Would school boards be asked to "purge" any and all courses in Dante, Chaucer, Milton, Tennyson, and most representative poets? "In fact, if the completely secular point of view represents the ideal in these matters," Cushing said, "then history and political science courses may have to rewrite the Declaration of Independence, Lincoln's Gettysburg Address, and the basic documents of our political, as well as cultural, tradition." [22] He was disturbed by the trend toward secularizing education.

It was to combat secularism, he said, that the church had created its own educational system: primary, secondary, and collegiate. To provide for religious and moral education, Catholics were willing to submit to a system of double taxation and other disadvantages, which one critic called "the most substantial and dramatic act of faith in education that is being made by any section of the American populace." [23]

In 1955, making it clear that he was speaking for himself and not for the hierarchy, Cushing said he would absolutely refuse any federal aid for the building of parochial schools. "Historically, and under the Constitution as it has been interpreted, we could not receive such aid." On the other hand, parochial school children should not be treated as second-class citizens. "When funds are available for the welfare of children, such as health and bus transportation and lunches . . . our children should not be excluded." Then he came out with a flat statement: "We do insist that no matter what people may say about private, church-sponsored, or parochial school education, this system is demanded by the natural law of God and, further, exists on its own right as a result of the Supreme Court interpretation of the Constitution." [24]

Over the years, Cushing has neglected no area of public concern: education, labor, current affairs, and politics. He has never dodged an issue because it was controversial, whether it was church-state relations, the church's attitude on divorce or on segregation. Cushing has no tolerance for middle-of-the-roaders who please neither God nor the devil.

chapter ten

THE PILGRIM

In 1946, Archbishop Cushing took Boston Catholics on an overland pilgrimage to the Shrine of St. Anne de Beaupré, outside Quebec. That year he told Emmanuel College alumnae that he was planning a pilgrimage to France and Italy. "I have never been in Europe, but my fame has reached England, borne across the ocean on two pairs of nylon stockings."

Two stowaways who had been detained at the House of the Good Shepherd to await deportation to England were among the girls attending Cushing's Christmas party. Motioning toward four piles of stockings by the Christmas tree, the prelate told each girl to mention her stocking size as she came up for a gift. Every girl in the institution received a pair of nylons, which were then replacing silk and rayon hose. A month later news clips sent to Cushing from England mentioned two stowaways who had come to America to seek a husband or a fortune and had been deported. When they tripped down the gangway they were wearing nylons, which, they said, were gifts from the archbishop of Boston. "Thus, while I have never been abroad, my fame has preceded me," Cushing told the college girls.

His fame had also reached Ireland where, in the spring of 1948, he was profiled in *The Catholic Standard*.[1] "Round about mid-March the spirit of Ireland comes to Boston," the story began. "Green ties appear in clothing-store windows. Sweetshops display green candy. Slogans hailing Ireland's national saint and the race that made Boston great, decorate the stores. . . . Warm-hearted Boston becomes one glorious riot of green and gold, liberally decked out with harps and masses of shamrock."

Recalling that Dr. Michael Browne, bishop of Galway, had been a recent guest of Archbishop Cushing, the author of one article said Boston's first bishop, saintly Monsignor de Cheverus, was French. "But as the years passed, Boston's growing Catholic flock became predominantly Irish. And today Boston is America's most Catholic city—and also America's most Irish city."

The archbishop first went abroad in 1948 under the auspices of the Confraternity of Christian Doctrine to promote the canonization of Pope Pius X.[2] Ten thousand persons jammed South Station to see him off to New York, where he boarded the *Queen Mary* with four hundred pilgrims. In Paris he spoke from a pulpit in the Cathedral of Notre Dame, the first Boston prelate to do so. During his visit Foreign Minister Robert Schumann presented him with the Legion of Honor.

Two days later he was in Lourdes, a picturesque little town in the foothills of the Pyrenees, which became a mecca that attracted two million pilgrims a year. Leaving Lourdes, Cushing had a pleasant reunion with his old friend Bishop Wade of Providence, remembered as "the fighting bishop of the Solomon Islands." The Cushing party stopped in Nice, where church and city officials welcomed them. "My hope," the archbishop told a crowd, "is that the present suffering of France will be followed by the glorious resurrection that France deserves." [3]

In Rome Cushing had a special audience with Pope Pius XII, whom he had not seen since his 1936 appearance at Boston College. On a side-trip to Assisi, the archbishop told reporters he knew what it was to be poor, "because I give everything away."

Back in New York, he told a welcoming group that he disliked traveling. "I'm happiest at my work. Coming home is the best part of it." [4]

In January, Bishop Wright went to Ireland to arrange for a "Come Back to Erin" pilgrimage in September 1949. This was the first trip to Ireland since Cardinal O'Connell in 1932 led a pilgrimage to a Eucharistic Congress. One purpose in 1949 was to bring back a group of Trappistine nuns of the Cistercian Order of the Strict Observance to their new foundation in the archdiocese. Cushing persuaded the Cunard Line to send the *Britannic* to Boston so that the five hundred eighty pilgrims traveling with him could sail from their own harbor. Among them were Governor Paul Dever, Bishop Wright, and Alfred Wasilauskas.

The *Britannic* dropped anchor at Daunt's Rock in Cobh, and the silvery bells of St. Colman's Cathedral pealed as a corvette brought the passengers to the pier, while adults and children, singing hymns and carrying flags, stood on the terraced hillsides, which have been likened to "sentinels in gorgeous green overlooking one of the world's most beautiful ports." A veteran Boston reporter said the reception the pilgrims received was overwhelming: "I never saw anything like it." [5]

Cushing leaned out the window of the carriage that took him from Deep Water Quay, shouting that Boston had more Corkonians "than you have in your city." A rousing cheer drowned out the rest of his words. He told another gathering that Boston had more Irishmen than Dublin and that they were more Irish than the Dubliners. Wherever he went in Ireland, he met folks who had relatives in greater Boston. "They all ask me if I know their relatives. If I said no, they would be disappointed, so I tell them I know them all."

On September 2, every resident of Ballyduff, whose villagers had dim memories of Cushing's mother, played some part in the reception given Cushing. The house in the town of Tournageeha, however, where Mary Dahill was born, was long since gone, and nobody who had known her was alive.[6]

In one speech in Ireland, Cushing said the country's greatest export was missionaries.

"Centuries ago, these holy men went to all parts of Europe and in our day, they have gone to every country in the world. I hope we can catch some of the enthusiasm of the missionary spirit, so that many of our young men and women may feel called to religious life." He advised nonmissionaries to stay home. "Wherever you go, you won't find a better land or a better way of living than you now enjoy. The far-off hills look green, but there are no greener fields in the world than those of Ireland." He advised Irish youths to stay home and marry colleens. "All must work to bring economic success and all must work and pray for a united Ireland."[7] The pride of Corktown Irish was acclaimed everywhere he went on a thousand-mile motor tour of towns and villages, where his warmth and humility made new friends. Once a member of a trade union, he told train crews and railway workers that he still had his union card.

Archbishop John McQuaid, welcoming him to Dublin, hailed him for his concern "for the protection, faith, and care of the people." Cushing answered that the Boston see would try to match Ireland's efforts in providing world missionaries.[8] After celebrating mass in the chapel at Holy Cross College, the prelate walked out to be nearly "crushed by admiring thousands, who tried to touch his hand or coat sleeve. Everyone wanted to see and greet the man they knew from countless stories and photographs as a paragon of charity."[9]

Among sites visited were the grave of converted alcoholic Matt Talbot, Dublin Castle, Trinity College, the ancient Kells Monastery, and the hill of Tara, where St. Patrick won from pagan kings the right to preach Christianity in Ireland. At the abbey of St. Mary at

Glencairn, County Waterford, Cushing made arrangements to bring back fourteen Trappistines—seven Irish, seven American—the twenty-fourth religious community he had invited to settle in the Boston archdiocese.

After a week's whirlwind tour, Cushing was honored at a farewell reception at City Hall in Cork, where Lord Mayor Sean McCarthy presented him with a silver replica of St. Patrick's Bell inscribed: "I was presented to His Excellency, Dr. Cushing, Archbishop of Boston, U.S.A., by the Rt. Hon. Sean McCarthy, Lord Mayor of Cork." [10]

Overwhelmed by the warm reception wherever he went, Cushing told one crowd in Cork city: "We are all the sons of working men, and you have given us a reception fit for royalty!"

The prelate was piped aboard the corvette *Cliona,* which took him to the *Britannic* at Daunt's Rock. On his return to Brighton, Cushing thanked the Lord Mayor: "From the moment you first saluted our party in Cobh, on the corvette, to the time you took leave of us on the *Britannic,* you did everything possible to make our visit memorable. The heart-warming reception over which you presided at City Hall will remain one of the most treasured memories of our all too brief visit to Ireland." [11]

Archbishop Cushing returned to Europe on the *Italia* for the Holy Year of 1950 with more than five hundred New Englanders and twenty-five nuns from Steubenville, Ohio. The pilgrims disembarked at Lisbon, Portugal, from which they went to the Shrine of Our Lady of Fatima, scene of the apparition of the Virgin to three children in 1917. During the Atlantic crossing the prelate was so grateful to Sister Angela Marie Connors for rising long before breakfast to wash and iron altar linens for the chapel and otherwise assist him that he called her "Sister American Express." One night at dinner when Sister Angela was sitting next to the prelate, she deftly hid under the table any visible liquor when photographers approached. Her most prized possession is a ring Pope Paul VI gave Cushing. Cushing gave another friend (Ralph Tedeschi) a zucchetto worn by Pope John XXIII.

Pope Pius XII received the pilgrims at Castel Gandolfo, the papal summer residence. In Rome at the Colosseum, Cushing, who was Episcopal Director of the Youth Department, National Catholic Welfare Conference, addressed six thousand young people who were attending an International Catholic Youth Rally. In a stirring talk he said: "Let the Colosseum be a symbol to you of the sublime lesson

you learn in Rome: Tyrants are here for a day—God is forever. . . .
Persecution is an hour, victory is eternal. Her enemies molest her for
a moment—the church does not die. Captains and kings come and
have their little say, go their way—but Christ conquers. Christ reigns,
Christ has the final word. Everything in Rome should teach you confidence in Christ and confidence in the church." [12]

Soon after the resumption of diplomatic relations between Spain
and the United States in 1951, Archbishop Cushing met with Generalissimo Franco in Madrid. After visiting Spain and Portugal, he
told reporters in Cherbourg that Franco was needed by Spain and the
world in general. "Under present conditions in Spain, it is not possible
to proceed as from one day to the next to the establishment of a
democratic government." Franco, he said, had force on his side, and
whether he was popular was less important than the fact that he was
indispensable because of the threat of communism.[13] Any effort to
replace his dictatorship, he went on, "would be to throw Spain into a
civil war and chaos." Others held that the war in Spain was "an in-
excusable and unjustifiable act of aggression by reactionary forces
against a popular government." [14]

In the summer of 1953, Cushing arranged for the *Nieuw Amsterdam*
to embark passengers from Boston for a trip to Ireland, as he had
when the *Britannic, Italia,* and *Constitution* called at the port. In
this second trip to Eire, he toured spiritual and cultural sites and
made a careful study of the methods of Irish missionary societies in
recruiting youth for the priesthood. More than seven hundred pilgrims
arrived in Ireland on his birthday and received another unforgettable
reception. Cushing visited the shrine dedicated to Our Lady of Knock,
whose only replica in America is at St. Patrick's Church in Roxbury.

In Cork city the whole town turned out to hear him speak from a
bandstand in the park. While receiving a thunderous ovation, Cushing drove through Fermoy to Glanworth in an organized motorcade
of two hundred decorated cars, through streets lined with children on
school vacation as bands blared. In Glanworth, eighty-three-year-old
Bishop James Roche of Cloyne, after officially welcoming him, introduced him to Canon Michael Hurley, pastor of Holy Cross Church,
who, when the Cushing homestead fell into rubble and dust, bought
the site, leveled it and put in a lawn with attractive boundary walls.
Cushing, in his gratitude, showered the Glanworth parish with gifts
over the years and, when in 1957 Canon Hurley came to Boston with
Father Martin Cusack of Blarney, gave them a warm greeting, ar-

ranging a cruise for them around Boston Harbor in Louis Perini's yacht, *Bostina.* "We enjoyed cocktails and delicious seafood," Hurley recalled.[15]

The Cushing party drove from Glanworth to St. Colman College Minor Seminary at Fermoy, where they were luncheon guests of Bishop Roche. Early the following morning they went to Mount Melleray Monastery, where Cushing addressed the Trappist monks. Pledged to eternal silence, they greeted him by ringing the chapel bell. Cushing again visited the Trappistine convent at Glencairn, assuring the nuns that their fourteen sisters were happy in their convent. He told the sisters to have a pipe organ installed and "send the bill to me." That night he rested in Dublin for a few hours before flying to Paris. Cushing had received the freedom of the city in Dublin, as well as in Cork, Galway, Armagh, and Mount Melleray. On signing the roll of Freemen of Dublin in City Hall on an earlier visit, he noticed that the last name on the roll was George Bernard Shaw, who had left a rich legacy to the museum in Dublin. Cushing also read the names of President Ulysses S. Grant, Frank Kellogg, Charles Stewart Parnell, and Douglas Hyde. John F. Kennedy would write his name later.

Back in Cork city the prelate spoke from the platform of the Cork City Corporation stage, normally used for symphony concerts. With him on the platform were Lord Mayor Sean McCarthy and his old friend Bishop Cornelius Lucey. The assembly was hushed as Cushing rose, pushed his robes back, walked forty feet to the front of the stage, and paused as American and Irish photographers and television crews milled around. While the photographers were checking their lenses, he told the story of a child in Boston who had dreamt that the archbishop had died and gone to paradise, where St. Peter received him at the gate. "We have been waiting for you, Archbishop Cushing, and want you to know you are most welcome." The prelate, however, refused to enter the Kingdom of Heaven, even when the Mother of God and St. Patrick tried to lure him over the threshold. Asked why he balked, he said: "I'm waiting for a photographer." Some of the dignitaries down front were jarred by his flippancy, but the rest of the assembly applauded, and even the august elders were visibly impressed by the time the archbishop completed his hour-long talk.[16]

Early in September, the prelate returned to the United States on the *Queen Mary.*

The Marian Year (1954) observed the centennial of the adoption of the Immaculate Conception dogma, the occasion for a pilgrimage

Cushing made that year. In June, five thousand well-wishers waved from Commonwealth Pier as the *Independence*, which had been delayed by fog for several hours in its passage from New York, slowly headed out to sea. Cushing and hundreds of pilgrims stood at the railing watching a spectacular display of colored streams of water shot into the air by fireboats. This time, the archbishop brought along priests, monsignori, and bishops, along with black-robed nuns, including Sister Shawn of St. Coletta's and Sister Gonzaga of St. Elizabeth's Hospital.

In his first newspaper report on this pilgrimage to Rome and Lourdes, Mayor Hynes, a special correspondent for the Boston *Globe*, wrote: "Everyone is amazed by the energy of Archbishop Cushing. He spent hours greeting people before we sailed, but came down to dinner looking refreshed and as enthusiastic as ever." Cushing was more relaxed than he had been for months during the nine-day crossing. Although June 26 fell on a Friday, he gave everyone, including the religious, permission to eat meat. Hynes took up a collection for Cushing charities on the way over. Walter Kirschner, president of the Klein stores in New York, said that although he was not Catholic, he would like to donate fifteen hundred dollars. Another big donor was Walter Goodman, owner of the Bergdorf stores in New York.

A Texan realtor enrolled the archbishop in the Texas Rangers, and he was guest of honor at parties given by Captain Switzer and by representatives of the *Globe*. "We ought to have a party like this every night," he told a *Globe* executive. Mayor Hynes noted Cushing's consideration for everyone in the party. Noticing a group of nuns sitting alone at a table, he sent them a bottle of champagne, and during the crossing gave the mayor a check for a thousand dollars to be used by Hadassah for children in Israel.

The pilgrims landed in Naples on July 2 and divided into three groups. Monsignor Edward Murray led one group to Rome, Assisi, Florence, Venice, Lucerne, Cologne, Amsterdam, and Cannes, while Monsignor Lally's pilgrims toured Ireland after visiting Lourdes and Paris. Archbishop Cushing, Bishop Wright, and his brother Dr. Richard Wright (Cushing's personal physician) went from Lourdes to Paris, where they attended a passion play in a huge outdoor area before Notre Dame Cathedral, with seating for ten thousand persons. Leaving Le Havre on July 14, the *Mauretania* stopped at Cobh to pick up other pilgrims.[17] When he came home, Cushing gave Ann Wasilauskas the Marian Medal which the Pope had given him.

The Marian pilgrimage surpassed all those of the past, he said in his final dispatch, datelined New York, July 21. "Some of our journeys brought us in the vicinity of Omaha Beach and similar places where our GIs landed for the liberation of Europe toward the end of World War II." Pillboxes of the enemy, ruined barges and vessels in the harbor, bombed houses adjacent to the seashore—all were grim reminders of the invasion and its terrible price.

Cushing found the pilgrimage for exceptional children rewarding, but there were problems with adults. "The trip was most pleasant and profitable," he wrote a friend, "but somewhat arduous and trying. The responsibility of bringing three hundred persons to Europe is tremendous." He thanked various donors for contributing to expenses.

During the pilgrimages, Cushing usually relaxed by promenading the deck, playing table tennis, and chatting with fellow passengers, as well as by writing chatty stories for newspapers. Reporters found him good copy, as usual. "Don't ever go on a pilgrimage with a bunch of old women," he said during one crossing. Commenting on a fire drill, he said: "If my opinion was asked, I would say that the women looked better in life preservers than they did in their so-called sacks."

The climactic trip came in 1958, when the archbishop returned to Glanworth to be greeted by a huge banner reading "Welcome Home." During this visit, he prayed at the grave of an aunt, Nora Cushing Morrissey, as well as at the Marian Shrine. For the first time he met David Gibbons, who recalled bidding a sad farewell to Patrick Cushing when he left Glanworth on an "ass cart." Using a gold key bearing his coat of arms, Cushing opened a six-classroom Cushing Memorial School dedicated to the memory of his father and unveiled a statue of St. Patrick on the school grounds. He also cut the first sod and blessed the site for a new church in Curraghalla in the hazy distance. He gave Canon Hurley forty thousand dollars toward the cost of the school.

Inside Holy Cross Church he read an inscription: "The pews of this church were donated by Most Reverend Richard J. Cushing, D.D., Archbishop of Boston, as a memorial to his parents." Cushing had also donated the public address system and the playgrounds on the site of the old village school. He was not present in 1959 when the church of Celtic Romanesque design was dedicated at Curraghalla. Canon Hurley later showed the edifice to Cushing's two sisters and a nephew and proudly recalled entertaining in the small dining room of his presbytery Archbishop Cushing and two Irish Bishops. "And twice have the archbishop's sisters been my dinner guests," he tells visitors from Boston.

After Cushing's visit, *The Catholic Standard* published verse by a local bard "in honour of the visit of Archbishop Cushing last week to his father's birthplace."

When sunset gilds the west in tints of red and gold
And evening spreads her cloak of grey the world to enfold;
When birds warble lullabies around Glanworth's ancient walls,
Those ivy-mantled castle ruins where once stood noble halls;
The abbey tower looms darkly against that red gold sky,
Once the home of Dominick's monks whom Cromwell doomed to die.

The stanzas were a pleasant souvenir for Cushing in their references to the "old stone bridge beside the mill," "the chieftains bold," the "castle tower," and "Our Lady's Shrine."

After the ceremonies, which were as colorful as in 1953, with bands blaring, Cushing drove to Cork city in a heavy rain. His party had to abandon their cars and cross the bridge over the River Lee on foot and walk to City Hall, where Lord Mayor McCarthy and members of the Corporation, wearing handsome red cloaks and fur-trimmed hats, greeted them. The Lord Mayor in a solemn ceremony made him a Freeman of Cork. The citation reads: "His Grace, Most Reverend Dr. R. C. Cushing, Archbishop of Boston, elected August 1959, in recognition of his practical goodwill towards Ireland and in particular towards the people of the County and City of Cork, and as a token of the affection in which our kith and kin in his archdiocese are held by the Lord Mayor Corporation and Citizens of Cork."

County Cork was indeed full of reminders of Cushing's largesse. On this visit he gave Bishop Lucey twenty-five thousand dollars toward the cost of five rosary churches being built in Cork city and opened the Church of the Resurrection on Spangle Hill opposite Cushing Street, named in his honor. On a plaque just inside the entrance of this church, which was dedicated in his presence, the prelate read the inscription on a tablet: "The Archbishop of Boston . . . has been most generous to the Church and deserves a special remembrance in your prayers."

During this 1958 visit, Cushing received an honorary degree of Doctor of Laws from the chancellor of the National University of

Ireland in the presence of the Prime Minister and of President Eamon de Valera. "I have never witnessed a scene of more academic magnificence," Cushing said. Dressed in a colorful gown and a large flat hat, Cushing said he felt like St. Thomas More when he was chancellor of England. In his acceptance speech, he said: "I stand here today as a man of action among men of ideas. I end by reminding you how much we need one another in times so perilous."

Archbishop Cushing took more pleasant memories home with him when he sailed from Cobh early in September.

chapter eleven

PREACHING FROM THE HOUSETOPS

As THE *magna vox* of the hierarchy in the United States, Cushing reached more people more effectively and eloquently than any churchman of his era. He did all this within the framework of the Boston Catholic reputation for book-banning and censorship, which was narrower than that of the Puritans who wrote the Blue Laws. Cushing rose to power at a time when the New England Watch and Ward Society was disturbed because limbs were beginning to be called legs. His authority was invoked at a time when he, a maverick prelate, was confronted by the fact that censorship was "one field in which both Catholics and Puritans agree and have an identical objective," as John Gunther put it.[1]

In 1938, Catholic bishops had established a National Organization for Decent Literature, and in 1955 they created a National Office of Literature to implement the moral forces of the nation against the "lascivious type of literature which threatens moral, social, and national life."[2] Censorship assumed various forms in Boston. There was the purely Irish Catholic type visible at the turn of the century when the Ancient Order of Hibernians and other Catholic groups succeeded moderately in eliminating strictly Celtic humor from the stage and in improving the image of the Irish middle class. In 1946 the hierarchy tried to bar "Duffy's Tavern" from a television network to prevent Irish Catholics from being lampooned. In that same year, the municipal censor of Boston expunged the phrase "Oh, God!" from *Life with Father* after it had played in Boston for several months. "Oh, fudge!" took its place.[3]

Before Cushing used public communications to enunciate his own views, he was called upon to silence the views of others. He refereed one hassle centering around Henry Morton Robinson's novel, *The*

Cardinal, published in 1950. Many thought the real life model was Cardinal Spellman, and when Otto Preminger filmed the book, he got no cooperation from the hierarchy. When the film was shot, Archbishop Cushing asked to see a screening, to which he invited Dr. John Spellman, the cardinal's brother. If there was any real-life resemblance, neither Cushing nor Spellman could find it. The prelate sponsored the premiere of the film and wrote a flattering preview for the *Pilot*.

"This movie doesn't seem to be about Cardinal Spellman at all," he wrote. "This cardinal . . . why, he's over six feet. Now that's not Cardinal Spellman,* and this cardinal goes down . . . south to get beat up by a bunch of racists. Now, that's not Cardinal Spellman, and this cardinal even had some doubts about his vocation to be a priest. Now, you and I know perfectly well that's not Cardinal Spellman." [4] Then came a non sequitur: "When I baptized Caroline Kennedy in New York, Cardinal Spellman was a witness. And that's how I know the baptism was valid."

When Cushing was asked to have *Forever Amber* banned in Boston, he sent Auxiliary Bishop Wright to discuss the matter with Mayor Hynes. The Catholic laity had tried to pressure Cushing into banning the film. In the late 1940s, Joseph Dever remembers an enraged Holy Namer, who while lauding Archbishop Cushing's anticommunist crusade, blasted liberals who had protested the picketing of the film by Catholic War Veterans, calling the liberals "pinkoes and stinkoes."

After Hynes and Wright saw the film, they found no valid reason for the banning, and it was shown.

Cushing did, however, condemn gutter-type nightclub shows and tawdry forms of burlesque. In a pastoral letter in 1951, he asked parents, news agents, and his clergy to stem the flood of objectionable literature in neighborhood stores, where, on clear view on racks, he said, were "garish comic books which glorify sex, horror, and the techniques of crime. For more sophisticated but still juvenile minds, there are slick magazines parading suggestive cover illustrations and featuring articles and photographs in which intrinsic vice is masqueraded as art and modern science." He warned parents to check literature read by their children. The prelate had in mind literary trash which has been called "erotic, neurotic, and tommyrotic."

---

* A priest aide to Spellman said: "Spelly was a shrimp in size, but you always talked up to him." See *The New York Times Magazine*, October 13, 1968.

"If Saint Paul were alive today, the archbishop said, "he would perhaps be the first and chief exponent of the use of radio and television to spread the Kingdom of Christ in the world." In 1954, the *Pilot* reported: "Having in mind the admonition of our Divine Lord to 'preach from the housetops,' the archbishop, early in his administration, went about the business of organizing the radio (and later the television) apostolate "That They May Know Thee, The Only True God, And Him Whom Thou Has Sent, Jesus Christ." Cushing had been doing this for ten years, beaming out presentations of the mass, the sacraments, the rosary, the Way of the Cross, and giving hundreds of talks on inspirational topics, which comforted and solaced thousands of shut-ins. By 1954, there were fifty radiocasts a week, more than half of them originating in local stations in the archdiocese. The others were prepared elsewhere.

One of his "firsts" in radio was a Daily Catholic Newscast, which he inaugurated in 1948. The first regional telecast was on Christmas Eve 1949, when the prelate celebrated mass in the cathedral. He was the first to have a mass televised in a studio, with a special altar and sanctuary built for the occasion. He also officiated at a televised nuptial mass, but refused to let advertisers turn the program into a bride and bridegroom show. His purpose was to explain the sacrament of Matrimony. On such solemn occasions, he is known to have told newlyweds: "Now you're on your own."

A few years later, after singing a televised mass at St. Clement's Shrine, he faced the TV cameras with some words that were not in the rubrics. How many of those watching at home, he asked, would like to see mass televised regularly? [5] Within forty-eight hours, more than twelve thousand letters approved the suggestion.

Cushing organized an archdiocesan industrial exhibit where two hundred manufacturers displayed and sold their products and raised one hundred thousand dollars toward financing a television studio. He put Monsignor Walter Flaherty in charge of the television center after the Federal Communications Commission granted it a commercial license, the first to be awarded to a religious group primarily interested in religion. The license permitted programs to be sponsored.

The original studios were in the former residence of Cardinal O'Connell on Granby Street. They included a chapel, complete with altar and tabernacle, mullioned windows, a Communion rail, and pews for thirty persons. The program permitted the shut-ins of New

England to "attend" mass every morning; Flaherty, in the control room, explained each part of the service. Cushing occasionally celebrated mass himself. His congregations included children in wheel chairs from Kennedy Memorial and his exceptional children from St. Coletta's. At the end of one mass served by two boys from St. Coletta's, he encouraged the handicapped children to "get closer to the hearts of viewers by waving directly into the camera." [6]

Flaherty studied television techniques in New York City and spent a summer in Hollywood, helping Father James Keller, M.M., founder of the Christophers, produce more than thirty films. Back in Boston, Flaherty conducted a program for station WMEX, the only daily Catholic newscast in the nation. In August 1955 he gave a five-day course on television techniques for nuns, an experiment that was featured on the "Today" show and in *Life* magazine.

Presented over the "Our Believing World" program was the first actual Confirmation and Ordination ever telecast. Cushing confirmed a group of children and ordained three young priests in the chapel of St. John's Seminary early in 1953. Other programs were "A Kindergarten Graduation" and "Mysteries of the Rosary." At Christmas in 1952, a color-sound film was made of a pontifical midnight mass telecast from St. John's Seminary, the only motion picture of its kind. During Sundays in Lent in 1953, when the archbishop celebrated a series of masses from St. Clement's Shrine, he gave Holy Communion to exceptional children from Kennedy Memorial Hospital.

Finally, in the fall of 1964, the prelate created an archdiocesan television station on Channel 38. It is a million-watt facility with a telecasting beacon on top of the fifty-two-story Prudential Tower. Station WHIS-TV-IHS competes now with major networks.

During the 1950s, Cushing promoted interfaith activities more than ever. In February 1956, a B'nai B'rith lodge in Lowell, Massachusetts, honored him for serving the cause of brotherhood. This was at a time when Catholic laymen were not encouraged to associate publicly with non-Catholics. In 1954, Samuel Cardinal Stritch of Chicago refused to let Catholics participate in a World Council of Churches meeting in Illinois, and many dioceses across the nation banned Catholic participation in the National Conference of Christians and Jews.

In 1956, when the archbishop was honorary chairman of the Boston chapter of the American Committee on Italian Migration, he welcomed more than two hundred Italian refugees into the archdiocese, finding jobs for the heads of families. One night he invited to his residence Louis Perini, Ralph Tedeschi, John Volpe, Joseph DeMambro, and Judge Anthony Julian—all leaders of the Italo-American community—and persuaded them to help the newcomers get settled in the community. Under the 1953 Refugee Relief Act, employment and housing assurances were necessary before the families could be invited. This was a magnificent effort by Cushing.

By the end of the decade, the archbishop could say, as he often did, that he collected decorations and honorary degrees "in bunches, like a stalk of bananas." At the centennial of Boston College High School in 1963, he said he had enough honorary degrees to paper the walls of the institution.

Honors reflected the broad range of his activities. In 1939, when Boston College gave him an honorary doctor's degree, he turned to his former professor, Father Keating: "You, of all people, Father, know that I do not deserve this." Six years later he was one of the college's three sons to whom the institution paid respects. The others were Bishop Louis F. Kelleher and Bishop Edward F. Ryan, D.D., who accompanied Cushing on some of his pilgrimages. In 1946 Cushing was made a Knight of the Grand Cross and Prior of the Eastern Lieutenancy of the Knights of the Holy Sepulchre. In the same year the Committee of Catholics for Human Rights at the Waldorf-Astoria gave the archbishop and Basil O'Connor an award for furthering human rights and interracial unity. Spain gave him the Grand Cross of the Order of Isabella the Catholic after he raised five thousand dollars for the children of Spanish sailors who went down with their ship. "I thought Franco might make me a matador or something," he said on learning of the honor.

The Silver Buffalo for Boy Scouts mirrored his "distinguished service to boyhood," and a gold medal awarded him in 1951 by the American Irish Historical Society was "in recognition of his services to the Republic." He was especially pleased with one unprecedented accolade. The Society of Jesus in New England named him a "Founder of the New England Province of the Society of Jesus," the highest honor it can give. By 1956 Cushing had also received the Knights of Columbus Lantern Award, Honorary Citizenship in Ireland, a command in the Order of Lebanon, a citation from Italy, and the New England Variety Club's Great Heart Award, given annually to the person who has done the most good for the greatest number. James Cagney flew a 6,000-mile round-trip to confer the honor at the

Statler Hotel in Boston. Stars of the theater and sports world were on hand for ceremonies during which Cushing lauded the club for its special charity, the Jimmy Fund for cancer research, originally sponsored by the Variety Club of New England and the Boston Braves baseball team. Sport greats included Joseph Cronin of the Boston Red Sox, Rocky Marciano, and Ted Williams. When Williams congratulated the prelate, Cushing said: "This honor belongs not alone to me but especially to all those for whom and with whom I have worked, in whatever position was entrusted to me." He thought of himself as the "agent and symbol of the warm-hearted, great-hearted public of this New England area." He did, however, claim one signal accomplishment: "No other man can make this boast. I persuaded Ted Williams to wear a necktie." It was the first time the baseball super-star had ever been seen wearing a tie at a public function in Boston.

Jim Bishop in a newspaper column wrote of a dull party when he was asked what he thought of Cushing. "He will never replace Ted Williams," Bishop said, an opinion he sharply revised later when he learned more about the prelate. If applause is any criterion, Cushing outshone Williams at the banquet, as he did another time at a Baseball Writers' dinner.

"I'm the only one who showed up in uniform," Cushing said to the delight of the athletes.[7]

Cushing, as archbishop, charmed another audience when the Boston Chamber of Commerce convened taxi drivers to hear themselves appointed public relations men for Boston. The prelate told of a Boston dowager who went to California to see a friend. "It was a matter of life or death or, of course, she would never have left Boston. One day as she sat with a friend on a beach, looking at the waves of the Pacific, she sneezed. 'I beg your pardon,' she said. 'It must be the air. I'll never get used to being three thousand miles from the ocean.' "[8]

More honors came in 1959. In January the *Jewish Advocate* gave him its "Man of the Year" award, praising him for his achievements as a churchman, orator, and administrator. "If the cardinal's noble thoughts against racial antipathy and creedal strife could be put into the hearts of every man and child, then verily would we arrive at the long overdue recognition that we are all children of one loving Father to enjoy the pleasantness of brethren living together in peace."[9]

In June, Fordham University, awarding him a doctor of laws, cited his "generosity and religious fervor manifested in the creation of such edifices as churches, religious houses, parochial schools, and institutions of higher learning which have risen through his large archdiocese." In 1937, when Harvard University conferred an honorary doctorate of laws on Cardinal O'Connell, the citation included the words "as a faithful shepherd of a multitude of devoted citizens." Harvard recognized Cushing twenty-two years later as "A prince of his church, ever mindful of the needs of the least of his flock." [10]

In November, Cushing accepted two medals that go with the award of Grand Officer of the Legion of Honor, the second highest that France can bestow. By this time he had indeed become the best known of the Cushings of Massachusetts.

In the late 1950s Elizabeth Cushing was living in South Boston with her brother John, an auditor for the John Hancock Mutual Life Insurance Company. Anna Frances, whose husband, William, had died, also lived in South Boston, and Mary ("Dolly") Pierce, widow of Richard Pierce (Pearlstein), was living in Brighton near the archbishop. Other close relatives were Cushing's nephews, the Reverend William Francis, Jr., and his brother Richard. The Cushings, a family friend said, "would do anything for one another, but they are not given to showing their feelings. That is their way." When Dolly Pierce was a subway change-maker for the MTA, she asked Mayor Hynes for a job. He said her brother, as archbishop, could do much better for her, but she refused to approach him. She finally took a job as saleslady at Best's store in Boston. Nobody has ever accused the South Boston Cushings of nepotism!

The prelate, who saw as much of his family as a tight schedule permitted, occasionally visited the Cushions in New York. The last surviving member was his Aunt Annie, who taught school in Rye for many years. When she died in 1960, Cushing went to Rye to conduct the requiem mass and officiate at committal services in the family plot. When it was over, he turned to Daniel E. Kelly, the family attorney. "Poor Annie," he said. "She's better off up there." [11]

An eventful year was 1959. Cushing was less concerned than his friends were when his life was threatened by an anonymous crank who said he was also planning to dynamite Holy Cross Cathedral. On the night of the threat a cordon of fifty policemen guarded the prelate on his rounds. Meanwhile, it was the end of the old order in Boston politics as a Boston newspaper noted on November 12, 1959:

"Former Governor James M. Curley of Massachusetts, last of the oldtime big city politicians, died today—eight days before his eighty-fourth birthday."

Curley was buried from the cathedral—the largest funeral Boston had ever seen. According to the Boston press, Archbishop Cushing had flown from Washington, D.C., to give the eulogy. Cardinal O'Connell had given one when Curley's first wife died, and Archbishop Cushing, who had said prayers and rosaries with groups while Curley was ill in Boston City Hospital, had eulogized the former governors' children (Mary and Leo) eight years before. He had also delivered the eulogy at the funeral of Curley's political rival, Maurice J. Tobin. This time the celebrant was Curley's youngest son, Father Francis Curley, S.J. Toward the end of the requiem mass, the prelate approached the coffin. "Then he prayed in the grating, honest South Boston voice that was his inheritance and that he was too proud to change." [12] High overhead Cardinal O'Connell's galero oscillated in the air currents. When the prayer ended, "everyone watched the archbishop's seamed face under the white miter, waiting for him to mount the steps to the pulpit. But the archbishop did not move. There was no eulogy." [13]

Curley's death signaled the decline but not the end of power politics in Boston. The end came a year later, and with it came a change in Cushing's fortunes.

By the turn of the century, the stage had been set in Boston for a mob master. Answering the call was James Michael Curley, one of the two most powerful Irish Catholic leaders during the early twentieth century. The other was William Cardinal O'Connell. Both, in different ways, encouraged a feeling of superiority and separateness among their followers, who turned to them just as earlier immigrants had turned to ward bosses and parish priests. Some of the stature Irish Catholics gained under O'Connell's leadership they lost under Curley's.

Both were conscious always of the cruelties inflicted on their people dating back to colonial times when Goody Glover was hanged as a witch on Boston Common for saying the rosary in Gaelic. In a conversation with John Gunther in 1944, Cushing mentioned the burning of a convent run by Ursuline nuns in Charlestown, a suburb of Boston. And Cushing knew as well as O'Connell that Protestant propagandists had lampooned Catholic convents and accused priests of being lechers.

When Cushing became archbishop, he at first considered parts of his archdiocese no man's land. When the Sisters of the Divine Providence suggested establishing a province in Kingston on the South Shore of Boston he warned of the futility of such an exercise in Protestant territory. He was delighted later with the success of the effort. Soon after he became archbishop he asked Bishop Cassidy, whose diocese included Hyannis what he could do to promote the church in the area. Cassidy asked him to send "a half dozen chapels to accommodate the 'swallow' that comes to Cape Cod each year," thinking of earlier years when swallows were rare on the Cape. Rarer were Catholics. By 1850, when the first tiny Catholic society was organized in Hyannis, a weekly newspaper ran a headline: "HORRORS!" [14]

If Curley was a peon among patricians when he became mayor of Boston and governor of Massachusetts, Cushing was charity itself. "From the prejudices directed against Catholics of early days we must learn tolerance," he said. "From the animosity shown the Irish in those days we must learn respect for men of every race. . . . From the rights denied our predecessors . . . we must learn to be constantly on our guard so that hereafter none of those rights shall be taken from us."

Cushing was at first amused by the antics of Curley, a vintage rogue in a vineyard of rogues, who ruthlessly if cleverly exploited racial and religious rivalries. The prelate's amusement faded, however, as he strove to lessen class antagonism and religious strife. A few weeks after he was ordained in 1921, Cushing witnessed a Curley tactic in his South Boston neighborhood, when Boston College students, masquerading as "Baptist ministers," rang doorbells asking devout Irish Catholics—immediately irate at the suggestion—to vote for the esteemed John R. Murphy, Curley's Irish Catholic opponent. The snide campaign won Curley a narrow but inglorious victory.

The prelate and politician were embarrassingly intertwined. Two days after his conviction for using the mails to defraud in 1946, Curley spoke at a dinner for a judge sponsored by Archbishop Cushing and attended by Governor Maurice Tobin. Months later His Honor was in a Danbury, Connecticut, jail. "What is important to a mystified country," *Commonweal* noted, "is that his long career has been possible only through the support of large numbers of God-fearing, good-living Catholics." Curley the mob master remained a burr under the saddle of the hierarchy.

Cushing, priest of the poor, had solid reason for admiring the Curley who was mayor of the poor—who had built so many schools, hospitals, free clinics, and beaches. But as the spiritual leader of a clergy-dominated society, Cushing was galled when Boston's municipal government, after more than half a century of scandal and bumbling efforts of reform, was repeatedly accused in print of remaining inept and corrupt. Periodic scandals, which muddied the image of the Catholic Church, kept Yankee Protestants hostile. Although Cushing was as concerned about the morality of Catholic leaders as O'Connell had been, he could take little direct action to curb their excesses. "I have often said that I would like to see more scholars who were saints and more saints who were scholars," he said at a testimonial dinner honoring the newly elected president of the Massachusetts Senate in 1959. "So, too, I would like to see more men in public life adequately equipped with knowledge, training, and experience who are at the same time examples of piety, and more men of piety who have the natural and acquired qualities for leadership in political life. We should approach this matter in much the same way as we would select a doctor or lawyer. . . . We should look for the candidate who adds up to a well rounded man on all levels."

Although he took no active role in the mayoral contest between Curley and Tobin in 1940, Cushing was pleased when the latter—an engaging young Irish politician who had first defeated his former boss in 1937—was elected. A few years later, Curley would be responsible for the political debut of another engaging young candidate named John Fitzgerald Kennedy. Tobin was a transitional political link between Curley and Kennedy.

By the end of the decade the Roman Catholic Church was the largest single denomination in the United States. Archbishop Cushing, who many insiders thought was being groomed for a promotion, was recognized as its leading spokesman.

chapter twelve

THE RED HAT

AN ANCIENT ceremony attending the election of a Pope is burning ballots in a small, dilapidated, cast-iron stove in a corner of the Sistine Chapel to the left of the entrance. After a round of voting, the scrutineer, who is last in rank, passes a needle through the center of each ballot and strings them together. The ballots, mixed with damp straw wrappings of hock or champagne bottles, after an inconclusive vote, send up the black signal of failure to the crowds waiting in St. Peter's Square, "surely the most ambiguous and ineffective signal ever devised," according to one observer.[1] Dry straw burned by the scrutineers creates white smoke, and the plume (*sfumata*) rising over the roof of the Sistine Chapel is the signal flashed to the waiting throng that a new Pope has been chosen. The feathery puff never fails to create a stir in the Eternal City.

The most significant puff of white smoke ever to curl up from the Vatican chimney was the one that signaled the election of Pope John XXIII on October 28, 1958. In the judgment of Vatican insiders, this paunchy son of a peasant farmer could be expected only to keep the papal seat warm, since he was seventy-eight years old. Nobody dreamed that he would spearhead the most startling religious revolution since the Reformation. In Cushing's opinion, there would have been no Reformation had Pope John lived at the time. "He could have kept Martin Luther in the fold."

Pope John's brief pontificate caused sweeping changes in the church and the modern world. John did more for the church in four years than had been done in the preceding four centuries. Soon after his elevation in January 1959 he convened Vatican Council II, the twenty-first ecumenical council held since the Council of Nicaea in 325 A.D., and the first to convene in ninety-two years. Asked the aim of the convocation, the Pontiff led visitors to a window in the Vatican and parted the curtains. "You see, that is why I called the council, to let fresh air come into the Church." [2]

Vatican Council II would make Cushing one of the best-known prelates in the world.

As early as 1948, when the bishop of Galway said there was "no more interesting person in the American hierarchy than Archbishop Cushing," the Bostonian was recognized as a world leader. A nation-wide poll taken by a national Catholic magazine to select the ten most outstanding contemporary leaders ranked Cushing high on a list that included such distinguished company as Winston Churchill. Later a group of newspapermen in a discussion sought a phrase that would best sum up his life. One suggested "The Bishop of the Missions," because of his worldwide missionary work. Another reporter, thinking of the hospitals and sanctuaries he had built, said a more accurate description would be "The Bishop of the Helpless." Then a non-Catholic spoke: "I'd call him 'Everybody's Bishop.'" That is an apt summary of a man of cosmic vision who is at the same time concerned with the least of his flock.

Brusque yet genial, this maverick prelate is totally unpredictable and often contradictory, and sometimes he is downright ornery. He is a complex personality who differs mostly from himself. Behind his many masks, he remains warm but aloof, essentially a lonely person with a few confidants. By 1959 he had received more publicity than any churchman in the world, and he was known to millions, yet of all who had a bowing or speaking acquaintance with him, few knew him intimately.

Among the top candidates for the College of Cardinals, according to *Time* magazine in 1951, was "Boston's strapping prow-jawed Arch-bishop . . . Cushing, fifty-five . . . whose able leadership of his 1,300,000 member flock has made him one of the best known members of the U.S. hierarchy." When Cushing was bypassed, some observers blamed it on the bizarre Feeney affair, while others thought Cardinal Spellman had blocked Cushing.

"Ridiculous," Cushing said years later. "Nothing could be further from the truth."

In the summer of 1953, John Hynes of Boston was one of a dozen American mayors who took part in the "Salute to Rome." In a hall overlooking a lake in Castel Gandolfo, Pope Pius XII greeted individually the mayors who were standing in a semicircle. Hynes was impressed by the way the Pontiff discussed El Paso with the mayor of that Texas city and was pleased, after the initial introduction, when the Pope returned to ask how Cushing was. During their brief exchange,

Cardinal Cushing's birthplace: 806 East Third Street, South Boston, Massachusetts.

Richard James Cushing graduates from Oliver Hagard Perry Grammar School, June 1908.

Above, Dick Cushing (*left*) and two friends in Marine Park, South Boston; below, Cushing (*right*) in college days, when he worked part-time in Hime Doherty's drugstore.

Cushing (*right*) as a seminarian.

Mary Dahill Cushing with a picture of her son Richard just after he became Bishop Cushing.

Bishop Cushing with President Marie (Mrs. Vincent) Green (*right*) of the League of Catholic Women after he addressed its Fourth Annual Congress.

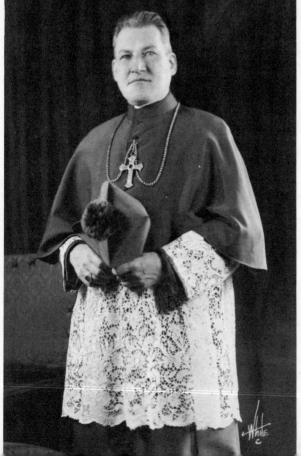

Cushing installed as archbishop of Boston, November 8, 1944.

Archbishop Cushing tries out for a concert arranged by the Sisters of Divine Providence.

The archbishop of Boston assists Mother Tharsilla at the groundbreaking for Sacred Heart High School at Kingston, Massachusetts, August 24, 1952.

In St. Peter's Basilica, Rome, Archbishop Cushing waits to ascend the steps to the Pope's throne, where he will be made a prince of the church, December 18, 1958.

Pope John XXIII places the biretta of a cardinal on Richard James Cushing's head.

Pope John XXIII and Richard Cardinal Cushing in Rome, 1958.

Santa Susanna, Cardinal Cushing's titular church in Rome.

Archbishop Cushing washes the feet of a parishioner on Holy Thursday.

The archbishop encourages a prisoner.

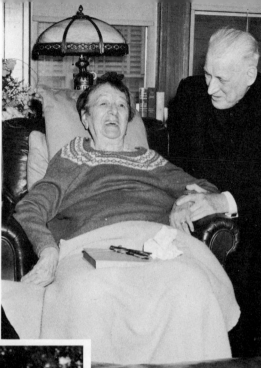

Above left, Cardinal Cushing carries a crippled child from the plane during the pilgrimage to Lourdes, May 1960; above right, he cheers one of his favorite senior citizens, Rose Stone Hull, 1967.

Mary Louise Redmond presents greetings and a gift to Archbishop Cushing on his birthday at Camp Mishannock, Kingston, Massachusetts, 1954.

Above, the archbishop takes to the saddle at an outing at Norumbega Park, 1952. Right, he and a nun ride the whip at Paragon Park, where, in 1963, he pours beer, below, for two old friends.

Archbishop Cushing is as much at ease with shipyard workers

WEARS MANY HATS

as with his young parishioners.

"Captain" of Louis Perini's yacht *Bastina,* July 1959.

Cardinal Cushing assists the chef at Paragon Park, 1963.

Cardinal Cushing preaches in the Church of the Holy Cross, Glanworth,
Eire, 1965.

Eire's President Eamon de Valera (*second from right*) sees Cardinal Cushing off at Shannon Airport, 1965.

Two great leaders meet in Harvard Yard, from which Irish Americans like them were once almost barred.

Cardinal Cushing in his Boston home with one of his most generous contributors, Joseph A. De-Mambro.

Francis Cardinal Spellman (*left*) and Richard Cardinal Cushing at the investiture of Ralph D. Tedeschi (*right*) as a knight of St. Gregory.

The cardinal's blessing on a young charge.

Cardinal Cushing finally gets a moment alone.

Hynes mentioned the great work Cushing was doing with centers like Nazareth. "Your Holiness," he asked, "Why don't you you make him a cardinal?" Pope Pius gave a quick summary of the procedures involved. When Hynes told Cushing of the incident later, the prelate said he didn't realize the mayor was on such intimate terms with the Pope.

In December, 1957, *Life* magazine noted that Cushing was "a likely choice for cardinal at the next consistory." Thus it was no surprise when Cardinal Roncalli, a few weeks after he became Pope John XXIII, chose Cushing as one of his twenty-three new cardinals.

At eleven P.M. on Sunday, November 16, 1958, Cushing, exhausted after a strenuous day, was writing his weekly column for the *Pilot* when Archbishop Cicognani called from Chicago to announce his elevation. In a daze, Cushing telephoned Monsignor Lally and a public relations officer but found them in bed. On the following day he told the press: "While I was saying mass this morning for the nine sisters of the household—I am a sort of mother superior to them—I heard the phone ring again and sensed that the news was known. My first reaction was that the people around here prayed me into it. I'm happy because they're happy."

The official Vatican document read: "He has the wisdom and prudence to converse with the professional. He has the simplicity to sing with the children and the understanding to encourage the old. But above all, it is his glowing charity and burning zeal for souls that has made him one of America's most loved shepherds."

Word got around quickly. Two nuns were in a parked car at Boston College when a mail truck pulled up. "Have you heard the news?" the driver asked. "They've made the archbishop a cardinal." [3] When a Massachusetts politician was asked whether he knew of the elevation, he solemnly nodded. "Sure, I knew it hours ago. I saw the white smoke coming up from Blinstrub's." [4]

The Right Reverend Anson Phelps Stokes, Jr., episcopal bishop of Massachusetts, said people of all faiths rejoiced at the appointment. "Certainly," said Mayor Hynes, "no prelate . . . has been more deserving and more worthy of the great honor." When seminarians from St. John's rushed over to the residence to congratulate him, the prelate came out to thank them. "Take the rest of the day off," he said.

Two days after the call from Cicognani, Cushing addressed the Ladies Catholic Benevolent Association at the John Hancock Building in Boston. The kitchen help and waiters joined in the wild applause. Monsignor Charles A. Finn, Cushing's old Theology professor, was awed to think that one of his seminarians had been named to what Cardinal O'Connell had called "an elector of the oldest and most potent throne in all the world." [5]

Monsignor Finn said he was honored to be able to present the new cardinal with his first check. Earlier in the day a reporter had asked Cushing why he didn't cancel the evening appointment. "I'm going to get a check there," he grinned.

Cushing told the assembly that never, in his wildest dreams, had he thought the student "would be elevated above the master. To men like Monsignor Finn and others who taught me in the seminary, I owe a great debt. . . . I have worked very hard here as your archbishop. I would have worked . . . much harder in a missionary diocese. Therefore I don't want anyone to conclude that I have been made a cardinal for work I have done." He credited the appointment to religious and laity of the archdiocese: "I see nothing personal in it whatsoever."

While he talked, four hundred seminarians formed a cheering section outside with help from bystanders. Old ladies cheered like school girls at a high school football game.

Cushing had misgivings about wearing the red hat because his background was unlike that of most princes of the church. "I'm no theologian, and I never did any formal teaching. The average . . . cardinal represents various phases of scholarship far different from anything in my experience." He told one audience that the "higher you go, the more difficult it becomes and the heavier crosses you have to carry," adding that psychologically and intellectually, he was "not equipped for this honor . . . and I know that as a result of this honor, my way will not be made easier."

He was primarily worried because he thought his new position would keep him from mingling with his "little people." The public would have to get used to the fact that he, as cardinal, would continue to visit jails and other places where prelates don't normally enter. "I want to do this, and must do it, for the simple reason that in today's welfare state we must keep in personal contact with all types—especially the poor, the wayward, the abandoned—lest they be lost."

Cushing felt more reassured when he learned that Pope John, the third of thirteen children who grew up in a little hill village, thought of himself as a simple pastor who counted his sheep one by one. "I come from humility and was raised amid modest and blessed poverty," he had said when he was patriarch of Venice. "I would like to recommend myself to your benevolence as a man who wants to be simply and above all your brother; amiable, easy to contact, and understanding." [6]

When Cushing saw a photograph of John's brother carrying a basket filled with corn, he called it a picture of a thousand words. Having never heard of Cardinal Roncalli before he became Pope, he was delighted to read of the Pontiff's visit to Regina Coeli Jail on Christmas Day, for it recalled his own visits to prisons. He was thrilled, too, to see photographs of John visiting orphans, delinquent children, old folks, paupers in slums, and even communists. "Good God, that's my man!" Cushing said. "For this is my own concept of the priesthood. My methods are somewhat akin to his. . . . Like John, I came from the poor, lived poor, and saw in both our lives a total dedication to a cause." [7]

The aspirations and activities of the two prelates were, indeed, astonishingly similar. "Since I was a boy," John said, "I never thought of being anything . . . except a priest." Cushing could say the same thing. Both felt at home in the presence of "the lettered and unlettered, people of world renown and the humble man of the street." [8] In his brief biography of Pope John, Cushing might have been speaking of himself when he wrote: "Cold formality and rigid protocol were two things directly opposed to the simplicity of John XXIII. Vatican tradition . . . dictated that the Pope had to dine alone. Not finding anything in the Gospels to support this tradition, John invited bishops and cardinals to dinner." Papal guests were invariably startled at the suggestion. Cushing was even more informal. "He has no more pretention than a cornflower growing in a ditch. . . . The only enemy he acknowledges is pomp. Cardinal Cushing fights it as though it were a vice, which it is," Jim Bishop wrote.[9]

"If Almighty God wills that a man like this who came from poor people and had extraordinary humility and a great sense of humor should be the Pope at one of the most critical periods in history, then I have this proof that I, too, am the archbishop of Boston by the will of Almighty God," Cushing told the press just after his elevation.

Their sense of humor is similar. Cushing likes the story about Cardinal Roncalli who found himself sitting beside a woman in a low-cut dress. When a bowl of fruit was served, Roncalli waved a finger as she selected an apple. "Be careful," he said, "it was only when Eve ate the apple that she discovered she was naked." Pope John, who did not trust Vatican elevators, told Giacomo Manzu, the sculptor, that the ancient lifts had one virtue. "They remind you to say your prayers."

Pope John and Cushing shared another uncommon virtue, even among churchmen who take time to console the sick and suffering. Despite their rank, they went out of their way, often arriving unannounced, at the bedside of an ailing or dying priest or friend. Again, Cushing might have been speaking of John or himself when he said in his eulogy of Cardinal Spellman: "Countless times, in the midst of the pressures of his busy life, he came home to visit sick or ailing friends or to be with them in times of joy and sorrow. He would cross oceans in the name of friendship, he would detour his journeys in the name of friendship, he would telephone and write letters without ceasing in the name of friendship."

There is a story of a Rhode Island priest who knew he was dying. In his last days he spoke often of the archbishop whom he had known when both were young priests. A physician summoned late one night during a raging storm found the pastor close to death. The nun who was taking care of him telephoned the archbishop at one o'clock in the morning. Ninety minutes later, the prelate was kneeling at the bedside of a friend whom he had not seen in years. And now his friend was sinking into a coma.

"Tom," the archbishop said, and the priest opened his eyes.

"Hello, Dick." It was a hoarse whisper.

The archbishop leaned over and rested his cheek next to the priest's for a moment. Then he rose and prayed until the priest died.

Only then did Archbishop Cushing put on his coat, pick up his hat, and go downstairs to his car, where his chauffeur was waiting. It was a slow, hazardous drive back to Brighton through the blizzard. Even as cardinal, Cushing remained the simple priest remembered by another simple priest who died in the upstairs bedroom of his rectory that night during the storm.

Cushing, who called "Papa Roncalli" the "greatest builder of spiritual bridges in the history of Christianity," loved him also because of his ability to melt prejudices and win the hearts of men. "Let there not be factions or division," John said. "We all live beneath one sky, all Catholics in one world. . . . The church is living. She is not just the custodian of a museum." [10] Cushing, who wrote a brief biography of John, concluded that he was "the Lord's answer to the confusions and misunderstandings of modern times, between those of other faiths and Catholics, and, equally important, between believers and those who have no religion at all." [11]

Cushing was uneasy as he prepared to go to Rome. "I don't take to protocol or socio-ecclesiastical standing or the high places that go with the robes of a prince of the church. . . . I don't think any man who has gone to Rome from this country ever knew as little as I do. I wasn't educated in Rome. I make more mistakes in Rome than anyone who goes there."

On December 10, Cushing left Logan Airport with cardinals-designate Cicognani of Washington, D.C., and John O'Hara of Philadelphia. Also in the party were bishops John Wright and Jeremiah Minihan and Mayor Hynes. Once more ten thousand persons jammed the lobby of Alitalia Air Lines and stood at the rail of the skyview promenade to see the official party of two hundred depart. Fifty state troopers formed an honor guard for the three cardinals, who walked on a red carpet from the passenger entrance to the ramp while the Boston Police Band played "Southie Is My Home Town" and "When Irish Eyes Are Smiling." Cushing waved to a group of parochial school boys carrying placards reading "Long Live Cardinal Cushing and His Fellow Princes," and as he ducked through the cabin door of the plane, he shouted back at the crowd. "Go home and get warm!"

Four aircraft flying papal and United States colors left one hour apart, starting at one o'clock in the afternoon. The yellow flight was followed by the white plane carrying Mayor and Mrs. John Hynes, John Cushing and his sisters Mrs. William Francis, of South Boston, and Mrs. Richard Pierce, of Brighton, along with public officials and reporters. The cardinals left on the red flight.

At Ciampino Airport in Rome, rain hampered the morning welcoming ceremonies. In a telecast from the apron at the airport, Cushing expressed his pleasure at receiving Santa Susanna [12] as his titular church and, in a typical aside, said he was glad the National Catholic Rural Conference was sending ten heifers and a bull of Aberdeen-Angus breed for the Vatican farm. Foreign reporters liked his informality. "Your cardinal is so refreshing, so human, so jolly," a reporter told Mayor Hynes, who had been commissioned by the Boston *Globe* to do a series of articles on the trip.

At his first interview at the Grande Hotel, where he stayed, Cushing put everyone at ease. "Hi, folks," he said to one group. "Sit down.

You'll live longer." There was a poignant moment in the lobby when he comforted a misty-eyed Boston *Herald* columnist, Bill Cunningham, who had lost his voice a short time before following a throat operation for cancer. In a column written on the day the Boston party flew to Rome, Cunningham told of the spiritual comfort he received from the prelate: "In the darkest depth of my recent trouble, they read me a letter that at first I could barely hear. But the words of faith and hope, and strength and love, began to reach me through the fog that was all but shut off from the world, and I seemed to feel myself being literally lifted back toward light and life. It was a personal letter from His Excellency, Archbishop Cushing—to me, practically a stranger, and of another faith." *

On his first day in Rome, a papal tailor measured Cushing for the brilliant scarlet robes of Office he was to wear the following week. Two days later, in the gloom of a rainy Sunday morning, after learning of the death of his sister Elizabeth in Boston, he went to the Grande Hotel to console his surviving sisters and brother and to instruct his nephew, Father Francis, to celebrate a requiem mass at St. Brigid's Church in South Boston. Cushing's sisters returned with the priest. In Rome Bishop Minihan celebrated the official funeral mass at Santa Susanna, the scene of eight simultaneous masses for Elizabeth Cushing. At five o'clock in the morning, the cardinal, hoping to slip unnoticed out of the hotel, found Rocco Paoletta, a Boston *Herald* photographer, waiting for him in the lobby. "Can't I keep anything from you, Rocky?" the prelate said as he went to speak to the Franciscan Missionaries of Mary before saying mass for his sister in the convent chapel in the presence of the cloistered nuns.

He also said mass at the Church of St. Cecilia in Trastevere, a 1500-year-old edifice in the heart of Rome's communist sector. His visit thrilled Monsignor Umberto Dionisi, famed for his "one-man" victory over the communists in his area.

"This visit is the answer to my prayers," he said. "This is one of the best bishops in America, who preaches with zeal and fire. Though I never met him before today, I admired him so that I prayed he would be made a cardinal and come to this church." [13]

Cushing gave Dionisi a five-thousand-dollar check. "I promise you that within three weeks after my return to Boston I will attend all masses at St. Cecilia's in Boston and ask the people there to send

---

* Cunningham, grateful to Cushing to the end, bequeathed his library to him.

contributions to St. Cecilia's in Rome." Monsignor Dionisi used the money to restore a newly discovered chapel, which dates back to the first century. He dedicated it to Cardinal Cushing.[14]

Italian photographers (*paparazzi*) have been known to trade punches as they battle for position during a consistory. American photographers and reporters who covered proceedings in 1958 were more like beagles on a scent. On December 16, Paoletta, posing as an official Vatican photographer, slipped into the private consistory at North American College and was snapping pictures of Cushing when a monsignor ushered him out, warning that the press was barred. After Cushing received his *biglietto* from a papal messenger officially notifying him of his elevation, Cicognani responded for the three American prelates. Afterward the guests, who included James and Thomas Dahill, cousins of Cushing, applauded, and the cardinals left in big black limousines to attend a private consistory in the Vatican Palace, where they received their mozettas and birettas.[15]

More than thirty thousand persons witnessed the public consistory held in St. Peter's Basilica on December 18. Edwin O'Connor wrote of the "solemn, spectacular, medieval, deeply moving pageant with the Pope on his throne, backed by the great tapestry with the madonna and the golden lions of Venice, waiting as the scarlet line of cardinals began their slow and reverent approach across the broad green carpet." [16] As silver trumpets sounded, the Pontiff, wearing a gold miter and flowing red cape, was carried to the throne. In the pageantry rich in purple and gold and white Cushing was tenth in line as Pope John, receiving the cardinals, bestowed on each the special badge of their rank—the galero, a wide-brimmed, tasseled red hat worn only at the consistory. It would not be seen again until the death of the cardinal, when it would be suspended from the roof of his cathedral. As Cushing slowly came down the aisle, an aide bent over to whisper to the Pope: "Here comes Cushing of Boston."

"The archbishop," the *Pilot* reported, "greeted the Pope in continental fashion, a buss on both cheeks. Words were exchanged. When the cardinal turned to take his place, the Pope is said to have whispered to his aide, 'Yes, Cushing of Boston is my kind of man.' " [17]

After kissing the papal ring, Cushing remained kneeling while two officials dangled the galero over his head as John intoned: "In praise of the Almighty God and as an ornament to the Holy Apostolic See, receive the red hat, singular distinction of the cardinalatial dignity, which signifies that you must show yourself intrepid even until shedding your blood for the exaltation of holy faith, for the peace and tranquillity of the Christian people, for the increase and honor of the Roman Church."

An observer recalled the words of Napoleon when he was crowned emperor. Turning to his brother, he whispered: "Joseph, if father could only see me now." In that solemn moment, Cushing, who was on the point of tears, may have been thinking of his parents and his sister Elizabeth who were not on hand to see the impossible dream come true.

The Boston pilgrims applauded as Cushing walked back to his place, his violet cape regally trailing behind him. It was an unforgettable scene as scores of cameras clicked and flashed and more than thirty motion picture crews recorded the historic event, some from stagings slung high up near Michelangelo's dome. As the procession passed, many spectators from foreign lands pointed toward the Boston prelate.

The silence following the words of Pope John was broken by cheers in Italian and English.

At dinner at the Grande that night, Cushing proposed a champagne toast to Pope John, and Bishop Wright in turn toasted Cushing. Spellman, who attended the dinner, was, according to Mayor Hynes, jovial, courteous, happy for Boston that a Boston boy was now a cardinal.

On the following day Cushing and fifty-five pilgrims who remained in Rome * had a private audience with John, whose words were translated into English.

"Your American enthusiasm will tear off my arm," the Pontiff said, after shaking hands with his visitors. "But I love it." In an aside to Cushing, he said: "We hope to meet again in Paradise and there we will speak English." The bond of affection between them shone. Cushing cherished the topaz ring John gave him during a traditional ceremony at the Vatican Palace.

Cushing formally took possession of Santa Susanna Church following the public consistory. The first time he had entered the church, according to Paoletta, he glanced around and said half to himself, "We'll have to fix up this joint." Among his donations were an organ and a new heating system. The present edifice was completed in 1599,

---

* According to Mayor Hynes, many of the Boston pilgrims had by this time left so they could see the Giants-Browns professional play-off football game for the eastern division championship.

and the façade was added in 1603. The Paulist priests who staff the church came to Rome in 1922 to organize a parish for Catholic Americans living in or visiting Rome. Cushing's oil portrait hangs on one side of the sanctuary arch, balancing that of Pope Paul VI on the other side of the arch. Cushing brought Paulist fathers to Boston in 1945 to establish the Catholic Information Center overlooking Boston Common.

During the ceremony of possession, the surplice of an Italian monsignor caught fire when he brushed past a lighted candle. "Nonchalantly he snuffs it out," Hynes reported. In a sermon on democracy, Cushing repeated words spoken by Cardinal Gibbons in 1887: "The civil government holds over us the aegis of its protection without interfering in the legitimate exercise of our sublime mission." Cushing said the words were just as true today, since the world recognized the papacy as a natural ally in the fight for freedom and democracy.

Cushing's last ecclesiastical act before leaving Rome was to ordain Vincent Daley of Belmont, Massachusetts, in his titular church on Piazza Bernardo. One of his first acts on arriving in Rome had been to give Cardinal Wyszynski of Poland a check for twenty-five thousand dollars for the education of Polish seminarians in Paris or Rome. "I would do the same for Cardinal Mindszenty of Hungary or Cardinal Tien of China," he said. Wyszynski, who had been released from prison in 1956, had been in Rome since John's election.

Cushing was unable to respond to all the appeals for help. "They thought I had the United States Treasury with me," he said on his return. "I came back from Rome with a red hat, a bad cold, and an empty purse. The honeymoon is over."

In the crowd at Ciampino Airport on December 20 were a group of children from the Don Orione Orphanage in Rome, which is supported in part by the Boston archdiocese. Cushing grinned as the youngsters paraded through the airport lobby with placards reading, "Viva il Cardinale" and "Long Live Cushing." After stooping to embrace the orphans, he waved a sign to the delight of the crowd.

His sisters and nephews were among those waiting to greet him when the party deplaned at Logan Airport in a bright, ten-below-zero Sunday morning. Lauding Pope John as a "very kindly and humble man," Cushing said he meant no irreverence in saying "he is somewhat my type. He likes people. He likes to be of service to people." Motioning toward the pilgrims, he said that because they were fatigued he would celebrate mass for them in Our Lady of the Airways

Chapel so they could fulfill their religious obligations. State troopers locked arms and escorted Cushing and his group from customs to the chapel as he let bystanders kiss the ring John had just given him. When Sister Malachy, mother superior provincial of the Franciscan Missionary Sisters of Mary, kissed his ring, he broke into a wide smile.

"Do you recognize me in this outfit?"

When a priest kept the group waiting outside the chapel, Cushing turned to the crowd. "You see, even a cardinal has to obey . . . his pastor." More than three hundred persons jammed into the circular edifice, with fifty troopers augmenting the ushers. After the service, Police Commissioner Leo Sullivan drove the cardinal to Lake Street, where a hundred seminarians were waiting.

He was glad to be home, as he told the crowd at the airport. "We are grateful. And now, back to work!"

Cushing helped Boston College earn the name "College of Cardinals." The institution was the alma mater of cardinals O'Connell, Cushing, and John Wright, who became a prince of the church in 1969. Like Cushing, Wright had gone from Boston College to St. John's Seminary. Three years after he became auxiliary bishop of Boston in 1947, he was named the first bishop of the new diocese of Worcester, Massachusetts. From there he went to Pittsburgh, then the tenth largest Roman Catholic diocese in the country. His elevation to cardinal was an unusual honor, coming as it did to a man who had never been an archbishop. Cardinal Cushing had to cancel his trip to Rome to witness Wright's elevation because of broken ribs suffered after he fell against a staircase in his residence. Despite the painful injury, Cushing bantered with his former secretary when the latter dropped in "to borrow some old clothes."

"The cardinal is giving me all his hand-me-downs," Wright said. "He had two full sets of choir robes, so he gave me one. I'll have to have them let out, because in the passing years I've become less thin." Wright, who is short and portly, had a quip for the press: "I didn't like that crack about you being tall and thin and me being short and otherwise," he told the cardinal just before he left for Rome.

Mentioning that Wright had lived with him for years, Cushing added: "I was always enamored of his extraordinary talents, and I looked on him as one of the most scholarly and best informed men in the American hierarchy. He will be tremendously missed." [18]

Bishop Wright, who had accompanied Cushing on the consistory pilgrimage in December 1958, was reminded of the trip on his way to Rome in 1969. During a brief stopover at Shannon Airport, he recalled an early pilgrimage: "The first pilgrimage we had from Boston was a 'Come Back to Erin' flight with Cardinal Cushing in 1948. The cardinal and I brought five hundred people from Boston. We were in Ireland for ten days and it was a wonderful trip."

In Rome, Wright was often asked about the health of the cardinal. "I heard he was not well," one foreign prelate said. According to a reporter who covered the trip, "If you're from Boston and in Rome these days that is the question you keep hearing over and over: How is Cardinal Cushing? Apparently anyone who ever met . . . Cushing here has never forgotten him, whether the person is an aristocratic Roman cardinal or a hotel desk clerk." [19] The clerk at the Grande Hotel well remembered the prelate: "He said hello to everybody." A reporter had another comment: "On these spring nights in Rome, newsmen gather in a sidewalk cafe and watch the people walk by and talk about the day Cardinal Cushing was elevated to cardinal. He approached the papal throne to receive the scarlet . . . hat. Pope John smiled broadly and held out his hand . . . 'Ah, Cushing! Cushing from Boston!' " This is a variation of a familiar story. Cushing, in any case, had little in common with Roman cardinals, who, in their dignity, speak formally and briefly. Cushing's "famous South Boston twang," wrote the reporter, "has rarely been heard in either a brief or a formal statement. So Rome remembers."

Old friends who remembered included the Reverend Ramon J. de Paegher of Tapei and Stephen Kim, the new Korean Cardinal, who characterized Cardinal Cushing as "very Irish and everybody here agrees."

During Bishop Wright's visit to Brighton on his way to Rome, the cardinal, to please photographers, draped a *ferraiuollo* over his shoulders. This is a bright red cape worn by cardinals on formal occasions. When John Cardinal Wright stepped forward to receive the vestment symbolic of his new rank, he slipped into the "old clothes" that Cardinal Cushing had given him.

chapter thirteen

A NEW KIND OF
PRINCE

JOHN COGLEY called attention to the fact that certain church traditions came into vogue when monarchy was the prevailing form of government and that although the church has outlasted the feudal era, feudal forms have persisted. Still in use are such titles as "His Grace" and "His Eminence," and the customs of genuflection and kissing the ring are still observed. "At times . . . to non-Catholics they must seem out of place on American soil," writes Cogley.[1]

A former priest gives a harsher appraisal: "Somehow in the world of emperors and kings my Church became arrogant, and it perverted the authority handed it by Christ. It forgot the image of the shepherd and mimicked the panoply of kings."[2] Noting that the President of the United States wears a business suit, eats hot dogs, and shakes hands, he adds that "only the mightily insecure must support their office with pomp and silk." Another priest considers it absurd for a clergyman to wear clerical attire "when dining out, at the movies or at a cocktail party. An off-duty mailman would look silly wearing his uniform to a concert."[3]

For years there has been a crusade against medieval pomp and pageantry and a demand for less ostentation in favor of the simplicity of the early church. "Poor Jesus!" a parishioner said. "He never owned a watered-silk dress of bright scarlet." Until recently, according to protocol, a cardinal's cassock is red: scarlet watered silk in summer, fine red broadcloth in winter. Over the centuries protocol has obliged Catholics to kneel to splendidly appareled cardinals with red cloaks three yards long.[4] The traditional wardrobe of a prince of the church included fifty items.

"This gave too much of an impression of triumphism," Cushing told millions of television viewers in 1968. "In other words, here comes the *Queen Mary*, down New York Harbor, and you other boats get out of the way. . . . Here comes the cardinal and archbishop and all of these robes. . . . All you ordinary people, scram." [5] Cushing said new rules issued by Pope Paul VI abolished "thrones" for Roman Catholic bishops and simplified their vestments in an effort to stress the spiritual and pastoral aspect of the cardinal's rank. Paul simplified robes even at consistories, dispensing with the huge trains of silk and white fur capes, as well as the red silk hats (galeros) and silver-buckled red shoes.

Unlike Cardinal O'Connell, who always stood on ceremony, Cushing jokes about the trappings of his office. He calls his official raiment "haberdashery" or "glad rags," his wide-brimmed galero a "sombrero." He told a television audience just after his elevation: "There is a saying in Scripture: 'Fear not, it is I!' " A visitor at the cardinal's residence was startled when Cushing handed him a portrait in which he was wearing a cappa magna. "Here," he said, "have a comic valentine. Nobody will know who it is. They'll probably think it's Napoleon." Cushing needs no cappa magna to stand out in any gathering, for few Americans are as colorful. He is colorful when his hair flies wild in a roller coaster or when he dons an apron and a zany-looking hat while playing the role of singing waiter at Blinstrub's Village.

While archbishop, he wore a double-breasted black suit and Roman collar whenever possible, refusing to wear a red patch at his throat or a pectoral cross around his neck. His normal attire makes him indistinguishable from a parish priest. Even as cardinal, he often dons black clericals. Just before he left to give the invocation at the Kennedy inaugural, he called in the nuns of his household to ask how they liked the Prince Albert double-breasted suit his tailor had just made for him. He was so delighted he said to the tailor, who had been driven to the cardinal's residence by Monsignor Lally, "Where have you been all these years?" When "Mike" Ferrara, who had made suits for Cardinal Spellman for years, sent the bill, the prelate's enthusiasm waned. On his way back from the inaugural, in a speech he gave in Baltimore, he amused the audience with an aside: "My tailor must think I'm rich. He charged me $350 for this suit." In 1957, he told a group: "If anybody wants to donate a tailor-made suit to a cardinal, send it to me, because I have no money for a tailor." He received shoes thereafter as he needed them.

The cardinal at first wore red watered-silk so his parishioners would not feel short-changed, but even then, he brushed aside pomp with quips. Once, glancing down at his square-buckled shoes, he asked an assembly: "Don't I look like one of the Pilgrim Fathers?" While guest of honor on Homecoming Day at Boston College,[6] he mentioned new problems: "How do you know when to wear which pair of shoes? And what about the black trousers showing beneath the red cassock?" The audience howled when he lifted his cassock to reveal red stockings, complete with garters, over the black trousers. "The Jesuits work miracles," he said. "Here I am—a cardinal!"

He explained why he had slipped into regal robes when he addressed fifteen hundred members of the Nazareth Guild of Telephone Workers: "You know, some of these people have never seen a cardinal, or even the robes of a cardinal, and now it is time for me to tell them of my gratitude for all they have done for me. He will also don rich red robes to please the young or elderly. When he was invited to a home for the aged, he asked whether he could wear a Prince Albert, "or must I come in a tall miter, red vestments and carry a crozier?" Advised that he should dress, he said, "Okay, I'll be there. And they'll get the whole show."

Another time he was wearing simple clericals when a photographer came to ask permission to take pictures in a Carmelite convent. She also wanted a photograph of him in his official vestments. He asked her to wait while he went upstairs to slip into them.

When fully robed, mitred, and croziered, he can be as solemn and dignified as the occasion demands. He can also be refreshingly informal. Once, while trailing a procession of acolytes down a nave, he turned to a group of kneeling women and smiled. "So how do you like my fancy red shoes? They cost me six dollars a pair." Another time an usher told him a parishioner asked who he was.

"Why, that's Cardinal Cushing," the usher said.

"That's him?" She looked dazed. "For the Lord's sake!"

"I don't know what she meant by that," Cushing grinned, "but I suppose she was shocked to see what I really look like." After celebrating a high mass, he went outside the church and waved to a Knights of Columbus Honor Guard, who saluted him with sabers.

"Why don't you fellows go home?" he said. "The roast beef's getting cold."

Cushing had so many varied appointments he sometimes changed vestments in the car. The pastors, curates, and laymen he met were flattered when he called them by their first name. He seemed to be everywhere. Children in parochial schools squealed with delight when he walked unannounced into classrooms. "How are you, children? It's Santa Claus," he sometimes said when in ceremonial robes. In formal processions he broke from the line of march when he saw a ragged looking youngster, put his arm around his shoulder and stooped to get the child's name and address. If the child came from a needy family, Cushing took care of them. No prince of the church had the knack of putting children more at ease. At a reception, the cardinal was moving casually among several hundred adults and children when a dirty-faced four-year-old nuzzled up, gazing up at him wide-eyed.

"Hello, little girl," he said. "What's your name?"

"Mary."

"My, what a nice name." As he patted her head, she broke the silence with her high-piping voice. "What's your name?"

"Richard." He exchanged a wave with her as his car drove off.[7]

Cushing was archbishop at that time. A similar story is told about him when he became cardinal. He tells friends about a little boy who lived near his residence. Occasionally when he went for a stroll, he met the youngster, who always solemnly said, "Hi, Dick." Then he would slip his hand into the prelate's and walk along beside him. Adults who took liberties, however, were apt to be rebuffed, although he was more amused than annoyed when they used an incorrect title, just as Cardinal Gibbons was when a parishioner greeted him as "Your Immenseness." One flustered person addressed Cushing as "Your Elegance," another as "Your Innocence," and others have confused "Your Excellence" with "Your Eminence." When, however, a man slapped him on the back with a "Hi, Cush!" he got a cold stare.

"But we were classmates."

Cushing nodded. "But I am also a cardinal."[8]

When a friend addressed him as "Your Honor," he smiled. "You must have a lot of contacts with judges," he said.[9]

Long before some modern cardinals began wearing a plain gold ring with a cross instead of the traditional ring with its sapphire, Cushing considered the ring an outmoded tradition, while realizing that the custom of kissing the episcopal symbol could not be changed overnight. But he avoids the practice whenever possible. He permits kissing of his ring only under ceremonial circumstances or by visiting priests or when he senses that a person might feel slighted if he denied him the privilege.

He handles the problem in various ways. At times the memory of drudgery in South Boston tenements comes to mind when women kneel to kiss his ring: "Save your knees for scrubbing floors." In a visit to the Chelsea Naval Hospital in 1961, he was embarrassed when a GI chipped a tooth when he kissed the ring, and he grinned one night at an amusement spot when a person in line shook hands with him instead of kneeling like the others. "I'm your heathen photographer," Torrey Capo said.

Cushing himself often raises his hands over his head or turns his ring toward the palm and shakes hands instead of following protocol. When recognized on the streets—usually wearing plain black clericals—he almost invariably manages to get his right hand stretched out thumb up in shaking position before the oncomer can kneel. If he is taken by surprise, misplays may result. Boston politicians have been seem bobbing to kiss the ring, only to end up by shaking hands.

In June 1959, Senator John F. Kennedy, as an overseer of Harvard College, was present when his old family friend, Cardinal Cushing, received an honorary degree from Harvard. While other Catholics prior to the ceremony tried to kiss his ring, the Senator shook hands. It was the way Cushing wanted it.

During Cushing's first two years as cardinal, Boston was racked by economic and political problems. It was a dying city of narrow, congested streets and was dotted with slums. Charges of political corruption persisted. Businessmen, politicians, along with educational and religious institutions, were blamed for not facing up to the problem. "Harvard and Massachusetts Institute of Technology . . . would just as soon forget the drab Gaelic city across the Charles," Peter Braestrup wrote. "Under the energetic . . . Cardinal Cushing the Boston Archdiocese stays collar-deep in its own affairs—fund-raising, building schools and churches." [10] Observing that roughly seventy per cent of the city's population was Catholic, the writer criticized the church for failing to "formulate a community-wide position for itself, and most of its top men agree that such a delicate and unfamiliar role will be long in coming." Cardinal Cushing, well aware of the problems, also knew that their solution depended more on the Catholic laity than the clergy.

In the 1959 mayoral contest, John F. Collins, register of probate, campaigned from a wheelchair against Senator John E. Powers of South Boston, president of the Massachusetts State Senate, who twice had made a strong showing when running against John Hynes.

Powers was a heavy favorite to win. Whereas Collins had little political backing and was running on a shoestring, Powers was supported by most of the powerful leaders of the commonwealth, including senators John Kennedy and Leverett Saltonstall. Far more experienced, and apparently more popular, Powers also had solid financial backing. Finally, in Cardinal Cushing, he had a strong, if silent ally.[11]

When a $100-a-plate testimonial banquet was held for Senator Powers at the Statler-Hilton Hotel on March 31, 1959, the hall was packed. Present were top Democratic politicians, Republican leaders, bankers, and prominent businessmen. Sitting beside the guest of honor at the head table was Cardinal Cushing. After other speakers had praised "the next mayor of Boston," Cushing counseled political candidates to avoid the calumny of whispering campaigns and to seek election on issues rather than on "character assassination, deceit, and fraud," an obvious allusion to Curley tactics. A person's religion, he said, was "no guarantee of political competence. . . . It is not enough to vote for a man or woman and then forget all about them or leave them to be led around by outside interests concerned only with their own welfare in terms of their vested interests."

The banquet raised two hundred forty thousand dollars of which one hundred thousand dollars went into Powers' campaign chest. The sixty thousand dollars remaining, after expenses went to Cushing charities. The largest gift (thirty-five thousand dollars) was earmarked for a pilgrimage for exceptional children to Lourdes in April.

On television, Collins hammered away at the theme: "Stop power politics: elect a hands-free mayor." The contest, he said, was one between David and Goliath—between the little people and the political professionals who run the city.

Four days before the election, Internal Revenue Service agents raided two locations in East Boston to smash an alleged bookmaking syndicate reputed to have been doing half a million dollars a week in gambling. Salvatore Bartolo, a former New England boxing champion, who owned one pub, was arrested.

That night on television, Collins branded Powers as a friend of Bartolo's. He waved photographs of Bartolo's ringside café with a large "Powers for Mayor" sign over it. The barroom also flaunted a huge Powers campaign sign on its roof. Photographs of Powers with Bartolo were not only shown on television but were also printed in large front-page advertisements in Boston newspapers the day before election, proclaiming: "Stop Power Politics! Vote for Collins!"

On the day after the election, which Collins won by thirty thousand votes, the Boston *Traveler* ran a front-page streamer: "Collins Victory Rocks Boston Politics." The Boston *Herald* called the victory "the most staggering upset in the recent history of the city," adding that "Collins demonstrated decisively that his 'Stop Power Politics' campaign had worked."

The decline of power politics did not, however, mean the end of corruption. In one of its apparently ineradicable forms—gambling—Cardinal Cushing would be an unwilling principal.

Cushing's personal interest in handicapped children was more evident than ever after he became cardinal. Late in April 1959, on the eve of his departure to Lourdes with sixty-three of his "forever children"—his "little angels with broken wings"—he unveiled plans for building "Lux Mundi–Lux Aeterna," a home for blind children. It would be the first religious school of its kind. He asked the Massachusetts Council of the Knights of Columbus, who since 1954 had donated two hundred seventy-eight thousand dollars to his charities, to make this a project.

"As the time approaches," Cushing said to nuns who were accompanying the children to the Shrine of Our Lady of Lourdes, "everyone is getting worried except me." On departure day, the big crowd at the overseas section of Logan Airport frightened some of the children, who turned to the sisters for reassurance as a police band blared away. "If God in His wisdom sees fit to cure any child we shall, of course, be grateful," Cushing told reporters, "but our trip will be primarily to honor Our Lady of Lourdes."

On the flight, the children, who included Protestants and Jews, as well as Catholics, were restless, and the cardinal stayed up all night with them.[12] After the "Pilgrimage of the Innocents," however, he praised them: "Our little charges have shown themselves wonderfully adaptable to air travel. For my part I cannot imagine normal youngsters behaving any better than our dear little exceptional ones; they have been an example and an inspiration to all of us." They traveled on his passport, and he carried most of them on ·and off planes in Boston, Dublin, and Lourdes.

President Sean T. O'Kelly of Ireland, who welcomed him at Dublin Airport, invited him to be his guest, but Cushing declined. "I am the leader of the pilgrimage and it is only right that I stay with my pilgrims." Onlookers wept at the sight of him shepherding the children from the plane onto a bus that took them to Our Lady of

Lourdes Hospital in Drogheda. An Irish Jesuit who witnessed the scene said: "The sight of that man, great in physical stature and great in mind and heart, carrying a little Negro girl of seven down the gangway in his arms, has moved and captivated all." The prelate, who explained that the bones of the child were brittle, showed by his tense expression "the love and anxiety he felt for her." [13] During the night in the hospital, Cushing patrolled the corridors to be sure the children were not frightened in unfamiliar surroundings.

Next day he visited every ward, talked to patients, presented each with an Irish horn rosary, and gave a special blessing to the seriously ill.[14] In the children's ward, he gathered youngsters around him so that they could pose for a souvenir picture, then put his biretta on the head of a ten-year-old. He gave one lad a rosary presented to him by Pope John. "Some day you may be a priest," he said. In his tour he autographed plaster casts of patients with broken limbs.

The next stop was Lourdes. At the airport, Bishop Marie Theas was waiting to take him to the rectory, but Cushing instead escorted the children to a convent in the village of Barters, where Bernadette Soubirous had had her vision of the Virgin.

After visiting the shrine, Cushing returned to Drogheda. Already a Freeman of Dublin and Cork, he became a Freeman of Drogheda in an enthusiastic setting as the villagers flocked to greet him. Before leaving, he cut the first sod and blessed the site of the proposed annex to the novitiate of the Medical Missionaries of Mary. "We will build that and will be back in the not too distant future to dedicate it."

Another crowd waited to see him off at Dublin Airport. "Come and see the children," he shouted. Many went out to the tarmac as he took each child, some with crutches and in wheelchairs, off the bus. "The most important people in Ireland are children," he said. A late arrival collared one of the American pilgrims.

"So you are from Boston? Tell me, how is your Cardinal Cushing, who gives so much money away?"

"He's feeling much better. What do you think of him in Ireland?"

"We think he is just wonderful."

The American waited until Cushing mounted the steps of the plane. "That was the cardinal standing right next to you."

"Lord forgive me," the Irishman said. "Do you think he heard what I said about his giving everything away?"

On the return flight, when one of the four engines sputtered, the pilot radioed ahead to Gander for permission to land. The plane settled smoothly on the runway, where emergency apparatus was waiting. Cushing telephoned to Monsignor Lally in Boston, asking him to notify the children's parents that their little ones were safe. A plane diverted to Gander had room for only forty-three passengers. Cushing waited at the airport with the other children until a second plane sent from New York took them to Boston's Logan International Airport, where they landed in a downpour twelve hours behind schedule.

"It was the most inspiring, the most successful pilgrimage I have ever sponsored," Cushing said. "Please God, we're going back again next year." [15]

In January 1959, the cardinal criticized the Eisenhower administration for inviting Anastos Mikoyan to tour the United States. If the Soviet leader came to Boston, he said, he would refuse to attend any function in his honor. "American business leaders . . . now singing the praise of Soviet Russia are drowning out the cries for help and sympathy for the Hungarian people upon whom, in effect, the United States has turned its back." [16]

In August he proposed a "crusade of prayer" during Khrushchev's visit, contending that his presence provided more opportunity for communist propaganda and "further discouragement for the people of captive nations." [17] A few days later, while officiating at mass for Massachusetts troops at Camp Drum, New York, he said: "Every foreign visitor of any rank who has come or will come to this country from behind the Iron Curtain is a master of deceit." [18] Before the year was out he also had harsh words for Fidel Castro when the Cuban government impounded church funds, a hard blow because of the shortage of priests in Latin America.

In October Cushing flew to Rome for the centennial of North American College. Here Pope John, who had been tutored by an Irish monsignor from Tipperary, gave his first public address in English on October 11. "I speak English like a child," he said. "Next year after practice I hope to do better." [19] Pope John was delighted when Sister Irenea, one of the nuns in the Cushing party, told him her community (Sisters of the Divine Providence) was in Kingston, just a few miles from where the Pilgrims landed. Cushing was devoted to Sister Irenea. Once, when he asked her when she was coming to Boston, she told him she was going to St. Anthony's Shrine a few days later for confession.

"Now, what have you done?" he asked.

In Rome Cushing dedicated the organ he had given to Santa Susanna Church and visited the cloistered Cistercian nuns, whose order had been stationed at the church for four centuries. The mother abbess, Alcide di Conti, gave Cushing a gold-embroidered stole and lacework alb and was delighted to receive from him a cake four feet long and three feet high surmounted by a replica of St. Peter's Basilica.[20] During the jet flight from Boston the airline hostesses had baked the cake for the prelate.

The pastor of the Church of St. Cecilia gave him a life-size replica of Stefano Madero's famed statue of that saint. In Rome Mother Mary Martin, founder of the Medical Missionaries of Mary, told him she was on her way to Africa. He loaded her baggage with gifts for her missions.

Waiting to welcome him at Dublin Airport on October 15 were Franciscan Missionary Sisters for Africa, who invited him to Mount Oliver Convent, Dundalk, their headquarters. As the clergy led Cushing through the cloister to the novitiate, a gang of children followed, each with a crisp dollar bill the prelate gave them. In his welcoming speech, Dr. William Conway, bishop of Neve, called Cushing "the greatest churchman of the United States, universally known as such; possessing a humility which his presence radiated everywhere he went." After the cheering and clapping, Cushing raised his hands for silence. "Take it easy," he smiled.

He told his old friend, Mother Alcantara, he would arrange for a chartered flight to bring them to the only American novitiate of the Franciscan Missionary Sisters in Brighton, near his residence.

Before returning to the United States, Cushing rested for a few days at Our Lady of Lourdes Hospital. On this visit, he pledged five hundred thousand dollars for a new training residence for those sisters.[21]

In July 1959, Cushing had been hospitalized for five days with a painful case of shingles, a skin ailment traceable to nervous fatigue. The prelate suffered a severe attack, his skin spotted with flaming sores. "I don't like to complain," he said, "but the pain is terrible. It's internal, like a raw nerve." [22] When he got out of the hospital he invited five nuns from Sacred Heart High School and a few girls at the summer camp run by the school to join him in a cruise on Louis Perini's yacht out of the Scituate Yacht Club. They cruised several miles out to the ocean to watch some Portuguese fishermen net fish.

Soon after returning from Ireland he went to Kansas City, Missouri, to address the National CYO Convention. It had been cold in the small private plane that flew him from Chicago to Kansas City, and the auditorium was hot. He felt faint before entering the auditorium and during the banquet pitched forward at the head table and passed out for about five minutes. When a doctor was unable to find a pulse, a stretcher and resuscitator were rushed in, and a priest was about to administer the last rites when the prelate suddenly sat up, waved away the physician and priest, and spoke for twenty minutes as if nothing had happened. "I feel fine," he said. "I've had these attacks before and they never last very long." [23]

On the following day, he addressed ten thousand CYO members. After attending a bishops' meeting in Washington, D.C., on his way home he found himself far behind schedule, especially in fund-raising. "Whenever I am away," he told a friend in a personal letter, "many benefactors seem to forget me and my very expensive charitable, educational, spiritual, and missionary program. I am months behind in payments on pledges and commitments that I have here at home and in Latin America, Africa, the Philippines, and elsewhere." Somehow he found the time on his return from the Midwest to give personal instructions to a Jewish girl who wanted to become converted to Catholicism.

On Christmas morning in 1959 he said mass at the new sisters' residence for student nuns and gave the sermon at a morning pontifical mass at the cathedral. That afternoon he celebrated another mass on television, giving another sermon. Meanwhile, he was completing a book, *Questions and Answers on Communism,* while keeping in close touch with the national political situation, which, for the first time since Al Smith's candidacy for the presidency, involved the Roman Catholic Church. More than that, it involved a personal friend, John Fitzgerald Kennedy.

On the Lourdes trip in 1959 Cushing could take only a fraction of the five hundred applicants. In May 1960, the Irish Airlines (Aer Lingus) provided facilities for eighty-seven retarded children, who were accompanied by nursing nuns, nurses, and several priests. Many were on crutches or in wheelchairs, and some wore leg braces. Again, the cardinal carried them on and off buses and planes. A few weeks before this trip, X-rays had revealed internal abcesses, requiring surgery. Nevertheless, the cardinal was on the departing plane, accompanied by Dr. Richard Wright. The prelate and nurses had their hands full during the flight when the restless children squirmed and babbled. A nun had to scramble after one child who rolled toilet tissue down the aisle of the plane.[24]

At Lourdes, the party, which included adult pilgrims, spent three days bathing in the waters, roaming the mountainside, and attending devotions. While the cardinal was giving a sermon, one retarded child mimicked his every gesture, capping his performance by making the sign of the cross with his left hand.[25] On the third day, Cushing led a procession of three hundred pilgrims through Lourdes. Here he joined volunteers who pushed wheelchairs bearing the handicapped children to the Grotto and baths.[26]

Then Cushing, with the children and thirty-three adults, flew to Dublin Airport, where he waved away a car waiting to take him to Drogheda. "I want to stay with my own people," he shouted from the bus. The half-million-dollar extension to Our Lady of Lourdes convent (called the Cardinal Cushing Wing), which he had promised to Medical Missionaries on his October visit, was ready to accommodate the children. During the dedication ceremony, he seemed amused by the Irish acolytes who were wearing cassocks, gold-fringed collars, and flowing ties. The prelate winked at the nuns as he passed them.

After the dedication, the youngsters present asked him to play ball with them. As fatigued as he was, he joined in the game to the delight of the sisters and nurses. Each child received toys sent by the Dominican Contemplative Nuns.[27] While in Ireland, Cushing took his party on a bus trip to Northern Ireland, with stops in Belfast and Londonderry, and entertained everyone after the trip at dinner at our Lady of Lourdes Hospital.

The cardinal lay down on an improvised bunk in the plane during the brief stop at Shannon Airport while the adult pilgrims browsed through the duty-free shop. When he became ill during the return flight, a bunk was set up for him in a compartment of the plane.

While Pope John XXIII was planning Vatican Council II, Cardinal Cushing was having domestic troubles. It was a time when Massachusetts was riddled by what Federal Judge Charles E. Wyzanski, Jr., called a "network of corruption."

Much of the corruption involved the state department of public works in connection with land damage settlements and lucrative contracts that invited bribery and graft. Newspapers and magazines

across the land aired the dirty linen to the shame and embarrassment
of church and civil authorities. Cardinal Cushing in his pastoral
Lenten letter in 1961 lashed out at the widespread corruption.

"When public officials who have proved themselves to be dishonest
are returned to office again and again, the voter emblazons before
the world his own indifference to the moral law," he wrote. "This is a
matter of gravest scandal. It is plain that the voting citizen in such a
situation encourages the spread of corruption and is himself a kind
of 'partner in crime.' When we hear murmurs of graft and bribery, of
'payoffs' and 'grabs', we know these charges are not the products of
. . . imaginations. They take their course in a sordid reality which
decent society cannot afford to tolerate."

One source of corruption was gambling.

chapter fourteen

THE KEY SHOP

A GAMBLING controversy in Boston which was headlined all over the nation involved the Boston Police Department, of which Cushing was chaplain. The entire force had long been devoted to the cardinal, providing him constantly with escorts, doing countless favors for his nuns and priests, and contributing generously to his charities. Thus the prelate was understandably upset when the Columbia Broadcasting Company produced a carefully documented, hour-long program, "Biography of a Bookie Joint," which impugned the honor of the department.

In the spring of 1961 the Boston *Herald*, referring to the opening day of the Massachusetts Senate investigation into gambling in the nation, ran a headline: "$50 Billion Bookie Empire Buys Police, Senators Told." The newspaper quoted Senator Henry Jackson: "You and I know what the problem is; they buy off the judge; they buy off the prosecutor and they buy off the law-enforcement officer."

A few months later, Ray McMullen, a CBS reporter who had been tipped off by the New England Crime Commission, set up a camera in a furnished room across the street from a small key shop on Massachusetts Avenue in the Back Bay. The shop was a front for a horse parlor. A cameraman, using telescopic lenses, stayed in the room for three days, photographing the traffic going in and out, including Boston policemen, who often left their cruisers double parked. Gambling stubs were shown being burned in a metal barrel on the sidewalk while a cop stood idly by.

Meanwhile, McMullen, with a concealed tiny 8-mm. camera and microphone picked up the action inside the shop as he placed bets and watched operations. He photographed eight uniformed officers, a motorcycle cop, and a detective attached to police headquarters. In one day, 1,246 persons entered the shop. According to the *Herald*,[1] the bookie establishment had an estimated weekly take of twenty-five thousand dollars.

Justice Department officials saw the documentary in Washington in the summer of 1961. On September 29, United States Treasury agents arrested eight persons in surprise raids on the key shop and three other bookie joints. The sight of a CBS cameraman photographing the action from the middle of Massachusetts Avenue ired the Boston press. Next day the *Globe* ran a headline: "U.S. Stages Hub Raids For T.V." The story told how twenty-eight agents hit four establishments as cameras whirred. The *Record-American* also splashed a headline on its front page: "T-Men Raid Four For T.V." Included in the storm of protest following the raids was the cardinal's blast. He was even more outraged early in December 1961, when the documentary was shown on a national hook-up. It was blacked out in Boston because of the cases pending against the men arrested on gambling charges.

The city was stunned. While the film had shown that illegal gambling was rampant all over the country, there was indignation that Boston was chosen as Exhibit A of the widespread breakdown in law enforcement and public morals.

Actually, there was nothing new about wide-open gambling and accompanying police corruption in Massachusetts. Cushing remembered when his personal friend, the ruggedly honest Thomas Sullivan, after becoming Police Commissioner in 1943, had been unable to weed out corruption. "Bookies operated openly on the sidewalks and used lunchrooms to place bets," Louis Lyons wrote, adding that the attorney general in an official report on corruption in 1945 had "presented photographs showing police cars parked in front of racketeer headquarters and police officers going into the building." [2]

The documentary, according to Fred Friendly of CBS, was one of the most maligned, as well as the most sensational, of any of his company's exposés. "Half a city cried foul, screaming that we were dishonest, that we had staged and rigged the program. . . . Yet the broadcast withstood the hostile scrutiny, and again proved that electronic journalism can be as accurate and responsible as any of the older media of reporting." [3]

Governor Volpe, after a private viewing, demanded the resignation of Cushing's friend, Police Commissioner Leo Sullivan.* Meanwhile, a

---

* Governor Volpe was set down hard in 1962 when, at the wake of Leo Sullivan, who died bitter and disillusioned, a member of Sullivan's family handed Volpe the flowers he had sent.

group of anguished wives of policemen went to the prelate to plead for assurance that their husbands were honest. Also shaken was the cardinal's part-time chauffeur, a Boston police officer of high standing in the Police Association.

Cushing refused to see a special showing of the film. "I want to see no part of it. Everybody has faults, but why hang them like dirty linens on a line stretching from one end of the country to the other?" Noting that the Protestant and Jewish clergy who had seen the film praised it, Friendly said "the worst attack and certainly the most difficult to bear came from our old friend Cardinal Cushing." [4] He referred to the night of December 5, 1961, when the prelate was spotlighted on the stage at the Boston Garden while police bands blared and the crowd cheered as Cushing defended the honor of the Boston police. "In my theology, gambling is not a sin any more than to take a glass of beer or hard liquor is a sin. It's the abuse that makes gambling evil or drinking intoxicating liquors a sin." This drew a gibe from a Protestant spokesman: "Gambling, Your Eminence, may not be a sin, but it happens to be a crime." Cushing was more apt to agree with a comment made by the late Heywood Broun: "If you make money at poker, that's gambling. If you make it at bridge, that's a social duty. If you make it outguessing Wall Street, that's a miracle."

"Someone betrayed us and I would like to know who," Cushing said in his speech at the Garden. "Whoever was behind it owes an apology to the city." His point was that gambling existed everywhere. "The United States Army wouldn't be a sufficient law enforcement body to stop people from gambling. Boston is as clean as any city in the nation . . . and even more so. How are you going to enforce laws in regards to gambling or to so-called bookies when the federal government will give these individuals a license to be in business so long as they return to the government a percentage of their profits?" He referred to the federal bookie wagering stamp and tax payments for illegal gambling income.

In his book, Friendly alludes to the power of Cushing who, unlike Governor Volpe and Mayor John Collins, backed the police commisosiner: "The Boston police, dishonored and humiliated, may not have *The New York Times,* the Boston *Herald,* the Boston *Globe,* the *Harvard Crimson,* CBS and all the Brahmins arrayed against them, but they had the cardinal in their corner." [5]

Michael Novak, an eloquent Catholic spokesman, in a letter to the *Harvard Crimson,* said the prelate's appearance at the policemen's ball made him wish Gilbert and Sullivan were alive to record the occasion. "The sight of the police band spontaneously breaking into 'For Boston! For Boston!' . . . the sound of the rifle butts of the honor guard pounding on the floor in enthusiasm; the sense of renewal, loyalty, pride and closing of ranks, should not be allowed to die unsung." Summing up the cardinal's position, Novak said he may have erred "in speaking only of the immediate morale of the force, and not also of the larger question of political corruption in Boston; some of his words like 'betrayal' may have smacked too much to non-Boston-Irish of local pride; but he showed his genuine humanity."

Marya Mannes, noting that the documentary had "aroused the thunderous ire of Cardinal Cushing," wrote that if he had seen the film he "would have been faced with a vivid exploration of the mighty river of crime which these small bookie tributaries over the country joined and swelled toward the corruption of society itself." [6] Pointing out that ten million small bets resulted in the breakdown of respect for and adherence to law, she accused the prelate of being "a religious leader extolling the very police who condoned this anarchy and soothing the conscience of the people who contributed to it."

Yet Cushing had strong support for his position. Writing in 1959, Chief Magistrate John Murtagh of New York said: "It is my firm conviction that gambling should be made legal. There is nothing inherently wrong in a wager." And nothing was easier to document than Cushing's statement that crime is endemic in American society.

Cushing may have been right when he said Boston was as clean—or cleaner—than any city in the nation.

The publicity resulting from the documentary forced Governor Volpe to appoint a special crime commission to probe corruption. The commission continued to function when Endicott Peabody was elected governor in 1962. Cardinal Cushing, who had earlier denounced the New England Citizens Crime Commission, a voluntary agency that had risen from the ashes of the Watch and Ward Society of the 1920s, felt no more charitable toward the Massachusetts Crime Commission. On a radio panel show [7] he said it was "too bad the commission was ever set up." In his opinion there were sufficient normal investigatory channels.

"If there was a crime commission in every state, . . . Massachusetts probably would have a better image than any other state," he said. Here, again, he was on firm ground, as California's Special Crime Study Commission suggested when it concluded: "No group of organized criminals has ever been able to achieve profits . . . without the friendship and toleration, if not the actual assistance, of politicians and public officials." Cushing erred, however, in underestimating the extent of corruption in the commonwealth when he tried to defend it against critics who charged that Boston and the state were crime-ridden at every level: "Somehow the people of the state and the city haven't enough loyalty to go about eliminating evil—real or imagined —without portraying them as places where crime and corruption are rampant. . . . You hear a lot of rumors, cheap talk with regard to these things. It is one thing to indict a man; it is another to prove the indictment."

It was nevertheless true that Thomas McArdle, chief counsel of the Massachusetts Crime Commission, when interviewed by CBS, said a bookie had offered him two hundred fifty thousand dollars if he would discontinue the commission's investigation of illegal gambling. Harrison Chadwick, a Republican member of the Massachusetts legislature, was censured by the House of Representatives for saying on the same show that some Massachusetts lawmakers were "actively involved with bookmakers." Although Chadwick could produce no firm evidence, there was substance to his charge, as the California probers indicated. Indeed, soon after Chadwick had mentioned that bookies had contacts with legislators, the capitol police in a raid on the document room in the State House uncovered a flourishing business in booking horses and numbers. A legislative aide, who admitted he was an "amateur handicapper," was fired after acknowledging that a dozen lawmakers dealt regularly with bookies.

As a guest on the Bay State Forum discussing the moral climate of the Commonwealth, Cushing blamed political corruption partly on "a society where everyone lives on credit." When tragedy occurs, he said, those who buy on credit may be so strapped financially as to resort to dishonesty. He said the church's teaching regarding honesty and integrity on the part of public officials would be pinpointed so there would be no charge of "a church of silence which fails to correct evils wherever they exist in public life." [8]

Trials resulting from "Biography of a Bookie Joint" were held in 1963. There were minor convictions, as well as reforms in the police department, but no police officer was either convicted or dismissed. The power to appoint the police commissioner passed from the jurisdiction of the governor to the mayor of Boston.

The documentary was not shown in Boston until 1964, and by then the Boston press was defending CBS. In Friendly's home is a silver bowl given to the executive producer of "CBS Reports" by the Boston Press Club as their award for television journalism in 1961. "But the prize from the Boston wars that I most treasure is a gift sent to me in 1964 when I was appointed president of CBS News," writes Friendly. "It is a copy of the biography of Pope John XXIII, *Call Me John,* and under the inscription ('To Fred: Congratulations on your promotion and prayerful good wishes for the future.') is the signature of the author, Richard Cardinal Cushing. There was no hint that His Eminence had forgotten, only that he had forgiven." [9]

By that time Cushing had forgotten to the extent of joking about the gambling scandal. In a letter to one friend he appended a footnote: "Keep away from the key shop, Joe." [10]

chapter fifteen

MISSIONARY TO LATIN AMERICA

"ON MY first official visit to Rome as archbishop of Boston in 1948," Cushing wrote in a leaflet,[1] "I informed Pope Pius XII of our 'Lend Lease' program for priests. It was a plan to send volunteer priests to missionary dioceses to ease the critical need for spiritual assistance in those areas. The Holy Father was greatly interested and suggested the possibilities of assisting Catholics in Latin America who had no priests."

Cushing's experience with Father Thomas Hennessey years earlier led to his lend-lease plan, which in 1958 was expanded to include the Society of St. James the Apostle, an organization of diocesan priests who volunteer to serve Latin America. "St. James was the reputed Apostle of Spain," Cushing wrote. "Latin America with its large Hispanic population—though the native Indians and Portuguese more than equal them in number—seemed the likely patron of this spiritual venture." [2]

Repeatedly the prelate has asked to be relieved of his archdiocesan responsibilities so that he might serve as a missionary in foreign lands, specifically South America, which has been one of his main preoccupations for years. It has been suggested that in the grinding poverty and illiteracy of the peasants who live in subhuman conditions, he saw qualities that made the church so vital to the Irish immigrants of South Boston in their bitter conflict with Protestant Yankees.[3]

Three-fourths of Latin America's population has an average life expectancy of thirty-five years; four of five are illiterate and are racked by disease and despair. The cardinal, deploring a social order that "has brought fortunes to the elect, and misery, starvation and premature death to forgotten millions," said a few years after launching his missionary program that unless conditions were improved, a "day of reckoning when, urged on by evil forces, the multitudes will arise and more Cubas will . . . result." He noted that the wealthy people of South America have never been trained to give.[4]

"Hundreds of missionary agencies in Latin America are looking for literature in English and Spanish and Indian to counteract the avalanche of literature emanating from communist sources," Cushing said.[5] In 1958 he sent missionaries large shipments of J. Edgar Hoover's book *Masters of Deceit* and financed the distribution of a hundred thousand copies of his own book *Questions and Answers on Communism*. Priests took the books down, fearing that communist longshoremen might throw them into the ocean. Cushing also sent Spanish primers at the third or fourth grade level. He knew, however, that education was not enough. Considering church landholding a hangover from feudal times, Cushing hoped the government would buy up land at a minimal cost, give it to the peasants, along with farm tools from American aid, and give them a chance to produce. Some critics labeled him a socialist for this suggestion.

Cushing was undaunted by basic problems of grinding poverty and scarcity of priests, who themselves lived on the mudsill of society in countries like Peru and Bolivia, which did not quite fit Voltaire's comparison of England to a glass of beer: "All froth at the top, dregs at the bottom, and good in the middle." There is no middle class in Peru and Bolivia. In his concern over the poverty of the church in Latin America, Cardinal Spellman had found that there were few rectories, forcing priests to board where they could. Priests in Puerto Rico received only thirty cents a month in salary. "And since these are not considered foreign missions, the priests receive no help from the Propagation of the Faith Society," Spellman said.[6] They did, however, receive financial aid from Cushing when he was director of the Propagation Society. In one trip to Puerto Rico, Spellman met Bishop Byrne of San Juan who "had words of praise and gratitude for another outstanding American priest—our Father Richard Cushing."[7]

By 1962, the Society of St. James had over seventy priests serving more than four hundred thousand Latin Americans. Sixteen priests took part in the first Ceremony of Departure in Holy Cross Cathedral in 1959—all but one were from Boston. After spending four months at the Maryknoll language school in Cochabamba, Bolivia, they were assigned to parishes high in the Andes. By 1962, American and Irish priests were staffing nineteen parishes—two in Ecuador, four in Bolivia, and thirteen in Peru. In the new rectories, every item from kitchen utensils to sheets and towels were supplied by Cushing. Even in remote areas luxuries included movie and slide projectors.

There was a central house in Lima for retreats. "Twenty-five minutes driving from downtown Lima brings you beyond the cloud umbrella which hangs over the city and into the sunny valley of Cieneguilla," Cushing wrote in a pamphlet. In the valley were modern school buildings with language laboratory equipment, and here bilingual teachers give intensive courses to prepare priests for missionary work. Peruvian seminarians mix with Americans in practice conversations. After four months at Cieneguilla, priests have a working knowledge of Spanish. Also available are refresher courses in Quechua for missionaries working with Indians.

Associated with the St. James project is the Missionary Society of the Sons of Mary, who built a house in Framingham, Massachusetts. After the death of its founder, the Reverend Edward Garesche, S.J., this society became Cushing's responsibility. Its members are priests and physicians.

Cushing, who thinks Catholicism can unite Latin Americans and raise their economic level, cites case histories in his leaflet, "Saving Souls in Latin America." There was Pedro Quispe, born high in the Andes, who lived with his parents in a jungle hut. He was underfed, and his home had no provisions for sanitation. When Pedro was fourteen, American priests took charge of the soup kitchen where Pedro had so often lined up mornings for his bread and milk. The padres built a large clinic and taught Pedro and his friends religion. "Wherever boys gather on a corner," Cushing writes, "a St. James station wagon will pull up and herd them down the block with other groups for catechism class. They help the padre set up his movie projector and steady the ladder while he cuts into city power lines. They enjoy the motion pictures and instructions, but even if they did not, they would stay anyway because they like their . . . padre." [8]

Juan Pinto, a communist studying to be a teacher, wanted to prove that religion was a sham. "When St. James fathers came to teach the normal school he gloated over how he would embarrass them." But he found that they welcome all questions and can answer them, too." Juan wound up unsure of his communism, Cushing writes.

Cushing was a papal legate to a national Eucharistic Congress sponsored by Pope John in Peru in August 1960. President Manuel Prado had sent a horse-drawn carriage to the airport to bring Cushing to a reception in Lima. A mounted bodyguard in full-dress uniform of red, black, and gold escorted the prelate to the noon function. Later that day he offered mass in a chapel just built by his missioners in a Lima slum. After receiving Holy Communion from the cardinal, the president's wife (Clorinda de Prado) accompanied him on a trip through Mendocita.

At dinner that night, Cushing told the religious that their presence in Peru was indispensable, and he urged them to make more use of the lay apostolate. "Protestants are pouring lay workers into Latin America, and Catholics must meet the challenge." The religious presented him with a large cake decorated with a map of Latin America in honor of his sixty-fifth birthday.[9]

Next day, Cushing and two prelates [10] flew to Piura, where they were greeted by half-naked children, rifle-bearing soldiers, bishops, nuns, and people from every walk of life. On a drive to the cathedral, the cardinal saw mud-walled, tin-roofed huts and other scattered shreds of poverty and ruin.

On a side-trip to Curhausi, a remote parish high in the Andes, President Prado told him Peru needed more Boston priests. In the tiny village Cushing found one—Father David Kelly. A later volunteer was his nephew, Father William Francis ,who worked in Lima slums.

In *L'Osservatore Romano*[11] Pope John lauded Cushing for his efforts in Latin America.

On his return, the cardinal said that at least a hundred thousand priests were needed there. "The people are very religious, but they are uninformed. There are hundreds of thousands who have no priests to guide them." Cushing's plan was to build new parishes or rebuild old ones, maintain them, and encourage native vocations. Meanwhile, thanks to Bishop Cornelius Lucey of Cork, Irish priests were joining the Society of St. James. Cushing paid each priest a hundred dollars a month, plus three dollars a day for "extras." As he built facilities, he encouraged his parishioners to contribute and tapped affluent donors to whom he made dramatic appeals. One was Joseph A. De-Mambro, owner of a large electronics company, which supplied the equipment for the society's language laboratories in Latin America and which, thanks to Cushing, got the contract to provide the amplification system along the inaugural parade route in 1961.* In a letter to DeMambro in 1963, Cushing wrote:

---

* DeMambro set up a massive and complicated public-address system to keep spectators lining the parade route informed of just what floats and VIPs were passing in the procession. The system also carried the inaugural address to nine loudspeakers along the route between the Capitol and the White House. The recorded music of the Boston Pops Orchestra was played over the system.

"I hope you found the two Irish priests, Mike Murphy and Father O'Connor, whom I sent to you, as interesting, capable and well-informed as I did. They are topflight men in the Missionary Society of St. James. One comes from Cork, the other from Meath. I don't want to impose on you, for you have been very good to me over the years, so send me the bill for anything they order. Also, send six transistor table model radios to Sister M. Michael Joseph, St. Joseph's Manor, Dorchester, Mass.

"During the weekend, I had a phone call from our priests in Peru at the request of the Peruvian Government to send a team of our missionaries to Latin America to go to the devastated area where part of a mountain of ice and rock fell, with the roar of lions, upon a series of villages and buried over three thousand poor inhabitants. The Superior of the Society in Peru called me.

"Their task will be to take care of the homeless kids who were not in the area when their loved ones were so deeply buried in the bosom of the earth that their bodies can never be recovered. I told our priests to do everything they could for the children and to begin immediately the construction of a large orphanage which the kids can call home."

Cushing saw that no child left an orphan in "this terrible tragedy" would be without a home. "Begging God's choicest blessings upon you and yours, and asking you, please, if you will be good enough to advise me when the TV sets will be sent, I am, your devoted and grateful friend."

While the cardinal was in Peru, six hundred delegates to Cuba's National Catholic Youth Congress staged an anticommunist demonstration, shouting "Cuba, yes! Communists, no!" The week-long meeting ended late in August with a pledge of loyalty to the church.

Cushing was one of the first Americans in high places to call Fidel Castro a communist. "When I see a bird that walks like a duck and swims like a duck and quacks like a duck, I call that bird a duck." In his early warnings about Castro, he mentioned signs of a build-up at the Guantanamo Naval Base in Cuba by iron curtain country technicians when he visited the base early in 1961. "When I got home and told them about this, they laughed at me," he said.

That summer Cushing served as Pope John's personal representative at another Eucharistic Congress at Santa Cruz, Bolivia. He brushed off State Department warnings that planes were being hijacked and that riots were feared to mark the beginning of a major revolution. "Unless Rome tells me not to go, I'm leaving."

Thousands of Bolivians gathered at an outdoor altar before a huge replica of "Christ of the Andes" to hear him speak of the unity of Catholics of all nations. He told President Victor Paz Estenssoro that he considered his welcome to the Congress a tribute to both the Pope and the United States. At the end of the session, highlighted by the giving of Communion to thirteen thousand men, Cushing told the crowd that Bolivia's Catholicism would save it from Cuba's fate.

During the trip he pledged thirty-five thousand dollars for the Pius XII radio station in the mining town of Siglo Veinte, which had twice been ravaged by communist mobs. He gave a check to the bishop of Santa Cruz to build a seminary and promised to help to restore two parishes and a secondary school there.

During his stay, he learned that Bolivian priests had refused to marry a couple who had twelve children born out of wedlock. Cushing officiated at their wedding: "I got all dressed up like St. Patrick for them. I wore everything. I waited twenty minutes at the altar, then they marched in—all the kids, followed by their mother and father. Outside, after the ceremony, the bridegroom said, 'I'm glad I waited twenty years. I got married by the Pope!'"

An infection the cardinal suffered in Bolivia raised raw sores on his arms and legs and took more than a month to heal. By this time he was used to living and working in pain. He came home from Bolivia in time to celebrate his fortieth anniversary as a priest. That day he filled his residence with wheelchair and stretcher cases and had a party for the children.

One member of the papal mission to the Congress in Santa Cruz was Archdeacon Thomas F. Duggan, former parish priest of St. Patrick's Church in Cork. This Irish patriot and chaplain in both world wars, who had been a prisoner of war, resigned as pastor of the largest parish in Ireland to devote his life to one of the poorest parishes in the Western Hemisphere. "Father Tom," as Cushing called him, was seventy-one when he joined the society of St. James. When Cushing had suggested he was too old, the priest reminded him that he had been asked to recruit Irish priests: "They are tremendously needed. The best way I can encourage them is to go myself. I know that God wants me to go."

Father Duggan, after returning to Peru in November, died a week before Christmas. Four days earlier, Mother Gemina Shelley, mother general, and Mother Dolores Ryan of the Missionary Sisters of St. Columban from Ireland, had met him during their visit to Peru with a view to starting their first Irish mission and schools there.

When Duggan died, Cushing, rising from a sick bed, met Bishop Lucey at Idlewild International Airport on the evening of the following day to fly to Lima. At a graveside there Cushing called Duggan a "martyr of charity" and "Ireland's greatest gift in honor of the fifteen hundredth anniversary of the death of St. Patrick." Later he transferred the body of the priest so he would be within the shadows of the language school in Lima, "at the foot of a mountain that symbolized the greatness of his courage and the power of his faith that could move mountains, in the soil of . . . the vineyard of God where the sun always shines and where saints like him are the greatest hope of the future."

Duggan wrote his own epitaph just before he died: "The work here is the most worthwhile we ever did." The best tribute to his memory is the succession of Irish priests who came to take his place.

While in Lima, Cushing was given special receptions at the American embassy and the residence of the papal nuncio. He took with him members of the St. James Society, including his nephew.

Back in Boston, he spent Christmas Eve consoling his "friends" at Walpole State Prison. He told them to live ever in a new day and to keep up their courage. "Being discouraged is a tool for the devil." After visiting each of thirty-seven prisoners on cell blocks, he posed for a photograph behind bars, saying, "This is where I belong." A few days later he told reporters about his new honorary degree designating him "a graduate of Walpole State Prison," as he motioned toward a banner bearing these words. "That's as good as any degree I ever received," he said.

Late in the summer of 1964 Cushing went to South America for the third time. "Believe me, I don't want to go," he said, "but I feel it is my mission, just as St. Paul 'stung his flesh,' and just as President Kennedy 'stung his flesh,' I must . . . to fight the enemies of decency and morality." [12]

The cardinal flew over the Andes to the tri-nation St. James Missionary area in buffeting air over mountains and desert. Bumpy trips by donkey or jeep over steep, rocky, and winding trails aggravated his emphysema and asthma, leaving him limp with exhaustion and at times even unable to talk as he traveled through the heat of coastal Ecuador and the chill mists of Peru. Yet he found the energy to lift the morale of priests and to make seventy speeches. Richard J. Connolly, a Boston *Globe* reporter, called him the best American public relations man ever to visit South America. His earthy humor, even when translated into Spanish, endeared him to the natives. While blessing a new brick church in a Lima slum, he said: "Mindful of the fact that you live in an agricultural country . . . you know what an ass is. We read in the New Testament that our blessed Lord road on an ass in triumph into . . . Jerusalem. Today the Lord rides on another ass: me." He told his audience that the only language he knew was "the language of the heart—that is, the language of love."

His worst bout came in La Paz, Bolivia, where the airport is almost fifteen thousand feet above sea level and where trains supply oxygen because of the prevalence of *soroche* (mountain sickness). "They had me stay in the plane. I needed oxygen for two hours," he said on his return.

"Cheerfulness took over when he visited priests, brothers, and lay assistants, along with "faceless" Indians, peasants, and the poorest of the poor. In one village he poured milk into the mugs of an army of urchins, and when they trailed him, he bought ice cream for them, paying the storekeeper twice the price so he could give them a second round next day. He took refreshments on every visit to orphanages.

One stop was at the anchovy-fishing city of Chimbote on the north coast of Peru, where a steel mill had been built a few years before Cushing founded the society. Indians who came down from their farms seeking jobs could not be accommodated, and one hundred twenty thousand moved into a community that could house only ten thousand. Here St. James priests opened a parish. "They must establish a colossal program of material and spiritual aid," Cushing wrote. "Instructions for First Communion, for example must be provided for four thousand. The challenge is great, but not overwhelming." [13]

The mission's church of the Virgin of the Poor was still under construction when Cushing visited it in 1964, but the revolutionary altar was completed, built so the priest can face the congregation, reflecting the updating of the church as a result of Vatican II. "Cushing has encouraged all his missionary priests to stay in tune with the times," *Time* commented. "For if there is a bit of the Last Hurrah in Boston's crusty and contrary Cardinal Cushing, there is also a generous measure of the new spirit of Pope John XXIII." [14]

Many priests and nuns were in the crowd that greeted him at Logan Airport when he returned with Dr. Richard Wright and Father Francis. When he pushed his way into the lobby of National Airlines he was welcomed by the self-styled Polish "freedom-fighter," Josef Mlot-Mroz, who was carrying a large sign that read: "Welcome Back Dear Cardinal, The 20th Century St. Paul." [15]

Although exhausted after his three-week trip, Cushing answered questions for reporters, who asked what he thought of the cover story *Time* magazine had just run on him. He said the profile missed the most important phase of his life—the nearly fifty years he had devoted to missionary work. "They portrayed a false image of me."

The *Pilot* in August in an editorial headed "Time Ran Out!" charged that "only the merest caricature of the churchman survived the famed *Time* process of collection, selection and interpretation. Combining a long look at the changing American church with a close look at the Boston Cardinal proved too much for both subjects: The church and prelate ended badly out of focus." Conceding that the magazine sensed lay American Catholic unrest and rebellion against clerical authoritarianism, the editorial pointed out that the surge of renewal does not include dissent with the Pope, lay election of bishops, and birth control against the law of the church. Cushing did not agree with these extremes in opinion or action.

Some readers of the profile, however, saw a larger significance in the prelate's work. "As a 'right-wing,' anti-ecumenical Protestant clergyman," one wrote the editor, "I tried to read your article on . . . Cushing . . . with proper disgust, but nostalgia got the best of me. Any Bostonian worth his salt cod has to be proud of this grand old man and his antics. Like our glorious Tea Party, he will always be a part of my Boston." [16] Another reader was equally enthusiastic: "If the picture you paint of that great guy . . . Cushing had been presented before the day of wonderful Pope John, we Protestants would have expected to see him excommunicated. Would that we had known of his clear insights, his impatience with outlived trappings and 'legalism in the church,' his attendance at non-Roman services, his wit and good humor, when he was so often publicized during Kennedy's White House years. What a man! What a human being!" [17]

The cardinal also sizzled when he read an article by Monsignor Ivan Illich in *America*.[18] The Vienna-born priest, who founded the Center for Intercultural Documentation in Cuernavaca, Mexico, a training center for Latin American missionaries, wrote that most North American Catholic efforts in Latin America were "thinly disguised colonialism" and that the pouring of millions of dollars, priests, and nuns into the area did more harm than good by making an alien church more foreign, an overstaffed church priest-ridden, and bishops into abject beggars. Illich, who trained priests, nuns, and laymen to become a kind of Catholic peace corps attuned to the cruel economic and social conditions of Latin America as well as its culture, branded American financial aid "the shady side of charity," thereby incurring the wrath of Cushing, chief sponsor of such charity.

Cardinal Spellman denied a request from the Mexican Bishops' Conference to recall Illich, but later the Vatican's sacred Congregation of the Doctrine of the Faith forbade Roman Catholic priests and members of religious orders to study with him. Meanwhile, he received temporary lay status from New York's Archbishop Terrence Cooke, thus depriving the Vatican of any effective power of suspension.[19] Illich, who still thinks social reform in Latin America must come from outside the church, remains at Cuernavaca, attracting Protestant missionaries, college students, and professors of all faiths.

In commenting on Cushing's violent reaction to Illich's article in *America,* John Reedy, C.S.C., editor and publisher of *Ave Maria,*[20] said Cushing's "vehement, emotional criticism . . . could have been predicted by anyone who understands the cardinal's Boston-Irish bluntness . . . and his openhearted dedication to the work of the Church in Latin America." The prelate was wrong, however, in inferring that the opinions of an author of any magazine article are necessarily those of its editors. "He failed to distinguish the editorial function of a publication from its function as a forum of public discussion and controversy."

Cushing is certain that his missionary work in Latin America, along with President Kennedy's Alliance for Progress, was headed in the right direction. In the spring of 1964, the prelate praised Kennedy's program in *Extension* magazine: "Despite the enormity of these problems and our heavy responsibility, the people of the United States have been asked to sacrifice relatively little in support of the Alliance. Less than one per cent of our federal budget is allocated to assist half a hemisphere." Crediting Kennedy with launching the program, he called it "the greatest task undertaken in our history."

After Kennedy's death, former Dominican President Juan Bosch wrote in his memoirs that "although the machinery of this Alliance for Progress survived him, the vitality and spirit of reform with which he imbued it died with him . . . and so I write about the Alliance . . . in the past tense." [21]

The cardinal thinks it will take more than a decade for the Alliance to achieve its goals. "Added to that program will be the know-how which the Peace Corps and others can give with more and more personnel in the future. Sometime, somehow, those who control the wealth of Latin American countries and those who govern them will see the necessity of giving maximum cooperation to the Alliance for Progress." [22]

Cushing returned from his last trip to South America with his usual fund of stories. He told the airport greeters about three Peruvian peasant women, each carrying a five-gallon can of water on her head, who had knelt to kiss his ring. After the first two had done so, successfully balancing the cans of water in an unfamiliar maneuver, the "third poor woman leaned over and the can of water fell all over me. I got out of the car and did a striptease in public. I kissed the poor soul and said, 'You are the woman of all centuries because you are the first woman who ever poured five gallons of water on a cardinal.'"

chapter sixteen

"WHAT'S THE WORD FROM LAKE STREET?"

In 1962, Frankland W. L. Miles, who was presiding justice of the Roxbury District Court when Father Cushing directed the Propagation of the Faith, visited the prelate. Cushing dropped on his desk a copy of Murray Levin's new book, *The Compleat Politician,* and fingered a paragraph. "Look at this, Frank. Some folks think I am the most powerful person in the commonwealth, except for President Kennedy. How ridiculous!"

Politics and the Boston see are inevitably associated in the public mind. It is true that the Roman Catholic Church in Massachusetts has a great political potential, but its power is seldom overtly used. "What's the word from Lake Street?" is a query often heard in the corridors of the State House, and there is basis for the observation that mayors and governors quake at the possibility of a ranking prelate's disapproval or even indifference. There is nevertheless no convincing proof that the church as such has ever been a decisive power politically.[1] That is not to say, however, that the Catholic Church—especially in greater Boston—is not a powerful pressure group.

A veteran political observer wrote in 1951 in reference to Archbishop Cushing that only "a brash authority" would "license a bar or nightclub handy to one of his churches, convents, academies, schools or hospitals. Censors never consult him about a play, movie or book: they know he would be astonished to be asked to define for them the difference between morality and immorality.[2] Archbishop Cushing's views were by then so well known that sexy television programs had lower ratings locally than elsewhere.

There is little clear evidence that either O'Connell or Cushing changed the course of political history on any level. Neither—by direct action—ever destroyed political figures whom they disliked. An amendment to the State Constitution that O'Connell attacked was easily passed in a popular referendum. If Cardinal O'Connell exerted more influence at times when public policy encroached on private morality, it was partly because most politicians consider such issues as birth control or book-banning unimportant. Thus O'Connell was more potent in the moral sphere. Two hours after the House of Representatives convened following announcement of his opposition to a lottery bill, the legislators switched their votes, and the measure failed to pass. "These supine legislators," Curley wrote, "feared that unless they kowtowed to the cardinal's wish, they would be voted into retirement by their constituents." [3]

Cushing, like his predecessor, normally uses his power only in a limited range of issues. Like O'Connell, he rarely intrudes directly in the field of politics and often remains silent on controversial issues. Generally, however, he takes a strong position on social and moral issues.

Clergymen in Massachusetts are not encouraged to voice political opinions. Many legislators consider churchmen naive in the field of politics and government. Cushing is an exception. The main basis for the belief in his power, however, stems from the fact that about half of the residents of the commonwealth are Catholic.[4]

When Paul Dever, in his first public act as governor of Massachusetts, made a courtesy call on Archbishop Cushing in 1948, some observers thought he was showing the deference all public servants pay to the most powerful social force in the state. This was probably true. Those who interpreted it to mean that the governor recognized the church as the most potent political force in Massachusetts drew the wrong inference.[5] It is nonetheless true that both Democratic and Republican politicians on St. Patrick's Day, often formally dressed and carrying canes, march in the parade and try to be photographed with the Irish Catholic archbishop.

When a Catholic principle or interest is attacked, it is Catholic laymen rather than the prelate who rush to the State House. "The narrowly Catholic view," Katherine Loughlin writes, "is often not the only factor to be considered in a situation. It is loyalty of that kind which called for blind support of a dictator like Franco because he had been against enemies of religion, apart from whether he was a just ruler." [6] Such a blind view acknowledges no loyalties except to the hierarchy.

Archbishop Cushing was powerful. When he became cardinal he was, in a broad sense—John F. Kennedy perhaps excepted—the most influential person in New England and a figure of national and international importance. Nonetheless, he was always careful to separate church and state. "Catholicism is not a religious sect," he said. "It is not a cultural system. Catholicism is not a political program, neither is it a social theory. Catholicism is not even a body of truths to be believed or of precepts to be obeyed." He defined it as "a form of life; it is a life to be lived." *

Cushing never considered political leadership to be in the purview of the hierarchy. The clergy can enunciate broad principles, but laymen must implement practical programs. In an unnoticed address given in 1948 to a convention of the Union of Holy Name Societies, Cushing told the priests to remember that these key parish groups were lay organizations that must have lay leaders. "If this organization ever fails, I don't want it attributed to you, my brother priests, or to me. I have absolute confidence in our lay leadership. I never interfere with the plans of the archdiocesan officers." He urged an active approach to community problems in which Catholic men must not remain segregated.

Cushing was far more influential than O'Connell partly because of his engaging ways, partly because of the exposure he received. For decades he made thousands of fund-raising appearances before Catholic men's and women's clubs, societies, guilds, fraternities, and sodalities, and as a commencement speaker, his record is unmatched. He has also spoken before hundreds of non-Catholic groups. His opinion, accordingly, is highly valued in the nonpolitical sphere in minor as well as major concerns. When the Boston Braves moved to Milwaukee, Louis Perini, the owner, was severely criticized by New England fans. Cushing quieted them: "Perini's move might inspire those with civic pride in this city not to take too much for granted," he told a Communion breakfast assembly. "The move to Milwaukee could arouse the citizens . . . to undertake several courageous projects." One was razing "that monstrosity of an elevated structure," which disturbed the serenity of Holy Cross Cathedral. There was a little joke that Cushing, with all his power, could do nothing about getting rid of the elevated tracks. In 1949 he endorsed a proposal to remove the ironworks to no avail. A concession is made on special occasions. For the funeral of Cardinal O'Connell and the memorial mass for President Kennedy the trains slowed down to lessen the din.

Critics complained when Cushing spoke out on some issues. He has criticized the Taft-Hartley Act, asked for labor-capital harmony, and

---

* Cushing once said "Nor do we consider salvation a product to be marketed."

urged labor leaders to oust communists and fellow travelers from unions. He has drawn criticism from management for his defense of labor. In 1945 at the cathedral he said: "In all the American hierarchy, there is not one bishop, archbishop, or cardinal whose father or mother was graduated from college. Every one of our bishops and archbishops is the son of a working man and a working man's wife. This is one reason it has been so difficult . . . for the saboteur to divide our people and us." [7] He said the same thing at the ninth annual convention of the CIO in Boston in 1947 as an indication of his sympathy for labor.

In a talk to the National Steelworkers Convention in 1948, he repeated this theme: "I belong here because mine is the church of the working people." [8] Observing that a bishop belongs with the workers, he said the proposition was equally true in reverse. "You belong to me. The workers belong to the church. Organized labor needs organized religion." He ended with a ringing appeal: "Workers of the world, unite—with God—that under God you may the more . . . successfully and safely unite with one another." [9]

As a champion of Fair Employment Practices legislation, he invited the Catholic Industrial Welfare Conference to convene for the first time in Boston and told five hundred labor representatives at a conference sponsored by the Massachusetts branch of the Jewish Labor Committee that a person's right to work "must not be contingent on such irrelevant or accidental factors as race, creed, or color." In a speech to the sixty-third convention of the American Federation of Labor he gibed at critics by telling a story of a school girl who had been asked to identify Socrates.

"Socrates was a Greek," she said. "He was a great philosopher. People used to go to him for advice. Socrates gave lots of advice. It was good advice. They poisoned him to death." Cushing said he had been invited to a banquet to give advice but would be unable to stay for luncheon. The implication was plain.

"Thousands of my brother priests in too many parts of the world stand in daily danger of prison, exile, or death for giving advice on this subject [labor]," he said. (In a sermon he said two hundred thirty priests in Yugoslavia had been murdered between April 1944, and May 1946).[10] "The men who hold in Budapest and Zagreb the position I hold in Boston are in prison for having given advice on this subject." He referred to Archbishop Aloysius Stepinac of Yugoslavia and Joseph Cardinal Mindszenty of Hungary. Their counterparts in Czechoslovakia, Lithuania, and elsewhere in Eastern Europe were also victims of constant terrorism, he went on, "for giving advice that I stand here to give you this morning."

Cushing told the assembly that it had become fashionable to accuse religious spokesmen "who have the courage to give moral advice on public subjects, of meddling in politics." That reminded him of a story of a jitney preacher in Dixie, who gave his first sermon to a packed congregation in a new church.

"Last night I noticed several empty bottles along the roadside leading to this church. Brethren, I'm tellin' you-all that drinkin' is the work of the devil!"

"Dat's religion, brother!" a man shouted from the choir loft.

"This mornin'," the messiah went on, "as the collection plate was passed 'round I seen some of the brothers take out of their pockets dice along with cash. I'm tellin' you, brethren, that gamblin' is worse than drinkin' and is the work of the devil!"

"Dat's real religion, brother!" the same voice said.

"Brethren, I come to a very touchy subject. Some of your wives have been 'round to see me. They tell me you ain't home nights and that there's a lot of runnin' 'round goin' on in this parish. Brethren, that stuff is worse than gamblin' and drinkin' both. It's the work of the devil!"

The momentary silence was broken by the same voice from the balcony. "Brother, dat's politics!"

Cushing said it was real religion "when you give out advice the boys want and when you preach only what the big shots care to hear. But it is politics if you put your finger on the actual vices of the hour and dare to preach against the evils on which big shots are growing fat." He explained that the heroic clergymen of Eastern Europe were accused of politics because they warned the people and workers about red fascism and were jailed for exposing communism for what it was. "When they criticize, as we all do, the limitations of democracy, the abuses of capitalism, the moral faults of Americans and of the Western World—then 'dat's real religion.' When we point out the appalling disasters which follow red fascism, then, 'brother, dat's politics!'"

Cushing did everything he could for labor, and his efforts were appreciated. In 1953, the Catholic Labor Guild and the official labor movement of the commonwealth filled Boston Garden for "United Labor's Reception to Archbishop Cushing."

Cushing was sometimes asked by those in high places to influence legislation. In January 1957, hundreds of persons, including medical students from Harvard, Tufts, and Boston University, attended a hearing on the "Pound Bill" at the State House. Dr. Paul Dudley White said Massachusetts, because of its attitude toward using animals in research, had become the laughing stock of the enlightened states. He asked "which should be considered first, the child or a stray animal that is about to be killed?" Dr. White and other leading physicians told the Committee on Legal Affairs that the lack of animals in medical schools was threatening to stifle further advances in medicine and surgery. There was a moment of levity when the chairman, warning the assembly to refrain from outbursts, was interrupted by a barking dog in the rear of the auditorium.[11]

A speaker pinpointed the issue: "People don't seem to realize that medical and surgical scientists of this state have worked for their fellow men, women, and children for many years under a severe handicap. This handicap is the serious restriction of the use of animals in medical research." It was pointed out that promising but hazardous methods of diagnosis should be painlessly attempted first on abandoned dogs and cats. Dr. Sidney I. Farber said the iron lung, so important in the treatment of polio, was first tried out on a cat.

Bishop Frederic C. Lawrence of the Episcopal diocese of Massachusetts; Rabbi Zev K. Nelson, president of the Rabbinical Association of Greater Boston; and Monsignor Augustine C. Dalton, director of hospitals for the Archdiocese of Boston, urged passage of the Pound Bill. "Certainly the attempt to relieve human pain and to prolong human life is supported by every religious principle," Bishop Lawrence said. "If this bill fails to pass, much human suffering, which might be prevented, will continue, and if it becomes law . . . the lives of countless human beings may well be saved."

The proposal allowed medical institutions to obtain stray animals from pounds for research, after a six-day period.

A few days before the hearing, President Nathan Pusey of Harvard and Dean George Berry of Harvard Medical School went to the cardinal's residence to give a lengthy explanation of the importance of the Pound Bill. Archbishop Cushing listened attentively until Dean Berry finished talking.

"How many votes do you have?" he asked.

Pusey smiled. "That's why we came to see you, Your Eminence." It was one leader speaking to another, as Theodore H. White suggests in his book *The Making of the President, 1968* in reference to the Nixon-Humphrey campaign: "It was impossible, Nixon's private polls said, for him to carry Massachusetts unless, inconceivably, Cardinal Cushing, President Pusey of Harvard, and the Boston City Council all publicly endorsed him; and even then it would be chancy."

The Boston *Globe* reported the hearing: "Joining many state and national medical research organizations in the fight for the passage of the bill are Archbishop Cushing and the heads of the various colleges and universities in the state." One proponent was Dr. John W. Spellman (Cardinal Spellman's brother), a close friend of the prelate, and chief of surgery at St. Elizabeth's Hospital.

The *1957 Annual Survey of Massachusetts Law* has a pertinent comment: "For many years medical scientists have sought a liberalizing of the laws on the use of stray dogs and other animals for scientific investigation, experimentation and instruction. Vociferous and politically significant groups with newspaper support have always defeated past attempts to change the law. This year, however, a very well organized effort of the medical schools and medical scientists succeeded in securing the enactment of a new 'Pound Bill.' "

There was another item of interest when Cushing built Sacred Heart High School in Kingston in 1954. At his suggestion, William Callahan, chairman of the Massachusetts Turnpike Authority, built an access road to the school. In deference to Cushing, whose motor registration (inherited from Cardinal O'Connell) bore the number 80, the chairman officially named the new roadway Route 80. It is more commonly known in local circles as "the Bishop's Highway" and "the Pope's Road." Local residents quip that it is the first highway to be plowed and sanded during the winter.

Cushing's suite at Sacred Heart High School includes an office, living room, bath, bedroom, and an alcove for a guest. On the lower floor is the "cardinal's dining room," the scene of many convivial parties, especially during the Christmas season. The prelate has often stopped for luncheon or a light supper on trips to Hyannis Port on his visits to the Kennedys, usually in the company of close friends like Judge Francis X. Morrissey or the late John Drummey, the archdiocesan accountant. Cushing and his friends stopped in one mid-afternoon after having luncheon with the Kennedys. He asked a sister if she could whip up a few club sandwiches. "You know how it is with those rich folks, sister. They don't give you much to eat." At Cushing's request, the Sisters of the Divine Word arranged one wine banquet for a "retiring" secretary. Four years later, the secretary was still on the prelate's payroll.

Although Cushing rarely pushes his weight around, his influence is felt in scores of ways. A Boston College hockey player he knew was permitted to play, although he was on probation for failing grades. When Cushing was spotted in a reserved seat, the player was ordered to suit up in a hurry. A Boston police commissioner gave a South Boston policeman a premature promotion to sergeant on a hint from Cushing, who wanted to help out his large family. One afternoon the prelate waved to the officer as he drove past him.

"Hey, sergeant," he shouted, "how do you like your banana stripes?"

Some political observers find it significant that the late Governor Paul Dever, a personal friend of the prelate, gave the keynote speech at the Democratic National Convention in Chicago in 1956, nominating Adlai Stevenson, who counted among his strong supporters Congressmen John W. McCormack and John F. Kennedy, both also close to Cushing. It was further noted that when Stevenson's divorce became an issue during the 1952 campaign, Cushing approved an article in the *Pilot* that stated that a Catholic would be morally sound in voting for a divorced candidate under certain conditions. Stevenson used a reprint of the article in the 1956 campaign.

Despite these isolated instances, Cushing has shown no interest in becoming a backstage Cardinal Richelieu. More than once, however, he has admitted his influence on legislation. Years ago, with his South End parishioners in mind, he backed a low-cost housing project. "And then," he said, "the tenants turned out to be largely Negro Protestants."

In 1962, Senator Joseph L. Murphy, who was seeking reelection, circulated a letter signed "Richard A. Cushing," in which the writer urged his "very dear friends" to vote for the incumbent—a man who so gallantly had fought for the parochial school bus law and who had helped defeat the birth-control bill in 1948." Murphy's opponent, George V. Kenneally, Jr., was the son of an old South Boston friend of the prelate (known to him as "Gigi"). Kenneally and a friend, Thomas McDonough, went to the cardinal's residence, where a nun came to the door and summoned a young monsignor, who took them to a waiting room on the second floor.

"The cardinal will be right in," the monsignor said.

A moment later, the cardinal, whose luncheon was interrupted when the monsignor gave him Murphy's letter to read, came storming down the corridor, muttering, "Boy Scouts, that's what politicians are, Boy

Scouts." (During the gubernatorial campaign that year between Volpe and Peabody, the Boston *Traveler* in a cartoon had lampooned the latter as a Boy Scout.)

When Kenneally tried to kiss the cardinal's ring, the prelate angrily pulled away and swatted him on the shoulder. McDonough tried to bring peace by saying his brother was a curate in a Chelsea parish.

"Oh, he is, is he?" Cushing said. "Well, he won't be a curate for long. And now get out of here, both of you."

The men were halfway down the stairs when the cardinal leaned over the bannister. "Kenneally," he said, "Are you Gigi's son?"

"That I am," the candidate said.

"Well, you go to your rallies and get on radio and television and tell the public I didn't write that letter, that it was all a hoax."

Kenneally won the election.

Mayor Hynes credited Cushing for helping to promote "The New Boston," which got off to a towering start when the Prudential Life Insurance Company of America built a multimillion-dollar business complex in the Back Bay. After Prudential had invested thirteen million dollars in the foundation, its executives sought legislation assuring them of an equitable tax situation. Cardinal Cushing, who had earlier conferred several times with a Prudential vice-president (Fred Smith), told the press that the proposed center would mean "a new lease on the economic life" of Boston. He made it clear, however, that no politician had approached him in the matter (none would have dared). In 1969, Mayor Hynes in an article he wrote praised the cardinal "for the graceful, efficacious manner in which he soothed and/or converted some of the recalcitrants of the community and for his ability to open doors for Prudential which might otherwise have been 'tightly bolted.' For the cardinal, Hynes recommended "the medal of Civic Conciliator."

The cardinal is amused by stories of his alleged political power. According to *Time*, Speaker of the House John McCormack "is enraged by the persistent charge that he is under the thumb of the Catholic hierarchy. He resents his cloakroom nickname, 'The Archbishop,' as an insult to the Catholic Church."

Although Cushing was never known to have asked James Michael Curley for a favor while he was on earth, he was indebted to him later, he said. "One of the first things Jim Curley did in heaven was to get me my red hat." If Cushing ever asked McCormack for a political favor, it is not a matter of record.

chapter seventeen

CUSHING AND THE KENNEDYS

CUTTING OR AMUSING adjectives suggest the progress of the Irish in America from the potato-famine refugees to their urbane descendants: shanty, lace-curtain, cutglass, two-bathroom, Venetian-blind, then fruit-in-the-house-although-no-one-is-sick Irish and year-round-suntan Irish. The Irish themselves in their self-deprecating way have used these terms, especially since the turn of the century when many of them became moderately prosperous. There were still plenty of Irish cops and firemen, but there were also Irish teachers, doctors, lawyers, and engineers.

They teased themselves about being Irish partly because they didn't really feel Irish any more. The neighborhood wake with its whisky drinking in the kitchen had given way to the funeral home. Gone were the muckers, clodhoppers, harps, and micks. Phrases like "kitchen canaries" and "pot-wallopers" began to sound nostalgic, if not hackneyed. By the late 1940s Irish Catholics were scarcely conscious of the discrimination that had once cemented them into an enclave.

Nevertheless, it was still an uphill push for this ethnic group in a WASP community, as Cushing noted in the mid-1940s when he told John Gunther that "Catholics in Boston today have very little *economic* power." [1] The economic picture had not generally brightened since the mayoral days of John F. Fitzgerald, who asked a Boston banker why he didn't put Irishmen on his board of directors. When the banker said two of his tellers were Irish Catholics, Honey Fitz bristled. "Yes, and I suppose the charwomen are, too." [2]

The story of Fitzgerald's son-in-law, Joseph P. Kennedy, is an eloquent example of stupid discrimination. Kennedy's success in New York and Hollywood after his frustrating experience in Boston delineated the bias. Nobody asked the Kennedy daughters to become debutantes. The Cohasset matrons on the South Shore riviera snubbed Rose Kennedy, the "First Irish Family" *mère de famille* who was driven around in a plum-colored Rolls Royce. Joe Kennedy? Wasn't he a barkeeper's son? The Cohasset Country Club, which had accepted as a member Edward Moore—little more than a trusted errand boy and general factotum for the Kennedy's—blackballed Joe Kennedy. When a Boston newspaper called him an Irishman, Joe fumed: "I was born here. My children were born here. What the hell do I have to do to be called an American?" He could have added that his father was also born here, and that he was not merely a bartender. He was the head of P. J. Kennedy & Co., Importers.

In 1927 Kennedy put his family and domestics on a private railroad car and regally moved out of Boston, which, he said, was no place to bring up Catholic children. He spoke of "Irish guys" who would have become "big men" in New York or Chicago. In Boston, however, they were side-tracked. He was proud when his son Jack was elected to the Harvard Board of Overseers (Robert Kennedy failed in his later try). If an Irish Catholic could join that elite society, he could join anything.

By the mid-1940s, there was some rapprochement between successful Irishmen and prosperous WASPs, but Brahmin Beacon Hill haughtiness kept the conflict of interests between Irish Catholics and Yankee Protestants simmering. Then, abruptly, came the glamorous young Kennedys. The rise of "Fifth Avenue Catholics" like Jack Kennedy, with the accompanying decline of Jim Curley, changed the picture in Boston.

By this time Curleyism no longer dominated the Democratic Party, as John F. Kennedy would note: "The people these days are no longer impressed by the politician in the Homburg Hat with the flowery oratory and the big limousine and the entourage of hard-boiled hangers on." [3] A social historian noted another significant change: "The internal dialogue between Irish cleric and Irish politician had changed, and the external conversation across socio-religious boundaries had broadened most distinctively at the top of the hierarchy as younger men, the contemporaries of John F. Kennedy's managerial world, have replaced older men, the contemporaries of Al Smith with their traumatic experience of the urban ghetto." [4]

It was ironic that Curley, who had ended the political aspirations of John F. Fitzgerald, helped launch the career of Jack Kennedy, Fitzgerald's grandson.

When Curley, after being elected mayor of Boston for the fourth time, retired from Congress in 1946, the vacancy required a special primary and special election that year, giving Jack a chance to run for his first office. Among veteran politicians who supported Curley in his fourth bid for the mayoralty was Honey Fitz himself, who thus blocked any potential opposition to his grandson's candidacy for the vacancy in the Eleventh District. This was the only contribution Joe Kennedy would permit Fitzgerald to make in the campaign, for Joe didn't want his son identified in any way with oldtime politicians. "You wouldn't last three hours with Honey calling the signals," he told Jack. [5] He made another revealing comment: "With the money I'm spending, I could elect my chauffeur." [6]

One of Jack's most ardent supporters was Archbishop Cushing, already known as "the parish priest of the Kennedys." As auxiliary bishop, he had visited Jack and Joseph, Jr., when they were Harvard students. He was then closer to the boys than to their father. After World War II, Cushing became more actively associated with the Kennedys. During the war, when Joe was ambassador to the Court of St. James, his son, Joseph, a navy lieutenant, was killed during a volunteer mission over the English Channel. Kathleen, his sister, was the Marchioness of Huntington when she died in an air crash over Britain. Lieutenant (j.g.) Jack Kennedy, called "Shafty" by his shipmates, was wounded in a heroic action in the Pacific while commanding PT-109. Rosemary Kennedy, retarded from birth, was in an institution. The Kennedy family needed a spiritual adviser.

"At first Joe and I didn't hit it off at all," Cushing recalled, "but we got along well enough later. Actually, I had nothing to do with the Kennedys socially; they came from a different background. . . . I have spent most of my time with little people, trying to help them. But the Kennedys have been good to me, and as their spiritual adviser . . . I have been good to them."

Tragedy kept bringing them closer together. Before World War II, Joe Kennedy balked at sending Rosemary to an institution. "What can they do for her that her family can't do better? We'll keep her at home." By 1941, however, she had become more withdrawn and difficult to handle, and when physicians said she would never completely recover, Joe went to Cushing for advice. When the ambassador offered to build a special cottage for Rosemary at St. Coletta's School, Cushing vetoed the idea. "I told him that most of our land down there was wooded, and if we had a separate building, people would ask, 'Who lives there?' So he asked me where she could be placed, under similar good care, and I told him of another St. Coletta's out in Jefferson, Wisconsin, and he agreed to that."   ,

Ambassador Kennedy recalled, when he gave Cushing a check for ten thousand dollars for charitable purposes, that a quarter of a century before, when he had four children and not much money, his son Jack was seriously ill with scarlet fever. "I decided that if this boy got well, I would donate half of what I owned to charity. Well, he got well." In 1946 Jack Kennedy, in the name of his family, gave the archbishop a check for six hundred fifty thousand dollars—the largest contribution until then in the history of the Boston see. During the presentation, Jack lauded the work of the Franciscan nuns who were to staff the proposed Joseph P. Kennedy, Jr., Memorial Hospital in Brighton, a two-million-dollar project to which the Kennedys had donated the money. In an aside he mentioned that the Franciscan order had made the baptismal clothes for his brother Joe. After presenting the prelate with the check, he had to borrow taxi fare from him to get to his next stop.

In 1947, Representative John F. Kennedy, at a Veterans of Foreign Wars breakfast in Boston, announced gifts of a quarter of a million dollars. Auxiliary Bishop John Wright accepted for Cushing one hundred thousand dollars for St. Coletta's, and fifty thousand dollars for the Christopher Columbus Catholic Center in Boston's North End. A check for fifty thousand dollars each went to Boston Children's Hospital and the Associated Jewish Philanthropies.

Cushing said Joe Kennedy turned philanthropy into warm charity and that many hospitals, homes, and schools, as well as social institutions would remain as his monuments. The prelate was not referring to the Joseph P. Kennedy, Jr., Memorial Foundation alone. There were anonymous private benefactions when Joe Kennedy was satisfied of the need. "He's not an open-handed Santa Claus," Cushing said, "but once he's convinced that you're sincere and that you're working for a good cause, he'll do whatever he can to help you." But Joe demanded a full return for every dollar he gave to charity.

Cushing said many persons working for homes and hospitals in the archdiocese were paid by Kennedy, who, when he heard about their case, would call the prelate, who found employment for them. In this way, they kept their self-respect. "Once," Cushing said, "he gave me the money for some land down in Hanover, where we were going to build our St. Coletta's School for exceptional children. Then, when he was able to see what we were doing down there, he gave me another four hundred thousand for a dormitory." [7] Kennedy also supplied the cash for a gym at the Boy's Guidance Center and for a school in Hyde Park named for his son Joe. Over the years, Cushing found Joe Kennedy a remarkable person, "and I know that he's done many things for a great many people without ever looking for any credit or publicity." [8]

"I owe much to Joe Kennedy, his wife, and family," Cushing wrote. "But the greatest debt I owe to Joe himself. He taught me by example the gospel of hard work, a love for the truth, a hatred for sham, and total dedication to one's vocation in life." [9]

It was Kennedy's example, he said, that motivated his children. When a stroke put Kennedy in the hospital, he told Cushing his ambition was not to amass a fortune, "but to train my children to love and to serve America for the welfare of all people." Another time Kennedy told Cushing he was more interested in the success of his children than in making money.

Until he died, Jack Kennedy was also a regular donor to the Kennedy Memorial Hospital, and royalties from his best-sellers, *Why England Slept* and *Profiles in Courage,* went to Cushing charities.

As the war against Japan waned, "Shafty" Kennedy, a boyish looking, tousle-haired naval officer, was mulling over his future. He had on the surface changed little since graduating from Harvard College, where his father remembered him as "rather shy, withdrawn and quiet. His mother and I couldn't picture him as a politician. We were sure he'd be a teacher or a writer." [10]

Journalism seemed to be a suitable training ground for an author, Joe Kennedy's friendship with William Randolph Hearst got his son a job with the New York *Journal-American* to cover from a "GI point of view" the founding of the United Nations in San Francisco. It was the death of Joe, Jr., who had his sights set on a political career, that changed Jack's mind about continuing in journalism. "My brother was killed and Curley stepped out, and there it was, a matter of events, and so I ran for Congress." [11]

The year 1946 was pivotal in Massachusetts politics. The Irish, having dethroned the Yankees, were being pressed by other ethnic groups, especially Italians. Just as they had been scorned by other groups, the Irish looked down on the later immigrants, who found their best friend in Archbishop Cushing as they went through the familiar upswing pattern, moving from ditch to dock to semi-skilled jobs on their way to the professions.

On a state-wide level, the Republicans were still strong. In 1946 when Maurice Tobin, the incumbent, ran for governor against Lieutenant-Governor Robert Fiske Bradford, it was a direct confrontation between the Catholic Irish and the Brahmins. Bradford won.

Jack Kennedy was two generations and several million dollars removed from his grandfather Honey Fitz, and the political milieu had drastically changed. Poverty, persecution, and religious and racial problems were no longer issues to be exploited. Joe Kennedy had done everything possible to see that his children had remained untouched by prejudice, an attitude that caused one Curley-camp critic to observe that the Kennedys "have forgotten where they came from . . . they think like Republicans."

According to other observers, the Kennedys were individualists with no real concern for the Democratic Party as such. Jack, hailed as the first Irish Brahmin, was, according to Governor Dever, "a lousy Democrat" because he lacked the common touch. But Curley read success in his tea leaves: "Kennedy! How can he lose? He's got a double-barreled name. . . . He doesn't even need to campaign. He can go to Washington now and forget the primary election." [12]

Jack set up headquarters in a suite at the Bellevue Hotel down the corridor from a suite occupied by his Fitzgerald grandparents. Judge Francis Morrissey, former secretary to Governor Tobin, and Joseph Kane, a first cousin of Joe Kennedy, were brought in to mastermind the campaign. Kane was "the old pro" responsible for the coup that had unseated Congressman John F. Fitzgerald because of fraud during his election in 1917.

As an unknown, Jack Kennedy had trouble finding rallying places for his appearances. The chairman of the Boston School Committee, Michael J. Ward, and Archbishop Cushing helped by introducing him to large gatherings as a war hero. Ward arranged for Home School Association meetings in crowded sections of the congressional district, and Cushing, who had recognized Jack as a presidential possibility even before he ran for Congress, introduced him at parochial school meetings, Holy Name and Communion breakfasts, and patriotic assemblies. He won still more votes for the twenty-eight-year-old candidate, still wan from malaria, at Bar Mitzvahs and various Jewish assemblies. Cushing's blossoming ecumenical spirit was an asset for an unknown politician.

"Jack was terribly shy and had trouble making speeches," Cushing recalled, "so I told his campaign managers to stress the idea of question and answer presentations, and you remember how effective he became eventually in press conferences and, of course, in the debates with Nixon." Later the archbishop introduced Jack to audiences at charity and church functions when he ran for the United States Senate. Cushing called him his "nearest and dearest friend—the most cherished personal friend I ever had," and the feeling was largely reciprocated. "The President felt closer to him than to any other clergyman," Robert Kennedy said. Cushing often expressed admiration for Jack. "I have known talented people all my life, but the case of another John F. Kennedy will not occur." It was obvious why the prelate became so attached to a handsome youth who was so far removed from the old-liners. Jack, with his Harvard background, wealth, and charisma, was far removed from the red-necked, rough-cut ward bosses of the gaslight era.

But despite Cushing's early appraisal, Jack scarcely loomed as a strong candidate. He was a "poor little rich kid" running in a blighted ghetto. Once the political haunts of his grandfathers, Honey Fitz and Patrick Kennedy (the highly respected boss of East Boston), the Eleventh District had become a slum lined with ugly yards. Jack seemed out of place in the district.

The archbishop was irked when some of Kennedy's Irish opponents brought bigotry into the campaign. Jack's sister Kathleen, they lied, had married a descendant of Oliver Cromwell, who had slaughtered hundreds of Irish soldiers, priests, women, and children in the Massacre of Drogheda. The blarney failed, and Jack received nearly double the vote of his closest rival. A friend patted Honey Fitz on the back at the Bellevue celebration. "Congratulations, John F. Some day—who knows—young Jack here may be governor."

"Governor?" Fitzgerald smiled. "Some day that young man will be President of the United States." Honey Fitz climbed onto a table and danced as he sang "Sweet Adeline." *Time* magazine commented: "That was the last real touch of traditional Boston Irish American politics in the career of Jack Kennedy, the most phenomenally successful Irish American politician of them all."

The archbishop agreed with Fitzgerald's appraisal, thankful that only race and religion linked Jack Kennedy with oldtime politicians. Dr. John C. Bennett of the Union Theological Seminary in New York succinctly expressed the change: "Boston is aggressively Catholic largely because it is aggressively Irish, and it is aggressively Irish because its people have not quite overcome their sense of being strangers in a hostile land. If this is the case, is it not natural to wonder if some of the aggressiveness will be lost as the Irish cease to have this sense of being strangers, when John Kennedy rather than James Curley becomes a symbol of the Irish leader in politics?"

While Curley was in jail in Danbury, Democratic leaders in Boston and Washington urged President Truman to pardon him. Democratic House leader John W. McCormack of South Boston, a long-time friend of the archbishop, drew up a petition to the President and obtained prompt signatures from both Democratic and Republican representatives. On the floor of the House, McCormack handed the petition to Congressman Kennedy who, against the advice of close advisers, refused to sign it. It was the beginning of a long rift between the two Massachusetts congressmen. Visibly upset when he returned from the confrontation, Kennedy told an aide: "Well, I'm dead now." Yet it was a measure of the man. His distaste for Curleyism counterpoised political expediency.

In 1949, Curley, a fading idol, lost the first of three mayoral elections to John B. Hynes, his former clerk at City Hall. Curley resented the new order. When Jack Kennedy in 1952 defeated Henry Cabot Lodge for the United States Senate, Curley supported Lodge. A generation earlier it would have been unthinkable for Curley to have preferred a Republican Brahmin to an Irish Catholic. There was more affinity between Kennedy and Lodge than between Kennedy and Curley. In South Boston late one night, Jack looked out his car window at Lodge, who was in a car in the next lane. He greeted his opponent, who waved back and shouted above the traffic din: "Jack! Isn't this a hell of a way to make a living!" [13]

There was another switch in the 1952 campaign when the Republicans used religion as a prop. Writes Joe Kennedy: "All I ever heard when I was growing up . . . was how Lodge's grandfather had helped to put the stained glass windows into the Gate of Heaven Church in South Boston, and they were still talking about those same stained glass windows in 1952." [14] According to one Lodge man, "When Archbishop Cushing baptized that baby in a special ceremony just before the election, that cut the heart right out from us." [15] Reference was to the

Robert Kennedys, who had just had their first child. Another Lodge supporter said his candidate had been "spilled out of his Senate seat in an ocean of tea," referring to the afternoon receptions for women voters held by the Kennedy ladies. The teas were another symbol of the change that had transformed Boston politics of the tumultuous years into a smoothly operating political machine dominated by Jack Kennedy, not really Irish, but "Harvard Irish." One of the oldtime backslappers told Jack: "You're a damned carpetbagger!"

Cushing's associations with the Kennedy's increased over the years. In 1953, in St. Mary's Roman Catholic Church in Newport, Rhode Island, the archbishop, who officiated at the nuptial mass, waited for Senator Kennedy and Jacqueline Bouvier to approach the altar, as Luigi Vena sang "Ave Maria" and "Panis Angelicus," his melodious voice contrasting sharply with Cushing's grinding monotone as he read a special blessing from the Pope during the ceremony. His words, in retrospect, were tinged with sad prophecy as he spoke of the couple's future "with its hopes and disappointments, its successes and its failures, its pleasures and its pains, its joys and its sorrows [which] are hidden from your eyes. You know that these elements are mingled in every life and are to be expected in your own. And so, not knowing what is before you, you take each other for better or for worse, for richer or for poorer, in sickness and in health, until death."

More than eight hundred persons from high social and political circles crowded into the church after a crowd of three thousand had broken through police lines and pressed in on the bride-to-be. Nearly half that number attended the reception at Hammersmith Farm in Newport.*

When John F. Kennedy was reelected senator in a landslide in 1958 after losing his bid as vice-president two years earlier, he raised his sights on the presidency in 1960. Some opposition to his candidacy came from Catholics. Father Juniper Carol, a Franciscan from New Jersey, wrote a widely circulated article in *Human Events* titled "Kennedy for President? A Roman Catholic Priest Says No!"

"I would not be at all happy to have a Catholic as a candidate for President in the next election," a monsignor said, explaining that although prejudices had melted to the extent of having a Catholic

---

* In 1914 Cardinal O'Connell officiated at the wedding of Joseph P. Kennedy and Rose Fitzgerald in his private chapel. Cardinal Spellman performed the marriages of Robert and of Edward Kennedy.

elected, "bigotry is still so strong that the average Catholic candidate would feel he had to underplay not just Catholic but generally Christian ideas in order to 'prove' himself a 'patriotic' American."

During the campaign, when Joe Kennedy telephoned Cardinal Cushing to express his concern over the failure of many Catholic bishops to come out for his son, the prelate told him their passive role was no sign that they were against Jack, "but I'm not sure Joe was convinced." Cushing also said Joe Kennedy had criticized Cardinal Spellman for attending a dinner at which President Eisenhower and Vice President Nixon were present, thereby giving the impression of supporting Nixon. "The brains behind the campaign was Joe," Cushing said. "Hour after hour, he was on the telephone, calling people all over the country."

Years later, [16] Cushing said on a CBS telecast that he agreed with Jack Kennedy's assessment that priests and nuns usually voted Democratic, while monsignors and bishops voted Republican, as Cardinal O'Connell often did. During the 1960 campaign, Cushing had "a pretty good idea who was supporting Kennedy within the clergy, and who was against him." Not all bishops favored the young candidate, thinking it was not the time to elect a Catholic. Cushing, however, considered Kennedy the only person in public life capable of dissolving the prejudice that only a certain type could be President. "My idea was to do everything I could to help him. . . . I would have done the same for a Jewish . . . or a Negro candidate as long as I could break through what . . . was a sort of iron curtain."

Some fears about having a Catholic candidate in 1960 were justified. There was more anti-Catholic propaganda in circulation than there had been in 1928, when Al Smith made his bid. Its presentation, however, as Lally notes, was different: "In 1928 the public had been subjected to propaganda that truly was scurrilous. It was 'Maria Monk' all over again, with revelations of ecclesiastical excesses drawn out in morbid and totally offensive detail. Caricature and even pornography were commonplace." [17]

Paul Blanshard and others stoked the fire by warning that the Catholic Church in America had by 1960 easily become the largest single denomination. It had increased from forty thousand at the time of the Declaration of Independence to forty million; it had the largest private school system in the world, on every level from elementary school to university. Thus the possibility of having a Roman Catholic as President was bound to rekindle old embers of prejudice.

At Creighton University, where he received an honorary doctor of laws degree in June 1960, Cushing said: "I hope and pray that once and for all we'll be able to eliminate the religious issue from politics." He had spoken along this line for years.

As early as 1947, Cushing had criticized Protestant ministers and editors who were warning of the danger to American institutions if Catholics occupied places of trust and alleging that Catholicism inevitably leads to despotism. He mentioned a Protestant spokesman who implied that Catholicism prefers tyranny to a democratic system. "Wherefore, he warns those who love liberty to beware of and to bedevil the organized Catholic Church." In the same speech, Cushing lauded the Reverend Douglas Horton, a Congregationalist leader, for warning his brother ministers to have no part of "the renewed anti-Catholicism which this good neighbor fears is sweeping America," adding that he shared Cushing's fear. "In the long run, only America stands to suffer from artificially fostered bigotry of the type promoted by these men."

After 1956, Cushing often spoke of the revival of religious animosities. At dedication ceremonies at the Joseph P. Kennedy, Jr., School in Hyde Park in 1957, he said it upset him to hear that a Catholic cannot become President. "I believe that people of all faiths think the same, that religion has nothing to do with a man's holding public office, the highest or the lowest."

On May 11, 1958, Senator Kennedy was in Boston for the sesquicentennial dinner of the archdiocese. In his speech, Cushing said he had never met a church leader who sought the union of state and church in America, "and I, for one, want absolutely no part of anything of the kind." In his talk, Kennedy said the founding of the archdiocese in 1808 had not even been mentioned in Boston newspapers. "Now, in an age when disintegration is our constant companion, it is good to be a part of an institution which has shown its ability to survive." He said Cushing's "example of devotion and faith will remain long after his buildings have crumbled away."

As in the congressional and senatorial campaigns, the prelate helped Kennedy in every legitimate way possible without trying to steer him politically. "Senator Kennedy would resent having a cardinal, a bishop, or a priest telling him how to act," he said at Creighton University. "I don't know anyone who would try to tell him." There was no Catholic vote, he said. "The only things Catholics agree on is the dogma mentioned in the Apostle's Creed."

Cushing was a Kennedy confidant whose political judgment was prized. Before and during the campaign, he had private chats with Jack, offering him friendly advice without trying to become identified with him on any political issue. He said in an aside that when they sat down for a cup of coffee, he usually had to pick up the tab. "The poor fellow never had a cent in his pocket." Neither the candidate nor the prelate saw any advantage in their being seen or photographed together, especially in publications circulating outside Massachusetts. Kennedy, who referred to his Catholicism as his "religious affiliation," even as President avoided being photographed with Catholic churchmen, "but he summons the photographers whenever a Billy Graham or some other Protestant churchman comes acalling" [18]

Kennedy's religion was an asset, for it brought him into prominence, as Arthur Schlesinger notes: "Looking as Jack does and talking as he does, a liberal-minded senator from New England who went to Choate School and Harvard, and comes from a wealthy family—if he were just another Protestant, nobody would pay much attention to him." [19] The writer concluded that people were interested in him because, as a Catholic, he was controversial.

In the spring of 1959, before a Communion breakfast audience of fifteen hundred members of the Catholic Telephone Guild, the cardinal introduced Kennedy as "the next President of the United States." The hope of the country, he said, lay in elected officials of the senator's caliber. "Youthful in appearance, mature on every level, of tremendous potential, he has the courage, the great hope of the future; not yet on the heights, but still climbing."

Cushing tried to silence a whispering campaign among Catholics themselves that the candidate was not a practicing communicant. He submitted to the senator and his father a statement he drew up denying the rumor. "Don't publish it," they said. Later the candidate explicitly asked the prelate not to involve the church in the campaign in any way.

The church did become involved, however. Three bishops in Puerto Rico tried to persuade Catholics not to vote for Governor Luis Muñoz Marín because he advocated government-backed birth control and interfered with the teaching of religion in schools. Cardinal Spellman, fearing that this church-state dispute might hurt Kennedy's candidacy, sent the bishops to other pastures,[20] but not before Catholic baiters triumphantly proclaimed the controversy as an example of the hierarchy's meddling in secular affairs. Monsignor Lally noted that it was not until Archbishop Egidio Vagnozzi, apostolic delegate to the United States, and Cardinal Cushing "had been heard on the subject that both Catholics and their neighbors were able to breathe easier." [21]

Cushing, who condemned Governor Marín's repressive measures, said American tradition encourages the discussion of moral and religious questions in helping voters reach intelligent decisions. "Our attitudes on various moral questions, whether it be gambling or liquor, or sterilization or euthanasia, or whatever else, are expected to influence our decisions in choosing candidates and parties and programs in the public life of our country." It was the American tradition, however, he said, merely to bring moral questions to public attention "and leave to the conscience of the people the specific political decision which comes in the act of voting." [20] In brief, he was against the tactics of both Marín and the three bishops, all extremists.

More criticism came from Catholic spokesmen in the spring of 1959 after *Look* published an article in which Kennedy denied there was any conflict between his conscience and the Constitution. "Whatever one's religion in his private life may be," Kennedy said, "for the officeholder nothing takes precedence over his oath to uphold the Constitution and all its parts." [23]

America, the Jesuit weekly, attacked the statement: "Mr. Kennedy doesn't really believe that. No religious man, be he Catholic, Protestant or Jew, holds such an opinion. A man's conscience has a bearing on his public as well as his private life." *America's* editor charged that the candidate in his statement had, in effect, violated the Constitution by submitting to a religious test.

Other Catholic periodicals joined the attack. The *Catholic Messenger* asked why a Catholic candidate had to submit to questioning by the likes of Paul Blanshard and Glenn Archer, a member of Protestants and Other Americans United for Separation of the Church and State. The *Catholic Review* pinpointed the issue: "We do not ask the Baptist President or the Presbyterian President or the Episcopalian President . . . to declare his stand on the Constitution. Why had not Protestants requested a statement of loyalty from Secretary of Agriculture Ezra Taft Benson, a Mormon bishop?" The *Review,* in rebuking Kennedy for submitting to a loyalty test for Catholics only and bowing to bigotry, said he had gone to extremes as an effort to placate the bigots. Theodore Sorensen writes that the candidate was called "a poor Catholic, a poor politician, a poor moralist and a poor wordsmith. Finally his closest friend in the hierarchy . . . Cushing, Archbishop of Boston—a man in whom the seeds of liberalism had been richly nourished through association with and pride in the senator—came publicly to his defense, stating that Kennedy's 'simple candor . . . has given way to other people's interpretations.' " [24]

Cushing, in a talk to the Lantern Club of Boston, a group of advertising representatives of national magazines, had said it was "a great pity that questions of this sort still have to be answered at all. They are certainly ridiculous when presented to a person who has been in public life as long as Senator Kennedy. The candidate's patriotism," he went on, was "written in dramatic and dangerous actions during the war; they were challenged by enemy conflict and finally honored by citation." Adding that Kennedy's patriotism had also been tested in peace, the prelate said that "from my personal knowledge of him I can say without hesitation that Senator Kennedy will always perform his public duties to the highest standards of conscience and his oath of office."

When Catholic publications blasted Kennedy, Bishop John Wesley Lord, a Protestant, told a New England Methodist conference that the criticism had surprised the senator. Lord praised Cushing for coming to his defense, and noting his remark that nothing would take precedence over his oath of office, he added: "If a man is willing to do this, I do not see how his conscience in other matters can be called into question."

When a national magazine asked Cushing to write an article titled "Should a Catholic Be President?" he submitted his draft to Senator Kennedy. Concerned about whether the piece would reassure non-Catholics, Kennedy let several articulate Protestant critics of Catholicism read it. "All agreed that publication of the article would be unwise," Sorensen writes.[25] When the candidate telephoned the prelate to ask him to kill the article, he did not mention that he had submitted it to men with whom the cardinal had often clashed. According to Cushing, Kennedy told him "the piece was the best of the kind he had read so far. 'But I don't want to get you involved. So forget the whole thing.' " Kennedy, meanwhile, refused to retract a word of the Look piece. "I gave this interview on my own initiative because I felt that the questions which were raised were matters which reflect honest doubts among many citizens."

On September 12, the senator answered questions put to him by the Greater Houston Ministerial Association at a televised meeting held in the ballroom of a Houston hotel. He said there would be no church

interference with his public actions, and that if there were, he would
oppose it. If the church tried to influence him "in a way which was
improper or which affected adversely my responsibilities as a public
servant, sworn to uphold the Constitution, then I would reply . . .
that this was an improper action . . . that it was one to which I could
not subscribe." He also said that if he found any conflict between his
conscience and the presidential responsibilities he would resign. He
repeated his belief in the separation of church and state and his belief
in a nation "where no Catholic prelate would tell the President
[should he be Catholic] how to act, and no Protestant minister would
tell his congregation for whom to vote—where no church or church
school is granted any public funds or political preference." He clearly
stated his position as he confronted the bristling group of Protestant
ministers at the Rice Hotel, determined "to kill the myth that a Catholic President would be an errand boy for the Pope and would trade
the gold in Fort Knox for a supply of Holy Water." [26] "I am not the
Catholic candidate for President. I am the Democratic Party's candidate . . . who happens also to be a Catholic. I do not speak for my
church on public matters, and the church does not speak for me."

Would he ask Cardinal Cushing, "his hierarchical superior . . . to
forward his endorsement of separation of church and state to the
Vatican?" He curtly answered: "May I just say that as I do not accept
the right of any . . . ecclesiastical official to tell me what I shall do in
the sphere of my public responsibility . . . I do not propose also to
ask Cardinal Cushing to ask the Vatican to take some action." [27]

Cushing backed the senator's position in the Houston confrontation, just as he had defended his statements in *Look*. There was general
approval of Kennedy's handling of the Houston Council of Churches
interview, although some judicial Protestants sincerely questioned the
ability of a Catholic President to resist church pressure in such matters
as federal aid to parochial schools. Kennedy reassured them: "There
can be no question of federal funds being used for support of parochial
or private schools. It's unconstitutional under the First Amendment as
interpreted by the Supreme Court. I'm opposed to the federal government's extending support to sustain any church or its schools." [28] As
for buses, lunches, and other fringe matters, he said that such issues
were social and economic, rather than religious, and that each case
should be judged on its merits within the law as interpreted by the
courts.[29]

The cardinal agreed and backed Kennedy when he shocked many

Catholics by saying he flatly opposed having an ambassador to the Vatican. "Whatever advantages it might have in Rome—and I'm not convinced of these—they would be more than offset by the divisive effect at home." [30] President Truman had failed in his effort to send General Mark Clark to the Vatican as a full ambassador when a militant group (Protestants and Other Americans United for Separation of Church and State) blocked the appointment.

The senator's wit lifted him over thorny situations during the 1960 campaign. In one forum someone asked whether he thought a Protestant could be elected President in 1960: "If he is prepared to answer how he stands on the issue of the separation of the church and state, I see no reason why we should discriminate against him." [31]

One night Kennedy spoke at the Waldorf-Astoria at a banquet to raise funds in memory of Al Smith, whom the previous speakers—Mayor Robert Wagner and Governor Nelson Rockefeller—had been praising. "Despite his successful record as governor," Kennedy said, "despite his plain-spoken voice, the campaign was a debacle. His views were distorted. He carried fewer states than any candidate in his party's history. He lost states which had been solid for his party for half a century or more." Kennedy added that the candidate had lost his own state, which he had governed so well. "You all know his name and religion." The assembly roared with laughter when Kennedy said, "Alfred M. Landon, Protestant." [32]

Nixon was at the dinner. Kennedy drew another laugh when he said: "Cardinal Spellman is the only man so widely respected in American politics that he could bring together amicably, at the same banquet table, for the first time in this campaign, two political leaders who are increasingly apprehensive about the November election—who have long eyed each other suspiciously and who have disagreed so strongly, both publicly and privately—Vice President Nixon and Governor Rockefeller." At the time Nixon and Rockefeller were daggers drawn. [33]

Kennedy made it clear that he did not want to be labeled a Catholic or the son of Joseph P. Kennedy. What a writer said of him could in every particular be applied to Cushing: "He wanted to accomplish the impossible by eliminating historic memories of fear and distrust from the minds of Americans. Before his death, and perhaps even prior to his election, he was to do more to blunt the ancient mutual hatred of Catholics and non-Catholics than any American had ever done." [34]

The cardinal raised campaign funds, tapping heavy donors. One was

Joseph A. DeMambro, who provided the sound equipment for Kennedy's New Hampshire tour. "Needless to say," Ted Reardon wrote DeMambro on September 16, 1960, "your cooperation contributed in great measure to the success of the trip." Jack Kennedy, who later quipped that his father could not afford a "landslide," was more serious when he wrote DeMambro early in 1960: "You have perhaps by now read that I have announced my intention of being a candidate at the July Convention. This is a tremendous undertaking and will require a huge personal effort. It will also require that large amounts of money be expended on my behalf for media, travel, and all kinds of activities to advance my candidacy. The federal laws deny me the full use of my family's resources, therefore I will be compelled once again to look to my good friends like you for help.

"To this end I have asked Howard Fitzpatrick * and others to take over this burdensome problem. They have formed a committee of which John Ford is treasurer. They will contact you in a few days to enlist your aid."

Three months later, Ford thanked DeMambro for a generous donation. It was one of scores of donations for which Cushing was responsible.

A few days before the election, Cushing addressed the National Council of Catholic Women in Las Vegas. Dr. Willard Givens, director of education of the Supreme Council of Scottish Rite Masons, Southern District, had charged that Cushing had induced Senator Kennedy to change his vote on federal aid to education. Cushing called the statement a colossal lie. "Never have I telephoned Mr. Kennedy in Congress, at his home, or anywhere else. Never have I requested him or any other person to change his vote on any matter." [35] In one instance, however, Cushing did use his influence.

In mid-March 1959, the cardinal, accompanied by Mayor Hynes, Judge Morrissey, and Dr. Richard Wright, flew to Pittsburgh to see John Wright invested as bishop of that city. Cushing knew Hynes was a friend of the Roman Catholic governor, David Lawrence of Pennsylvania, who had been mayor of Pittsburgh. Cushing also knew that Lawrence felt that Kennedy was inexperienced and that, because he wanted a winner, was uncertain of his chances of being nominated or elected.

"See if you can get Lawrence to come to this hotel at nine o'clock

---

* Sheriff Fitzpatrick of Suffolk County, a caterer who serviced Cushing benefits, was a generous donor to Cushing charities.

tomorrow morning," Cushing told Hynes. Lawrence called the mayor back at four A.M. "I just got in," he said. Nevertheless, after four hours' sleep, he conferred with the cardinal at the hotel. Cushing's party concluded that the prelate had told Lawrence how crucial Pennsylvania's vote would be on the first ballot at the convention. In any case, Lawrence swung his support to Kennedy.[36]

The cardinal was delighted with Kennedy's victory, for it not only erased the bitterness of Al Smith's 1928 defeat but also capped more than a century of Irish social and political activity. "If only subconsciously," wrote Lally, "each Catholic was aware that at that moment a stigma of second-class citizenship had been removed." [37] Cushing observed that "what Catholic men in public office do and say, and even in some measure their conduct in their personal lives, will have enormous influence on what their fellow citizens think of the . . . Church." As President, Kennedy had one basic concern, Cushing said in a 1964 telecast: "What kind of image am I going to make in history as the first Catholic President of the United States?" [38]

In Cushing's opinion, Kennedy "made for history the greatest possible image. He couldn't have left a better impression than by laying down his life for all of us." The prelate said that when Kennedy made his statement, "he was probably thinking of a future Jewish President or a future President of any faith and nationality. I recalled this and much more during the course of his funeral, and I said that, for all the people of the United States, he has left for history the greatest image that could be bequeathed to the future." [39]

A sociologist, noting that the oppressed Irish Catholics had once needed a leader like Curley, along with patrician persecutors, "to fuse their ethnic, religious and social loyalties into political solidarity," added: "The efficacy of . . . Curley's political ethos died when . . . Kennedy achieved the Presidency." [40] Irish Catholics finally had their first statesman. "The Kennedys," wrote Joe McCarthy, "have power, money, glamor, and—what is more important to the Irish—class and respectability. By identifying with them, the Irish of Massachusetts can fulfill in fantasy the American dream of economic, social and political success." [41]

Cushing noted that responsible Republicans did not approve any of the anti-Catholic propaganda distributed during the campaign by bigots—both Democratic and Republican—and that Nixon had kept a promise made at the beginning of his campaign: "Religion will be in this campaign to the extent the candidates . . . talk about it. I shall never talk about it." [42] The cardinal praised him for his gentlemanly tactics: "If I were asked to name the Goodwill Man of 1960," he said a year after the election, "I would unhesitatingly give the accolade to Richard Nixon. . . . During the recent campaign, which tested and taxed all his powers, physical and mental, he never exploited the religious or any other issue that would tend to divide the American people." [43]

On the eve of the inaugural, the cardinal told the National Catholic Camping Association in Boston that he had arranged to stay in Washington with Archbishop Patrick A. O'Boyle, "because I think one of the things it takes to become an old soldier is to stay away from the big guns." At three A.M. on January 19, the prelate flew with Monsignor George Kerr, and when a storm forced the plane back to New York, they took a bus to Pennsylvania Station, where no redcaps were available because of a strike. "I spent more than an hour sitting on my suitcase waiting for a train. . . . In an attempt to get warm, I ordered some oyster stew . . . that did not have any oysters in it." [44] The two churchmen faced the prospect of sitting up all night in a coach until two Boston men invited them to share their roomette. Cushing didn't have enough money to pay for the accommodation. "It's a good thing Kerr was going to stay with relatives when he got to Washington, for it was Monsignor who paid," he said.

Archbishop O'Boyle, who had stayed up all night waiting for them, served them coffee (which he made himself) in the rectory. "Now, you get the worst coffee in the world in convents and the second worst in rectories," Cushing recalled, "but Bishop O'Boyle makes one of the best cups of coffee I ever had. He has the magic touch. He told me I would not be able to get any sleep because I was scheduled to say mass at the National Shrine of the Immaculate Conception."

From the mass—well attended despite a storm—the prelate went to the inaugural, "and I have never been so cold in my life. When I got to the inaugural, the crowd was assembled, and I was sitting next to a protocol officer of the State Department. Just before I got up to give the invocation, I said to him, 'There's a fire in that lectern, can't you see the smoke?'"

The official dismissed it as "just steam."

"Well," Cushing said, "I guess it's being made by the hot air from all these politicians." The thought crossed his mind that a bomb was hidden in the lectern. "I said to myself, here's where I steal the show. If it's a bomb . . . I'm going to land over on Washington Monument." [45]

Senator John Sparkman, chairman of the Inaugural Committee,

introduced Cushing after Marian Anderson sang "The Star-Spangled Banner." During the invocation, smoke continued to curl around his feet, and behind him he noticed a fireman with an extinguisher. "I decided that if the extinguisher went off, the spray would turn me into one big icicle. I've heard of a lot of people being under fire, but this was the first time I found myself . . . over a fire. I finished my little assignment." As he spoke, he was distracted by Secret Service men huddling around his knees.

An electric heater, placed inside the lectern to keep the speakers' feet warm, was housed behind a locked panel, and it took time to find the man with the key (Joseph DeMambro). By then, as *The New York Times* reported, "smiles were spreading through the gathering of notables. President Kennedy and ex-President Eisenhower shared in the relief and the smiles." Eighty million people saw the mechanical failure on their TV screens.

Cushing, who had been more puzzled than worried about the smoke wafting up, later jokingly introduced DeMambro at a meeting as "the man who tried to electrocute me." After he asked God's blessing for the nation's thirty-fifth President, he was followed by Archbishop Iakavos of New York, head of the Greek Orthodox Archdiocese of North and South America; Dr. John Barclay of the Central Christian Church of the Disciples of Christ in Austin, Texas, which Vice-President Lyndon Johnson attends; and a rabbi. All offered their prayers for the new chief executive. Then the great American poet, white-maned Robert Frost, hatless like Cushing, recited an original composition from memory when he was unable to read his dedicatory poem in the sun's glare.

Never before had so many Americans seen Cushing's ascetic, seamed face and heard his voice, which McGeorge Bundy called "the harshest in Christendom." The prelate didn't mind, "I was no sooner home than I got a message from a man in California: 'Your prayer was too long. You saw smoke coming up from the podium when you were reciting the prayer. It signaled the fact that the devil was asking for equal time, because where there's smoke, there's fire.' Well, I took an awful lot of kidding on that, I'm telling you." [46]

A story has made the rounds that some Boston confessors require penitents, as atonement for their sins, to sit through one of Cushing's sermons, "which seem to be measured in units of eternity rather than time." Cushing, who can laugh at himself, enjoyed the ribbing he received because of his long, ear-shattering inaugural prayer. "Someone told me I was fine for about fifteen minutes," he wrote in the *Pilot*, but when I get to the half-hour mark, you are more interested in physical survival than spiritual sustenance. From then on, you just live in hope. . . . I will have to bring someone along with me at future engagements with a bell or a buzzer. When I hit the fifteen-minute limit, I will get the gong." [47] Once, when Cushing spoke too long at a drum and bugle corps competition, the band drowned out his words by striking up a march. In a *Pilot* column he wrote: "As most of you know, I am a man of a few million words. I think this is a family trait. All the Cushings were great talkers."

Years later, the cardinal had a more somber recollection of his invocation at the Kennedy inaugural. "I thought it was a pretty good prayer, but less than three years later Jack was killed. So it didn't seem to do any good."

During Cushing's second trip to Peru in 1961, Ambassador Kennedy suffered a stroke while playing golf at the Palm Beach Country Club. Earlier in the day, President Kennedy, after a trip to Venezuela, Colombia, and Puerto Rico, had stopped in Palm Beach to see his parents on his way to Washington. He heard of the stroke an hour after returning to the White House. That afternoon, accompanied by his brother Bobby and sister Jean, he flew to Florida on *Air Force One*, joining other members of the family at the bedside of his father, who had received the last rites. The founding father recognized his family the day after he was stricken. Then, when pneumonia developed, surgeons performed a tracheotomy on Christmas Eve to ease his breathing.

A few days before Christmas, the cardinal, who had rerouted his return trip from Peru, rushed to the hospital, thinking that the ambassador's coronary attack had resulted from overwork during the nomination and election of his son. Cushing in the hospital bedroom waited until Joe Kennedy awoke. He blessed him. "Keep up your courage, Joe; you're going to be all right." Later Cushing told reporters Kennedy had answered: "I know I am."

"The cardinal," writes Richard Whalen in his biography of Joe Kennedy, "had interpreted hopefully the guttural sounds he heard. These, along with smiles, frowns, and movements of his left hand, were the extent of Kennedy's ability to communicate." [48] And he was crippled, paralyzed along his right side.

"Actually," Cushing said afterward, "when I saw him I wasn't sure he would pull through. He didn't look well at all. But you could never discount the courage this man has. I could tell that he wasn't ready to give up; he had too much courage for that." [49]

As the cardinal prayed, Joe Kennedy appeared to be in a coma. "Mr. Ambassador," Cushing said, "you have been through many crises in your life. You have survived them all. You can conquer this one if you have the will and the courage of the past. All I can give you is prayer, and especially the prayers of the retarded children whom you have helped so generously. Those of the latter will fall from innocent lips and stainless souls. They will be answered."

Later, the cardinal said: "Whether he understood me or not, I do not know, for he was then within the shadow of death. But, thank God, he did survive and never since did I hear a word of discouragement or a gesture or complaint as he fought his way back to health in mind and body."

By New Year's Day 1962, the ambassador was past the crisis, just a week after his wife and children had remained for hours at his bedside, afraid the end was near. By May he was well enough to move to New York, where he took therapy in a clinic for several weeks before going to Hyannis Port. Here the cardinal often visited him, going with him on cruises in the *Marlin*. Kennedy always made sure that the prelate's favorite food, lobster, was in the refrigerator.

"He was always conscious of time," Cushing recalled. "He would spend just so long on the boat and, when the time was up, he would motion for us to go back to shore. There was always something he had to do, and he didn't want to waste a minute." [50]

In the spring of 1962, Cushing told a thousand members of the Society of St. Vincent de Paul of his plans to bring a hundred Cuban refugee children from Miami to Massachusetts. A few months later they were in the care of Spanish-speaking Marist nuns in a convent in Framingham. The sisters taught them English and sent them to public schools to prepare them for placement in foster homes.

The prelate was a sponsor of and adviser to the Cuban Families Committee, made up of friends and relatives of those captured at the time of the abortive invasion in April 1961 of their native land at the Bay of Pigs. The ransom, which Castro demanded for the release of sixty of the more seriously wounded of 1,112 prisoners, among whom were three priests, had to come from private sources, since the United States could not officially deal with Castro in a matter stemming from the attempted invasion. Before the situation was resolved, the Cuban dictator had raised the ante to include fifty-three million dollars in drugs and medicine.

At five A.M. on the day before Christmas, a negotiator for the release of the captives called Attorney General Robert Kennedy from Miami, saying the ransom had to be raised by three o'clock that afternoon. Kennedy telephoned the cardinal at Lake Street.

"Castro wants an extra two million nine hundred thousand dollars, and everybody wants to get the prisoners home to Miami by Christmas," he said. *Time* reported: "Bobby had good reason to think he could depend on Cushing. The cardinal had known Joseph P. Kennedy for twenty-five years; old Joe managed to say his first words after his paralytic stroke last winter when Cushing visited him in Palm Beach. Cushing baptized Caroline Kennedy,[51] both of Teddy's children, and one of Bobby's sons."

The cardinal, who promised to help raise the money, told Bobby to call him back. He had already raised two hundred thousand dollars for a tractors-for-prisoners deal, which fell through. "I was saving the money until I was sure it would be used for the purposes intended. It was my reserve." [52]

In a massive telephone operation, Cushing tapped donors for a million dollars, and General Lucius Clay raised the rest of the money, soliciting contributions from major American corporations. The largest single donation Cushing received was a thousand dollars. Not a cent came from Joe Kennedy. "I do not believe that he was aware of my fund raising." The money came from benefactors of the St. James Society, who, during the previous five years, had donated more than a million dollars a year for missions. "I, too, wanted the prisoners home with their loved ones before Christmas Day," Cushing said.

Early in January 1963, a reporter called him: "We have a story that you are the donor and that you are head of Catholic charities for the whole country."

"They'll be saying next that I'm head of Fort Knox," Cushing said. Asked if he headed the Kennedy Foundation, he added: "Mister, I wish I did!"

The Boston *Globe* hinted that there might be a Republican probe of the ransom money, which could turn into a congressional investigation after a rumor circulated that the money had come from a racketeer. Although it had been simple blackmail on Castro's part, none of the principals thought of it in that light. Cushing did not like the idea of paying ransom. "However, we are living in an entirely new age and I think the payment saved the prisoners from languishing in prison and possible death. I wouldn't call it ransom, just an exchange." He was delighted when the prisoners were on American soil by Christmas

Eve. Three days later he received a telegram from the Cuban Families Committee inviting him to attend a reception given by President Kennedy for the Cuban Freedom Fighters.

On January 12, 1963, a newspaper quoted Cushing as saying he would go to Cuba for the release of twenty-three other American prisoners, "if I were invited by Castro. I'd go to China if I were asked to intercede for Richard Fecteau and John Downey."

The day before, in his column in the *Pilot*, Cushing identified himself as the mysterious benefactor only to stifle "rumors crediting this gift as coming from sources with which I have no identification. I alone am responsible for the collection of this extraordinary sum." Later he further unraveled the story: "I warned those in charge of negotiations with Castro that he was going to hold us up for money. I was head of the Human Family Relief Committee trying to get these men out of Cuba. . . . I was telling the poor Cuban people there isn't a man in the United States who could collect sixty-two million dollars. That's what Castro wanted." He added that something had to be done, "because these men were dying a slow death."

Through the Kennedy administration, he explained, he established contact with a lawyer who had dealt with Khrushchev in releasing two CIA agents from Russian prisons. "So he began to do business with Castro for sixty-two million dollars worth of supplies, much of them drugs." Cushing said Castro had the United States "over a barrel."

He had another comment later: "Whether we should have gone into Cuba at the time of the Bay of Pigs without umbrella support by the Air Force, I don't know. I have my own reasons for believing why we didn't go in there, and, if my reasons are correct, it's a good thing we didn't, because by this time we'd be in a third war if we weren't all wiped out." He told this story early in 1964 to a mixed congregation in a Methodist church in Sudbury, Massachusetts.

The year 1962, one of the most eventful in the prelate's career, was climaxed by a significant political struggle and the opening of Vatican Council II.

The senatorial contest between Edward Kennedy and Edward Mc-Cormack was hailed as a test between the Montagues and Capulets of Massachusetts. It was a battle that forced the cardinal to divide his loyalties at a time when Democratic politics in the commonwealth was a tangle of economic, religious, and social alliances.

Cushing's interest in Ted Kennedy was obvious. He had persuaded Ted to visit Latin America to broaden his knowledge and understanding of hemispheric developments.

"Look here, Ted, please go!" Cushing said. "The on-the-spot impressions you gain will be of great value."

There was a saying that running against the Kennedys in Massachusetts was like running against the Catholic Church. This time, however, Kennedy's opponent in the primary was an able nephew of Speaker John W. McCormack and a classic example of a successful Boston Irish Democrat. The close ties between the cardinal and the Speaker of the House of Representatives were bolstered by their common allegiance to their beloved South Boston. Once, when asked whether he liked John McCormack, Cushing said: "Of course we're friends. I'm from South Boston, he's from South Boston." Ed McCormack and Ted Kennedy, moreover, represented the New Boston Irish, of whom Cushing was proud, even when his seminarians and young priests privately called him "the Curley of the hierarchy." Their collective backgrounds included "Harvard, Annapolis, and the University of Virginia, sport cars and chic wives, jet trips to Europe and Brooks Brothers jackets." [53]

Kennedy represented "floating" Catholics, while McCormack was a "parish" Catholic. Accounting for the transition from parish to floating were such factors as mobility, the drift to the suburbs, and the prosperity of many of the Irish. When Cushing was a priest, Catholics were identified by long-time family association with parishes and a common interest in church suppers and parochial schools. Much of that had changed by 1962, when "mobile" Catholics like the Kennedys contrasted with "rooted" brethren like the McCormacks. Stewart Alsop classified Ted as one of the "rich, wellborn Eastern seaboard politicians whom he called 'People's Dukes.' " [54]

Noting that there had been a social ascendancy among Irish Catholics during the two decades preceding the 1962 contest, Professor Earl Latham says, "The Kennedys are better examples of it than the McCormacks." He points out that the history of politics in Massachusetts since the turn of the century has in many respects been an acculturation of second, third, and fourth generation Irish Americans to the Yankee Protestant political ethic. Thus politicians like Kennedy, who have been able to slough off the traditions of shanty politics, have done well at the polls, even when scorned by old-line politicians, because Irish Americans in general sought to disassociate themselves from these traditions. Ted Kennedy, like his brother Jack, was obviously a new charismatic political product with no tinge of Curleyism. The McCormacks were less marketable. During the 1962 contest, a worker said the Irish Catholic middle class sought to identify themselves with the glamorous Kennedys.* "When they hear Eddie McCormack speak, they think of South Boston and their parents' homes. When they see Ted Kennedy, they think of Palm Beach, Beacon Hill, the Virginia fox-hunting country, and their children's future." [55]

McCormack seemed better qualified for the office, but he lacked his opponent's vote-getting ability. A poll taken in Massachusetts early in 1962 showed that Attorney General McCormack would defeat Ben Smith (the incumbent who filled the vacancy when John F. Kennedy resigned his Senate seat) for the Senate nomination in the Democratic primary, but would lose to the Republican candidate, George Lodge, son of former Senator Henry Cabot Lodge, whom Jack Kennedy had unseated in 1952. The same poll showed that Ted could beat both McCormack and Lodge.[56]

One legislator, after a sit-down with Ted, said, "Teddy's been an assistant district attorney for a year or so. He's completely unqualified and inexperienced. He's an arrogant member of an arrogant family." He grinned. "And I'm going to be with him."

Ted went out of his way to have himself photographed with the cardinal when he ran against a fellow Catholic, while McCormack, who had often been photographed with Cushing, did not think such material should be used in a political campaign. The prelate gave Ted no overt support during the contest, nor did he later when Ted ran against Lodge. When Robert Kennedy and Lawrence O'Brien went to the cardinal to solicit aid for Ted, he reminded them that Jack Kennedy had not been elected by Catholics and also that in 1962 a Harvard-educated Episcopalian grandson of the founder of Groton was running for governor against an Italo-American Catholic (Endicott Peabody versus John Volpe). And, paradoxically, Peabody was a Democrat; Volpe, a Republican. Peabody won.

The Peabody-Volpe battle put a further strain on Cushing's loyalties. He knew that President Kennedy wanted to dislodge Volpe, the incumbent. There had been no Democratic governor since Joseph Ely was elected in 1932. Peabody, who was worried about the negative effects of ethnic and religious aspects of the contest, was pleased when thousands of copies of a warning against "voting your own kind" were reprinted from a *Pilot* editorial written by Monsignor Lally.[57] The editorial mirrored Cushing's support of Peabody, who, meanwhile,

---

* Senator Edward Kennedy lost some of his glamor after the 1969 tragedy at Chappaquiddick.

gave persons with Irish Catholic and Italian Catholic names important posts in his organization. His campaign got all the impetus it needed when Thomas O'Neill, Kennedy's successor in his old Cambridge congressional seat, became Peabody's campaign manager. The campaigns of Ted Kennedy and "Chub" Peabody were combined with common billboard advertisements and joint appearances. Ted's donors and workers helped push the Yankee Protestant uphill to victory.

Backstage, the cardinal solicited support for Ted Kennedy, introducing him to well-heeled friends. Ted hit it off with Joseph DeMambro, who gave him a recording machine to improve his elocution. "I am never off that recording machine of yours," Ted wrote to Joe on March 7, 1961. "If I ever develop into a Clarence Darrow, I know whom to thank." In mid-November 1962, Ted again thanked his friend: "I want you to know how much I appreciate your very generous assistance to my campaign. I am deeply grateful for your support."

In the contest, in which Ted received 79 per cent of the vote, the parish versus floating Catholic issue did not appreciably affect the election. McCormack, indeed, did well only among the academic community, the wealthy non-Irish suburbs, and with civil libertarians, while Kennedy, as an *America* article noted, benefited from the "support from those who remember that it was his brother's election in 1960 which lifted the ancient burden of Non-Acceptance from the Irish Catholic mind, festering since the defeat of Alfred Emmanuel Smith." [58]

It was, in a sense, an election the cardinal couldn't lose. And he could sympathize with a bitter Eddie McCormack, who said after the election: "If this is politics—if they can get away with this—then I don't want any part of politics." [59] Cushing knew, however, that Ted had a better chance in the November election against George Lodge.

And when Ted did trounce Lodge in November 1962 and took over his brother's seat, Joe Kennedy's dream had come true. "The Kennedys, all of them," writes his biographer, "had won all that was worth winning." [60]

On the day of the election, Cardinal Cushing was in Rome attending the first session of Vatican Council II.

On July 19, 1963, Cushing baptized Christopher George Kennedy, the eighth child of the Robert Kennedys. The President and his daughter Caroline were among thirty Kennedys and guests who crowded into the sacristy of St. Francis Xavier in Hyannis. "If you don't become a priest, bishop, or cardinal, it won't be my fault," Cushing said to the infant. Caroline kept interrupting the service with her chattering. The prelate, who was wearing a white mitre with his ceremonial robes, wondered whether the little girl mistook him for St. Patrick. Finally he turned to her. "My dear Caroline, if you don't be quiet, I'll take up a collection and the whole crowd will be dispersed, because that's the only way of dispersing a crowd." [61]

It was a sadder occasion a few weeks later when Jacqueline, the birth of a child imminent, was rushed to the hospital at Otis Air Force Base. The President and a few friends flew to the Cape to find that the baby had been born suffering from hyaline membrane disease. Patrick Bouvier Kennedy died less than forty hours after birth in the Children's Hospital in Boston.

Evelyn Lincoln, Kennedy's secretary, thought this was one of the hardest blows the President experienced during the entire time she was with him.[62] Kennedy, who had been peering through the thick glass of a pressure chamber, lost control when the baby died. He pounded his fist against the wall in his anguish. Bobby, Dave Powers, and Pierre Salinger were with him when he got the news. "He walked away from us through a door into the hospital's boiler room," Salinger writes. "There, he wept for ten minutes, finally coming back to the three of us where Bob put his arm around his brother's shoulders." [63] It was an agonizing moment for a man never known to have had an emotional outburst. The cardinal said of the infant: "He now lives in the nursery of the children of heaven."

On August 10, the President's helicopter landed on the baseball field at St. John's Seminary at 9:55 A.M. Three other helicopters brought other members of the family to Patrick's funeral mass, including Mr. and Mrs. Hugh D. Auchincloss with their children, Jamie and Janet; Jacqueline's sister, Princess Lee Radziwill; Attorney General Robert Kennedy, and Senator Edward Kennedy and their sisters, Mrs. Peter Lawford and Mrs. Sargent Shriver, who was with her husband. Also at the mass were Cardinal Spellman and Judge Morrissey.

The cardinal, following his crucifer, began the service by sprinkling the flower-covered coffin with holy water while intoning: "Blessed be the name of the Lord, now and forever." The President wept again during the Mass of the Angels, during which the cardinal, wearing white rather than the usual black vestments of requiem, prayed: "Almighty and most loving God . . . as soon as they leave this world, You give everlasting life to all little children reborn in the font of baptism, and we believe You have given it today to the soul of this little child.

Because of my innocence, You have received me and given me a place in Your sight forever." The prelate offered the mass in his private chapel, which seats eighteen. After the other mourners had left for Holyhood Cemetery in Brookline, the cardinal, trailing the president, watched him encircle the tiny coffin with his arm, as if he wanted to take it with him. "The President had tried hard to reach that baby, to touch his hand," Jim Bishop wrote. "From his neck he had taken the gold St. Christopher Medal his wife had given him and thrust it inside the white casket beside the newborn." [64] Cushing, also weeping, consoled the President, who was still in tears as they were about to leave the chapel.

"My dear Jack, let's go, let's go. Nothing more can be done." [65]

The cortege moved slowly toward the cemetery, where the Kennedys have a family plot on a knoll. At graveside, the President rested his hands on the coffin. Cushing read the committal prayers: "Bow down Your ear to Your servants, upon whom You have laid the heavy burden of sorrow. Grant that they may not languish in fruitless and unavailing grief, nor sorrow as those who have no hope, but through their tears look meekly up to You, the God of all Consolation."

Then President Kennedy touched the coffin and said "Goodbye." Dave Powers saw him touch the ground and whisper, "It's awfully lonely here." [66] He lingered until nearly everyone had gone before he flew back to the Cape to comfort his wife. Manchester writes that Secret Service agents were often frustrated because the President, "like Lincoln, refused to live in a cage." One worried agent turned to Cushing at Patrick's funeral. "How do you protect this man?" he asked.[67]

Two months later, Kennedy visited Harvard University to choose a library site for his state papers. He addressed a morning assembly at the University of Maine, saw the first half of the Harvard Columbia football game at Harvard Stadium, then slipped quietly away to visit Patrick's grave, praying silently for a few minutes. He left a yellow chrysanthemum bouquet at the grave site.

That day, Holyhood Cemetery seemed lonelier than ever.

chapter eighteen

A TIME OF GRIEF

EARLY IN THE AFTERNOON of the black Friday in November 1963, Cardinal Cushing, in his ceremonial robes, was waiting to greet the new naval commander of Boston when word came that President Kennedy had been shot down in Dallas.[1] Cushing felt like an aging father who had lost his only son. Closer to the President than any other churchman, he had baptized, married, and buried Kennedys. He was their confidant. "At dinner with them, he could raise his codfish voice in louder dissent than old Joe or young Bobby or laugh more heartily at the antics of the family than they could," Jim Bishop writes.[2]

The rear-admiral who had come to pay his respects saw the tears in his eyes as the prelate ran his tongue over his parched lips. "Jack Kennedy has been assassinated." The cardinal finally got the words out. There was no courtesy call. The admiral left. The tough, gnarled prelate, inured to tragedy, was crushed. He went to his private chapel to weep and pray on his prie-dieu, facing a golden statue of Christ, as his household nuns, heads bowed, knelt in the pews to say their beads. When he regained his composure, he gave a brief eulogy before television cameras in his garden after passing word to every parish in the archdiocese to pray for the President.

The next day, at a memorial mass telecast nationally from his archdiocesan network, studio WHIS, he said: "I have been with him in joy and sorrow, in decision and in crisis . . . and I know of no one who has combined in more noble perfection that quality of greatness that marked his calm, cool, calculating intelligence and his big, brave, bountiful heart. Now, all of a sudden, he has been taken from us, and, I dare say, we shall not see his like again."

There was heartbreak in his voice that quavered when he mentioned touching domestic scenes: "Charming Caroline 'stealing' the publicity, jovial John-John on all fours ascending the stairs of an airplane to greet his 'daddy,' and the loving mother, like all mothers, joyfully watching two children of her flesh and blood, mindful always of two others in the nurseries of heaven." He had lost his best friend, he said. "History will never record how close we were in life."

Mention has been made of Cushing's "warrior shoulders, square jaw, and penetrating eyes," which made him look "more like a Cherokee than a saint. He carried himself like an ancient Hamite chieftain, and he spoke in the imperious tones of command." [3] The warrior who had heartened the Kennedys throughout years of anguish, himself needed comfort the day after the assassination. "My heart is broken with grief over his martyrdom for the cause of the free world."

It was a consolation, at least, to have seen his closest friend run the country for a thousand days, "not as a partisan Catholic, but as a patriotic President." [4] And he could treasure the memory of Kennedy's last kindness. A few weeks before the Dallas tragedy, Cushing had met Kennedy to sign a contract under which the President's bestseller, *Profiles in Courage*, would be televised with all profits going to Cushing charities.

The Kennedy family thought that Jack should be buried in the family plot in Brookline, but Cushing advised against this when Ted Kennedy called him from Hyannis Port.

"It seemed to me that it was just not practical to have a national shrine here. We faced the problem of bringing the body back to Massachusetts. The body would be unburied another night, and then the family would have to endure another ceremony here." [5]

The cardinal also told Ted that because of the narrow streets in Boston and Brookline, a presidential cortege would create an impossible traffic jam. According to Manchester, either the cardinal or several members of his staff, who were on the line (Cushing later had no recollection of this), suggested that the President be buried in the heart of Boston Common. Ted left the matter open and discussed plans with his mother. [6]

The family took the cardinal's advice. The President would be buried in Arlington Cemetery. Cushing recommended a low mass, since it would take only forty minutes, as compared with at least ninety minutes for a high mass.

Cushing, chosen to celebrate the funeral mass in Washington, had a stormy meeting with Archbishop Vagnozzi, the apostolic delegate. A Catholic head of State, Vagnozzi argued, was entitled to five absolutions at the end of a funeral mass. Cushing, who later described the discussion as a "hassle," flatly rejected the idea.

"If there are going to be five absolutions, you'll have to say them yourself. I won't do it because they'll last twice as long as the mass itself. In the popular parlance, this family has had it." [7]

There was more friction that evening at the home of Archbishop O'Boyle, where Sargent Shriver and Theodore Sorensen, representing the Kennedy family, met with the two prelates. A surprise visitor was Judge Francis Morrissey, who later denied crashing the party as some writers have alleged. Shriver invited him, he said. Cushing, in any case, thought that Shriver and Sorensen had asked the jurist to come, since neither he nor O'Boyle had.

"Your Eminence, this is how the family would like it done," Shriver said, turning to Sorensen. Cushing listened to Sorensen "with growing dismay. His chieftain's face was set." [8] O'Boyle was appalled by Ted's apparent ignorance of Roman Catholic ritual. Among his proposals were secular music in the cathedral and Kennedy quotations and biblical readings during the service. Shriver, before the session, had wondered whether a cardinal should be addressed as "Your Eminence" or "Your Holiness."

Where was the mass to be celebrated? The hierarchy preferred the cavernous Romanesque Shrine of the Immaculate Conception, which had ample parking and could seat twenty-five hundred people. Jacqueline Kennedy insisted on St. Matthew's because of its pleasant associations involving her husband. When Bobby Kennedy told her the seating capacity was only eleven hundred, she shook her head. "I don't care. They can all stand in the streets. I just know that's the right place for it." [9]

The invitation list presented problems. Writes Jim Bishop: "De Gaulle? Yes. Queen Elizabeth? Yes. Harold Wilson? Yes. Richard Cardinal Cushing? Oh, yes. He would say the mass; it didn't matter that Archbishop O'Boyle was the ranking Roman Catholic churchman in Washington. He would step aside for a family friend." During the autopsy of the President, according to Bishop, Shriver, after telephoning Cushing in Boston, had clapped a hand to his forehead: "My God!" he said. "We forgot to invite Truman, Ike, and Hoover!"

Jacqueline agreed that O'Boyle would be the second prelate at the altar, but if any clergyman besides Cushing was to speak, it would be Auxiliary Bishop Philip N. Hannan, whom she considered "sort of a Jack in the church."

At the evening session, there was talk about a lay speaker—Sorensen, McGeorge Bundy, or Robert McNamara. Even if a decision had been reached, "Cushing would have scuttled it anyhow," Manchester said.[10]

Cushing refused to change the text, insisting that he would follow liturgy, and he was relieved when Jacqueline settled for a low mass and the most simple ceremony possible. "We'll bury him like Jesuits are buried in a pine box, with a low mass," Cushing said.[11] He frowned when Shriver said Bobby and Ted might quote from Jack's speeches. "It'll sound like politics; you'll be tying a rope around his coffin."

While the prelates discussed vestments, Ethel Kennedy called to say that Bobby wanted Communion offered. When the two prelates vetoed the proposal because it would take too long, Shriver said he would persuade Bobby that only the family should take Holy Communion. Cushing was to celebrate the mass, with O'Boyle in charge of music. Bishop Hannan would speak and read material Sorensen provided.

The two-hour session ended around midnight.

President Johnson, Jacqueline, and the Kennedys walked the eight blocks from the White House to St. Matthew's, followed by the most dazzling array of world dignitaries in American history.[12] In the hush of the cathedral, the choir sang Latin hymns, drowning out the band music in the oncoming procession. Luigi Vena sang Gounod's "Ave Maria" at Jacqueline's request, reminding Cushing that Vena had sung the same hymn at the marriage of Jack and Jacqueline. The cardinal, as he led a file of prelates to the door of the church, could hear the bagpipes over the muffled tattoo of the drums. The procession drew closer, and the cardinal wept softly when he heard the strains of "Hail to the Chief," set to the cadence of a dirge. Vested in red and black under his white mitre, he sprinkled the coffin with holy water and intoned a long prayer as the eight-man casket team halted on the church steps. Cushing departed from the usual procedure when Jacqueline and her two children drew near. To Jacqueline he looked "enormous" as he descended the steps, "looking to his credit, a trifle irritated with God," Murray Kempton wrote; "we would be grateful for the Catholics and grateful to them for providing one cardinal who looked like a prince of the church." [13] Opening his arms to comfort Jacqueline as she came part way up the steps, he kissed her on both cheeks "and gave her my heart's full measure of condolence and sympathy." [14]

After kissing the flag that draped the coffin, he reentered the church, pausing on his way down the aisle to embrace Rose Kennedy, who motioned for him to go on when he offered to escort her. Chanting in Latin, he followed the crucifer who, flanked by two candle-bearing acolytes, was slowly returning the cross to the altar. Behind him came the casket team, followed by President Johnson and Jacqueline, leading her children by the hand. After the family was seated, the cardinal chanted "with the harsh, dry inflection of the Boston Irish homeland. For those in the cathedral, this is the moment of passing." [15] After chanting the 129th Psalm, Cushing recited verses from Paul's Epistle to the Thessalonians and completed the mass.

Ted Reardon found the mass "beautiful, typically Cushing; he was so great, and I know how the Boss loved him so, that I was half in and half out of the world." [16] Caroline consoled her mother, who was shaking and weeping. "Everything was unbearably evocative—the 'Ave Maria' in the balcony, the prayers she had shared with her husband for ten years of Sundays, the celebrant who had married her and christened her daughter." [17] The cardinal intoned a prayer over her and each member of the Kennedy family as he offered Communion.

After the choir sang "Sanctus" and "Benedictus," Bishop Hannan mounted the ambon and read five scriptual passages selected by Jacqueline and an excerpt from Kennedy's inaugural address. Then the cardinal, circling the coffin three times, sprinkled each side with holy water as the congregation chanted the Lord's Prayer.

Suddenly the grating voice became almost a wail as the prelate, forsaking Latin prayers, improvised: "May the angels, dear Jack, lead you into Paradise. May the martyrs receive you at your coming. May the spirit of God embrace you, and mayest thou, with all those who made the supreme sacrifice of dying for others, receive eternal rest and peace. Amen."

The misty-eyed cardinal's impulsive words, which he later said were a sudden inspiration, moved Jacqueline. Cushing, about to change vestments near the altar rail, saw Caroline comfort her again as tears streamed down the widow's face. In the poignancy of the moment, he had consoling words for John-John and Caroline, and when he knelt to kiss Jacqueline, she said, "Thanks for calling him 'dear Jack.' " [18]

"He may be brusque and *very* informal at times, and sometimes unpredictable with his ad libs," an observer said, "but I have never seen such tenderness as . . . he displayed for the children of John F. Kennedy on November 25, 1963. . . . When I saw him comfort the children and Mrs. Kennedy, I was moved beyond words." [19]

Caught up in the heartbreak was John-John, whose military bearing amazed one of the largest television audiences in history. "John, you can salute Daddy now and say a good-bye to him," Jacqueline said. When Cushing looked at the boy's face, he "saw the shadow of sadness crossing it and felt a burning sensation in his chest. Eight months later he could scarcely speak of it. 'Oh, God,' he whispered hoarsely, 'I almost died.' " [20]

As the President's coffin was borne away, Jacqueline, now dry-eyed, watched her son salute. A veteran reporter who witnessed the scene, said: "God, I wish we were a monarchy and the kid was taking over and that woman was the regent."

At Arlington Cemetery, Cushing, O'Boyle, and Hannan stood near the head of the coffin, facing General Charles de Gaulle, who was near the foot of the grave. In his improvised committal prayers, Cushing chanted, "Oh God, through whose mercy the souls of the faithful find rest, be pleased to bless this grave and . . . the body we bury herein, that of our beloved Jack Kennedy, the thirty-fifth President of the United States, that his soul may rejoice in Thee with all the saints, through Christ the Lord, Amen." [21]

Standing solemnly at the grave site on the slope of Arlington Cemetery were the Irish Guards and Black Watch, Third Infantry troops, green-bereted honor guard of the Special Forces, and a United States Marine detachment. Ten minutes before three o'clock fifty Air Force jets, one for each state of the Union, flew over, followed by *Air Force One*, the presidential plane, in a final salute. Cardinal Cushing sprinkled the flag-covered coffin with holy water when it was lowered to the ground and led a prayer. Guns thundered a twenty-one-gun salute, and while the Marines played "Eternal Father," Cushing improvised a prayer for the eternal flame, which Jacqueline, Bobby, and Ted had lit. After the band finished playing, Cushing gave a general blessing. Then he and John Metzler, superintendent of Arlington Cemetery, walked over to Jacqueline, who was standing near the grave with Bobby and Ted. Metzler presented her with the coffin flag, which had been "stretched and snapped into its ceremonial triangle folds." [22] Cushing steadied Jacqueline. "If you want my advice," he said, "I wouldn't have any other ceremonies." [23] She nodded.

Before leaving the cemetery, the cardinal embraced Rose Kennedy. "Good-bye, my dear," he whispered. "God be with you."

Joe Kennedy was at Hyannis Port when his son was assassinated. When Ted broke the news, he bore up surprisingly well. On the day of the funeral, Joe, who was too weak to go to Washington, drove through Barnstable with his niece, Ann Gargan, revisiting some of Jack's favorite haunts. Later he and Rose went to Palm Beach, where Cushing witnessed a poignant scene.

"Joe was sitting in a wheelchair when the newly widowed Jacqueline came into the room with Caroline and John-John," a biographer writes.[24] " 'Granpa!' the children cried in delight as they ran to him and kissed him wetly on the cheek. Jackie, too, went to his side and kissed him." Although Joe Kennedy could not speak, tears rolled down his cheeks.

That year, Cushing bypassed the usual Thanksgiving celebration for the aged and handicapped at Blinstrub's Village. Instead he told the gathering the Bible story of a valiant woman. "That valiant woman . . . was reproduced in the twentieth century by Jacqueline Kennedy." [25]

Just before Christmas Jacqueline sent the prelate a book titled *Inaugural Addresses of the United States, from George Washington, 1789, to John F. Kennedy, 1961.* The gilt-edged, leather-bound volume, one of eighty-five copies published by the United States Government Printing Office, was inscribed: "For Your Eminence—Jack was going to give you this for Christmas. Please accept it now from me. With my devotion always—for all you were to our 'dear Jack' and to me. Respectfully, Jackie."

On December 29 Cushing celebrated a private mass at the winter home of Joe Kennedy in Palm Beach. Later he told three thousand persons at a memorial mass in Miami that the shadow of death hovered over Jack Kennedy throughout his life before it finally "touched him on Black Friday." The Boston *Globe* quoted his statement that Kennedy "had the presentiment that he would be assassinated . . . he often said he did not want to go to Texas, but he went and the tragedy occurred." [26] The prelate told the religious editor of the *Globe:* "I've never believed it was the work of one man. The Warren Commission Report is not complete. Much of the evidence has not been published." [27] Another time the cardinal voiced his suspicion of a conspiracy. "I am convinced there is someone behind all this. No one can convince me that Oswald was alone in the assassination of President Kennedy." [28]

In a press conference in Miami, he called Jacqueline "the most extraordinary woman I have ever met. I wish I could say to the young girls of the future that I think instead of looking to motion picture actresses for ideals, they should look to Jacqueline." [29] In Palm Beach, he was about to get into a boat to go for a spin with Joe Kennedy when Jacqueline came over. "I have a memento of Jack for you. It is his dog tag, and I want you to have it." The inscription reads: "Kennedy, John F., Commander in Chief of the Armed Forces." There is also the letter "O," which was his blood type, and the words "Roman Catholic," which identified the one man in American history who was a Catholic President.

"She could not have given me anything more personal and more meaningful," Cushing said, "because I loved the man and knew he loved me. May God be good to him." [30] Cushing said he would wear the dog tag until the Kennedy Memorial Library was completed and promised Jacqueline that "they would never get it away from me."

After the tragedy, the cardinal comforted the Kennedys at every opportunity. He lauded Joe Kennedy for his dignity and fortitude. Ted Kennedy later wrote: "Dad considered himself most fortunate to have both the close friendship and the spiritual inspiration of Cardinal Cushing for more than twenty years." [31]

In cooperation with the Boston Symphony Orchestra, directed by Erich Leinsdorf, the cardinal officiated at a ceremony in Boston more solemn than the one held in St. Matthew's Church. Musical accompaniment included the St. John's Seminary Choir, the New England Conservatory of Music, the Boston Pro Musica, the Harvard Glee Club, and the Radcliffe Choral Society. Reporters, television crews, and a few spectators watched the final rehearsal on a chill Saturday morning in January 1964 in Holy Cross Cathedral. The musicians and priests, rehearsing Mozart's Requiem Mass in D Minor, were tense on a poignant occasion that rekindled so much sadness. Just as the rehearsal began, Cushing wished the conductor luck. "I'll do the best I can," he said, "but I don't know much about music and I've got a voice like a fish peddler."

"Your Eminence," Leinsdorf said, "it's the heart that counts, rather than the voice."

For a moment after the rehearsal, John Fenton writes, the participants "seemed to freeze like so many wax figures, their drawn faces reflecting fatigue." [32] Dully, they watched the cardinal mount a high altar and rest his elbows on a lectern.

"We shall now take up the collection," he said, lifting the tension as the cathedral echoed with laughter. "Jack Kennedy would have laughed with the rest, at a good joke to end a good day's work," a reporter observed.[33]

Henry B. Cabot, president of the Boston Symphony Orchestra, had suggested having the orchestra play at the memorial service—an idea that would have been flatly rejected by Cardinal O'Connell and even by Pope John, who disapproved of blending modern or secular music in sacred services. When Monsignor Edward G. Murray passed along the suggestion to Cushing, he was delighted. Equally pleased was proper Bostonian Cabot when he shook hands with the prelate at their first meeting. "Hello, Henry!" Cushing said, as if they had been friends for years. A battery of microphones encircled the fifty-four-member orchestra to provide a stereophonic reproduction of Mozart's Requiem, and television cameras were ready for the memorial mass, which would be viewed by millions.

On Sunday morning, January 19, Cushing greeted Jacqueline Kennedy on the front steps of the cathedral. The congregation of eighteen hundred persons included Ted and other members of the Kennedy family. Just before ten o'clock, Cushing escorted Rose to a front pew. Also present were Protestant and Orthodox clergy, rabbis, purple-robed monsignori, and priests in black clericals. The first service of its kind in 334 years of Boston's history had reunited the city.

The cardinal, wearing the rich and heavy robes of his office, celebrated the long, pontifical requiem mass with great dignity and with his intuitive sense of the significance of the occasion. Next day a reporter called the prelate "a kind of one-man pontifical parade of quips and sudden punchlines in which he is forever poking fun at himself. Yet this same archbishop held the nation in awe as he celebrated the mass of the Mozart Requiem before television cameras in memory of President Kennedy." [34] A *Globe* correspondent was equally impressed: "A prince stood tall . . . to bid farewell to a friend. . . . For two hours he led a nation honoring the memory of . . . Kennedy. And for two hours he showed America a side of him seldom seen . . . a side of pomp and grandeur, or near-awesome solemnity appropriate for a prince of the . . . church." The scribe noted that even his voice, which he compared to a fish dealer's seemed to change. "The prayers drifted on clear, echoing notes throughout the giant cathedral."

From the lectern after the service, Cushing thanked Cabot for offering the orchestra, adding that the day had a special meaning because of the presence of Jacqueline, "who has taken herself from her sorrow for a few hours to pray to God with us in sacrifice and song." Jacqueline had wept as she listened to the mass, and tears flowed down her face as she went to the altar rail to receive Communion.

"We are grateful, too," Cushing continued, "for the presence of the mother of our departed President, a resolute symbol of maternal strength, for the company of his brother and sisters and all of those of his family and friends who came from near and far to honor his memory."

The prelate explained why the Requiem was appropriate: "Separated by centuries, these two men were touched by a creative instinct uncommon in any generation: both brought out of their youth a shining light which will illumine the ages; both were summoned to eternity at a moment which to mortals must seem untimely. Mozart died before he finished his immortal Requiem. President Kennedy died before he finished his first term in office. Yet the memory of men will enshrine their names."

The cardinal introduced Jacqueline and Rose to Leinsdorf in the sanctuary after the service. Both seemed spiritually refreshed.

"It was magnificent," Jacqueline told Cushing. "I will never forget it." [35]

In May 1964, Cushing spoke at a luncheon commemorating the issue of Kennedy Stamps. Dr. C. Gordon Brownsville, an associate of the Billy Graham Evangelistic Association, recalls another instance of Cushing's thoughtfulness: "Cardinal Cushing was to have given an invocation before luncheon, but he arrived late. It was Friday, and the main course was prime ribs of beef. To make up for his tardiness, he gave the priests and nuns a special dispensation so they could eat the beef, which they were drooling for. The orator was an honor student from a new Catholic high school. He sat next to me, mentioning that his school needed a gymnasium. Later, when I asked the cardinal to autograph my program, I told him what the lad said and asked why he didn't build a gym for the school. His blue eyes sparkled. 'Let them go out and raise the money as I have to do.' He is most magnetic." [36]

"In the stamps issued today," Cushing said, "we seek to record for all time some part of the inspiration which his leadership gave to America, some memory of that grace and style which is now no longer with us. We pray that these stamps, as they cross the globe in international exchange, will carry with them some of the spirit of that stalwart President whose image they bear. His pursuit of peace, his strivings for harmony among nations, his strength in time of testing, his youthful hopes for a better world—all of these find wings in these stamps to touch anew the hearts of men in every place where people communicate with one another." [37]

In that same year he asked: "What could be more eloquent of the way in which 'God writes straight with crooked lines' than the way in which men of every faith were brought closer . . . at the time of

the . . . President's death?" In 1966 he had another comment: "John
F. Kennedy fought the good fight for the God-given rights of his fellow
man and for a world where peace and freedom should prevail. He
fulfulled unto death the pledge he made on the day of his inauguration
as the thirty-fifth President."

Cushing said he doubted that Kennedy "would want me to say he
was a very religious man. As a matter of fact, I wouldn't want anybody to say I was a very religious man." Kennedy had become more
prayerful after his election, however. He would often, during sleepless
nights, Cushing said, "get out of his bed and kneel down and pray.
How do I know this? His father told me!" He added: "We had a President with one hand in the hand of God; but for some reason God
permitted him to be taken from us." [38]

Cushing feared Kennedy might not have been reelected because he
had pushed civil rights action too far. Cuba, he thought, might have
been an Achilles heel, and "he had a far vaster plan for containing
poverty than Johnson . . . big business knew it and was out to get
him." His major goals, Cushing said, were "no war, because no one
could win, and the real losers would be the little people; he was also
anxious to create a lasting image as the first Catholic President."

On June 19, 1964, Senator Ted Kennedy wired the Democratic
State Convention in Springfield, Massachusetts: "Don't nominate Joan
[his wife] until I get there." With him on the flight in a private plane
were Edward S. Moss of North Andover, Massachusetts, his administrative aide, and Senator and Mrs. Birch Bayh of Indiana.

"You should make some kind of spectacular entrance into the convention," Moss said to Kennedy just before the plane took off.

"What do you want me to do, crack up the airplane?"

"No, just parachute out of it into the convention." Everyone
laughed.[39]

Shortly after eleven P.M., the plane clipped the tops of several trees
as it came down into an apple orchard in Southampton, near Springfield, and swerved to a stop after banging into trees. Edwin T. Zimny,
the pilot, was killed instantly. Moss died the following morning at
Cooley Dickinson Hospital in Northampton. Senator Bayh pulled Ted
Kennedy through the escape hatch and covered him with his wife's
raincoat. Ted, in severe pain, had fractured several bones in his back.

Joan Kennedy called Cardinal Cushing. "I was up with asthma
when I first heard the news of the plane crash at three-thirty in the

morning," he told the press. "My heart goes out to the entire Kennedy family." [40]

On the following night, Cushing accepted a check from a thousand members of the Massachusetts Court, Catholic Daughters of America, at Blinstrub's. During the preceding year they had donated more than one hundred twenty-five thousand dollars for the Pius Society of St. James the Apostle in recognition of Cushing's Silver Jubilee. On that Saturday night, each of sixty-three courts paraded in purple and white academic robes and mortar boards. The prelate turned the meeting into a somber occasion.

"It was miraculous that Ted . . . survived such an accident. . . . The Kennedy family has had more tragic deaths and more family troubles than any family of my acquaintance. A few weeks ago, I buried Joan's and Ted's baby at Holyhood Cemetery." The cardinal told the assembly he planned to attend the national convention of the Greek Orthodox Churches of North and South America in Denver, Colorado.

The prelate visited Ted Kennedy at Cooley Dickinson Hospital and drove to Andover with Monsignor George Kerr to join Joan at the wake for Moss at a funeral home. Mrs. Moss was so upset he took her out to his car and consoled her, then drove her home, where he comforted the three Moss daughters, telling them he was sure their father was in heaven and that they should be happy, not sad. Then Cushing and Kerr visited Mrs. Zimny and her two children, none of whom was Catholic.[41]

"What a brave and wonderful man your husband was," he told Mrs. Zimny. "He saved Ted's life." Judge Morrissey, who witnessed the touching scene in the Moss home, said it was one of the cardinal's finest moments. "In tragedy and sorrow," he said, "Cardinal Cushing rises to his full stature as a prince of the church."

Cushing and the Kennedys continued to be intertwined. After his third trip to South America, he told the press that he had "private thoughts" about Robert Kennedy running for the United States Senate, as he had explained to Joe Kennedy. "I heartily endorse the idea that Bob Kennedy should stay in the political picture on a national level, by what means I do not know. I think Bob . . . should have announced his candidacy for Vice-President weeks ago. My idea is that the people should elect their own candidate for Vice-President, even if a man from a minority party should be elected."

A short time later, Cushing was innocently involved in a dispute when Bobby ran for the Senate against the incumbent, Kenneth Keating. When Kennedy charged that his opponent had fought federal aid to education and the test-ban treaty, Keating appealed to the Fair Campaign Practices Committee, of which Cushing was a member. Bruce Felknow, chairman of this committee, wrote to Bobby that his charges were "not only false and distorted, but also appear to be either a deliberate and cynical misrepresentation or the result of incredible carelessness." [42]

"Instead of retracting," writes Ralph De Toledano in his biography of the candidate, "Bobby applied pressure on Felknow. Ralph McGill, editor of the *Atlanta Constitution,* and Cardinal Cushing, a Kennedy family friend, resigned from the Fair Campaign Practices Committee, and Felknow was forced to apologize to Bobby." [43]

In March 1967, Cushing relived tragedy when he stood with members of the Kennedy family as the late President was reinterred in the National Cemetery at Arlington, Virginia. "Bob stood on the edge of the grave and looked down at the President's casket and I feel sure that he relived every moment of his past life, the tragedy of the assassination and the funeral and the years since." Cushing, admitting that Bobby was controversial, felt for him. He was tempted to go forward to pull him back from the edge of the grave. Not until he had finished his prayers did he notice that President Johnson was present. "He looked like the saddest person there," Cushing said.

The cardinal had flown to Washington on the invitation of the Kennedys to officiate at the graveside rites and had stayed at the site for more than seven hours while workmen prepared the graves for the late President and his children.

He spent the night with the Edward Kennedys and returned to the cemetery at 6:40 the following morning with Defense Secretary Robert McNamara. The cardinal had taken one of the two small caskets at midnight from Holyhood Cemetery by car to the Naval Air Station at Newport, Rhode Island, and had turned over the coffin containing Patrick Bouvier Kennedy to Jacqueline's mother aboard *The Caroline,* the family plane. It was placed beside another tiny coffin which contained the remains of the daughter who died at birth. "When I saw the two caskets I relived that midnight journey. . . ."

The cardinal told this story to the press in the library of St. John's Seminary just after the event. To add to the bleakness, he said, it has rained "like a monsoon in Vietnam." Never before had he seen such a downpour. It was one of the saddest moments in his life. "I don't know how they can stand it," he said.[44]

A month later, on May 27, 1967, the cardinal gave the invocation at the launching, at Newport News, Virginia, of the aircraft carrier *John F. Kennedy.* During the ceremony, in which he called Jacqueline the "queen of the household where there will always be a vacant chair," Caroline broke a bottle of champagne over the bow of the ship. Her mother handed her a handkerchief when the wine splattered over her and streamed down her face. In an aside, the cardinal told Jacqueline he didn't like to see her wearing a miniskirt.

During these bleak years, he thought often of his favorite Kennedy. "If you put all the Kennedys in the world together, you'd never get another Jack." [45] During the discussion of a site for the Kennedy Memorial Library in Cambridge, he made a deadpan remark to the press that his friend would have appreciated. "They are going to need egress from it, access to it. I don't see how they can do it without taking over Harvard Square. It looks like the Scollay Square * of old, anyway." [46]

Less gaily he discussed another memorial for another Kennedy in January 1969.[47]

At dawn on June 6, 1968, a telephone call told the cardinal that Robert Kennedy had been shot in Los Angeles in an assassination attempt. Cushing immediately called Judge Morrissey, who drove him to the Kennedy Compound in Hyannis Port. His eyes were red-rimmed when he arrived to comfort the ailing father and sorrowing mother.

Rose Kennedy, arising early to attend the seven o'clock mass at St. Francis Xavier Church, as she had done faithfully for years, heard the news on the television set in her bedroom: "Senator Kennedy lies in critical condition . . . shot in the brain."

"The great thing about the Kennedys," a columnist noted, "is not just that they have courage but that they give it. And the sad thing, which is also the glory of it, is that they give it in greatest measure in the manner in which they meet trial and tragedy." [48] "Pope Rose," as some Hyannis parishioners call her, has shown remarkable courage every time tragedy has struck. With her serene faith, she is the power and the glory of the clan.[49] Cushing himself has said she "has more courage than any woman I ever met. She has more confidence in Al-

---

* A picturesque part of Boston, now gone, popular when the fleet was in, with its bars and burlesque shows.

mighty God than any priest or religious I have ever met. She's taking everything in stride and leaving it all to the Lord." He said this after learning of the shooting of Bobby, adding, "She's an extraordinary woman. She accepts everything as the will of God for His own particular purposes."

Arthur Krock, an old Kennedy friend, doubts that Rose ever recovered from the deaths of Joe, Jr., and Kathleen, who, he said, "was the star of the family, a blithe spirit with more wit than anyone but Jack." [50] When tragedy struck for the fourth time, Rose was in constant touch with Ted, and she telephoned her daughter, Eunice Shriver, in Paris. She also talked to Cardinal Cushing, who was on hand, and was grateful when he promised to return in a day or two.[51] Cushing told Jim Bishop about her fortitude: "She wound up consoling me." [52]

That morning, sparing her invalid husband the news, she prayed at church for her second son gunned down. When she returned, Joe Kennedy was quietly weeping in his chair, having just overheard part of a telephone conversation in which Ted had told his mother details of the tragedy. Rose tried to hide her own grief to keep Joe from becoming more upset. Cardinal Cushing, who spent twenty minutes with them, came away with tears in his eyes, amazed at how well they were taking the news of Bobby's fight for life in California.

"I've been with his family more in sorrow than in glory," he told reporters. "I've never met a family comparable. They take everything as the will of God." When he went up to the ambassador's room to comfort him, Joe, unable to speak, understood everything said to him. "He let a few tears drop. I kissed him and said, 'Don't get discouraged now.' " [53] Cushing fumbled for consoling words for Rose. "We all have our troubles, but why should the Kennedy family have all these troubles—why, why, why? I just cannot understand all the troubles your family has endured over the years."

"I have confidence in God because He knows all things, because He's all powerful, because He's all loving," she said.[54] She remained placid. Later she told a *Look* writer: "I've had so much, a son as President, two as senators, a son-in-law who's an ambassador . . . perhaps God doesn't permit that much. Why should the Kennedys be so special? Why shouldn't a Nixon or a Humphrey have his chance?" She refused to be beaten by a series of tragedies. "I have four children left, grandchildren to think of. I don't intend to be laid low or pulverized. If I collapsed, the morale of the family would be lowered." [55]

Cushing, who stayed for dinner, offered to take Rose to Los Angeles, but since there was little she could do there, she preferred to stay with her husband.

Back in Boston, Cushing asked people of all faiths to pray for Bobby's recovery and for the anguished Kennedys, as well as for a solution to the national crime wave, "the height and depth, the length and breadth of which is beyond full comprehension." [56] During the day, he told reporters of the need for a deep-rooted congressional probe of the control of firearms and of the necessity of immediately passing more gun control laws. "People who carry firearms are criminals or would-be criminals." He also urged better protection for political figures. "The bodyguards could not keep Jack in line, and Bobby, much like him, is gregarious and loves to mix in mobs. There must be provisions made to stop them or any candidate." He said emotional mobs could not be controlled without calling out the marines.

The cardinal, who had started the day saying mass for Bobby in the same chancery where in 1963 he had sung a Mass of the Angels for Patrick Bouvier Kennedy, later that day said a mass in a Somerville church for the brother of a monsignor. As he entered the church, he told reporters he was so shocked he could scarcely think. "One wonders what this country is coming to. Are we going to run a political campaign with bullets or debates?" The nation, he went on, was beset by war, racism, politics, and unemployment. "Congress must stop fooling around and start doing something about all of these things—especially guns. This is a sad day in the history of our country. It's obvious we did not learn our lesson with Jack's death. I hope we learn it now."

Cushing was worried about America's image throughout the world. That same day, when he confirmed fifty-seven children at St. Vincent's Church in South Boston, he asked: "How can we explain this to people in other lands? How can we explain the late beloved President Kennedy killed by a bullet? How can we explain to them that at half past three this morning, his brother, running for the office of President, was shot. At the present time, it is doubtful whether he will live. . . . Latest reports are not encouraging. Even if he should live no one can tell in what condition his brain will be . . . whether he will have speech or sight.

"I don't know any family, wealthy or poor, that has suffered more than the Kennedys. They are all dedicated people and look at all the suffering they have had." [57]

Boston newspapers published his statement on Bobby's death. He said in part: "The violent death of . . . Kennedy . . . rends the heart of America, already scarred by earlier sorrows. The madness of men, once again, grieves our nation and brings us to our knees in prayer. . . . Like his brother, he did not know the meaning of fear and even where duty was wedded to danger, he embraced it. . . . For both of them, life was an adventure which summoned each man according to his abilities." The cardinal loved Bobby primarily because he was, as a columnist put it, "the perfect Irish-American, a gut fighter with brains and a heart that could truly bleed for a cause." [58]

In June 1968, when Cushing offered a special mass for the senator's recovery, he sounded anguished: "I will pray that it will never happen again." His face was pale and drawn. "We did that before, too, but it didn't do any good."

The tragedy left Ted Kennedy the clan leader. Polls showed that only he could save the Democrats from defeat in the 1968 presidential campaign. But, still in mourning, he refused to run, although he had no intention of dropping out of public life. "A few close friends, even one archbishop, had counseled precisely that," William H. Honan wrote in *The New York Times Magazine*, "for the sake of his family and his brothers' families." [59] The archbishop was Cushing.

"The smart thing for Ted Kennedy to do is to get out of politics and take care of the kids," he told reporters.

In *This Week* magazine in January 1969, the cardinal discussed a suitable memorial for Bobby Kennedy that would reflect his concern for young people, "especially the disadvantaged and discriminated against. Like Ethel Kennedy, when I think of Bobby . . . I think of his closeness to young people. They identified themselves with him, and he had them with him." [60]

chapter nineteen

A SECOND REFORMATION

After Pope John xxiii announced early in 1959 that he would convene Vatican Council II, Catholic bishops were polled for suggestions, and from twelve thousand items recommended for discussion, seventy topics were prepared for three sessions of the council to be held beginning in the fall of 1962. Soon the Christian world hummed with talk about "winds of change" that would sweep aside ancient traditions and rituals once deemed sancrosanct. Pope John established a Commission for the Promotion of Christians United and met with the archbishop of Canterbury and the patriarch of the Eastern Orthodox Church to reevaluate papal doctrines promulgated only half a century earlier.

Cardinal Cushing, whose favorite world leaders were the "two great Johns," played a prominent role in an unfolding drama involving Pope John and President John Kennedy, between whom there was a warm feeling of rapport and respect. Cushing, so close to Kennedy, was almost equally devoted to Pope John: "There was something supernatural about that man, because he was the only one in Vatican circles who understood me, and I don't understand myself."

In 1962 *Time* broke precedent in naming Pope John "Man of the Year," the first churchman to be so honored. The Pontiff was acclaimed for launching Vatican II, which his successor, Pope Paul VI, would continue. Vatican II dealt with the renewal of the church through revision of its discipline and organization and for laying the groundwork for closer Christian unity.

On October 11, 1962, in St. Peter's Basilica at the Vatican, twenty-six hundred Roman Catholic bishops and fifty observer-delegates from other Christian churches heard Pope John say: "There burns in my heart the intention of working . . . to hasten the hour when for all men the prayer of Jesus at the Last Supper will have reached its fulfillment: '*Ut unum sint*—that all may be one.' "

This dream Cushing shared. He had already used parables to show his ecumenical bent. One concerns two Protestants who were happy in paradise until they came to an insurmountable wall. St. Peter explained: "Catholics are on the other side of that wall. We musn't let them know there is anyone in heaven besides them." In that talk Cushing recommended the examination of "our conduct to see if we make strangers of those who believe as we, love Christ as we, want to do His will as we, yet somehow 'followeth not us.'"

Cushing was attuned to the mood of rethinking history long before the Council aimed at uniting those of differing faiths. Often he had said: "It never made any sense to me that people were classified in this great pluralistic society . . . as Catholics, Protestants, Jewish, Orthodox, or atheist. . . . We are all children of God and should understand one another and love one another." He preached this message from alien pulpits, in *Pilot* columns, and in pastoral letters. He thought of Pope John in the same affectionate way as did President Kennedy, who quipped to friends at a White House dinner that he doubted that the Pope was all that the press pictured him to be: "You Protestants are always building him up."

The Caritas Club feted Cushing at Blinstrub's on the eve of his departure to Rome. He turned the evening into a surprise party for an old friend, Arthur Godfrey: "A genuine American with a philosophy of life akin to the new climate I expect from the council. Here is a man who loves all people, preaching racial justice for over a generation." Surprised and moved, Godfrey went aside to chat with Cushing, who left that night with six thousand dollars to present to Pope John.

In an informal talk, Cushing said he hoped Vatican II would spread among all faiths love for the dignity of man. "I do not want Catholics disliking Protestants or Jews or atheists or communists, and I do not want them to dislike us for any reason of our belief." Leaving Logan Airport next day, he told well-wishers that the council would step toward Christian unity but warned against overoptimism.

When he arrived in Rome, *Il Messagero,* a daily newspaper, described him as "a tall clean man, with the look of a pioneer of the West." [1] Partly because of his health and partly because he wanted to go home to raise money for his charities, he did not stay for the complete session. "I'd better stay at least three weeks," he told Pope John. "If I go home earlier, the people will think I've been excommunicated." [2]

"You seem to get thinner and thinner every time I see you," the Pope said during one conversation.

"I'm feeling as well as can be expected, Your Holiness. But I can't do as much as I'd like for the poor back in Boston, because I have bleeding ulcers."

John suggested that he try bicarbonate of soda before going to bed. "I do, and it's marvelous."

"Your Holiness, thank God you're not infallible in prescribing medicine. That's the worst thing you can take for ulcers." *

Cushing told the Pontiff in another chat that all the theology he knew was in Cathechism Two, which is taught to students in intermediate grades in parochial schools.

"Shake hands," John said. "You'll never be in trouble."

Cushing thought it absurd that the council had no translation system comparable to the one used at the United Nations. At his suggestion, an electronics system for simultaneous translation of Latin into various languages was installed a year later at the second session. Cushing told Pope John he was displeased with the organization of the council, arguing that not enough of the prelates understood spoken Latin. At a preparatory meeting, when he was reproved by a monsignor for speaking in English, he told a cardinal at his side to tell the gathering in Latin that he represented "the Church of Silence." It was only when discussions were translated into English, Spanish, French, Italian, German, or Arabic that many bishops knew what was being debated.

The language barrier left Cushing feeling uncomfortable. "Only the scholars knew what was going on. I was physically present, but my mind was at home thinking of those to whom I owed money." At one point, he motioned toward Monsignor Thomas Ryan, his temporary interpreter. "He is my teacher. I am the best pupil in his English class." He grinned impishly. "Do you know why? I am the only one he has."

Admitting that his Latin was abominable, he said he had never before heard a lecture in Latin, "and it was all Greek to me. For once in my life I kept my mouth shut." Even Cardinal Spellman, who had studied in Rome for years, could understand only about half the spoken Latin. The more Cushing mentioned his dilemma, the more he elaborated. He wasn't sure, he said, that the language he heard was

---

* President Kennedy asked Cardinal Spellman what he should say when asked about the infallibility of the Pope. "I don't know. All I know is he keeps calling me Spillman."

Latin. "I didn't know whether it was Chinese or Eskimo." He told another group in Boston: "If you ever heard Frenchmen, Spaniards, Germans, Americans—even Italians—speaking Latin, you'd think they were all speaking Russian. I would sit there and listen, and when it was all over, I'd go over to chat with my friend, the dean of Harvard Divinity School. And he's the only one who would tell me what went on." [3] Cushing referred to an observer-delegate, Harvard Professor George H. Williams, who later said: "Cardinal Cushing long anticipated and implemented in his diocese, the pastoral and ecumenical principles of Pope John's pontificate and council."

"Even the Russian observers . . . were better off than I was," Cushing said. "At least they had interpreters."

Speeches had to be written in Latin and submitted for approval three days in advance, and speakers were limited to ten minutes. But bishops, like everyone else, said Cushing, were long-winded, and some spoke too long. Even when the senior cardinal elected daily gaveled a speaker to silence, he might keep talking. Alfredo Cardinal Ottaviani, head of the Congregation of the Holy Office, the branch of the Curia that deals with faith, morals, and heresy, walked out in a huff when, to silence him after he had been warned, his microphone was turned off. Finally the Pope, who had been watching proceedings over closed-circuit television, ruled that speakers would have to add something new on any given subject and would confine their talk to five minutes. [4]

Cushing was bored, sitting for three hours or more daily without understanding what was going on. The Negro Laurian Cardinal Rugambwa of Tanganyika, Africa, told him too late that he could join other prelates who left the session for the morning coffee break to escape the drone of oratory. Pope John had set up a coffee shop off a corridor leading from a side entrance to St. Peter's, and here churchmen could have a little ecumenical council of their own and exchange views with non-Catholic observers from all over the world. Since coffee shops are often called "bars" in Italy, some prelates thought liquor was served. Cushing said he didn't know whether "they had anything else out there," because "I didn't even see the bars. But, in any event, the observers would go out and in a very friendly, fraternal atmosphere, they accomplished wonders by breaking down barriers." [5]

One day, when Cushing was crossing the chamber to sit with the observers, an old cardinal accosted him. "God bless you, Cardinal Mindszenty," he said. "You've been an inspiration to us."

"I'm not Cardinal Mindszenty, Your Eminence. He's over there on the other side. I'm Cardinal Newman."

The first session, which ended on December 8, 1962, sanctioned the improvement of public worship to make it more vital. At this session, the bishops had criticized the monolithic church for shutting itself into a cultured ghetto and for perpetuating medieval attitudes and practices that meant little in a modern society. They felt the time had come to take a fresh look at rigid rules. Cushing was among prelates who found the following rules, observed in some parishes, absurd: it is wrong for a Catholic to play the organ in a non-Catholic church as a help to the religious service or to be a member of the choir during religious services; in Protestant marriages in a Protestant church, a Catholic should, in general, not take part as witness; Catholic servants who must accompany masters and children to a Protestant service must not take part in the services.[6]

Cardinal Cushing stayed at the session for two weeks. Late in November, he said that Augustin Cardinal Bea, head of the Vatican Secretariat for Christian Unity since Pope John founded it in 1960, would lead panel discussions at Harvard Divinity School during the following March and that he and Cardinal Bea would speak to any congregation to "preach our gospel of love and mutual cooperation, a gospel that will respect rights of conscience of all individuals." There were close ties between Cushing and the gentle Jesuit who, under two Popes, spearheaded the drive for Christian unity.

In January 1963, Cushing and Bishop James K. Mathews, resident in the New England area of the Methodist Church and president of the Massachusetts Council of Churches, appeared on a television program moderated by Dean Samuel H. Miller of Harvard Divinity School, author of *Religion in a Technical Age*. The theme was "Christian Unity—Dream, Plot, or Possibility?"

Both Mathews and Cushing discussed the thawing religious climate in which, said Miller, it was possible to "talk more freely with less bitterness and misrepresentation and with more open-mindedness and mutual respect than ever before."

"There is now with an increasingly clear voice being heard," said Mathews, "across what might have been termed an abyss of separation, the cry 'Brother,' and that's a cry that has been directed from both sides, and we find that that abyss perhaps isn't as broad or as deep as we supposed."

"I'm for Catholics being identified with Protestants and Jews," Cushing said, "and all others and all kinds in every possible friendly way. Nobody is asking them to deny their faith and they shouldn't be asking anybody to deny their faiths."

Dr. Miller, an eloquent champion of the ecumenical movement, in a speech a few years later,[7] stressed the profound changes occurring in Catholicism, while chastising other denominations for their self-concerns. "What is needed is a major explosion which will blow off the church roof and shake ourselves out of our complacency. Man's collective knowledge has created a universe, yet he does not have the wisdom to cope with the myriad problems which surround him." In a new world, he continued, everyone would have to learn to live in harmony, "for we can no longer say, 'East is East, and West is West, and never the twain shall meet.' "

It was the first such congenial religious confrontation on television.

Early in April, when Cushing spoke at the Community Church in Westwood, a Boston suburb, the minister [8] who introduced him said: "The wall that separates us is breached." Cushing, who was wearing street clericals, told of progress made during the first council session but warned that there was nothing in the ecumenical movement to get people to change religious beliefs. "The idea is to let us speak to one another, understand one another, love one another, and have respect for the conscientious beliefs of one another." [9]

In April 1963, Cardinal Bea received an honorary degree of Doctor of Canon and Civil Law at a convocation marking Boston College's centennial. The previous month the prelate gave the first lecture opening four ecumenical seminars at Harvard Divinity School on the first full day of its historic colloquim. The dialogue was the first in the history of the 300-year-old university and was attended by one hundred fifty Roman Catholic and Protestant scholars. Cardinal Bea gave two more lectures on subsequent days, composing the Chauncey D. Stillman lectures. He spoke of the need of healing "the scandalous worlds of separation that prevent all Christians from a perfect internal communion of faith and love, from the external professions of the same faith, from the use of the same sacraments and from the same direction of the same ministry and order." There would be no search for compromises, he said, in overcoming differences. "Faith must not be confused with politics."

In 1945, Cushing had brought Paulist fathers to Boston to establish the Catholic Information Center overlooking Boston Common. Over the years, the Paulists brought in progressive cardinals to speak on Vatican II at public lectures, beginning in 1963–64, when Cushing entertained them at his residence. The three liberal cardinals were Bea, Franz Cardinal Koenig of Austria, and Leon Joseph Cardinal Suenens of Belgium. When Cushing met Suenens at a railroad terminal in 1963, he gave him a wrestler's hug for the benefit of photographers. Presiding at one lecture given by the Belgian prelate, Cushing supported his plea that nuns take a more aggressive role in secular affairs. "The constitutions of many of our congregations were drawn a hundred, two hundred, or three hundred years ago, and have been in the deep freeze ever since," Cushing said.[10]

The new religious climate brought Cushing and Harvard closer together. As the years passed, old animosities had been forgotten, and the prelate no longer considered Harvard the Kremlin on the Charles or an incorrigible foe of Boston College and Holy Cross. In 1958, Cushing approved the Charles Chauncey Stillman Professorship of Roman Catholic Theological Studies. The first to hold the endowed chair was Christopher Dawson, an Englishman, who taught at Harvard Divinity School from 1958 until 1962. The present incumbent, Father Joseph H. Fichter, S.J., who will have taught for five years when he leaves the faculty in the summer of 1970, wondered at first whether he could get used to living with Protestants. It proved to be no problem.

Vatican II has been largely responsible for the increase in the number of Roman Catholics and women (including one nun in 1969) at Harvard Divinity School. In the spring of 1969, there were thirty-seven religious groups represented in the student body. The largest single denomination was Roman Catholic (twenty-eight). There were twenty-three United Methodists and between sixteen and nineteen Episcopalians, American Baptists, Presbyterians, members of the United Church of Christ, and Unitarian-Universalists. Dr. Charles William Eliot, in his wildest dreams, could not have foreseen that one day there would be more Roman Catholics than Unitarians at Harvard Divinity. Times had changed since World War I, when Archbishop William O'Connell was exercised because Father George LaPiana, a secular priest from Palermo, Sicily, accepted a teaching post at the Divinity School. Even as cardinal, O'Connell would never have suspected that one of his promising priests—Father Cushing—would later donate five thousand dollars to the Divinity School's library, while encouraging the activities of the "Friends of Harvard Divinity School," sponsored by the League of Catholic Women, whose president was Mrs. Vincent Green.

Stories are told of the new spirit of understanding. According to one, perhaps apocryphal, President Nathan M. Pusey was showing Cardinal Cushing around Harvard's famed Widener Library when the prelate asked for a standard textbook on canon law. Pusey was embarrassed when a librarian couldn't find a single volume. Surely, not all the books were in the Harvard Law School library? A closer check revealed that books on canon law were listed under ballistics.

Another story (true), gives a clue to Cushing's mellowing attitude toward a university once considered heretical by Irish Catholics. Between the halves of the Harvard–Holy Cross football game in 1965, stadium fans were startled to see an Episcopal bishop in rich vestments walk onto the field to bless the Holy Cross football team. The Anglican bishop turned out to be a Harvard senior, whose ruse was discovered when the robes were found in his dormitory closet.

"Please forget about it," Cushing wrote the chastened prankster, who had sent a contrite apology to the president of Holy Cross. "Don't worry about it in any way whatsoever. I perfectly understand the situation and your intention. I hope and pray there will be no disciplinary action taken against you." [11]

Father Fichter tells how the Divinity School contributes to the renewal of churches by training both a learned ministry and a learned laity: "If this is the 'age of the laity,' the number of our graduates going into academic life or into the 'unconventional' ministries is bound to have an effect on the *aggiornamento* of organized religion. The ecumenical thrust of the school has been of increasing significance. Self-renewal had previously been the internal concern of each separate church. But the rivalries and antagonisms are now out-of-date. As a Catholic, I have personally witnessed the school's influence through the Stillman Professorship, the active presence of Catholic students, and the growth of love and respect across the creeds. This is a current example as well as a source of future renewal."

In 1964, *Time,* noting that Cushing's "distrust of Harvard having long since died," hailed the Catholic-Protestant ecumenical dialogue held at Harvard the previous year as a landmark in the history of Christianity and gave Cushing most of the credit for making it possible. Soon, according to a historian,[12] visiting cardinals would be "taking up residence amidst the intellectual Protestant walls of the Harvard Divinity School. Moreoever, the old rapprochement between Lake Street and Harvard Yard is channeled into new political, administrative, and intellectual alliances."

There is a warm rapport between Pusey and Cushing, who was a towering figure at the colloquium. Dr. Scott Francis Brunner, of the United Presbyterian Church in Philadelphia, wrote of the cardinal's speech at the closing dinner at the 1963 session: "Cushing is a massive, muscular man with deep etched lines in his face. Hearing him I thought first of all of Al Smith, and looking at him, of Abraham Lincoln. Then, as the impact of his words gripped me, I thought of Albert Schweitzer. Smith, Lincoln, and Schweitzer—put them together and you have Cardinal Cushing. . . . Without him there would have been no colloquium—because of him the colloquium will continue. What a man, with a heart as big as the heart of God." [13]

A year later, an Episcopal minister [14] startled the Christian world by suggesting that Cardinal Cushing be made presiding bishop of the Protestant Episcopal Church in America. "Here is a man like the early Apostles—rugged and down-to-earth; frank and impetuous, but a saint in the New Testament sense of the world." While Cushing retained his current post, the minister believed the cardinal could preside at Episcopalian conclaves of bishops and give them "his fine leadership with his own peculiar, special, unique ecumenical orientation."

"It's impossible," Cushing said. "They have better men than I to head up their church."

In April 1963, Pope John's encyclical *Pacem in Terris,* capturing the imagination of the civilized world, called for the settlement of controversy through negotiations and meetings. John asked nations to overcome racial and national barriers, urging general disarmament among world powers—all with an eye to human freedom and dignity.

At about the same time, President Kennedy told a Boston College assembly that the importance of Pope John and his encyclicals was that "we are learning to talk the language of progress and peace across the barriers of sect and creed." The President, after reading the encyclical, had said: "As a Catholic, I am proud of it; and as an American I have learned from it." The treatise, he said, was not strictly Catholic, for "it closely matches notable expressions of convictions and aspirations from churchmen of other faiths, as in recent documents of the

World Council of Churches, and from outstanding world citizens with no ecclesiastical standing." [15]

People of all faiths grieved when Pope John died in Rome on June 3, 1963, just before the second session of Vatican II. When Monsignor Lally called to tell him of John's death, Cushing said: "Today the whole human family is desolate; we have lost our common father." He spoke of his dear friend who had "erased the oldest prejudices and had captured the hearts, as well as the imaginations, of people everywhere. Pope John was the best human reproduction of Christ that I ever met."

In Call Me John, his biography of the Pontiff, Cushing recalled something John had said a few days before his death: "My bags are packed and I'm ready to go." Nor could he forget John's last words to him: "You are a consolation to the Church."

Reactions to Pope John's death reflected the powerful impact of Cushing and the Kennedys. By the twentieth century, when Greater Boston had become cosmopolitan, prejudices began to fade, especially those rooted in the social, religious, and political life of the late nineteenth century. By the time John Kennedy was elected President, a new ecumenical spirit was creating a warm climate of brotherhood that melted ancient hostilities. For Cushing what is essential is the fatherhood of God and the brotherhood of man. "More changes have been made in the church since the second Vatican Council than in all the years since the Protestant Reformation," he said in 1968. Most of the credit for this goes to Pope John.

Cardinal Cushing, declaring an archdiocesan day of mourning, celebrated a televised mass at the cathedral, which was jammed with nuns and priests, while another fifteen hundred followed the ceremony on television in the lower church. Outside, the sidewalks were crowded. Elevated trains slowed to a crawl to keep down the din. Cushing, in black vestments and a white mitre, hailed the Holy Father as the "builder of bridges between Catholics and Protestants, between East and West, and between Christians and non-Christians. He lifted the Catholic Church from its moorings of past ages into the bewildering chaos of the twentieth century. His goodness will live forever." At the close of the service, the cardinal embraced with the "kiss of peace," Bishop Frederic C. Lawrence, suffragan of the Episcopal diocese, and Bishop Gerasimo of the Greek Orthodox Church, who were seated in the sanctuary.

Time, commenting on the dramatic change that came when Cushing began visiting synagogues and Protestant churches,* added: "The instinct for renewal has always lived in Cushing, and Pope John gave it form. One reason Cushing was so partial to church renewal is his scorn of what one reform-minded layman called 'Chancery Catholicism.' " [16]

Cardinal Cushing was the second Boston prelate to help elect a Pope, a privilege rated the highest prerogative of his rank.[17] A thousand persons waved good-bye when he flew out of Logan Airport in June 1963. When a Milan newspaper speculated that Cushing might be a possibility for Pope, he laughed. "I'm afraid not. If I were ever elected Pope, that would be the end of the apostolic succession. All I want to do is help people." Despite other talk about electing the first non-Italian Pope for 440 years, it was not practicable. "Cardinal Cushing," wrote a British reporter, "as outspoken a critic of Roman hegemony as it is possible to imagine, dismissed it as wishful thinking. A non-Italian would never be able to find his way through the intricacies of the existing Curia. His nationality would condemn him to impotence." [18] Cushing, who felt there were too many aristocrats in the Curia, told Boston reporters he didn't think a non-Italian would be chosen. "He has to be head of the Vatican state." He reminded them of a saying: "The man who goes into the election a pope, comes out a cardinal."

Cardinal Spellman, although not the most powerful or representative prelate at the conclave, was at the time the best-known American churchman—the primate of the United States and the diocesan of the wealthiest see in the world. He had painted himself into a corner at the first session of Vatican II because he took a dim view of most of Pope John's initiatives. Whatever he said when he called on Giovanni Battista Cardinal Montini the night before the first balloting, he was certainly not speaking for all American cardinals, as a reporter noted: "Cushing of Boston, Meyer of Chicago, and Ritter of St. Louis regard him as a reactionary whose lead they would not think of following." [19] Although Spellman could not count on the American block, he did command votes other than his own, including that of the conservative Cardinal McIntyre of Los Angeles, a former Wall Street stockbroker who received a late vocation. Other powerful allies were cardinals Tien Ken Sin, Wysyznski, and Bea, who was anxious to carry on with

---

* Cushing spoke in more than fifty Protestant churches and in more than a dozen synagogues.

the job Pope John had given him and "whose influence was power-fully applied at a wide range of crucial points." [20] While they differed with Spellman in so many ways, Cushing, Meyer, and Ritter joined him in supporting Montini, as did Paul-Emile Léger of Canada. Cush-ing, who expressed regret that he did not have Joe Kennedy's organiza-tional talents available to him in Rome, was, said a reporter, "perhaps the most extreme of this group." Léger, he added, was "perhaps the most influential." [21]

Cushing was a close friend of Montini when he was archbishop of Milan. In June 1960, the Italian cardinal had come to the United States to receive an honorary degree from the University of Notre Dame. Arriving in New York, he was met at the airport by Cardinal Spellman and Archbishop Vagnozzi. After spending the night with Spellman and attending a luncheon in his honor on the same day, he flew to South Bend, Indiana. While in Boston, he stayed with Cardinal Cushing and visited the Kennedy Memorial Hospital, worker chapels run by Franciscans in downtown Boston, and the Don Orione home for Italian-Americans in East Boston. Here, Cushing spoke warmly of "these people who came to this country in their youth, gave their all to their adopted country, and now, through no fault of their own, are unable to take care of themselves." Cushing and Montini dined with three hundred persons in the home.

When Montini as Pope Paul VI came to New York in 1965 to ad-dress the U.N. Assembly, his secretary told reporters that the Pope owed his knowledge of English to three Bostonians: Cardinal Cushing, Joseph DeMambro, and Ernest Siciliano, a Boston College linguist. When Montini came to Boston, Cushing asked DeMambro to serve as interpreter, and when the Pope expressed an interest in learning to speak English, the electronics executive arranged for Siciliano to pre-pare tape recordings, which were shipped to the cardinal's home in Milan and from which he learned English.[22] The tapes recorded dia-logue from English to Italian to English.

While DeMambro as interpreter was holding forth in his "hog Italian," as he put it, Cushing told him in an aside: "Be good to him. He'll be our next Pope." [23]

At ten minutes past five P.M. on Wednesday, June 19, the doors of the Sistine Chapel were locked and the conclave opened. Most of the eighty cardinals assembled to elect a successor to John had been ele-vated to the purple during the Pontiff's brief reign; twenty-six were created by Pius XII, eight by Pius XI.

Between each two rounds of voting, the cardinals left the Sistine Chapel for the more informal confines of the conclave area, where they were waited on by servants if they dined at the long table in one of the Borgia rooms. The first voting session was held on the morning of June 20.

According to the Vatican correspondent of *Il Messagero,* Cushing tried to elect Montini by the "inspiration" method, one that requires that at the beginning of the first session of the conclave, a prince of the church can rise and suggest that in view of the extraordinary eminence of a particular candidate he should be immediately elected by having all cardinals except the one designated giving their assent. There had been no record of the inspiration method having been used in modern times. If Cushing had (unsuccessfully) attempted this dramatic maneuver, the London *Observer* speculated, what were his motives?

"He is a man of generous, aggressive, almost brash temperament. There is no doubt that he regarded the result of the election as of crucial importance for the whole future of the Church, and in a few days beforehand he seemed by no means confident of a progressive victory." [24]

Cushing was as interested as the Curial Cardinal Bea in electing a person who would continue John's policies. According to the *Observer,* if the story in *Il Messagero* were true, Cushing must have concluded that "a clear call from a notable and progressive church leader, speaking as it were from the world to the city, could do no harm at that stage. It would not escape notice . . . that Cushing, apart from his other attributes, is the diocesan of by far the most powerful Catholic layman [President Kennedy] alive today." [25]

The speculation raised questions. Since Cushing was deficient in Italian and Latin, in what language did he speak? His South Boston English would certainly have been incomprehensible to most of his colleagues. Did he fail in his effort because he tried to deliver it in faulty Italian or Latin? Nobody will ever know. Consistory proceedings are secret.

After two rounds of voting on Thursday, black smoke curled over St. Peter's Square at 11:52 A. M. The prelates reconvened at four o'clock, and after two more inconclusive ballots, at 5:49 the crowd in the square moved away at the sight of more black smoke.

The first ballot on Friday morning elected Montini overwhelmingly. When Cardinal Ottaviani proclaimed the election of the son of a prosperous lawyer and journalist, who had been a member of the Vatican secretariat since 1922, a roar went up from the hundred thousand persons assembled in the square. Cushing afterward referred to the throng that heard Ottaviani make the announcement from the center balcony of St. Peter's.

"That square was loaded," he said when he stepped out of the car returning him from the conclave. "I wanted to take up a collection, but they wouldn't let me." [26]

Cushing considered Montini the best possible choice. "I am confident that we have what I wanted, a mission-minded Pope, a Pope who has visited the United States and has a great admiration for the Catholics of our country. He speaks English well enough. He stayed with me at Lake Street for two days the last time he was in the country and gave a Latin address to the seminarians at St. John's." [27]

When John was elected Pope, he said *"Horrefactus sum"* ("I am horrified"). Paul VI's calmer words were *"Deo volente"* ("God willing").

On his return to North American College, Cushing laughed when he met reporters. "Well, I didn't make it," he said.

Between the final obsequies for Pope John and the balloting, Cushing learned that the United States Supreme Court had banned the reading of the Bible and the reciting of the Lord's Prayer in public schools, a decision he called a victory for communism. He urged an amendment to the Constitution to offset the ruling. "To me, it is a great tragedy that the greatest book . . . ever published and the best-seller of the ages, cannot be read in our public school system." The decision was made on June 17, 1963.

America magazine called the decision a step toward secularization, adding that there had been "disturbing hints of heightened anti-Semitic feeling" since it had been made. *America* cited the danger of a minority group in a pluralistic society painting itself into a corner of social and cultural alienation." [28] The *Pilot* joined the attack, whereupon the *Jewish Advocate* accused both publications of harping on a sour note: "that Jews who fight against religious intrusions in public schools are ganged up with secularists and atheists. . . . Since when has a group lost the right to its opinion . . . and by what right does anyone, especially editorialists for a church group, issue veiled threats against fellow Americans of another faith."

In the *Pilot,* Cushing called the decision "ridiculous" but stayed out of the debate. He found it hard to imagine how civic morality of an enduring kind could be taught on any other basis than that of religion and was alarmed by the rift that threatened ecumenical calm, especially when Rabbi Roland B. Gittelsohn, president of the Jewish Community Council of Greater Boston, wrote in the *Advocate:* "When Catholics of Boston stood behind their youngsters who were expelled from the Elliot public school some years ago for refusing to participate in religious exercises, they served their church well, they served God well, and they served America well." As for the issue of anti-Semitism and unpopularity, Gittelsohn reminded Catholics that they had survived such an ordeal.

Cardinal Montini was crowned Pope Paul VI on June 30. During the nine days after his election, Cushing in Rome made his usual round of visits and donations. Observing the need of repair in a youth center, he borrowed a pen from a reporter and wrote out a check for five thousand dollars. "I hope this doesn't bounce," he said, handing it to a priest. At the Queen of Apostles Hospital for nuns at Albano, twenty-five miles south of Rome, he left three thousand dollars with Sister Thecla, mother general of the Daughters of St. Paul, who staff the hospital. At his specific request, each nun received ten dollars, a bottle of wine, and a pair of shoes or a garment. He said at the hospital bedside of a dying nun: "If the prayers of a fool like me can help you, you'll get better. I'll see you in Boston."

"No," the nun said, knowing she had terminal cancer. "Some day I'll see you in paradise." She was serene. "It's a good place to die, and I know where I'm going."

Cushing would have left Rome before the coronation, but he remained until President Kennedy arrived. "He won't be here for the coronation," Cushing told reporters, "but he may want to see me. I hope he wants to see me," he winked, "because if I stay in Rome any longer I'll be in the poorhouse." He told the press that he had to collect eight million dollars a year to keep operations of his archdiocese and his Latin American program going. "When I'm home, I can raise it. But I've learned . . . that our charity alms are reduced to a very low level when I go away . . . they drop off about sixteen thousand dollars a day."

Cushing was on the steps of North American College when President Kennedy arrived with his sister, Mrs. Stephen Smith. The prelate kissed her on both cheeks. "Hi, Jean! My, you look good." After shaking hands with the President, the cardinal kissed him, Latin style, on both cheeks. Kennedy was startled when Cushing jabbed him on the chest and raised his fists in a simulated ring pose. "It was getting awful formal there," Cushing said afterward, "so I wanted to shake him up a bit."

The cardinal handed the President gifts Pope John had personally intended to present to him, including an autographed copy of *Pacem in Terris,* and two sets of silver, bronze, and gold medallions commemorating another encyclical, *Mater et Magistra.* Soon after the death of Pope John, Cushing received a package from Archbishop Angelo Dell'Aqua with the words: "I have the honor to forward to you the enclosed pectoral cross which was destined by the Holy Father John XXIII for Your Eminence. This cross was used by His Holiness during the years of his service for the Holy See in the Orient, in Paris and in Venice. It was also used by him when he was Pope." When he told reporters he had received one of the two papal crosses used by John, Cushing winked. "I got the better one," he said, refusing to tell who got the other.

Soon after his return from the second session of the council, Cushing told a mixed congregation that he gave the cross away "because I didn't know what would happen to it if anything happened to me. I gave it to a community of nuns in Mexico who cannot even wear the religious habit. They are as poor as Job's cat." [29] He asked the sisters, who were devoting their lives to the poorest of the poor, to pray for Pope John. If he was not in heaven, he said, "then God help the rest of us. I wish a man like John had been Pope in the fifteenth century. I doubt that Luther would have left the Catholic Church."

In another talk, the cardinal said he had received the cross from John "because of the help I gave, the love and admiration I had for him, and because of his gratitude to me when he needed help for unity among all Christians and non-Christians in the days when few helped him." Cushing wore the pectoral cross for the first time at a Boy Scout ceremony at Holy Cross Cathedral. He rarely wears one, however. "I have crosses enough without carrying one adorned with jewels."

Cushing joined Kennedy in an audience with the new Pope, later describing the meeting as a magnificent tribute of affection and esteem by the Pope to the President and American citizens. The Pope gave Kennedy a solid gold rosary for Jacqueline, who, because of the impending arrival of her third child, stayed home.

After giving away most of his clothes in Rome, Cushing on the eve of departure was down to one pair of wrinkled trousers. The nun housekeeper who pressed them ironed them as if they were pajamas, with no crease. Next morning, while officials and reporters waited at the airport, Cushing asked the nun to press the pants with a neat crease down the center. This time she burned them so that his knee showed through a wide split. He donned a cassock so he could deplane in Boston without causing a mild sensation.

The cardinal returned to Rome late in September 1963 for the second session of Vatican II, when the revival of the order of deacons was discussed. At one time, deacons performed important functions, but the rank had become little more than a steppingstone for seminarians on their way to ordination as priests. Many prelates, because of the increasing shortage of priests, thought deacons could be trained to assume most of the pastoral functions of the priesthood. This raised a question: Should deacons be allowed to marry? The church had not demanded celibacy of deacons or priests until the fourth century, and Christ had not demanded celibacy of his apostles.

Latin American prelates for the most part favored the marriage proposal, and Cushing sided with them against the dissent of Cardinal Spellman, who asked how celibate priests could live happily in a community of married deacons. Cushing favored the revival of the diaconate so married or unmarried deacons could substitute for priests in all phases of pastoral work except those pertaining to purely sacerdotal functions. Spellman's supporters argued that easing celibate standards would bring chaos. Some seminarians might prefer to remain deacons rather than become priests, if they could marry. Were not thousands of seminarians the world over already deserting classrooms for this reason? Cushing had a facetious comment: "The bishops will govern the church, the priests will do all the work, and the deacons will have all the fun." [30]

According to one story, a perplexed young priest told Cushing he had just received a gift of "His" and "Her" towels. "What shall I do with them?"

"You better keep them. The way things are going, you may need them."

Although the vote against permitting deacons to marry was 1,364 to 839, the spadework paved the way for Pope Paul's decision a few years later, on June 18, 1967, when he granted an authority that permitted married or unmarried Roman Catholic men to be ordained as permanent deacons. It was specified that they would be separate from the seminarian's temporary diaconate. The Pope set a minimum age of twenty-six and further stipulated that unmarried men who became deacons would not be permitted to wed after they were ordained. Married men accepted could not remarry if they were widowed. Deacons may now administer baptism, dispense Holy Communion, administer sacraments and officiate at funerals and burial services.

Before the Second session of the council, Cushing had told an *America* editor [31] that the Vatican should do something about problems of mixed marriages. He had often argued against extracting an agreement from Protestants that all children in mixed marriages be raised as Catholics. This struck him as a violation of conscience. Catholics, he said, must esteem as well as respect the religious values of others.

In June 1963, a national magazine [32] reported his views on relaxing church laws on mixed-faith marriages, particularly in answer to a query as to whether he expected changes in church law to result from Vatican II.

"Yes, if the council is faithful to the pastoral approach . . . there should be considerable changes in church law." Canon law, he said, is the result of pastoral needs, which change. Past laws may not be of much help to later generations. "In fact, they can sometimes be a hindrance in the care of souls." If promises, often made in bad faith, were no longer required, he went on, "we would not be revoking any divine law; we would not be changing any dogma of the church." Another time, he said: "When I was ordained a priest, mixed marriages were so frowned upon, that 'erring' couples could be wed only in a five-minute ceremony in the rectory. As soon as I became archbishop, I said to myself, 'I won't stand for that kind of thing: in the future they will be married in church.' " [33]

Cushing's eloquent appeal was rejected at the council. "While Protestants throughout the world appreciated the attitude of Cardinal Cushing and other liberal leaders," writes Paul Blanshard, "they were not disposed to forgive or forget the failure of the council to effect a reform in this elementary matter of interdenominational fair play." Religious leaders doubted whether there could be any meaningful improvement in interchurch relations unless the Roman Church relaxed its rules on mixed marriages.

Cushing, impatient with the so-called "service-station liturgy" in Latin favored by unimaginative priests, had been one of the loudest American voices in urging Rome to conduct services in the vernacular, and he was pleased when the second session ruled that the major part of the mass and of the sacraments should be in the vernacular.

The session also dealt with the layman's role in the church. Again,

Cushing was a pioneer, for he had often pleaded with the laity to become more active in church affairs. "If you don't, who will? You see the deadwood I have here in the clergy." In another of his frequent comments on his concern over the role of the layman, he said long before Vatican II: "For many years, the Catholic layman was all right to take up a collection and run beano games when they were legal and sell chances on the pastor's hat, but they had no part in the structure of the church." There was a saying that the role of the Catholic layman was to "pay, pay and obey." 34

As early as the spring of 1962, Cushing had announced plans to have laymen participate in an archdiocesan synod soon after the council ended. It marked the first time in the 154-year-old history of the Boston see that laymen took part in such a gathering of priests held to make regulations and disciplinary laws for the area.

The Roman Catholic Church had always been considered an institution built around its hierarchy. Vatican II changed the conception. It described the church as "the people of God," a revolutionary concept. "The church, in brief, is a living community of men who share in governing it." 35

The council recommended that pastors seek the laity's "prudent advice" and urged them to give them freedom of action in duties assigned them in the service of the church. Since Vatican II, this movement has gained momentum. In 1967, a Commission for Studies of Justice and Peace was formed in Rome, with six women on its board, the first time in history that women were permitted in the Curia. Later that year, Pope Paul convened a worldwide congress of the lay apostolate, with nearly three thousand delegates present. One resolution was the abolition of stringent rules on mixed marriages, another wish fulfilled for Cushing. Today laymen dominate many diocesan school boards, once completely clerical, and have a powerful voice even on the boards of leading Catholic universities.

The second session recessed on December 4, 1963, soon after the tragedy in Dallas.

At the third session, opened in September 1964, Pope Paul, continuing John's policy of *aggiornamento*, shook up the Curia, the entrenched bureaucracy of ultraconservative Italian cardinals, who administered the Holy See. For four centuries, all vital authority had been vested in the Pope and Curia, whose principal members were cardinals appointed for life. Paul persuaded some of the older prelates to resign, limited the term to five years, and arranged to have members drawn from all parts of the world, rather than just from Italy.

Vatican II also established the principle of "collegiality," by which bishops, acting in union with the Pope, are the supreme authority of the church. This new power extended the responsibilities of bishops beyond their own dioceses.

In the spring of 1962, Cardinal Cushing said that if the council did not make a pronouncement on religious freedom, the ecumenical movement would "fall on its face." Cardinal Spellman had given his strong support on this issue to John Courtney Murray, the theologian who had been a principal architect of the religious liberty declaration. In his address to the United Nations in April, Pope Paul said: "There is every reason to expect the promulgation of a text on this matter, which will have great consequences."

There was, however, powerful opposition to such a declaration among certain Spanish and Italian prelates, who met in a private conclave early during the last week of the session, under the leadership of Cardinal Bueno y Monreal of Seville, to draw up a petition opposing the declaration and asking for postponement of the vote. It was clear that American bishops would have to spearhead the move to achieve a declaration on religious liberty. Cardinal Spellman was so sure of the success of the measure that he did not attend the crucial session when the issue came up.

On September 17, under Cushing's guidance, 170 of the 240 American prelates met at North American College, not only to press for collegial (collective) rules but also for pronouncements on religious freedom and exoneration of the Jews. He spoke only twice at the third session: once to plead for freedom of conscience for all mankind, the other time to argue that all men of all times were responsible for the death of Jesus, not merely Jews. Each time he spoke, the prelates in St. Peter's Basilica broke rules by loudly applauding.

The formidable Cardinal Ruffini, challenging the theological basis of the Declaration on Religious Liberty, said that since the Catholic Church was the only true religion, Catholics alone were entitled to complete freedom. He was backed by Cardinal Quiroga y Palacios, archbishop of Santiago de Compostela, Spain. Then came a series of speeches by cardinals Albert Gregory Meyer of Chicago, Joseph Ritter of St. Louis, Paul-Emile Léger of Montreal, Silva Henriquez of Chile, and Cushing. This group seemed to support the thesis for curial argument that the matter was primarily American and political rather than theological and should not, accordingly, be settled by a council, especially because of the central point they raised: that freedom of conscience, a concomitant of human dignity, should be respected alike by church and state.

"The debate," wrote Xavier Rynne in *The New Yorker*,[36] "was the occasion of Cardinal Cushing's first speech at the council, and he was listened to with considerable interest as he filled the aula with flawless Latin periods in his high-pitched Boston twang." It was at this point that Cardinal Ottaviana first spoke to object to the declaration.

In his religious speech on September 23, Cushing, in recommending "a decent respect for the opinions of mankind," cited Lord Acton's statement that "freedom is the highest political end." Cushing said the church "must show herself to the entire modern world as the champion of liberty, of human liberty, and of civil liberty, specifically in the matter of religion," and he scored the fact that "the doctrine of the church on religious liberty in modern civil society has not yet been declared clearly and unambiguously." He noted that "throughout her history the Catholic Church has ever insisted upon her own freedom in civil society and before public powers," adding, "that same freedom in civil society which the church has ever insisted upon for herself and her members she now in this our age also champions for other churches and their members, indeed for every human."

"As a clincher," wrote Blanshard, "he quoted from Pope John's general endorsement of liberty in *Pacem in Terris*. He sat down to the reverberation of loud applause." In his encyclical, John had written that "every human being has the right to honor God according to the dictates of an upright conscience, and therefore the right to worship God, privately and publicly." According to Blanshard, Cushing and Cardinal Meyer made the best appeals.

Cushing was delighted when Cardinal Silva Henriquez, speaking for fifty-eight Latin American clerics, agreed with him, reminding the council that not all South American bishops followed the Spanish line. He stressed the need of endorsing religious liberty "to win back the unchurched masses of Latin America." The shrewd and powerful Cardinal Ottaviani appeared to make few converts when he emphasized the primacy of supernatural rights and the church's claim to absolute knowledge of religious truth over the natural right of freedom of the human conscience. Then came the blow, which stunned the American prelates.

On November 19, the next-to-last business day of the third session, the American bishops, exhausted after ten weeks of effort, were awaiting the vote on the declaration when Cardinal Tisserant spoke: "It seems proper to the presidency that we should not proceed to a vote as scheduled. This declaration will be examined at the next session. The fathers are invited to submit their textual suggestions by January 1st."

Not since an enraged bishop pulled another's beard at the Council of Trent, wrote Xavier Rynne, was there so much disorder in the Basilica. The Americans, stunned, reacted violently. One of them, according to Henri Fesquet, writing in *Le Monde*, muttered, "The bastards," referring to the small but powerful minority of curial and Italian prelates whose Machiavellian maneuvers had paved the way for Tisserant's bombshell. Vatican officials were amazed at the violent American reaction. "If anyone was at fault," Cardinal Ritter said later, "we were, for being too trustful. . . . We had been too sure of a vote, which we would have won by a big margin." Cardinal Meyer, furious at the cavalier way Tisserant had scuttled the declaration, said of him, "That man is hopeless!" (Cardinal Tisserant, speaking of Cushing, told Milton Lord: "He's one of the best bishops we have.")

Although Cushing was crushed when the proposal was sidetracked, he would later be able to say: "The recent Declaration on Religious Freedom leads me to believe that I do not hope in vain. The Declaration . . . on the right of man to religious freedom has its foundation in the dignity of the persons, whose exigencies have come to be more fully known to human reason through the centuries of experience."

On September 29, Cushing told the council: "We cannot judge the leaders of ancient Israel. God alone is their judge and most certainly we cannot dare to attribute to later generations of Jews the guilt of the Crucifixion of the Lord Jesus or the death of the Saviour of the World, except in the sense of the universal guilt in which all of us men share." He was glad to find the council strongly repudiating anti-Semitism. Cushing voted in favor of the declaration holding that "the Jewish people should never be presented as one rejected, cursed, or guilty of deicide. What happened to Christ in his Passion cannot be attributed to the whole people then alive, much less to that of today. Besides, the church held and holds that Christ underwent his Passion and death freely, because of the sins of all men and out of infinite love."

The declaration echoed words Cushing had written in the Boston *Traveler* in the spring of 1964: "The spiritual ancestry of Christians is Jewish. We are the sons of Abraham, Isaac, and Jacob, even as they. The Cross is a point of separation in our spiritual traditions, but we must all be keenly aware of the essential Christian doctrine: Christ died for the sins of all men, those prior to his time, his contemporaries, those who came after him. Anti-Semitism is a profoundly un-Christian attitude."

In Rome during the third session Cushing said to a Jewish reporter: "Who killed Christ? Whether it was the Romans or others we don't know, but the point is we can't change history. We can't change what is recorded in the Gospel. All of us—Jews, Gentiles, everyone—crucified Christ, because he chose to die for all our sins, to make atonement for our sins." [37] He went on to say he hoped his Jewish friends would be satisfied with the declaration from the council. "No one went as far as I did on behalf of the Jews and I'm tremendously fond of the Jews and they of me. I've received thousands of letters from Jews all over the world on my statements at the . . . council. I did not make those statements in any special effort to befriend the Jews. They can take care of themselves."

Boston Jewry was elated by the prelate's efforts. Dr. Alexander Brin, editor and publisher of the *Jewish Advocate,* said Cushing's "magnificent call at the ecumenical assembly has evoked a deep reverberating echo in humanity's collective heart. He gave a living demonstration as a great human being who possesses the moral power and spiritual idealism of such immortals as Roger Williams, Thomas Jefferson, and Abraham Lincoln." Brin nominated the cardinal for a Nobel prize.[38] "Rarely has a religious leader of any denomination in this country won such a commanding position in the life of the nation and won the universal regard of leaders in all creeds, as well as the respect of millions of their followers, as has Cardinal Cushing," Brin said. Rabbi Bnai Moshe also had a comment: "Richard Cardinal Cushing is a facet on the face of God."

Vatican II adopted another recommendation that Cushing had been making for years. It phased out the *Index Expurgatorius,* the Catholic Index of Prohibited Books. Between the final two council sessions, *Time* reported that Cushing had called the Index of Forbidden Books meaningless, recommending that "they should get rid of the whole thing." [39] One of his reasons was to give teachers and students more latitude, especially in the study of communism. While a bishop's imprimatur on Catholic books is still required, "it is a law more noted these days in breach than in observance. Books dealing with controversial issues fall from the presses like leaves in autumn, many of them frankly critical of the structure of the church." [40]

In 1962, the cardinal had returned from Rome feeling that he had been ineffective. "Sensing the importance of the moment in history," Albert Duhamel wrote in *The New York Times*, "he returned in 1964 and twice within three weeks rose to deliver to tumultuous applause petitions for the recognition of religious freedom for all mankind and the exoneration of the Jews." [41] And this, says Duhamel, was "the constant prayer of his life." Without being overoptimistic, Cushing visualized further steps toward Christian unity, knowing, as a modern priest said, that "Vatican II is only a spark, a beginning—but it marks the future with a ray of hope." [42]

Cardinal Cushing, who dominated the third session, emerged from Vatican II as one of the most forthright and progressive prelates in the entire conclave, which generated changes that directly affected the religious life of six hundred million Roman Catholics. The monolithic church that had stood pat for centuries was rocked to its foundations. "For nothing in the church—literally nothing—is being allowed to go unexamined or unquestioned. A questioning so pervasive and so intensive will . . . have large social consequences. And not only for those who regard themselves as Catholics." [43] Vatican II proved that the church, static until the Reformation, had an unhoped for vitality and capacity for change, and thousands of Catholics welcomed the gusty winds of renewal. Many, insisting on the primacy of their individual conscience—a view backed by some bishops—began to challenge outmoded concepts of monarchical papacy, dogma, infallibility and the confessional box. Laymen long taught to think of non-Catholic Christians as schismatics and heretics were suddenly told to consider them brothers.

After reading a profile of Cushing in *Look*, a Catholic wrote the editor as one who since childhood had been "spoon-fed the catechism answers as the be-all and end-all of religion." She had equal praise for Pope John and his "outspoken and good-humored disciple, Cardinal Cushing. The day of the tightly compartmented, of so comfortably barricaded minds of the born-and-bred bead-sayers, has passed." Other readers, citing Cushing's broadmindedness, predicted that if the church had more prelates like him, lost sheep might return to the fold. One reader of the profile suggested a "Be Like Cushing Week"—perhaps "in the dead of winter when things get dull." During this week, all bishops and cardinals would "embrace his philosophy, his earthiness and his dislike for worn-out mannerisms." [44]

When Cardinal Montini became Pope Paul VI in 1963, most Catholics heard mass largely in Latin, ate fish on Friday, and read no books condemned by the Vatican Index. The stodgy Roman Curia was packed with aging Italian cardinals, and official dialogue between Catholics and atheists was taboo. Married deacons were unknown, and bishops wore ceremonial robes reflecting medieval splendor.

Among rules relaxed at Vatican II were meatless Fridays, the Lenten fast, and the prohibition against joining such groups as YMCAs, YWCAs, and Masons.

The first English mass in the United States was celebrated in August 1964, in St. Louis, when more than ten thousand priests and laymen assembled for the annual North American Liturgical Week. Now the practice of saying mass in the vernacular is common. The Curia has been invigorated and a Vatican secretariat for nonbelievers encourages contact with communists and atheists. In the spring of 1968 the first (five) married candidates for the diaconate were ordained in Cologne, Germany, and one hundred ten more were in training in Germany alone. Cardinal Cushing was further pleased when Pope Paul ruled that non-Catholics no longer had to make written promises, when marrying Catholics, to rear children in the Catholic faith. The Pope also, recognizing changing circumstances, simplified the princely finery of cardinals.

Eliminated altogether is the red broad-brimmed, flat, thirty-tasseled galero. The red hat for centuries had been a symbol of the rank of cardinal. The trend is to reduce the use of red and to encourage optional choice of black, with no red trimmings. Showy attire discarded includes red shoes and silver buckles; the mantelletta (a red silken or woolen sleeveless knee-length garment), and the ordinary red felt hat. The scarlet cappa magna, a flowing silk cape worn by cardinals on ceremonial occasions, now optional, may be worn only outside Rome.

Pope Paul further ruled that cardinals may be addressed as "lord cardinal," instead of "your eminence," and archbishops and bishops may be called "monsignor," instead of "your excellency." In a letter to a friend Cushing wrote: "I don't like the idea of being called 'lord cardinal.' Just call me Father Cushing. I have been a father to the poorest of the poor all my life."

Many Catholic orders now permit sisters to wear secular dress. The first day Sister Ruth Marie wore the contemporary garb adopted by her order, she noticed the boys in her mathematics class ogling her legs. She turned to face them. "What did you expect—wheels?" [45] One prelate who objected to change was James Francis Cardinal McIntyre of Los Angeles, who took a dim view of the Sisters of the Immaculate Heart of Mary when they abandoned their traditional habit in favor of civilian attire. The cardinal has been called a frost who keeps his eyes fixed on the thirteenth century. Nevertheless, the Vatican backed him up to a degree by ruling that if the progressive nuns wanted to continue as an approved order, they must renounce secular garb and wear "a recognizable habit." [46]

Until Vatican II, the hierarchy was content to see its communicants "hatched, matched, and dispatched," and rarely did priests or laymen question the authority of the church. Thus it was news when a priest in Los Angeles in 1963 demanded the removal of Cardinal McIntyre, charging him with autocratically ruling the "Church of Silence." [47] Catholic lay organizations backed the priest, encouraging rebellion in church ranks. Elsewhere conservatives were jolted when priests and nuns joined civil rights picket lines. One conservative was Monsignor Joseph McCaffrey, pastor of New York's Holy Cross Church, who retired in 1969 at the age of seventy-eight after lamenting "the awful changes in the church—young priests leading civil disobedience, going to jail, burning draft cards." [48]

The American Catholic renewal, *Time* reported, stemmed from the "spiritual fallout from the Vatican Council and the church-wide modernization unleashed by Pope John," adding that the renewed church, in the opinion of progressive theologians, seemed "more credible to men as it sheds no longer relevant trappings of past ages." Cardinal Cushing, the report said, while neither deserving nor getting the credit "as originator, rebel, theologian, theoretician or organizer of change," emerged "as the intuitive old party in a high place who gave renewal a hearty push just because it seemed the right thing to do." [49]

Pushing for renewal is the educated laity, who, while accepting the church's basic mysteries and matters of faith, question the way theologians translate these dogmas in term of practical behavior.[50] There are still laymen, however, who resist renewal. "I left the Baptist Church for Roman Catholicism, and now it is being dismantled all around me," a housewife said. "At the rate they are going, it will look like the Baptist Church before long." [51] *Time* concluded that church renewal has "been most actively supported by . . . Cushing." While the cardinal approves of renewal, he does not endorse the concept of the church wherein "authority is shared by all people, not simply those in special offices, and in which the differences between believers and atheists are considered minimal." [52]

The principle of collegiality adopted by Vatican II paved the way for regional and national episcopal conferences in the United States. The pattern was a Bishop's Synod (197 cardinals and bishops from around the globe), which convened in Rome in 1967 as the first parliament of the church. In the decentralization that followed, most dioceses in the United States established senates of priests to help bishops administratively. In 1966, in the Boston see, forty priests were elected to the senates to serve as liaison between 1429 priests and Cushing.

"Their first demand was for a $200-a-month salary," Cushing said. "Why, when I was a priest, I did that kind of work for nothing."

Some priests and laymen now demand the right to elect their bishops, and there are liberals who would even elect the Pope. "After all," one said, "if local bishops come to be elected by the people of God, it would seem that the bishop of Rome should be, too." [53]

Typical of the spirit of renewal was the sit-down Cushing had in October 1964, with Billy Graham, whose crusade in Boston the cardinal endorsed, urging Catholic students to go to the Boston Garden to hear the evangelist. "His message is one of Christ crucified and no Catholic can do anything but become a better Catholic after listening to him. I only wish we had half a dozen men of his character to go forth and preach the gospel. He is extraordinarily gifted."

Graham, who called Cushing "the leading ecumenist in America today," said he felt much closer to Roman Catholic tradition than to some of the more liberal Protestants. In a 1967 television documentary, Billy Graham said ecumenism started in Boston long before anyone heard of Pope John. "I remember fifteen years ago when I was here, it had already started. It had already reached down to people in your area," he told Cardinal Cushing, adding that Catholics believed in his message. "This has been a great encouragement to me," Billy Graham said.

"No Catholic can listen to you without becoming a better Catholic," Cushing told the evangelist.

In the late 1940s, Cushing had invited Protestant and Jewish clergymen to sit down with him at ecumenical luncheons and engage in informal civil and religious discussions. Rabbi Joseph Shubow, then president of the Greater Boston Rabbinical Association, was delighted when the archbishop called him: "Rabbi Joe," he said, "I'd like to have you and Dana Greeley be my guests at a series of luncheons." According to Shubow, the Protestant and Jewish clergymen who attended these sessions got an extraordinary insight into Cushing's lovable character and saintly spirit. "In the marvelous discussions," Shubow said, Cushing pointed out that it was time for those who believe in God to unite against those who don't, adding that in the history of civilization "we have reached something of a stalemate." When Shubow noted that too much emphasis had been put on the "stale," and too little on the "mate," Cushing pounded the table: "Joe, that's just what I was thinking about."

Thirty years ago, before ecumenism was commonly known, a Jewish couple about to be wed told Rabbi Shubow they would like to invite four Irish Americans to serve as ushers. Shubow asked if they were friends. "Close friends," they said. "Then that's all that matters," the rabbi said.

Bishop Stokes had heard of Cushing long before he came to Boston. In 1956 he sent the archbishop a Christmas card and expressed a wish to see him. In the 1967 WNAC television documentary, Stokes recalled that when he and Suffragan Bishop Frederick Lawrence went to the residence to visit the prelate, his first words were: "Well, boys, how are things going?" Stokes, observing that Cushing was known the world over, said doors were opened to him when he visited the English bishop of the Fiji Islands. The bishop of Fiji recalled the time Cardinal Cushing requested permission to celebrate mass in a small room behind the altar of Westminster Cathedral in London. The minister asked Cushing whether he had the necessary permit. When Cushing said no, the English clergyman explained that he could give permission to say mass only to visiting priests who had permits. Learning that the name of his visitor was Cushing, he asked whether he happened to be related to his eminence, Richard Cardinal Cushing of Boston."

"I am Cardinal Cushing."

"Oh, I'm terribly sorry, Father—Your Eminence." In his embarrassment, he asked why he didn't wear something so that he could be recognized as a cardinal.

"What do you want me to look like, a ruddy monsignor?" Cushing said, putting the minister at ease.

After returning from the second session of Vatican II late in 1963, Cushing told a congregation at St. Benedict's Church in Somerville that he would speak in Protestant churches, at that time almost un-heard of for a Catholic prelate. "Nothing like this has ever happened before. I am accepting invitations from ministers and will make these talks in the ecumenical spirit." He addressed Jewish congregations, as well as Protestant, making strong pleas for brotherly love as he laced his talks with earthy wit and humor.

The Reverend Blaine Taylor, head of the Sudbury Council of Churches, was one of the first Protestant ministers to take the prelate up on his promise. On January 19, 1964, on the afternoon of the Kennedy Memorial Mass, Cushing, after a light lunch, slipped into his scarlet-piped black cassock and drove to the Methodist Church in Sudbury. He shook hands with a reporter in the vestibule. "My name's Cushing," he said. "What's yours?" The Catholics and Protestants who heard him speak in the church were charmed and astounded by his candor and humor. He accepted the invitation, he said, "because of the godly examples of two Johns—John XIII, Pope, and John Wesley," the founder of Methodism.

In his ninety-minute talk he told the attentive audience that he was in trouble by the end of his first year in high school, that he was hopeless as a curate, and that he had never earned a college degree. His blunt remarks amused, shocked, and moved the gathering. He drew the first laugh when he said, "This is not a speech. This . . . paper I'm holding . . . I have taken from a speech by a Methodist bishop." A moment later he said he wouldn't favor an ambassador to the Vatican. Then he criticized divisions in religion: "They come to me . . . and say, 'We want a Protestant minister and a Catholic priest and a Jewish rabbi to plant a tree on Boston Common.' Time and again . . . some group wants a priest and a minister and a rabbi, and the Orthodox lately makes four of us. Pretty soon the atheists will want to get into the act." The end result was confusion. He went on to tell of a visit by Khrushchev's daughter and son-in-law to Pope John.

"What beautiful hands he has," the daughter said during the interview, in which her husband said he was an atheist. Pope John, who understood a little Russian, asked if he would "take the blessing from the beautiful hands of an old man for yourself and your wife and your children." John's charm, Cushing said, "struck the heart of the couple." In his concluding remarks, he told the congregation to recognize the conscientious religious beliefs of everyone and erase any semblance of bigotry.

That evening, he addressed the fiftieth anniversary banquet of the

Catholic Daughters of America, an event that had been postponed because of Kennedy's assassination. Early the next morning he flew to Chicago to address the Catholic Inter-American Corporation Conference.

In March he told several hundred Congregationalists in suburban Wellesley: "Organic unity of the faiths is not possible in the foreseeable future, but the ecumenical movement can achieve the unity of love. In the past we have been living in ghettos. We have hardly talked with one another, but sometimes we were fighting." Later that month, with President Pusey of Harvard present, he called for "the unity of love" at Christ Church Episcopal in Harvard Square. In what is considered the first such ecumenical service in the United States, Auxiliary Bishop Thomas J. Riley, representing Cushing, and Bishop Anson Phelps Stokes, Jr., took part in a special service in the same church on the first Sunday of Advent. Both gave a brief sermon and used Catholic and Protestant prayers. In another service, Bishop Stokes, after presenting Cushing as "our cardinal" before the prelate, spoke at Trinity (Episcopal) Church in Boston, later explained the reference to a group of Catholic women: "It was no affectation, because we of the Protestant community have come to love Cardinal Cushing and consider him in a special way our own."

Cushing did not endear himself merely to Protestants. In May 1962, he had spoken at the consecration of Archbishop John Bassoul of Homs, Syria, at Holy Cross Cathedral. Garbed in vestments of the Eastern Rite Church, donated by a Greek Orthodox priest, Cushing presided at the ecumenical occasion. In July 1964, the cardinal, who had donated one hundred thousand dollars to the Greek Orthodox Seminary in Brookline, spoke to a Greek Orthodox conference in Denver. A few years later, in Istanbul, Turkey, Patriarch Athenagoras I of Constantinople, leader of the world's 150 million Eastern Orthodox Christians, called Cushing the "Universal Man."

"Cardinal Cushing has love and understanding for all mankind," he said. "He is a strong man, a big man, a courageous man who has worked hard and long to help bring unity to all Christians. He was the first to bridge the nine-century-old schism between Catholicism and Orthodoxy." [54]

Athenagoras had met Cushing in Boston in 1947 at a dinner to launch the Greek War Relief Association's fund-raising campaign. As they were introduced, Cushing reached forward to give the patriarch a fraternal embrace, a gesture that stunned and delighted the assembly, who wildly applauded. "I'm often in correspondence with the cardinal and read with joy his forward-thinking articles and comments," Athenagoras said in Istanbul. When Pope Paul invited non-Catholic churches to send observers to Vatican II, the patriarch sent his personal confidant, Father Andre Scrima, a noted theologian, with orders to seek out Cushing.

"My brother from Boston was most helpful to my representative," he said. When he first met Cushing in Boston, Athenagoras was archbishop of the Greek Orthodox Church of North and South America.

Cushing also established close ties with other churches. He donated two thousand dollars to the Armenian Cathedral in New York and was principal speaker in 1968 at a banquet held at the Statler Hilton in Boston in honor of His Holiness Vasken I, Supreme Patriarch-Catolicos of All Armenians. Cushing received this prelate at his residence. In 1969, the cardinal sent two thousand dollars to the Cardinal Cushing Center in Galilee in memory of the mother of Lawrence Stone, a frequent donor to Cushing charities. Half of the money came from Temple Shalom in Newton. Stone, who is Jewish, had a simple answer when a rabbi asked when he was going to have himself photographed with him rather than with Cushing.

"When you do as much good as the cardinal," Stone said.

In 1964, President Chiang Kai-shek of the Republic of China presented Cushing with the Special Cordon of the Order of Brilliant Star for "invaluable contributions toward higher education in China . . . eminent service to the cause of human freedom." Cushing was cited as "a great leader, renowned humanitarian, and a staunch and true friend of the Republic of China." The cardinal got credit for reestablishing Fu-Jen University on Taiwan after the communists forced it off the mainland.[55] Cushing had encouraged his wealthy friends to contribute to the university. Just before Christmas in 1961, one of them received a note from a university official: "Here in Free China, our Fu-Jen University is slowly rising, thanks to the leadership and generosity of the Holy Father and of Cardinal Cushing; and thanks also to the goodness of friends and benefactors like yourself. Already our graduate school of philosophy is functioning in temporary quarters." [56]

By 1964, Cushing had received awards from more than ten sovereign nations, along with two from the state of the Vatican City, all in recognition of his humanitarian ecumenical spirit. When Brandeis, a Jewish-sponsored, nonsectarian university, gave him an honorary degree in 1964, the citation neatly summed up the prelate's achievements:

"For twenty years Archbishop of Boston, he wears the Red Hat of the College of Cardinals in a fashion all his own. He cherishes, with Franciscan tenderness, his special flock—the aged, the unprotected, above all, the exceptional children. Transcending the parochial, he reaches out to the shanties of the poor and the forgotten of Latin America. In affection called 'His Elegance,' he watched a beloved young friend rise to presidential eminence and shared with burning sorrow a family's and a nation's grief. Early a patron of this young university, he blessed and named the Bethlehem Chapel. His gift of microfilmed Vatican Hebrew Codices . . . synthesizes his reverence for the inseparable heritage of Judaism and Christianity. With John XXIII, he announces himself to the Jewish world as 'Joseph your brother,' and carried forward the ecumenical banner of Pope Paul. Impatient as Theresa of Avila, yet descended from Philip Neri, Saint of Holy Laughter, he would have men dissolve dissension in the cenacle of the human heart."

Jewish leaders had approached Cushing before founding the university, which Cushing said was greatly needed. He lent his talent and strength to Brandeis when the Jesuit president of St. Louis University arranged for Brandeis to be the only institution in the nation to reproduce the microfilm of Judaic manuscripts in the Pope Pius Library in St. Louis. Cushing raised twenty thousand dollars for the project. "I got it from the people I come from—working people—who'd give me one dollar, ten dollars, fifteen dollars, the grassroots people who prayed me into office."

Cushing's ecumenical reputation brought in more invitations than he could handle. In April 1964, he spoke at an Episcopal church in Meriden, Connecticut: "Remember that I am not a theologian or a scholar—just a man who loves people," he said.[57] Early in June, because of his known love for Jews, Cushing was asked to present an honorary degree to Sidney Rabb at the Boston College commencement. Drowned out in the applause were his words: "I've been wanting to do this for a long time, Sid." Later Michael J. Walsh, president of Boston College, chuckled over the incident. "Cardinal Cushing had absolutely nothing to do with your getting the degree," he told Rabb.

A few days later, as Cardinal Bea's host, Cushing was admitted to all academic festivities at Harvard University. After Bea received his honorary degree, Cushing walked with him to Sever Quadrangle in

Harvard Yard and up the high and straight steps of Fogg Museum, where a luncheon was held in the courtyard inside the museum. Cushing, spent after the drawn-out ceremonies during which he successfully patted back a yawn, had a Scotch highball, but both cardinals left before the luncheon. David Mittell, a Harvard graduate assigned to attend to the needs of the two cardinals, had a car waiting. It took them to Lake Street, where a few of Cushing's friends, including Ralph Tedeschi, joined them in a more relaxed atmosphere. It was the last time the two great ecumenical cardinals were together.

Cardinal Bea, who died in November 1968 at the age of eighty-seven, remembered Harvard Divinity School and Cushing in his will. To the library of the Divinity School he bequeathed part of his personal library (exhibited behind glass in the summer of 1969); to Cushing, his pectoral cross, the symbol of his episcopal office. "What shall I do with the . . . cross?" Cushing asked reporters. "Have you any suggestions? I must wear it for a while—then what?"

Cushing hopes that both Pope John and Cardinal Bea will be memorialized in the calendar of saints. In a speech at the Medford Jewish Community Center a few days after Bea's death, Cushing compared him with President Kennedy: "They both tried to sow the good seeds of love for one another." The Jewish center was sold out long before Cushing addressed five hundred persons, without a glance at his prepared text. He received standing ovations at the beginning and ending of his talk. Just before his speech, a Jewish father standing outside the door of the hall, took his son by the arm. "Come on inside. I want to show you a great man." David Susskind, who has interviewed hundreds of celebrities, agrees. Once, when asked whom he most admired and would like to emulate, he said, "Cardinal Cushing."

Cushing opened his talk with his own humorous twist: "I'm somewhat handicapped this morning because I have no teeth. I can't eat and I can't talk. As for the latter, it may be a good thing. Because every time I talk I get into trouble."

Cushing's respect for and understanding of the beliefs of others brought visitors of every faith to his residence, another departure from the days of Cardinal O'Connell. Seven Protestants, who had a private audience with the cardinal while the Lutheran Laymen's League convened in Boston, introduced "the son-in-law of Theodore S. Haffenreffer, who donated the mullioned windows to your private chapel." Haffenreffer, who manufactured Pickwick Ale as well as beer, at a time when Pickwick was known as "the poor man's whisky," was an old

friend of the cardinal, although non-Catholic. Cushing amused his
guests with a comment: "I told Theodore once that he made the ale
and we Irish accounted for his profits."

A Baptist minister from Duxbury, a South Shore town once the
home of Myles Standish and John Alden, told a Catholic curate that
he had no trouble getting in to see the cardinal. "It would take a
Catholic priest a month to get such an appointment," the curate said.
The Baptist came away with a deep admiration for Cushing's homespun manner. The prelate called his attention to a bust of him made
by an Italian sculptor. "How do you like that nice fellow?" he asked.
Another sculptor, Suzanne Silvercruys Stevenson, was commissioned
to do a head portrait of the cardinal. On her way to Boston from
Connecticut to have the bust cast in bronze, she drove through a red
light deliberately, rather than risk a jarring stop. A traffic cop asked
whether she realized she had gone through the light.

"Oh, yes, officer. You see, I have Cardinal Cushing's head on the back
seat, and I didn't want it to roll on the floor."

The Irish cop, shaking his head, waved her on. "Glory be to God,"
he said.

A Congregational minister who came to the residence to discuss a
religious issue brought along his twelve-year-old son. The cardinal
spent most of the time discussing Ted Williams' batting average with
the boy. A few days later Cushing telephoned the minister's residence,
not to speak to him, but to invite his son to a Red Sox game. Cushing
blesses the Boston Red Sox at the beginning of each season, and he
checks now and then to see that God keeps his word.

The prelate's generous invitations sometimes make his residence
look like the Grand Central Station. Once he gave a reception for a
large delegation of French sailors who wanted to meet him, and he has
welcomed dozens of other groups from Europe, often taking time to
conduct moving ceremonies, as he did for a group from Poland and
later for some Lithuanians. In a tour of Massachusetts Memorial Hospital in 1963, he invited the entire crew of the missile frigate *U.S.S.
Boston* to Lake Street. "I don't know just how I'll entertain them," he
said, grinning and glancing around the ward before turning to the
nurses. "Would you like to come out and meet the boys from the
Boston?"

Nobody has ever called Cushing sanctimonious, as deeply spiritual
as he is. A crusader who sometimes said, when offered a cigarette, "No,
thanks, I'm no degenerate," dropped in one afternoon to discuss the

moral implications, as well as the harmful effects, of smoking, when Cushing abruptly ended the lecture. "Well, I smoke," he said.

When he can think of no other way of entertaining unexpected guests, he shows them around his residence. "What do you think of my bedroom?" he asked one group. "I have no closets. I have no place to put my pants on." He startled two visitors when he asked them, twisting his cassock. "Do you know of anything that can be done to get the electricity out of this thing?"

As the *magna vox* of the American hierarchy, he can speak with a dignity that holds a nation in awe, yet his random comments can be shockingly candid. He openly agreed with the Beatles that they are more popular than Christ. He shrugged when told that Governor John Volpe went to mass daily in the company of two state troopers. "Once a week is enough." He has used Volpe, as well as other Massachusetts notables, for target practice, as proud as that public servant is of his personal friendship with him. In the spring of 1964, Paul Dever, a mutual friend, roared with laughter when the cardinal told him that Volpe, who had been elected governor that year, had come to see him after having an audience with Pope Paul in Rome. Volpe, the cardinal said, mentioned that Pope Paul had asked him to run again for governor. "But the conversation probably went like this," Cushing said. "Paul probably asked Volpe what he did for a living, and John said he was the former governor of Massachusetts. The Pope then nodded politely and asked him if he was going to run again." Cushing teases, but there is no malice in his teasing. Actually, he enjoys poking fun at himself.

"I met a woman who knows the Book of Psalms by heart," he told a congregation. "I don't know one Psalm by heart." When a priest explaining that he had lost his faith, told him he was taking off his frock, the cardinal didn't blink. "Neither you nor I have brains enough to lose the faith. Don't tell me you lost the faith. You need brains for that. Martin Luther had brains. All of the great heretics of the past and the great reformers of the past—they all had brains."

A prelate who calls himself "a fool as well as a tool for Christ," he picks up the telephone late at night to accept a call from a tavern roisterer who asks him to settle an argument. A souvenir for a visitor to his residence may be a cardinal-colored packet of matches inscribed: "These matches were stolen from Richard Cardinal Cushing." Over the years, Cushing has been called the people's priest, the world's greatest missionary, a pontifical Casey Stengel, a one-man ecumenical council, a maverick cardinal, "hip," "an action man," and "the cardinal of the young and old."

Just before his last trip to South America, he welcomed an Irish Teachers' Workshop. "He greeted us in his own abruptly warm way, showed us around the lower part of the palace, and posed for pictures on the lawn," one teacher said. "After mass he said, 'I'll show you the joint upstairs.' " He took his visitors into his bedroom, which he calls a hospital ward because of the oxygen tanks beside the iron bed.

When a priest gave him a replica of St. Patrick's Bell, he unwrapped it. "I thought it was a quart of Irish whisky," he said. Then, glancing around at the young ladies, he dropped a bad pun. "We've got too many bells around here, both bells and belles." A vocational teacher presented him with a leather volume of tributes paid to President Kennedy after the assassination. Cushing will give it to the Kennedy Library.

Few visitors leave the episcopal residence without a memento. To a nun, who was passing out Silver Jubilee medals to the Irish teachers, Cushing said: "Sister, you know these cost two and a half dollars apiece, so make sure nobody gets more than one." One guest told a reporter after the visit: "This great, blunt, gentle and generous man left us with a request: 'Kiss the ground of Ireland for me,' and a word of advice that everyone in America needs: 'Take it easy, you'll be dead a long time.' "

Later that year, the Bunratty Castle girl singers from Ireland stopped by during their tour of the United States, and Oona Kelley, their leader, gave the prelate a harp. He couldn't resist a tired gag. "I can't even play on the linoleum, but I will treasure this."

The cardinal may meet out-of-town visitors at a railroad terminal or airport—sometimes after midnight—while his aides are relaxing at the residence. The hierarchy itself finds some of his activities unorthodox, if not incredible. The *Pilot*, refusing to believe that he took a visiting New York police delegation into a bar for a round of beer, as *Time* reported in 1964, spoke of the unbelievable error of "placing a mitred bishop in a Boston tavern."

But nobody in the hierarchy has doubted the sincerity of his humility. One afternoon, after introducing a cleric as a canon of a great Roman university, he grinned. "I'm a canon from South Boston." And that is a fair appraisal of his self-opinion, for he has no more pretensions than a simple priest.

He does, however, have more problems than a simple priest. Some, in the 1960s, were particularly nettlesome.

chapter twenty

MAKING THE ROUNDS
WITH CUSHING

THE 1960s WERE LOADED with church controversies. The cardinal stepped into one fight during "The Thousand Days," when Catholics were blamed for killing the educational aid bill in 1961. When the measure was reintroduced in 1962, Cardinal Spellman opposed it on the grounds that it discriminated against Catholics. The bill threatened religious independent schools with extinction, he said. Cushing made his position clear soon after the educational-aid furor died down, stating that aid to Catholic schools should not be made a condition for permitting passage of any general aid to education. The Washington *Post* and *The New York Times* applauded his stand.

Cushing, although not convinced that the Constitution forbids all subsidies to private education, felt that as long as most Americans opposed such use of tax money, Catholics, while trying to prove their right to such assistance, should neither force such legislation through at the expense of national disunity nor use their political influence in Congress to block other legislation beneficial to education.

The cardinal, privy to most Kennedy secrets, often served as the family's intermediary, as well as their spiritual adviser. When Joe Kennedy tried to get President Kennedy to name Boston Municipal Judge Francis Morrissey to a vacant federal judgeship in the Boston area, the Bar Association, with help from the Boston *Globe*, blocked the appointment. According to Cushing, Joe felt bitter about this. On a cruise out of Hyannis Port in the *Marlin*, Kennedy took the prelate aside and told him to ask Morrissey to accept a trust fund for his children in the amount of seventy-five thousand dollars as balm for his wounds. During the drive back to Boston, Cushing discussed the matter with Morrissey, who refused the offer. The judge had been close enough to the Kennedys to have the power of attorney for the President until his death.

The trips to Hyannis Port were for the cardinal escape vents from a stifling archdiocesan schedule. While cruising on the *Marlin*, he wore a straw sombrero to offset the sun's glare and over a Ballantine Scotch or three spun hilarious yarns. According to Judge Morrissey, some of Cushing's best stories centered on nuns, whom he loves. During one stay in St. Elizabeth's Hospital, when he was attended by sister nurses, it took two of them to arrange for operation bedpan. The first entered the room holding a sheet over her head; under it, the second nun slipped the pan onto the bed.

On his sixty-seventh birthday, the prelate amused four thousand nuns at the closing of the fifty-third annual Archdiocesan Teachers Institute at Boston College when he said: "I am the dynamic type. I have to keep working. I don't like the position I now hold. I never have. There is too much 'plutocol' to it all, for me. How I have survived so far, I don't know. If it were possible . . . I would like to dedicate all my time to the recruiting of diocesan priests in the United States, Ireland, Australia, and other English-speaking lands to work in Latin America."

Earlier in the month, he presided at Nun's Day at Fenway Park, home of the Boston Red Sox, in keeping with a custom he had established years before when he sent letters to all mothers superior in the archdiocese offering to take their sisters to a baseball game, with choice seats in a reserved section. "It is presumed," he gravely noted in the invitation, "that they like peanuts, popcorn, hot dogs, ice cream, and tonic. I'll be there and will root for the home team. Meanwhile, we thank the Red Sox management for making this wholesome recreation possible." [1] In 1962, wearing his "straw skimmer" cockily aslant, he borrowed a bat from the nearest Red Sox player and wore it long enough for photographers to get a shot. Newspaper and television audiences are familiar with his clowning in crazy hats—firemen and construction worker hats or a miner's helmet. He has even been seen wearing an old lady's flowery Easter bonnet, ribbons and all. Hats for him are a symbol of a collection box. At a fashion show sponsored by Catholic women at the Statler Hilton in Boston, the color scheme was cardinal red. Cushing, who waited until the show was over before addressing the group, complimented the ladies, then asked why—with all the hats in the show—no one had copied a cardinal's hat.

To make it an occasion, the cardinal will, as *Life* mentioned, pose as a pilgrim in carnival plumage, as a minuteman, marine, or Peruvian or Spanish naval cadet. Newspapers and magazines have run scores of photographs of the prelate dancing a jig in an old folks' home, kissing the oldest person present, kneeling down beside a recluse to recite "The Face on the Barroom Floor," or clowning under an outlandish hat. Nuns, as well as oldtimers, love him for his unpretentious gaiety.

"For twenty years I have lived in the archbishop's house," he told a group in 1964, "and in all those twenty years I have never been above the second floor of that house. I am a kind of mother superior to the nuns * who live on the top floor. I have never dared penetrate the third floor. Even the Holy Ghost couldn't get up there."

One favorite ploy is to have his picture taken with clusters of nuns. He will strike any pose requested by photographers, exchanging quips with them meanwhile. He almost invariably leaves head tables to dignitaries who need them and will walk over to sit with nuns at their table.

On a visit to Rome, he spent an hour chatting with two hundred nuns hospitalized at the Daughters of St. Paul in Castel Gandolfo. He gave each a gift basket and a five-dollar-bill. "Spend this on yourselves," he told them. "Don't give it to your superiors." He told one nun to get a permanent wave. "Saving this bed for me?" he asked a bed-ridden sister. "What are you doing here? You look better than I do." Older sisters smiled when he greeted them with a "Hello, girls." On this trip he gave two small parishes in the hill town of Varsi life-sized marble busts of himself and the late President Kennedy.

The night before he turned sixty-eight, he took four busloads of old folks and nuns from the Little Sisters of the Poor homes in Roxbury to Paragon Park on the South Shore. Table-hopping for four hours, he sang, poured beer, bit ends off cigars and lit them for old men. He gave a box of candy kisses to each nun, warning them that they were the only kisses they would ever get. After taking a dozen nuns on a roller coaster, one, who had sat beside him, apologized for having clutched his arm in her excitement.

"Forget it, sister. I'm old enough to be your father."

Lawrence Stone, owner of Paragon Park, told Monsignor George Kerr it wasn't too safe for a person of Cushing's age to sit on the front seat of a roller coaster.

"I know," Kerr said. "But who's going to tell him that?"

Stone said Cushing was the only cardinal he had ever seen on a roller

---

* Sisters of the Joan of Arc order.

coaster. Cushing is probably also the only cardinal who has been on a ride-a-glider. In 1964 he led a pilgrimage to the World's Fair in New York and spent a few minutes in the Vatican pavilion where he rode the rail-less train. Juan Cardinal Landozurro Ricketts, of Lima, Peru, paid him a surprise visit at the pavilion and wound up more surprised than Cushing, whose slapdash informality charmed the crowd as he picked up a baton to lead a band, led singing, and joked with young-sters. "Hi, girls," he called out to a group of women. Introducing him-self to fair-goers inside the New England Pavilion, he said, "Hello, there. My name is Cushing." [2]

In one excursion to Paragon Park, he picked up the heavy hammer at the mallet-swing concession when he was in his mid-sixties and shot the striker gong-high to register "Strong as a truck driver."

Guests helping celebrate his sixty-eighth birthday at Paragon Park credited him with a peak performance. With two priests and a profes-sional entertainer, he organized a barbershop quartet to sing "Sweet Adeline" and other nostalgic tunes. Then he encouraged the group, ranging in age from seventy to ninety-eight, to sing the birthday song as he donned a chef's cap while plunking his straw hat on the head of an old woman. The cardinal varied the routine by clowning around with the hat on. At the end of the act, he bowed. "Have you had enough penance, or do you want more?" Although it was Friday, he let the old folks have hot dogs and hamburgers. "The diehards," he said, "can still have fish chowder." On the bus-ride home, he pointed out scenes of his childhood. "Here we are in good old Southie, and there's Columbia Point, the Boston *Globe* (not there when he was a child) and Boston College High" (in its new location).

The cardinal, who considers himself the personal shepherd of the nuns in his see, attends to their every need. The sisters at St. Coletta's, he said, "don't know enough about a lot of things. We have a super-market man [Ralph Tedeschi] on the board who helps them with tips on how to buy so they save money." Dropping into a nearby an-tique shop one afternoon, Cushing teased the sisters about "spending their money on junk" instead of contributing it to his charities.

Investigating a report that the Marist nuns in Bedford were desti-tute, he found they didn't even have a clothesline. When they asked for a deep-freeze, the prelate made a prayerful appeal on his weekly radiocast, after putting his favored dealers in a generous and pious mood by saying the rosary. He gave a plug to an appliance dealer, knowing he would receive no bill for the item after he praised the quality of the merchandise. But what good is an empty deep-freeze? Another plug for another merchant, and the locker was full of provisions. Cushing raised money for the Marists, edited their magazine, and remodeled and furnished their convent, not forgetting to put a clothesline in the backyard.

For years, whenever Cushing wanted to send an electronic gift to anyone, he turned to his friend, Joe DeMambro, who often, at no charge, air-conditioned homes for nuns and the aged and provided radios, televisions, stereos, and hi-fis for scores of Catholic institutions in and out of the archdiocese. He provided long-playing records of classical music for the hi-fi he gave to the Cardinal Cushing Villa in Gloucester, sent three transistor radios (to be used as prizes at a bazaar) to Father William Francis in Peru, and, also at Cushing's request, delivered a stereo and records to Ann Wasilauskas Mulligan in memory of her father, the prelate's friend and employee for many years. A Dominican bishop from Ecuador received a television set while convalescing in St. Elizabeth's Hospital, and two nuns from Lourdes, who visited the cardinal, went home with a tape recorder.

"A priest friend of mine here from Pakistan would like two transistor radios to take back with him," Cushing wrote his friend. "He will pray for you forever, and, believe me, you need his prayers. I was talking to the mayor of Worcester Sunday; I told him how wonderful you are. You will get some business from him." In another note, the cardinal, in thanking DeMambro for sending a station wagon full of Christmas gifts to the cardinal's residence, said he was keeping one radio for himself, "because the last time I brought nuns to the second floor of my house they walked away with the radio."

After the Kennedy assassination, Cushing was victimized by crank calls and door-bell-ringing in the wee hours of the morning. The FBI persuaded him to move his offices up to the second floor and told him to have a loudspeaker installed, which would enable him to speak to anyone outside without opening the door. One night there was a banging on the front door.

"Christ is risen, Christ is risen," a swaying figure shouted when the cardinal opened the door.

"Listen, fellow, you're two days early," Cushing said. When the drunk kept yelling, the cardinal told him to pass on the news to residents of the next building. Next day an aide mentioned a man who had kept him awake with his shouting.

"You don't say," Cushing said deadpan.[3]

One Christmas Eve, a Negro came to the door and told Cushing he had several children and no presents to give them the next day. He left not only with a roll of greenbacks but also with two large bags of provisions the cardinal took from his kitchen.

Cushing is so fond of the Trappistines in Wrentham he delights in teasing them. One morning while going over plans for two new high schools with architects, he was called to the telephone and was told there had been a tragedy. He would have to come to the nunnery at once.

"So it's yourself, is it?" a sister said when she opened the door. "Well, the reverend mother is having her nap, so you go into the parlor and wait for her. The quiet will do you good." She raised her hands in protest when he told her he was rushed. "You can tell her yourself if you wish, but I have to live here after you're gone."

Finally, the mother superior appeared, and he gave her permission to speak. The tragedy?

"All our cows have gone dry." She shook her head sadly.

He saw that she was serious. "You brought me all the way down here to tell me that?"

"Now, Your Eminence, you don't understand. If there is no milk, we can't sell it. Then we get no money to buy our food. The nuns will starve and you'll have to close up this place and we'll all have to go back to Ireland where you brought us from."

Explaining that he had grown up in a leaky-roof tenement and knew nothing about cattle, he told her to buy twenty cows. When a bill came for six thousand dollars, he wondered whether they had golden horns.

"They're wonderful milkers that we got at a bargain of three hundred dollars apiece, praise God. And God bless you, Your Eminence," the mother superior wrote. "If anything else comes up, we'll call you." Something did come up. The mother superior, more hesitant than usual, asked a special favor of his eminence. Was it all right for the nuns to buy corsets and girdles? It was.

On one visit to the Trappistines, the prelate told of the Little Sisters of Jesus. "They don't live in nice convents like this. They live in tenements. Two of the nuns work in a garment factory and another works in the kitchen of a home for unmarried mothers. The three live together on the fourth floor of a slum building in South Boston. They live with the poor as the poor." He said he hoped they could get some sleep while he talked. (The rule of silence does not preclude laughter in cloisters.) As they lined up to kiss his ring, he told them to stay on their feet. "Some of you look too heavy to pull up." Having granted them a one-day reprieve from silence, the first the entire order had had in years, he asked the mother superior whether she approved of masses being conducted in English.

"Oh, I should hope not," she said.

"Well, I'm certainly glad you're not one of the council fathers," he smiled.

Just before leaving, he splashed some of the sisters with holy water. "That's to get the devil out of you." They couldn't wait for his next visit.

When Cushing was invited to speak at Notre Dame University on Father Patrick Peyton, who produced a film on the rosary mysteries, he learned that a few sisters in Kingston were scheduled to attend a five-day seminar there at the Institute of Spirituality. A travel agent met the sisters at the airport in Chicago and led them to a limousine that took them to the Palmer House, where Cushing greeted them and provided a suite for them. He paid most of their expenses while they were in South Bend.

Nuns are more pleased than embarrassed when he focuses attention on them. While dedicating a chapel at Newton College of the Sacred Heart in 1963, he lauded Mother Sweeney for her fund-raising ability. "She has more gall than I have," he said, "and that's a lot of gall." Observing his twentieth anniversary as archbishop on November 9, 1964, he laid the cornerstone for a Catholic elementary school in Somerville, part of a complex ranging up through high school.

"Never underestimate the power of a nun," the cardinal said. "The original plans called for the elimination of the high school—until a visit from the provincial of the Notre Dame nuns. Everyone knows you can never win an argument with a woman—certainly never with a mother provincial. The high school remains."

Cardinal Cushing tells the story of two nuns who visited the Unemployment Compensation Department in Washington, D.C., to see how it operated. A man at the desk applying for unemployment compensation turned to the clerk: "You can say what you like about opportunities for work, but when Cardinal Cushing is laying off nuns, that's proof of unemployment."

The cardinal lives frugally at his residence, usually too busy to spend much time at table, particularly because of his steady banquet schedule. Supper may be a banana or a few grapes, a sandwich and a carton of milk, or perhaps a custard. On his way to appointments, until ulcers caught up with him, he might lunch on a hot dog or a chicken sandwich and a soft drink. On a blander diet in recent years, he sometimes tells hosts in advance what to prepare. One list [4] included "good clam chowder, shredded lobster on lettuce with mayonnaise on the side, fresh oysters, and a corn muffin or popover, along with tea without sugar." There are times when he prefers fortified tea. One afternoon a few years ago, the cardinal addressed a group of male nurses at a capping ceremony at McLean's Hospital. At four o'clock, a Harvard University overseer, who had served as master of ceremonies, brought the prelate a cup of tea.

"What is this," he asked, "plain tea?" The overseer brought another cup laced with medicinal Scotch.

In his study, while reading correspondence or dictating to one or two secretaries, the cardinal may listen to recordings or watch a baseball or football game on television. He is such a baseball fan, he not only blesses the Red Sox organization, but sometimes says a prayer for the team on his radio program. They usually need it.

The silence in the household is occasionally broken by groups of visiting children of all races and colors. Christmas parties are joyous occasions for both Catholics and non-Catholics. Once, when a Roxbury priest brought about thirty boys from a foster home, Cardinal Cushing, too busy to entertain them, sent them to Anthony's Pier Four, a restaurant on the Boston waterfront frequented by celebrities. This time the kids stole the show, pelting one another with hard and soft rolls as their priest proctor tried to restore order. Children, because of their love of and respect for the cardinal, behave better at parties in his residence or on the spacious grounds. At such times, Cushing forgets his loneliness.

"This is the most lonely life imaginable," he said on a 1968 telecast. "Nobody wants to . . . visit a cardinal-archbishop. What are you going to say to him? A man with such power?" [5] Another time he said: "I have no close friends. Because of what I have to do day in, day out, I go it pretty much alone." In 1965 in Galway, he told a crowd that he was probably the loneliest man in the hierarchy, "because I find I have to hide myself away to avoid publicity. I do not want to talk about myself." He told one community of nuns: "I am sort of a shy guy, you know. I put on a big front and sometimes I say the wrong thing."

He forgets his loneliness, however, when he takes nuns and old-timers on outings or accompanies children in rides on swan boats in the Boston Public Garden, as he did in spryer days. On one trip he was dunked while stepping onto a boat. Sometimes, when depressed, he drops in to talk to an aide or takes a drive with one or two friends.

As a prince of the church, he gets involved in national issues, yet he has never lost his eye for detail. When an old priest, who was an authority on canon law and pastor of a local church, died, he left the financial affairs of his parish in a mess. Cushing, annoyed, told an aide to find a priest who had graduated at the bottom of his class at St. John's Seminary. He wanted no more of famous scholars heading parishes. In a wrathful mood, he can be unreasonable. During one conference involving a land conveyance, he told a lawyer that he should go back to the kindergarten.

For Cushing is complex. He may have his associates cheering for him one moment and cursing him the next. An aide said his hatred of sin and love of sinners often leads him into odd situations, "such as being on both sides of an issue. These are mere follies of the heart." While he is basically kind, he can, in an irascible mood, turn around and crush, in one damning statement, an aide or priest who steps out of line, as he did with the attorney. Sometimes after an impulsive action, he is quick to apologize. A notable example happened on February 16, 1969, when the cardinal, after a radio talk show, apologized to the broadcaster. "Maybe I should keep my mouth shut," he said, calling himself "a thick Irishman." He followed with a non sequitur: "Most of my relatives are Protestant." *The National Catholic Reporter,* ten days after the broadcast, ran a transcript of the program.

"The cardinal, according to this newspaper, is a 'radio talk-show fan,' to the discomfort of Donald J. Trageser, manager of the news and talk station, WEEI. After the latest of the cardinal's calls, Trageser lamented, 'I wish the cardinal liked music.'"

The prelate cut into a Sunday afternoon program while Father Henry P. Oullette, chairman of the psychology department at Emmanuel College, was on the "Howard Nelson Show." Cushing—over the air—accused the priest of upsetting Catholicism and of downgrading the church and threatened to pull off the air both Father Oullette and Father Robert White, another archdiocesan priest who appeared on another program, "Topic Religion." Trageser dropped both priests after the incident because, as he told Cushing in a note, "It is not worth the abuse and personal attacks to have such men on our air, even though everything they have said on our air has been the essence of mature, enlightened Christianity."

Trageser, who acted on his own initiative, still respects the cardinal: "Whatever his faults may be, lack of charity is not one of them. . . . And he has a heart as big as all outdoors. He is a very human man."

During the stormy program Howard Nelson telephoned Cushing at his residence. Part of the conversation follows:

Cushing: Do you mind, if we are going to demand from WEEI one of our own priests—and you're one of our priests—to go on simultaneously with you? You are upsetting the people of the Catholic church, my dear father. We've paid for your education. Do you represent Emmanuel College or the archdiocese of Boston or the priesthood of the archdiocese of Boston? What do you represent?

Oullette: As you know, Your Eminence, ah, I was asked to come here as a psychologist. And as you also . . .

Cushing: I know, but you've all the people upset. These . . . poor people are calling me up. . . . You've, you give them a lot of stuff. They don't know what a psychologist is from a theologian. For goodness sake, you get off that program or we are going to put a man alongside. . . .

Nelson: Cardinal Cushing. Cardinal Cushing. I'm Howard Nelson. I, I've never had the opportunity to meet you. We are on the air. But one of our functions, Cardinal Cushing, is to inform, and to bring all kinds of information to a radio audience.

Cushing: Wait a minute. He's confusing all the Catholic people. . . .

Nelson: Cardinal, respectfully . . .

Cushing: I don't care what you represent. I've been very good to that station WEEI. . . .

Nelson: Cardinal Cushing, Cardinal Cushing . . .

Cushing: Wait a minute. Don't, don't, don't try to outtalk me.

Nelson: Well, no but—Your Eminence, may I just have a word with you? May I just suggest . . .

Cushing: Yes, you can. Have it.

Nelson: Thank you, please. I, I speak to you as an individual who's been in broadcasting for a great number of years, dedicated to the proposition . . .

Cushing: Forget about the speech. Come to the point.

Nelson suggested that perhaps the discussion should not be aired, and when Father Oullette tried to cut into the exchange, Cushing went on: "You're wrecking—you're downgrading the Catholic church." After another abortive interruption, Cushing said: "And you—wait a minute till I tell you something. The only program you people have that amounts to anything is a quasi-religion program. . . . The country's in bad shape. Why don't you talk about politics? Why don't you talk about taxes. . . . Why don't you talk about Cuba." He went on to ask why the program had to bring in the Catholic church.

Father Oullette denied ever having discussed the Catholic church, adding that "any manner of theology is referred to the evening program."

"Wait a minute," Cushing broke in. "I have great admiration for you people." When Nelson thanked him, he continued: "But I want to tell you one thing: We're going to pull this guy off."

The cardinal relented in the taped but unheard (by the radio audience) part of the conversation with Nelson, explaining that he would not remove Oullette from the program. When Nelson said he had been broadcasting since 1932, Cushing said, "You're as crazy as I am." A moment later, he told the broadcaster: "I'm a hundred per cent for you. I'm an old man now, and get upset." Admitting that he had faults, he said he was "a very liberal cardinal," and when Nelson told him he was in his "corner," Cushing said: "The Lord knows, I need someone."

Cushing can be contradictory. Two weeks after he honored a physician, with warm praise for his profession, he spoke at a parish south of Boston, where a ninety-eight-year-old priest was celebrating the seventy-fifth anniversary of his ordination. The prelate told the audience that the best way to live long is to stay away from doctors. He has been known to drop prescription pills down the drain instead of swallowing them.

He may contradict the brightest of his priests. When Governor Christian Herter created fourteen juvenile court judges and was backed by Monsignor Lally, Judge Frank Tomasello said the appointments were unnecessary, and Herter talked about impeaching the jurist. Cushing publicly sided with Tomasello. When many bishops were denouncing Moral Rearmament as a false super-religion, Cushing wrote a glowing foreword for a book of essays by Moral Rearmament's director, British journalist Peter Howard.

Cushing has strong opinions. He has called college board examinations "a lot of nonsense," and thinks "geniuses are a nuisance." He admits that he does not get a hit every time he goes to bat. While his supreme achievement has been his success in wielding the schisms of Catholics, Protestants and Jews, along with his worldwide missionary work, he has not always distinguished himself in the racial-social upheaval. He has, however, rectified most of the mistakes he has made.

Cardinal Cushing celebrated his Silver Jubillee on June 7, 1964, on Jubilee Sunday. As a sentimental gesture to mark the occasion, he ordained two deacons in Gate of Heaven Church, the first time there had been an ordination in his native parish since 1869. On the following day, he ordained twenty-three more deacons at the cathedral. He had hoped to ordain four times that number on his twenty-fifth anniversary as bishop.

Cushing took time out that year to celebrate a requiem mass for Nora Harrington of South Boston, who died at the age of eighty-nine. Nora, who reputedly had regularly contributed twenty-five dollars a month to the Society of the Propagation of the Faith, had letters from Cushing thanking her, but she had no way of proving they were authentic until a few years before her death when Cushing came to St. Vincent's Church for a Confirmation.

"Himself came out of the church, with his mitre high on his head, swinging his brass walking stick," a parishioner recalled. "Down the steps he came, dignified as the high altar." Then he saw Nora in a crowd across the street. He crossed over to embrace her.

"Hello, Nora! It wouldn't be St. Vincent's without seeing you."

According to the parishioner who mistook a crozier for a cane, when "himself" said this, bystanders heard him.[6]

During the mass, the cardinal said Nora for forty years had greeted him at the church door when he went there on assignment. "For all my work with the missions, I believe this little woman did more. She died penniless, but deep in our affection and with the richest treasure known to man, she died in the love of God." She would have been delighted to get all the attention," he added. "A prince of the church in his scarlet robes, five monsignori, and a dozen priests have come to pay her honor." [7]

During the week of his Silver Anniversary, Cushing blessed the fishing fleet in Gloucester amid a wild demonstration of parade and tribute. Then he vaulted aboard a trawler and asked the captain to sail him to Boston. On the way to the Boston Fish Pier on the *Grace & Salvatore,* he ate lobster with the fishermen, cracking open the claws with a monkey wrench. A few weeks later he was in Hollywood, Florida, to thank the Catholic Daughters for fifty thousand dollars they had donated to his Latin American program. In his convention address, he said the Knights of Columbus had reneged on their promise to give him the million dollars he had asked for the same program. Then he reassured the ladies that he would seek no more money at the convention.[8] "There are others here who need money more than I do, and it's easier for a cardinal to beg for money than for someone of lower rank."

On his arrival he had told the Florida press that he was a "distinguished beggar." Pushing through a crowd in downtown Miami, he called out to a priest: "Don't stand there, man. Take up a collection." Reporters liked his candor and breeziness but were startled when he criticized their semi-tropical weather. "This climate doesn't agree with me. . . . I'm exhausted. . . . My asthma is bothering me a bit today."

Back at the Diplomat Hotel, there was no trace of his vigor. He sank onto a divan, pale and almost gasping for breath, completely spent after the day's activities.

chapter twenty-one

IN THE EYE OF A
HURRICANE

IN A TELECAST, Cardinal Cushing said: "I would rather be out among the poorest of the poor or selling the cause of the missions, or at the present time, the cause of human rights and related subjects in the field of social justice, than in the mansion out on Commonwealth Avenue." [1] Another time he said that the church "had always been Christ-like in its dealings with the poor, it would not be in the trouble it is today."

The prelate, who was a central figure in a civil rights controversy early in the decade, admitted also that his church had occasionally been guilty of race prejudice in America, citing segregated schools, missions, and churches. Until the twentieth century, indeed, the church had at times been anti-Negro in certain respects. In 1890, Archbishop Patrick Ryan of Philadelphia told the archbishop of New York: "Archbishop Ireland has created a sensation in Washington and through the country by declaring that Catholics should admit the Negroes to *social* as well as political equality. His enthusiasm sometimes leads him too far, but his purity of intention is unquestionable." [2]

Cushing has long been a vocal advocate of civil rights. Early in his bishopric career, he established the Blessed Sacrament Mission in Roxbury, where sisters ran a school for Negroes. He attended functions there and passed around refreshments in parties in the school garden. While directing the Society of the Propagation of the Faith, he contributed to the construction at Bay St. Louis, Mississippi, of a seminary for Negroes and over the years paid for the tuition of other Negro seminarians. He would gladly accept a Negro as auxiliary bishop, and long ago he outlawed segregation in Catholic institutions. He tells the story of a little white girl who sat next to a colored girl on the first day of class at an integrated school. Her mother asked how things went.

"We were so scared," the white girl said, "all we did was sit and hold hands."

At times, however, Cushing has been understandably hesitant about taking action as complicated problems of integration arose. After World War II, South Bostonians tried to bar Negroes from a public housing project, and violence flared in the summer of 1964 in the Italo-American neighborhood of East Boston, when a Negro family moved into a public housing project. Again, Irish Catholic blocs, who themselves had moved from docks and tenement backstreets of immigrant ghettos, aired their contempt for their alleged social inferiors.

During a time of racial turmoil in Boston in 1963 and 1964, Cushing in leaflets, pastoral letters, radiocasts, and public announcements, expressed views that were contradictory. In a pamphlet on "Inter-Racial Justice" written in 1963, he said social attitudes rather than biological make-up were the core of the problem. "Whatever superiority one group may have over another is completely the result of environmental factors, or of hereditary factors, which have no relation whatever to racial differences. The superiority of one group . . . must therefore be regarded as temporary."

When the Boston School Committee denied there was *de facto* segregation in certain schools, NAACP and CORE pushed for action, and Negroes, supported by many clergymen and civil-rights groups, staged two boycotts. Instead of attending public schools, colored children in the first boycott heard lectures on Negro history and racial problems at "freedom" schools.

Cushing, who had written so widely on civil rights, said in one pamphlet that Negroes "must not even shrink from the difficult course of demonstration, denunciation, witness, and testimony, when these are required of them." Later, because of methods used by both black and white extremists, he argued for gradualism, convinced that Negro children were more victimized by economic and social under-privilege at home and in their neighborhoods than from school segregation. Louise Day Hicks, chairman of the Boston School Committee, agreed, charging that Boston schools were being used as scapegoats for those who failed to solve the housing, economic, and social problems of blacks.

In a local telecast early in 1963, Cushing called the proposed boycott of *de facto* segregated schools "a very, very dangerous thing. . . . I am all for human rights—for every living, breathing human soul. But I think there is a better way of attaining these rights than by violating laws of society and by endangering the community by sending a number of children, emotionally upset, through the streets of the city." Whereupon a critic asked: "Does he read his own writing?"

Negro comedian Dick Gregory, who in February 1964 came to Boston to support a second boycott, expressed disappointment at Cushing's opposition, for the prelate, above all others, he felt, was one person blacks could completely trust. In a letter to Gregory, the cardinal paraphrased what he had said on the air. Home study under dignified and decent conditions was at least half the problem, he wrote. He agreed with novelist James Baldwin that the best educational facilities would not help children enough if they continued to be ill-fed, ill-housed, and held down in unsavory, congested ghettos. He said demonstrations tend to "throw emotional obstacles in the way of expert study," adding that children should be educated, not exhibited.

Clergymen in the archdiocese who opposed Cushing's stand on the boycott included Father Robert Drinan, dean of Boston College Law School; Father Walter Kenneally, a former professor at the law school; and Father Richard Twomey of the Department of Theology at Boston College. In a panel discussion, Michael Walsh, then president of Boston College, apologized for the disagreement among the churchmen. Cushing, in a light vein, said he might buy a couple of houses across the street from the law school and put Negroes in them. "Let's see how they'd like that," he said. The offhand remark was intended as a joke, but some took it literally.

Cushing gave more than lip service to his convictions. He financed a Montessori method program for Negro children of working mothers, providing a skilled lay teacher who worked hand in hand with the Catholic Inter-Racial Council in a South End Mission. It became a day-care center partly supported by federal grants of food. Here children receive hot meals and loving care.

In a Pentecostal letter written in the spring of 1964, the cardinal told employers, landlords, educators, and pastors to implement charity and understanding, counseling all to "love all men and especially love Negroes because they have suffered so much from lack of love. Make yourself truly color blind and, if you think of color at all, let it be to love the more." Just before leaving for Latin America that summer he said: "I commend and encourage the clergy who have involved themselves in the toils of the Negro and have made witness of their Christian faith. To those who have held back, I issue a call to action. Let no pulpit be silent, no wrong left uncondemned; let every altar be a place before which we dedicate ourselves anew to that brotherhood of redemption in which we were all born in the blood of Christ. In this hour, if the men of God are silent, the very stones will cry out."

Later Cushing wrote "Thoughts to Remember" for *Good Housekeeping:* "It is not enough to preach and teach the dignity of man and his equality before God and the law; we must take steps to see that our words are matched by effective action in the life of the community." [3] He warned against the poison of prejudice in housing, education, employment, and every area of opportunity and advocated programmed education and action.

In his December 1966 pastoral letter he pledged his commitment to "Project Equality," noting that all who did business with the diocese had to agree to observe all federal fair employment practices; also, to make positive efforts to employ Negroes who need jobs.

Unfortunately, as the Boston *Traveler* noted in the spring of 1963, the program was not implemented. "This week, however, in a letter to the Boston Priests Senate, the cardinal repeated his pledge to adopt and implement Project Equality and to do so as part of a state-wide ecumenical program."

Churchly ecumenicism was not enough, Cushing said. It was not enough to build bridges from church to church. Also needed was secular ecumenism—"one which is directed toward a more effective service of God in the world and for the world." The *Traveler* observed that the moral evil of racism could be fought in the purchasing office as well as from the pulpit. Cushing operates a central archdiocesan purchasing division.

The loudest screams of protest over alleged *de facto* school segregation came from Roxbury. Meanwhile, bulldozing by the Boston Redevelopment Authority (BRA) angered residents of the South and West Ends of Boston, and again Cushing found himself in the eye of a hurricane of protest.

There had been confusion and heartache since the enactment of the Housing Act of 1949, which had been designed to give federal aid in the renewal of run-down cities. In the West End, bulldozers and wrecking balls had forced nine thousand residents to· scramble for any available quarters, and now they were razing homes in the South End, which had become a slum. Negroes and some Puerto Ricans had replaced white Catholics and others who had moved to the suburbs. The residents, including some white tenants, complained that the church had done little for the blacks, a charge that distressed Cushing, who on Confirmation days urged young white Catholics to practice religion daily: "Should a colored family move into your area, welcome the family. Be nice to the colored children. We all belong to the same race, a human race, no matter what our color may be." The prelate came out strongly for better housing.

But with mounting concern, he watched the progress of the BRA, whose members Mayor John Collins had appointed. Monsignor Lally was chairman of the authority. In the spring of 1964, Cushing told three hundred Protestants in Old South Church that he could not understand why the BRA insisted on demolishing homes before new homes were readied for the displaced families. "The authority should encourage owners of salvageable homes to fix them up." After criticizing urban renewal as practiced in the area, he expressed hope that churches would be spared and that more compassion for little people would be shown, a concern shared by Suffragan Bishop John Burgess of the Episcopal diocese of Massachusetts. When Bishop Burgess told Cushing that the BRA's intention was to tear down homes "beyond redemption," the cardinal said: "This is information even Monsignor Lally hasn't given me." [4] The *Pilot* did not publish this comment. Edward Logue, then director of the BRA, told the cardinal that the authority was renewing and redeveloping certain home and apartment blocks in the South End but was careful to add that it had great respect for the architectural values of churches.

It was because of the slow implementation of the civil rights program—especially in housing—that the cardinal did another turnabout in 1967, coming out flatly for demonstrations: "A dedicated nun struck on the head with a stone while walking in silent protest through a segregated white neighborhood is dramatically fulfilling the mission of Christ, threatening men in their selfishness and challenging them to a genuine manifestation of life." He had already [5] told nuns to take a more active part in secular affairs. Nuns on picket lines were reflecting their concern with practical questions of morality and Christian living rather than with abstruse theological problems.[6] "A joyous revolution is in the making among U.S. nuns," *This Week* magazine reported.[7] "The tall headdresses, starched wimples and flowing robes that long symbolized the nuns' 'no' to secular society are beginning to disappear. As the cloister door swings open, there is a new sense of sisterhood . . . toward the human family." Nuns were becoming militant.

"When you take the vow of obedience," a Poor Clare nun in New Orleans said, "you don't abdicate your personality." In Milwaukee, sisters, like determined suffragettes, marched with Father James Groppi's black commandos, while others demonstrated in Washington, D.C., against the war in Vietnam. Discarding their traditional habits in favor of blouses, skirts, suits, and knee-length dresses, nuns have been working directly with the urban poor. They are moving from convent seclusion into apartments, helping housewives organize against greedy landlords and merchants, and marching in civil-rights demonstrations.[8]

Cushing encouraged them to fight for peace and civil rights and to combat poverty. In the summer of 1968 he gave the Urban Sisters working in those fields ninety thousand dollars to develop programs allied to education. In 1966, he had sponsored a Human Rights Commission Seminar at St. John's Seminary for more than five hundred nun superiors and principals. The Sisters' Committee at that time launched two inner city programs: an experimental education project at Hawthorne House in the South End and a summer volunteer program, working with people of every faith and color.[9] Cushing had become more liberal since the spring of 1965 when he dedicated a giant bronze statue of Mother Julie Billiart, founder of the Sisters of Notre Dame de Namur, at the order's new novitiate in Ipswich on the North Shore. Warning nuns that they were teachers, not marchers, he told them they belonged in the classroom, adding that Mother Billiart would never have been found "out on the highways and byways."

In a national telecast in 1968, Harry Reasoner of CBS told Cushing: "You've taken a number of very strong stands throughout your priesthood. Sometimes you've been called too liberal, sometimes too conservative. Does it make any difference to you whether your ideas are popular or unpopular, Your Eminence?"

The answer was no. Cushing said he was both liberal and conservative to a certain degree: conservative "in matters in which I'm not fully acquainted . . . in which I am not at least a quasi-expert. But once I've made up my mind, everything about me is very liberal."

The cardinal's ambivalence puzzles those who don't understand the remark made by French philosopher Renan: "Woe unto those who do not contradict themselves at least three times a day." The prelate's conclusions sometimes fluctuate because he is constantly reevaluating and reassessing issues. His liberal attitude at Vatican II marked him as a leading progressive in church matters. His dread of communism at other times made him reactionary—a right-wing conservative. Thus he found himself embarrassingly aligned with such "darkening firebrands" as Joe McCarthy and Robert Welch, who founded the John Birch Society in 1958. As a life member of the NAACP, Cushing found himself in the strange position of twice publicly endorsing the society. An odd sequence began in 1960, when, in answer to a query, Cushing wrote to C. M. Crawford of Los Angeles, noting that he knew of nobody who was a "more dedicated anticommunist in the country than Robert Welch. I unhesitatingly recommend him to you and endorse his John Birch Society." Although Cushing liked Welch personally, he privately conceded that Birchers were fanatics and "a bunch of nuts." In his talk to the Methodist congregation in Sudbury, he called Welch "a good Baptist who has gone to extremes occasionally." In general, however, he applauded the society for its sincere anticommunism, while objecting to its methods.

Disenchantment first set in when he learned that the Birchers had compiled a dossier on the Comsymp derelictions of the *Pilot*. Then, on April 19, 1964, he received a telegram signed "Gretchen van Heussen," an alleged New York correspondent for Swiss and Italian newspapers, asking whether he endorsed the John Birch Society, "and, by inference, statements that Presidents Franklin D. Roosevelt and Kennedy were communists." [10] According to the telegram, two editors of *American Opinion*, the Birch Society's organ, on the Long John Nebel New York all-night radio program had quoted Cushing's letter to Crawford while denouncing the two Presidents as communists. That Sunday night Cushing telephoned Station WNAC, which carried the discussion program, and demanded equal time. On the afternoon of April 21, the cardinal was a special guest on the "Haywood Vincent Show," another discussion program.

"I would prefer imprisonment and death under a slave state than membership in an organization which has branded a martyred president . . . a communist," he said. "If it is true that two members of this society called my nearest and dearest friend . . . a communist, they and their associates owe the people of all nations who loved him and who will never forget his tragic death a profound apology." If the two Birchers identified him with their incredible remark, he went on, "I cannot dignify them with an answer save to say—shame, shame for attempting to blight the character and mar the memory and distort the image of a martyr for his country to that of a traitor."

The discussion on the "Long John Nebel Show" had mentioned an article in the February 1964 issue of *American Opinion*, which said Kennedy had collaborated with Khrushchev to stage a sham embargo of Cuba, adding that when Kennedy became a political liability to the communist conspiracy, he had been liquidated. The mythical writer of the telegram, familiar with such charges, including the fantastic attacks on Roosevelt, had linked them with Cushing's 1960 endorsement.

Robert Welch said the telegram contained "outright falsehoods," and Scott Stanley, Jr., and Thomas Davis, who were on the staff of *American Opinion,* repudiated the charge that they had called the Presidents communists. The *Irish Press,* noting that Cushing had publicly retracted a letter he wrote in 1960 endorsing the John Birch Society, reported that Welch had also branded President Dwight Eisenhower "a dedicated communist."

After a conference with Davis, a Roman Catholic, at his residence, Cushing, realizing that he had been hoaxed, wrote a letter of apology and gave it to Davis for publication. In it he said the charges he had made on the Haywood Vincent program resulted from misinformation. "I now feel that many of them were unjustified. Because of my own dedication to the fight against the atheistic communist conspiracy, I certainly do not want to do any harm to fellow battlers in the same cause. While I think the Crawford letter is now too out of date for continued use . . . I would be glad to have Mr. Welch print this letter in his Bulletin of the John Birch Society if he wishes to do so." [11]

Thus his hatred of communism led him to endorse, for a second time, a smear group that advocated many causes which he opposed. He also lost track of the fact that the late President "advocated every cause which the Birchers despise." [12]

He finally reached a definite conclusion: he no longer wants, in any way, to be identified with the John Birch Society.

chapter twenty-two

LAST LOOK AT
IRELAND

"THE PEOPLE OF THE UNITED STATES owe a great deal to Ireland," Cushing said in 1965. "The archdiocese of Boston in particular—150 years old and young in comparison with the dioceses in Ireland—was given its greatest impetus by Irish emigrants. We are now the second, even the first, archdiocese in the United States. . . . It is generally said that the archdiocese of Chicago is the largest, Boston . . . second, and New York . . . third. Somehow, I have the conviction that Boston is fairly close to being the largest in the United States. We have over two million Catholics here." [1]

In his seventieth year, the cardinal continued to administer his sprawling archdiocese and to look after spiritual life in his 411 parishes. By 1965, he was overseeing the work of more than a score of colleges and universities, a dozen hospitals, homes for the aged and convalescent, charitable organizations, and more than a hundred religious orders in the area—all the while visiting prisons and scores of institutions and lecturing to groups of every faith all over the country. When he visited the prison in Walpole, Massachusetts, a young inmate asked: "What is he coming here for?" "Simply because he cares," a long-termer said.

When Pope Paul VI named Cushing a special legate at the dedication of Galway's two-million-dollar cathedral in August 1965, there was renewed speculation over the prelate's health. A few weeks earlier, he had revealed that in 1956 doctors had given him eight months to live because of cancer. "Somehow or other I survived. The Lord chooses the foolish to confound the wise." In 1963, while comforting an old man during his Christmas visit to Boston City Hospital, he said: "Eight years ago they gave me eight months to live, and I have

15

buried half of them." There was a time early in 1965, he admitted, when it looked as if he wouldn't reach his seventieth birthday. He had a major intestinal operation in the spring of that year. Just before flying to Ireland, the cardinal gave the commencement address to the graduating class of St. Elizabeth's Hospital's School of Nursing. "Everyone knew what my trouble was but myself," he told the girls. "Truth to tell, I don't yet know what my trouble was."

There were days, as he approached his seventieth birthday, when he looked years older, he was so gaunt and haggard. Some inner strength enabled him to rise to any emergency. On days following sleepless nights, he knew how wan and spent he looked. "Don't tell me, I know," he told a lay sister. "I look like Lazarus after four days in the tomb." [2]

So many inquiries poured in about his health, he issued a medical report in verse:

> I live out in Brighton, close to B.C.
>   And I'm just as healthy as I can be.
> I have arthritis in both my knees,
>   And when I speak, then I talk with a wheeze.
> My pulse is weak and my blood is quite thin,
>   But I'm awfully well for the shape that I'm in.
>
> I need arch supporters to strengthen my feet,
>   My ankles are swollen; I'm white as a sheet,
> I toss in my bed without sleep every night,
>   No wonder each morning I look like a sight.
> My memory is failing, my head's in a spin
>   But I'm awfully well for the shape that I'm in.
>
> Diverticulitis is a word hard to spell
>   But it's a disease from which I'll never get well,
> Ulcers that keep me on a diet with Maalox
>   Prevent me from resting in a funeral box
> The length of my sermons brings yawns or a grin
>   But I'm awfully well for the shape that I'm in.
>
> The moral is, friends, as this tale I unfold
>   That for you and for me who are fast growing old
> It's better to say, "I'm fine" with a grin
>   Than to let people know of the shape that we're in.

In his correspondence there are hints of his physical suffering, which escape the notice of reporters and photographers who cover him. "Asthma kept me awake most of the night," he said in one letter.[3] "But for those who are hoping for my demise, let me say I've fooled them all my life." It is not generally known that he began to sleep in a hospital bed soon after he became archbishop, and even with an oxygen tank beside him, there were nights when he was lucky to doze off for an hour or two. When a patient in City Hospital told him she couldn't sleep, he said, "My dear, neither can I." Instead of complaining about his afflictions in public, he is more apt to joke about them. He likes the story of a parochial school girl whom he showed around the residence when she came with her parents on a visit. At school the next day, the thirteen-year-old girl told a sister about seeing the hospital bed that could be cranked up and down. "And I saw the archbishop's pajamas on the bed."

The nun looked horrified. "Don't you ever again dare mention that you saw Archbishop Cushing's pajamas," she said.[4]

When he became archbishop, he had two choices: "I could either adopt an easy, calm, and beautiful way of life, or go to work. I chose to do the latter. I do it the hard way and know as well as the doctors do, that I have paid the price." [5]

Cushing has indeed been living on borrowed time since the mid-1950s. The worst crisis came in December 1953, when he underwent two operations at St. Elizabeth's at a time when it was rumored that he was suffering from an incurable ailment. Not until 1964 did he publicly admit that he had had cancer. On December 8, his prostate gland was removed, and fourteen days later he had a kidney removed on which there was an eight-pound malignant tumor. It was at this time that physicians gave him eight months to live. His weight dropped from about two hundred pounds to 146. After the two operations, Mayor Hynes and Governor Herter issued public appeals for prayers.

Cushing went back to work, although church authorities wanted him either to retire or become a coadjutor bishop.[6] Early in January 1954, the cardinal released a statement: "Now that I am home, a period of convalescence lies before me. How long it will be I do not know. If it were only a week I would naturally be impatient to be done with it so that I might be about my Father's business." He went on a bland diet. "I have to. I bleed and sleep with an oxygen tank beside my bed." Before oxygen tanks were in use, he occasionally slept in an old-fashioned oxygen tent. Now he sometimes uses an oxygen mask.

On March 17, 1954, Cushing and Bishop Cornelius Lucey attended a St. Patrick's Day celebration given by Bishop John Wright in Worcester. While addressing two thousand persons in a program sponsored by the Friendly Sons of St. Patrick, Cushing, after a backward glance at Wright, collapsed on the platform and remained unconscious for a few minutes. Taken in his car to the hospital, he insisted on leaving two hours later.

The incident gave further cause for concern, but he quipped away his worries. "I'm dying fast, but I'll bury you all." If told he looked fit, he brushed aside further discussion. "I guess you can get used to any face if you look at it long enough." In the mid-1950s he said he felt as well as he ever did for about ten minutes a day. He told one group that he felt fine, "only the doctor is trying to make a mummy out of me. He has me holding my weight down." He said this in 1965, when he weighed 140 pounds. At various times in recent years he has assured friends that there is nothing seriously wrong with him, "except that I have all the diseases there are."

In 1954, however, despite his levity, he realized the seriousness of his two bouts with surgery. On May 1, the *Pilot* quoted him: "I came within a glimpse of heaven. I didn't get in, so I came home." He added that "life is too short for tears."

Early in 1960, he was back at St. Elizabeth's, this time with a severe case of laryngitis. "You have to suffer," he said. "Nothing good comes without suffering." Another time, when he was discussing the efficacy of suffering, he said "suffering pain has tremendous power before the throne of God."

In recent years he has spent some nights dozing in a leather chair beside his bed to ease his breathing. During the winter of 1964, his asthma and migraine headaches almost drove him out of his mind. One night, he said, "I went down and knocked on Father Joe Maguire's door, woke him up and asked him if he had a bottle in his room. He gave me a couple of good shots of rye, but it didn't do any good." [7] There were more and more references to ailments in his letters. "This note is brief, for I am sick," he told a friend, repeating the words in a penciled footnote. "Better tomorrow." In the spring of 1961 he wrote the same friend: "I was exhausted after my hurried trip to Washington, where I preached at the Pentagon. I have so many things bothering me that I am worse off than a one-armed paperhanger with the shingles. Truth to tell, I have already had that disease, but fortunately I still have two arms." [8]

By 1965, he felt his energy waning, and knew the trip to Ireland would be his last. Leaving Logan Airport on August 4, the "most popular prince of the church walked an emerald carpet leading to his plane," the Boston *Herald* reported.[9] An honor guard of Catholic Boy Scouts flanked the green strip that led to the boarding steps of the Shamrock jet, *St. Brendan,* which bore the cardinal's crest on its fuselage. The same crest was on special menus for the flight.

In Ireland, Cushing spent most of the time on the twelve-day tour making more friends in towns and cities, where cheering crowds lined the streets, rain or shine. In the smallest hamlets, the sight of his Austin-Princess pulling to a stop quickly brought excited neighbors to his side, as if there had been advance notice of his coming. He used his pat greeting: "My name's Cushing."

In the tiny community of Inistioge, a farmer's wife caught his eye. "I have a daughter," she said, "who works on a weekly news magazine in the States—*Time.*"

"You have, have you?" Cushing got out of the car. "Well, you tell her to tell them I didn't like the picture of me they ran on their cover and I didn't like the article they wrote about me, either." He then gave an earthy disclaimer of being earthy when he referred to a *Look* piece on American cardinals that had been published in 1964. "*Look* called me 'the Irish Cardinal . . . as Irish as a boiled potato'. . . . I'd like to get my hands on the guy who wrote that." A minister * who read the account had a different opinion: "The article about Cardinal Cushing was very good. Would that St. Paul had fared as well!"

Pulling up to a roadside in Charlesville, Cork, the prelate exchanged the usual amenities. "I'm going to have a birthday on August 24. Can anyone guess how old I am?"

He beamed when a girl said he would be at least sixty. Then a boy piped up: "You'll be eighty-four." Cushing tapped him on the head with his hat. "May God forgive you." He smiled. "I'll be seventy." [10]

"Never before in my forty-five years of priesthood have I experienced such a reception," he said when he drove into Galway. He told a crowd it was the first time in history that a Pope had assigned a personal legate to dedicate a cathedral. It had taken seven years to build it, the first cathedral in four centuries. The towering structure, built of Galway limestone, rises majestically on the site of one of Ireland's

---

* The Reverend Virgil Geers, O.F.M., Peoria, Illinois.

British-built jails notorious for imprisoning hundreds of patriots during the rising against British rule in 1798. "We're closing up our jails and making cathedrals out of them," Mayor Michael Tierney of Galway said.[11] The structure accommodates three thousand persons.

In a speech to Irish bishops at dedication ceremonies, Cushing asked them to encourage their young priests to volunteer for the Society of St. James. "I want to keep the wolf from the door in Latin America. I have a feeling that the problems there are not sufficiently understood. . . . I still consider myself interested in the universal church, not just in the archdiocese of Boston. We want all the lay missionaries we can get, too."

During the dedication, Cushing whispered to his friend, Bishop Michael Browne of Galway: "Come on, Mickey, let's get the hell on with it." Bishop Browne in his talk said "even Boston has not been large enough to contain his [Cushing's] energy and activity. He has sponsored a special missionary effort for Latin America. He has been a benefactor of many causes—not merely our cathedral, but many religious and missionary institutes in Ireland."

Months before the trip, Cushing had telephoned the *Irish Press* about an item he had read in the newspapers to the effect that Ireland was planting trees in memory of President Kennedy. "You Irish are living five hundred years behind the times," he told an editor. "If you want to put up a memorial, why can't it be a living memorial which will benefit poor people?" He was thinking of a modern maternity hospital that would cater to the poor. During his visit, he discussed construction of such a hospital with the son of President Eamon de Valera, a professor of midwifery and gynecology attached to a hospital in Dublin.

The cardinal officiated at the first baptism held in the new cathedral, when the fifth son of the Galway mayor was named Richard William Holland for Cushing and William Cardinal Conway of Armagh, primate of all Ireland. In a dual ceremony, the two cardinals were made Freemen of the ancient borough in John F. Kennedy Memorial Park, Eyre Square, after it had been dedicated by Cushing. After the ceremony, he unveiled a bust of Kennedy.

"I don't know what this freedom means," Cushing said, having been made a Freeman of Dublin, Cork, and Wexford, as well as Galway. "Maybe it means I don't have to pay taxes. . . . I remember that when President Kennedy received similar honors . . . he said he was the greatest Liberator in the United States." The inference, he explained, was that Kennedy had received the freedom of so many cities in Ireland, "he looked upon himself as a great liberator."

In an interview by the London Catholic weekly, *The Universe,* during his stay in Galway, Cushing urged the creation of a Vatican secretariat that could help channel resources to underdeveloped nations. But he did not favor a central missionary fund available to bishops from all impoverished dioceses, since it would be impractical. "Who would control such a fund? How would the money be allocated? How could it ever have enough money?" Even the United States, with all its wealth, he said, could not overcome the hunger of the world.[12]

There was a moment of excitement for the Presentation Sisters when Cardinal Cushing, in the presence of Cardinal Conway and other dignitaries, opened the magnificent new Our Lady's College in a woodsy setting overlooking the River Boyne. In 1813, a tiny band of sisters had come to Drogheda to establish their first school with a ceiling so low no one could stand upright. For their first mass, these pioneer sisters borrowed a chalice from the Dominican Fathers in Drogheda. Conway told the assembly that eight years earlier the reverend mother was worried about the prospects of finding money to build the college. Her story, he said, read like a fairy tale in which Cushing was the prince. Cushing donated two hundred ten thousand pounds for the project,[13] which replaced six Nissen huts once used by the Irish army. Cushing also dedicated a nurses' hostel for the Medical Missionaries of Mary in Drogheda, to which he also handsomely contributed.

"Everywhere he went, the happy smiling cardinal won the hearts of all who came in contact with him by his informality and love of children, the poor, the aged, and the sick," *The Catholic Standard* reported. "His regular greeting was, 'Hi, folks!' " When a student in the boarding school run by the Presentation Sisters read a welcoming address, he embraced her. "This is the first and last time you will get a kiss from a cardinal." When Dolores Smith, a student, bent to kiss his ring, he told her he didn't have the strength to pull her up. Noticing her embarrassment, he put her at ease. "I like your hat," he said.

When he sprinkled holy water on the premises, smilingly assuring the sisters that it would drive the devil out of them, a tiny nun whispered to a shocked bystander: "Isn't that what holy water is for?"

Earlier in County Wexford, Cushing met Mrs. Mary Ryan, a cousin of the late President Kennedy, and her family at Duganstown, home of Kennedy forebears. The only photographer he let accompany him into the Ryan home was John Murphy of the Boston *Record-American*, who during the tour had to drive over seventy miles an hour to keep up with the prelate's Austin-Princess.

Murphy took pictures of Cushing and Mary Ryan at the homestead. She gave the cardinal rosary beads and showed him a tree planted by President Kennedy during his visit. In the cardinal's party was Sister Mary of the Nativity, a Wexford-born nurse in the Congregation of the Medical Missionaries of Mary, who had nursed Cushing at the time of his last operation, in February 1964. Cushing had lunched in Taghmon with Sister Mary's mother and relatives before visiting Duganstown.

Thousands of cheering Corkies, many waving American flags and pictures of the cardinal, greeted him in Cork City. "Happy birthday!" a woman shouted, and when the crowd took up her cry, he shouted: "Okay, let's sing it." After the song, the prelate took a head scarf from a girl and waved it, adding to the informality of the occasion by whipping off his biretta as his car proceeded slowly down the South Mall. A Garda marching alongside the car didn't realize that Cushing was holding a biretta over his head.

That same day Cushing received another "homely" welcome from fifteen hundred villagers, when he revisited Glanworth. He chatted with natives, whose grandparents had known his father, and had a pleasant reunion with Canon Michael Hurley, who was then eighty-one years old. John O'Driscoll gave him an ancient anvil that had been used as a forge by the Cushings in the nineteenth century. O'Driscoll also gave him a hammer his father had used in Glanworth when he was a nail-maker. As Cushing spoke, a member of a Boston television crew recorded his remarks. Thomas Riley of the *Record-American* asked a farmer in rubber boots what he thought of the cardinal.

"If ever another St. Patrick were needin'," he said, "that would be him." [14]

"A different situation prevailed when my parents emigrated," Cushing said to the gathering. "There was a famine here then. My father perfected his trade as a blacksmith and in the days of horsecars in Boston he worked as a blacksmith for the old Boston El." [15]

As on previous visits, the cardinal knelt alone in silent prayer before the Marist shrine at the site of his father's home.

When he boarded the Aer Lingus Boeing jet at Shannon for the return trip, Celia Moran, a senior hostess, presented him with a birthday cake with seven lighted candles. President de Valera was on hand with members of the hierarchy to see him off as a huge crowd watched from balconies. As he walked to the tarmac, the cardinal received the same twenty-one-gun salute that had been given to President Kennedy on his last trip to Ireland.

He told the press it was probably his last look at Erin. "I am an old man now and not very strong, and there is so much for me to do at home, and particularly for South America. You live in a land of tremendous history, and future generations of this country could be the bulwark of the western world, of the free world. Ireland has everything to offer." [16]

Oona Kelley, of Dungannon, the harpist with the Bunratty Castle Singers, gave the prelate a replica of the Irish harp she had played when her group entertained at the cardinal's residence in 1964. "I have received many gifts in my time," he told the crowd, "but this means more to me than any others of its kind. Ireland is the only country in the world which has such a beautiful musical instrument as its national emblem, and I think there is nothing more beautiful in the world than the harp." [17]

On August 24 at his residence, Cushing celebrated his birthday by inviting Joe Kennedy and the ambassador's seventeen grandchildren to a party. Joe flew from the Cape in his private plane with Ann Gargan, and Judge Morrissey brought a busload of Kennedys, including John-John and Caroline, who chose her middle name (Joan) after she saw a picture of Joan of Arc in a corridor of the cardinal's residence. "I took her name in confirmation because she was killed like my father," she said. The cardinal, who tells friends this story, added that John-John prefers to be called simply John.

The prelate embraced Joe Kennedy and kissed him on the cheek. "He looks to be in good shape," he told a reporter. "I told him to keep up his courage. He's my type of guy; he likes to run the show, but he no longer can." Asked whether he was going to run the show, he grinned. "I don't think so. I think the kids will take over." [18]

In the group were five of the Bobby Kennedy children, three Shrivers, four Lawfords, two Smiths, and one of Ted's children. Caroline, as usual, was the starlet. "Caroline, honey, how are you?" Cushing asked as she and the other grandchildren lined up for the "Happy Birthday" song.

"Let's give three cheers for your grandfather," Cushing said when they finished. He led them in a "Hip, hip, hooray!"

"You're the most important one here today," Cushing told Joe Kennedy.

Thus did the cardinal confound some physicians by reaching the age of seventy. "No matter how weak the body," Jim Bishop wrote, "the voice is strong enough to bend windows, and the spirit is youthful and athletic." If Cushing was worried about an impending operation for a nonmalignant tumor, he didn't show it. He told friends he would survive the surgery, although it was, he said, serious. "After all, God doesn't kill Santa Claus or fools like me." After the operation in mid-October, he was soon up and around.

Ten days earlier he had gone to New York to hear Pope Paul VI address the U.N. Assembly. He stayed at the Waldorf-Astoria, where Pope Paul met President Lyndon Johnson. Cushing was one of the first five cardinals to greet the Pope at Kennedy Airport. Later he was asked about Paul's detour to talk to him a moment after he landed. "My only fear was that he was going to tell me to come back to Rome," Cushing said.[19]

Heads turned at the United Nations when Jacqueline Kennedy, dressed in black, entered to take her seat, escorted by Cardinal Cushing and her brothers-in-law, senators Edward and Robert Kennedy. Cushing sat on her right in the front row of seats reserved for VIPs. The climax of Pope Paul's speech centered on John F. Kennedy's imperishable words: "Mankind must put an end to war or war will put an end to mankind." *The New York Times* reported that the "words were deeply moving and meaningful."[20] When the Pope mentioned Kennedy, Jacqueline "blinked back tears and Cushing, sitting next to her, reached over and patted her in a fatherly manner."[21] As he moved through the crowd in the Delegates Lounge after his speech, Pope Paul spotted Cardinal Cushing, who was talking to Cardinal McIntyre of Los Angeles. He stepped off the red carpet to embrace them, kissing them on both cheeks. He also greeted Jacqueline.

During his fourteen-hour visit to New York City, the Pope celebrated mass in Yankee Stadium. It was cold, and "I didn't even have a coat," Cushing said, when he returned to Boston. Referring to the African cardinal who had sat next to him, he said Rugambwa nearly froze to death. "I had to get him three overcoats." He added that he came home to get warm. Cushing said Paul's visit created "an atmo-sphere the like of which I have never experienced. It was a day full of charity to all and love for one another." [22]

Two weeks after his operation, the cardinal made more history. He was the first prince of the church to give a sermon in a Masonic Lodge—the Grand Lodge of Massachusetts, the oldest in the United States. Addressing himself to his familiar theme of unity of love, he called for respect for all people and their beliefs. Irving H. Gale, the lodge master, introduced him as "Richard the Open Hearted of Boston."

In December, he spoke at a "Festival of Faith" in a Congregational church in New Haven, Connecticut. As he mounted the pulpit, he ran his hands through the pockets of his black cassock and looked around quizzically: "Is Monsignor Maguire [his personal secretary] in the house? In my overcoat pocket I have some notes." Maguire, a former football great at Boston College, found the notes, but it really didn't matter, for the cardinal is often at his best when speaking extemporaneously.

chapter twenty-three

SHADY SIDE OF
THE HILL

In a letter to former Lord Mayor Sean McCarthy of Cork after his final trip to Ireland, the cardinal spoke of retiring in 1970 at the age of seventy-five. "The burdens of the archdiocese," he said, "are too much for a man of my age." He also set 1970 as the target date for a fifty-million-dollar fund drive.

In 1967 he said he would be "tickled to death" if he could join Paul-Emile Léger, of Canada, who resigned from the second largest Roman Catholic diocese in North America to work as a simple missionary among the lepers of the Republic of Cameroon on Africa's west coast.

To end queries about his declining health, Cushing quipped that he still played football. "I look like a quarterback for the Boston Patriots," he told a reporter. Cardinals should be permitted to resign when they reach seventy, he added, especially in his case. "People are sick of hearing me and worrying about me. They need new blood. Who knows? I am liable to be the first applicant for the home for retired priests when it opens in the West End." [1] He was seventy-two when he told an audience at Symphony Hall that he had no yen to live as a cardinal or bishop. He preferred to be a simple missionary in South America. "When I reach seventy-five, I'm resigning. I'm all through."

Meanwhile, he provided a retirement home for senior priests. "I'm going to throw them a big party at a downtown hotel—all of them," he said during his Silver Jubilee in 1964.

"Will you give them a drink at the dinner?" a reporter asked.

"More than one," he said with his "fetchingly crooked smile." [2]

In the summer of 1968 he opened Price Institute at Maryknoll's Ladycrest in Topsfield. It is not enough to provide retirement homes, he said.[3] He wants strong programs to involve those retired in cultural and intellectual development so they can remain a part of the community. That summer he did not feel well enough to go to Waterville, Maine, to receive an honorary degree from Colby College. The college president conferred the degree at the cardinal's residence a few days later after the trustees, for the first time in history, honored a recipient *in absentia*. In December, Cushing received another award, along with a substantial purse, at a dinner when the New England Dale Carnegie Institute named him, in the presence of Governor Volpe and Senate President Maurice Donahue, "Man of the Century." [4]

By this time, the cardinal was tired, and despite all the honors heaped on him, he knew more than ever "the loneliness that surrounds a bishop." [5] There were times when he could no longer conceal the pain that tortured his days as well as his nights. In 1966, he halted a sermon in a Protestant church, raising his hands to tell a startled congregation that it was "too warm for any more." [6] The occasion was a concelebrated mass marking the centenary of the church.

During his talk on the shortage of priests, he had called the preceding Friday his "worst day." His pallor reflected a strain he had been under since a few days earlier when he told a crowded Columbus Day congregation in Holy Cross Cathedral that he wasn't sure whether he could finish the mass. He survived it but passed up the breakfast that followed at the Cardinal Cushing Center for Spanish Speaking Peoples nearby and skipped two other scheduled appearances on the holiday. He apologized for missing the appointments. "If I wasn't forced to bed, I would have been there."

In his early seventies, however, he was, for the most part, outwardly as jaunty and cheerful as ever. On his seventy-first birthday, he gave a large party for convalescent and handicapped children, introducing an Irish harpist who played accompaniment while the children sang "Galway Bay," the prelate's favorite song. On his following birthday anniversary, he took the Little Sisters of the Poor on an outing, this time on a cruise around Boston Harbor.[7] "We have plenty of food and plenty of beer to drink," he told the group as the *New Boston* shoved off from Rowe's Wharf. "The main thing I wish is that you go back to your home sober." The eighty-five guests this time ranged in age from the sixties to ninety-seven; many were in wheelchairs. Cushing gave the men cigars and promised the women hair-dos. As the ship approached the pier after a cruise of almost three hours, he asked if anyone wanted "one for the road."

That year (1967) Cushing hosted the last Thanksgiving celebration before Blinstrub's Village burned down. "The reason I started this custom several years ago," he said, "is that in my travels throughout the archdiocese I found too many of the aged who had no one to visit them, no one to give them that love, that affection which all of us crave, but which is especially the solace of the elderly. They are in the evening of life, and they have a right not only to rejoice in the memory of happiness gone by, but to feel that they are still wanted and needed and loved." [8] He spoke of the "unconscious tyranny of youth toward the aging," adding: "Give them the care, the attention, the love that they deserve, and that we ourselves will desire in the sunset years." The prelate said he would like to eat turkey with his guests, "But now I have only false teeth and they feel like horseshoes in my mouth." [9]

After the fire that razed the nightclub, Mayor Kevin White of Boston said Stanley Blinstrub, who had never asked charity for himself, "has offered charity to everyone. The city will do everything it can to help him." Blinstrub was grateful. "I've had hundreds of people offer help . . . and Cardinal Cushing above all."

Early in May 1968, sixteen thousand persons attended the Blinstrub fete at the Boston Garden. The Cardinal, standing next to Blinstrub in the lobby, greeted guests before he and the nightclub owner walked down to their seats to the music of "The Bells of St. Mary's."[10] Mayor White and Governor Volpe were present. Jess Cain, of station WHDH, the master of ceremonies, introduced silver-haired actor Pat O'Brien as the "former coach from Notre Dame."

"Your Eminence, Cardinal Cushing, what an honor to be here tonight," O'Brien said. "You're looking at a man who wouldn't give a spot to a Dalmatian dog, but just look at the talent here tonight." Swinging into "I'm Getting Married in the Morning," the actor added his own inimitable soft-shoe touch. Then he dedicated the "Rockne Locker Room Talk" to Cushing, winding up with the Notre Dame fight song.

The cardinal told the assembly of the South Boston drunk who fell into an open grave on his way home one Saturday night. When he awoke to the dawn's light and heard birds singing, he murmured: "Glory be, it's resurrection day . . . and I'm the first one up!"

"I've had a hard time speaking tonight, because of my teeth. Today the dentist gave me a temporary upper and . . . lower set. If I talk the way I usually do, both may go flying down the middle aisle. My

dentist told me, 'If you are true to those teeth, they'll be true to you.' "
Thanking all for being there, he said he had written to all the per-
formers present, even though he had never met any of them. "I
asked them to help out Stanley Blinstrub and look how they responded. To show my gratitude," he quipped, "I'm going to send
them my picture with my autograph."

The talent, he reflected later, must have been pretty good to keep
him quiet for three hours. The line-up included Arthur Godfrey,
Wayne Newton, Brenda Lee, Connie Francis, Mike Douglas, Norm
Crosby, Bobby Vinton, and Al Martino, a former bricklayer who said
he wanted to lay the first brick in Blinstrub's new nightclub.

"The day of the fire was the saddest of my life," Blinstrub said.
"The cardinal called me at the height of the inferno and offered to
help. That day he started what happened tonight." [11]

More than seven hundred persons feted Cushing on his seventy-third
birthday at a $100-a-plate reception at Tara, the hilltop estate of
Ralph Tedeschi, against the musical background of Lester Lanin's
orchestra. "I can't socialize too long," Cushing said. "I have work to
do." He was scheduled to speak the next morning at Cathedral-in-the-
Pines in New Hampshire. One of the affluent guests * on leaving the
party handed Tedeschi an extra check for a thousand dollars for
Cushing charities.

The cardinal interrupted his table-hopping to clear the bar of
loiterers, shoving two or three of them away in his impatience.
"Here's another beautiful young lady," he said as he made his rounds,
resting his hand on the head of a state senator's wife. When he removed his hand, he accidentally knocked her wig on the floor, much
to her embarrassment.

The pièce de résistance at the formal dinner was roast sirloin of
beef à la Cushing *au jus naturel*. Slices were served from a huge
four-tiered birthday cake topped with a biretta-shaped icing. Cushing
sent most of the cake to nearby St. Coletta's.

Less publicized was a $1,000-a-couple dinner given a month later
by Mr. and Mrs. Rubin Epstein of Brookline, also in honor of the
prelate's birthday. This testimonial, which added fourteen thousand
dollars to the kitty, was duplicated on Cushing's seventy-fourth birthday. In mid-October 1968, Catholics, Protestants, and Jews combined in an unusual tribute to Cushing at the Elliot L. Richardson

---

* Irving Usen.

Charity Ball at the Statler Hilton, raising fifty thousand dollars for the Cardinal Cushing Medical Center in Galilee, Israel. "As this glorious institution of healing rises from the hallowed sands of the Holy Land to serve men of all religions, creeds, and races," the toastmaster said, "we all are privileged to witness a truly eloquent testimonial to the ecumenical spirit for which Cardinal Cushing stands." [12] He called the prelate "the greatest Catholic churchman in the world." A month later, on November 23, in the same hotel the cardinal was honored at the Labor Guild's Cushing Awards dinner.

In the fall of 1968, Cushing invited eight thousand underprivileged children from ghettos to see an exhibition football game between the Boston Patriots and the Philadelphia Eagles at Harvard Stadium, with entertainment at half-time provided by Revere's 27th Lancers Drum and Bugle Corps. Cushing made thousands of dollars from advertising revenue in the program, not to mention from the ticket sale. After the game many of the children ate hot dogs with the players in Harvard Field House, through the courtesy of the cardinal and the Caritas Guild, which sponsored the game.

Cushing seemed to be everywhere in 1968, involved in a wide range of activities. Between April and October he sponsored six separate pilgrimages to seven foreign countries, as well as to places in New England and the East Coast. The "Cardinal Cushing Boston Pilgrimages" included trips to Canada, Ireland, France, England, Norway, Denmark, and Sweden, plus two excursions to Lourdes. A third overseas tour visited shrines and sites associated with St. Botolph (patron saint of Boston) in England and Scandinavia.

The first of two domestic pilgrimages included trips to Philadelphia, Washington, and New York during Memorial day week. The second took pilgrims north through Albany, Buffalo, and Niagara Falls into Canada and the shrines of Ontario and Quebec. It was almost as if the prelate, racing against time, wanted to pack everything he could into his schedule in his last years of service.

Another project in 1968 was an urban affairs office designed to develop specific proposals for better housing, with liaison between parish officials and social agencies. Cushing, during a controversy over the relocation of the University of Massachusetts, backed an in-town site and offered the use of Holy Cross Cathedral for cultural purposes. He said he would sell land around the church to the university as it became available.

He continued to speak out on issues. He called for an end to the

war in Vietnam, approved the ratification of a nuclear nonprolifera-
tion treaty, and in his New Year's message warned against the deteri-
oration of universities and colleges into greenhouses for flowering
anarchists. He said the "sacred forum" of the college and university
campus must be preserved, but that "it is the function of the total
academic community to avoid becoming slaves to slogans . . . so mes-
merized by the immediate as to become insensitive to the long range
and the enduring." The university, he said, is central to building a
new world which should be the aim of all in "the last year of the
turbulent 1960s." The world, he added, faces a "crisis in integrity,
asking for the discovery in 1969 of the spiritual significance of science
and technology." [13]

The August 1968 cover of *Yankee Clipper,* the journal of the First
Naval District Reserve, showed his eminence pulling on a sailor's
white cap, a salty shot on the occasion of the July commissioning of
the *U.S.S. O' Callaghan,* at which Cushing was the main speaker. Noting that war makes men into brutes, he said "out of it can also come
achievements that expand the human spirit and remain an inspiration
for all future time."

Cushing continued to visit hospitals. In Chelsea Naval Hospital the
chaplain introduced him to a young marine who had lost a leg.
"What were you doing?" the cardinal asked.

"Going for a walk."

As glum as he felt on hearing the sad news, Cushing joined in the
laughter.[14] Marine Lance Corporal James Shea, nineteen, of South
Boston, another wounded veteran of the Vietnam campaign, recalled
his first meeting with the prelate seven years earlier at Fenway Park,
when he cut his lip while kissing the ring. Cushing told a GI who lived
in Brockton about the modern Cardinal Cushing General Hospital.
When he dedicated it in 1968, he said it was for people of all faiths:
"There is no Catholic appendix, no Protestant liver ailment, and no
Jewish kidney disease." While chatting with a youth from South Boston, he picked up the boy's hat. "I could use this as a Sunday collection
basket," he said, turning it upside down to autograph it. He also autographed casts.

"This is not my first visit here," he told a rear admiral at the end
of the tour, "nor will it be my last. This is the least I can do for these
brave men whose devotion to duty and their country can stand as examples to all of us."

Cushing's wit, candor, and lightheartedness continued to lift the pall of gloom from institutions housing the neglected or forgotten. In a home for the aged, he passed out jiggers of whiskey. "Holy water— that's what it is! But don't sprinkle it around. Pour it down." He assured the group that the holy water would cure everything "from falling hair to sore toe nails" and would help them to live to be a hundred. "Come here, my good mother," he said to the sister who was opening the carton containing jiggers of whiskey; "you haven't been drinking the holy water, have you? Santa looks as though he's been drinking it. Well, it won't harm him." Referring to himself as the bartender, he added: "Do they give you this every day, or only when I come? Well, I should come more frequently so you won't have hardening of the arteries. Come on, sister, you're kind of slow."

And the elderly, the bleakness of their days temporarily forgotten, love him for his gaiety and compassion. He might go unannounced into a hospital ward to find half a dozen men idling. "I hope I didn't break up a crap game," he says, shaking hands with everyone. "It's the cardinal in person," an aged woman in another ward said. "I saw him face to face."

In one surprise visit to the Soldiers Home in Chelsea, where the honor guard of the Fourth Degree Knights of Columbus greeted him, he moved through all the wards. "Hello, Jake," he said, kneeling by the bedside of an old man. After singing with him, "Smile the While, I Kiss You Sad Adieu," he told the patient he was celebrating Passover "with the best Jew in Boston."

"Who is he?" Jake asked.

"You."

When Jake thanked him, he said, "Okay, kid."

When he learned that a grandnephew of 91-year-old John Mc-Carthy was soon to be ordained, the prelate told the patient that he would give the young man permission to say mass "right here at the foot of the bed, facing you. And if he can't do it, I'll come myself."

In 1968, Cushing made his anniversary visit to Boston State Hospital and his regular rounds to homes for the poor. In April he dedicated the new five-million-dollar sixty-story Sancta Maria Hospital in Cambridge. "Make way," he quipped as he moved around the facility. "Here comes the *Queen Mary*." He wore his ceremonial robes to please the patients.

That month a respiratory infection aggravated by exhaustion sent him to St. Elizabeth's Hospital for several days, forcing him to cancel an appearance for the Easter Sunday mass at the cathedral. He scotched rumors that he was seriously ill by answering telphone calls. He did admit a few months later that cancer had been found in 1965 when he underwent surgery for intestinal polyps. The malignancy was removed.

The cardinal was weary by the end of the year. In mid-December, he canceled an appearance at the sixtieth anniversary mass of St. Brigid's parish, where he had said his first public mass. He stayed home with an acute case of influenza and a high temperature. Although indisposed for the rest of the month, he officiated at church events, including a Christmas mass at the cathedral and the St. Nicholas Cotillion two days after Christmas.

Cushing founded the cotillion in 1957 to aid homeless and afflicted children through Nazareth. Parents of each debutante donated five hundred dollars (later seven hundred and fifty) to the fund. Cushing would have preferred a larger donation. "That kind of money won't even pay my expenses for a single day," he said at a time when he needed sixteen thousand dollars for daily operations.*

He planned the social as a pleasant evening for young ladies and their parents and escorts, with a dinner followed by a reception at which each girl is photographed beside the cardinal in his full regalia. The girls in their white evening gowns carry red bouquets and tread a red carpet leading up to the stage of the Sheraton Plaza, where they form a semicircle behind the prelate. "Inspired by the occasion and the cause, flower genius Ruth Traynor goes to Rome for the marvelous setting, and the Sheraton Plaza is a fountained garden, with camellias, trees and plants especially grown for this society." [15]

In 1968, the cardinal, escorted by the Knights of Malta, crossed the ballroom to the stage to await the procession of seventeen debutantes. In his brief talk, the cardinal urged the young ladies on to full and rewarding lives and left after giving each debutante a traditional charm.

Cardinal Cushing over the years has rewarded faithful donors to his charity appeals by having them honored by the Vatican. A typical note to a candidate might read: "I am interested in having you made a Knight of the Holy Sepulchre. This is an honor which you richly deserve for all your kindness to me and your devotion to the church;

---

* The original sponsors of the St. Nicholas Cotillion were Mmes. Hester Pickman, John T. Bottomley, Alvan T. Fuller, and James J. Phelan. Mrs. Phelan, the lone survivor, lives at the Ritz Hotel in Boston.

also, in recognition of the fact that you are an exemplary Catholic gentleman. I am happy to obtain this honor for you." When Ralph Tedeschi was made a Knight of St. Gregory, Cardinal Cushing celebrated a private mass in the spacious living room of Tedeschi's home (Tara). One person declined the honor. When, on the plane flight to Pittsburgh, the cardinal told John Hynes of his intention to make him a Knight, the mayor graciously declined. "I can't afford the fifteen hundred dollars the vestments cost," he said.

chapter twenty-four

MORE PRIESTS AND
FEWER BABIES?

CARDINAL CUSHING HAS OFTEN SPOKEN of the worldwide need for more religious vocations and in recent years said it was "from every point the most important problem you could . . . consider at this moment in history. Unless we think of every ordained priest as part of the universal church, we shall have a flock of spiritual millionaires who will rot from within. We cannot keep the faith unless we propagate it." He has reached out for converts by radio, television, in public appearances, and through the press.

"When I was first made a bishop," he said in 1968, "I looked forward to the day when I would ordain a hundred priests a year. This year I'm ordaining only thirty-four men, and we need at least sixty." [1]

The Catholic Church is falling far short of his goal of supplying one priest for every eight hundred communicants. By 1968, the worldwide ratio was about one for every thirteen hundred, and since then, the situation is worse. The shortage is especially acute in France, Spain, Brazil, Argentina, and the United States. Many priests who quit are long-time men ordained for fifteen years or more, while the majority have been priests for three to twelve years. According to figures released in 1969,[2] there were marked decreases in the previous year in the number of clergymen, nuns, teachers, schools, and places of worship—and the smallest membership growth in a quarter century.

Part of the frustration in clerical ranks—the chief cause of the decline in numbers—stems from the slow rate of implementation of Vatican Council II promises. Many priests who started as assistants in a parish at the age of twenty-five have to wait until they are in their fifties for promotion to pastor. Some prefer the quicker satisfaction they find in government service in poverty programs or in social service.

Among theologians who think the traditional priesthood is dying is Monsignor Ivan Illich, who argues that Pope Paul's insistence that priests remain celibate is hastening the death of the clergy. Defections of the clergy were unusual until the early 1960s. Now they are common. "Tomorrow they may be the pattern," Illich says.

A recent survey by the National Association for Pastoral Renewal bears him out. A poll showed that seven thousand of the nation's thirty-seven thousand diocesan priests want freedom to marry. Some priests and nuns are marrying without Vatican permission, and many who defect do so to marry. Of 711 cases reported in 1966 and 1967, 322 of the men have married. It is obvious that an increasing number of priests firmly believe that Catholicism must eventually allow its clerics to marry. "What eventuality will not take place during the papacy of Paul VI, who last year reaffirmed the rule of celibacy for the church," *Time* reported in 1968. "Nevertheless, many former priests continue to informally practice their ministry and still consider themselves priests. For them the truth is that they have not left the church; they are simply ahead of it."

One priest attacked the rule of celibacy in a magazine article, noting that while Protestant ministers are allowed to marry, Catholic priests are "presented as a class of men not subject to the same desires and interests as other men. To suggest that a whole class of men share such a mystical quality is to sustain a myth at the price of honesty." [3] He added that two years earlier, when James Kavanaugh, an ex-priest, in the same magazine had expressed a wish to marry, he had to do so anonymously, "because it was considered shocking for a priest to have such desires." [4]

At Notre Dame—the leading Catholic university in the United States —Kavanaugh was loudly applauded when he said: "I don't know how I, as a man, can find God and meaning without marriage. I need the close personal relationship of a woman. I need it, and I intend to have it." He renounced his priesthood, said the institutional church could "go to hell," and wrote a best-seller, *A Modern Priest Looks at His Outdated Church.*[5] Although many of his former colleagues denounced him for his stand on marriage, birth control, and divorce and for his disregard for the teaching authority of bishops and popes, he found strong support among Catholic clergymen, who agreed with his statement: "Don't you see, the priesthood as a state of life is false? You don't institutionalize sanctity. Not any more."

Kavanaugh is married. Among those who commended his book

were an Uruguayan priest, who married a former nun, and an ex-nun, who wrote him that she was in love with a priest: "I feel soon that our relationship will come to a head; it must; we cannot live under this strain much longer. I want at times to write to him and tell him he does not have a celibate vocation, but I feel this must come from his own realization." [6]

In 1968, Gregory Lemercier, a former Catholic monk, who led his entire monastery out of the church in a dispute with the Vatican over psychoanalysis, married a former nun in a civil ceremony while surrounded by other former monks of the one-time Benedictine Monastery of St. Mary, Cuernavaca, Mexico. The bride was once a nun in a convent attached to the monastery. Lemercier and his colleagues turned their monastery into an "Amaus Psychoanalytic Treatment Center." They wear blue jeans and T-shirts instead of robes and cowls and support themselves by making and selling religious art and treating clients with psychoanalysis.

In that same year, *Time* published a letter from a former priest, Thomas R. Melville, which says in part: "Sister Marian Peter and I have been married. We could have gotten permission from Rome, but decided not to. We want the church to know that it is time that her hierarchy began preaching and living the Gospel of Christ's love for all mankind, and forget their frantic defense of a legalistic system that has only served to alienate the clergy from the poor." [7]

The cardinal takes a liberal stand on this issue. Soon after Vatican II, he received permission from Rome to ordain a Lutheran convert, Ernest Beck, who later took his vows in Mainz, Germany.[8] At about the same time the cardinal sponsored the priestly studies of a married former Episcopal priest. In 1964 in a television interview he was asked what he thought about married priests.

"I wanted to ordain one for Boston. . . . I don't think in the foreseeable future they will accept them in the United States, although I am convinced that we should accept at least topflight men. The Holy See has said that at . . . present . . . they would not give permission to any bishop in the United States to ordain a married priest with children. But it may come." [9] Three years later in an informal talk, he predicted that never in the lifetime of those present would they see priests in the western world marry.[10] Then came a typical one-line non sequitur: "For that matter, who would ever marry the likes of me?"

Another time he smiled when asked if he favored ordaining women to ease the shortage of priests. "I've supported many lost causes in my lifetime," he told a community of nuns, "but this one is not for me. I could never confess my sins to a woman. It would be like doing it on television."

The cardinal is alarmed over another ominous trend—the sharp dip in seminary enrollment. "We are losing vocations that should be going to the seminary and are not, and frankly, it's a serious problem to keep seminarians in the seminary itself." [11] He blames the situation on the widespread worldliness of the clergy, characterizing it as the great weakness of the modern Catholic Church. Seminary enrollment in the United States in 1967 fell by 5,541—more than twice the decline of 1966.[12] According to Cushing, many potentially good priests leave seminaries rather than submit to petty rules and a boring curriculum. Father Kavanaugh, recalling his seminary years, says he was "shielded from the fleeting pleasures of the world. [*] I could not leave the grounds, see a girl, read a magazine, drive a car, escape the iron discipline that bound me in its arms. . . . I heard what I was supposed to hear, and said what the administration expected me to say." [13]

Even after ordination, which you can reach "as naive as a twelve-year-old," prospects are often dismal. A Colorado priest agreed: "Some of the bitchiest old women in the United States are wearing cassocks, not dresses." Still another factor that is eroding the will and ambition of young clerics is a growing anticlericalism in this modern age of the layman. This happens when the layman thinks he knows more than the clergy.[14]

Cardinal Cushing, in another pioneer move, in the summer of 1968 updated seminaries by inaugurating a four-year college course for Catholic seminarians, with the integration of the archdiocesan major and minor seminaries. The move set the stage for a stronger liberal arts training for future priests, in accord with directives of Vatican II and American bishops. The seventeen-year-old Cardinal O'Connell Minor Seminary in Jamaica Plain merged with the eighty-four-year-old St. John's Seminary in Brighton.

Cushing also arranged for seminarians to have more freedom on evenings and weekends. Instead of taking a two-year college course and six years of seminary training, men now divide the eight years

---

* One Catholic *Time* reader (Rosalie C. Boyle) nominated Kavanaugh as "Man of the Year" (1969) as "the man who helped to unshackle our emotionally crippled minds that has us wearing out the kneeler in the confessionals."

equally, receiving a bachelor degree for the first half of the course. During the second phase they take seminary courses, with emphasis on theology and philosophy. And they are allowed to enroll in other colleges. Cushing explained the radical change:

"Revision of administrative structure and curriculum . . . will find closer bonds with the American educational system insofar as that system may offer the best preparation for the study of contemporary theology and be able to alert seminarians to the complex society in which they will minister." The cardinal's aim, in line with Vatican II, is to prescribe a scientific and humanistic education for seminarians appropriate to the culture of their respective countries and the directives of the American Bishops' Committee on Seminaries.

The prelate has done some soul-searching since his unfortunate experience at St. John's Seminary in 1966, which led to the expulsion of eight rebels from the campus. It was a time when there were rumblings in seminaries all over the nation.

In the spring of 1966 Cushing tipped a hornet's nest. Noting that his residence and chancery in Brighton is the headquarters for New England's five million Roman Catholics, *Newsweek* reported: "There St. John's shepherds future priests from Massachusetts through their final six, essentially isolated, years, prior to ordination." [15]

St. John's was virtually under siege during Holy Week, when a cordon of police guarded its doors. Outside, three hundred Catholic laymen marched in an unprecedented protest against the cardinal, who had abruptly expelled eight seminarians the week before. Inside, scores of seminarians held a holy fast in support of the ousted students. In the administrative office, the cardinal conferred with archdiocesan officials in an effort to resolve the most explosive confrontation ever held in an American Catholic seminary.

"The crisis was not limited to Boston," *Newsweek* said. "Throughout the United States Catholic bishops faced a problem of integrating the spirit of freedom generated by Vatican Council II with their antiquated seminary systems that treat students like mischievous teenagers." [16]

Students objected to a new spartan regime imposed by Monsignor Lawrence J. Riley, whom Cushing had named rector in 1965 to succeed the progressive Monsignor Matthew Stapleton. Riley, an old-school disciplinarian who cheerlessly viewed the seminary as a "closed" institution where candidates for the priesthood should be withdrawn from the world, reinstated the all-Latin mass and rejected a list of outside lecturers whom students wanted to hear. They accused Riley of creating an atmosphere of dusty medievalism by inquisitorial means. They were further frustrated when Riley ended the ecumenical exchange with Protestant clergymen and theologians and forbade students to voice opinions, not only in public forums, but even within the confines of the school itself unless permission was granted. No longer could they publish their ideas, take part in demonstrations, leave the grounds without permission, take a course in another school, or sign a petition relating to social or political issues.

Such stringent rules did not reflect Cushing's ideas. In a radio talk in June 1964, when asked whether he allowed seminarians to read newspapers and keep up with current events, he had said: "We are doing that today, and I will build a library at the archdiocesan seminary in Brighton and they will have access to all the newspapers of the country."

Monsignor Stapleton, who had permitted students to have dialogues with their Protestant counterparts and to listen to visiting theologians of all faiths, also had given them off-campus freedom as settlement house workers and let them take part in civil rights projects. Riley restricted off-campus activities to four hours a week, refused to discuss policy with student leaders, and turned a deaf ear when they presented him with a four-page statement of grievances. Listing a dozen complaints, the seminarians appended an appeal from the Book of Acts: "Come and help us!"

When the ired seminarians used the confessional to seek guidance from liberal faculty members, Riley countered by restricting their confessions to selected advisers. During the winter, the students appealed to the cardinal, asking him to discuss policy changes. The prelate, who at the time was miserable with migraine headaches, kidney problems, and his other ailments, did not respond.

Late in March, when he was addressing Boston pastors in St. John's auditorium on the meaning of Vatican II, 125 seminarians silently protested outside, carrying signs reading "Freedom in the Seminary Now and the Truth Shall Set You Free." Cushing, already annoyed by a student charge that he was an "intransigent cardinal-archbishop" living "in an aura of Byzantine splendor," rushed outside to warn the protesters that strong-arm tactics would avail them nothing. His wrath was understandable. For a prelate living up to a vow of Franciscan poverty, it was too much to be called a hedonist.

He asked newsmen not to report the incident, but it was too good a story to kill. That night the prelate told a student delegation that their bold defiance might close the seminary. Three days later, Riley expelled eight ringleaders. Cushing, normally sympathetic with the plight of aspiring priests, had become stiff-necked when the students exploited the situation, and he approved the expulsions.

In doing so, he grabbed a tiger by the tail. Six rebels, after seven years of study, were only one year from ordination. Early in April, lay Catholics twice picketed the cardinal's residence and the nearby seminary and organized a four-day Easter prayer vigil on behalf of the students. Local Catholic university professors and students formed an ad hoc committee to urge Cushing to appoint a board of inquiry.

"In the next two months, the whole ecumenical stance of the church in this area will be decided," predicted committee leader Patrick Hill, a graduate student at Boston University. "If the eight students are not reinstated, Protestants will lose faith in the renewal of the church, and seminarians will go elsewhere." The furor died down, but not until a seminarian said 150 of his colleagues would resign over the dismissals, a prophecy that did not come to pass. "In five years," another said, "St. John's will be a girls' dormitory for Boston College." That did not happen, either.

Many veteran pastors agreed that stern discipline was an integral part of seminary life. "The young men seem to be taking it," one said. "You've got to take a lot more in this league that you probably don't have to take in other leagues," said another pastor. "In some ways, the seminary should be harder even than West Point."

The cardinal stood firm, feeling that the students had overstepped the bounds of protest, even after his talk to a Communion breakfast sponsored by the Holy Name Society in New York in April, when he championed the right of dissent as "among the most precious of our national values" and as a right that must be guarded at any cost. Back in Boston, he rejected personal appeals for reinstating the seminarians. He told one, who had given an interview on television, that he would bar him from every Catholic seminary in the world, "even behind the Iron Curtain."

Christian Century magazine, in its April 13 issue, ran an article titled "Please Reconsider, Cardinal Cushing!" It said the cardinal had an ideal opportunity to put his democratic convictions into action, noting that the eight seminarians had been harshly dealt with for exercising the same right that the cardinal upheld in his New York speech. "We earnestly hope the cardinal will reconsider, will, while there is still time, rescind his decision—a decision contrary not only to the mind and spirit of Vatican II, but, of his own career and recent remarks." [17] But the prelate, calling it an internal matter, did not budge. He felt that with church authority under increasing attack, he would worsen the situation by yielding to pressure.

Time assessed the impasse: "The battle between the liberal prelate and freedom-seeking students symbolized one of the unresolved problems of the new spirit of freedom in the Catholic church: the reformation of a seminary system basically unchanged in centuries." [18]

Cushing's dilemma came at a time when other bishops gave in to protests by recognizing student councils, offering new courses in pastoral psychology and sociology (instead of medieval philosophy), including courses in Protestant theology, and replacing Latin lectures by small-group give-and-take seminars. They also ended compulsory curfews, swinging away from student segregation from the outside world. For the first time, seminarians could study secular culture, with which they would live after ordination. At Chicago's St. Mary of the Lake Seminary, once the nation's strictest, students could have their own radios, attend plays, concerts, and lectures in town. In San Francisco, the rector let two seminarians tour the city's homosexual bars with vice-squad cops for a sociological survey.

Criticism of seminaries nevertheless continued. When a three-day consultation on the black church was held at Boston University School of Theology in 1968, McKinley Young, chairman of the consultation and a student at Andover-Newton Theological School, complained that white seminaries do not provide adequate training for an effective ministry within the black community. "Christ is a white Anglo-Saxon and the American Christ has to die," Young said. "Christ can't be the Jesus of Nazareth anymore. He must become the Jesus of Watts and of Harlem." He added that Christianity must be liberated from the kind of culture imposed on it in America, and the structure of seminaries must change to make Christianity relevant for the black as well as the white student.

Earlier in 1968, Cushing had been harassed when a Catholic Inter-Racial Council Commitment Vigil staged a three-day fast outside his residence, seeking concrete commitments by the archdiocese to aid the inner city and the black community. The council said the vigil was "in reparation for the share of all white people in this diocese in the death of Martin Luther King and in reparation for the great gap between the rhetoric and the actions of the archdiocese." The council urged the archdiocese to commit four per cent of the fifty million dollar Jubilee Fund to the inner city and asked that all money from the sale of church property in the inner city under urban renewal or highway construction projects remain in the inner city. It was not a demand that the cardinal could easily meet. Even when the fifty million dollars was collected, his archdiocese would still be in debt. Early in 1969, he said he owed forty million dollars.

The cardinal, shaken by the assassination of Martin Luther King, in an impulsive moment urged that he be canonized. "We have trifled too long, all of us, with words and admonitions," he said on April 8, "we have done so little when so much was required. In this dark hour, with our whole nation in mourning, we must judge ourselves, and take the measure of our failings. We were all in Memphis, one way or another, on Thursday night, and the violence and death there must touch the conscience of every citizen. Dr. King summons us now to a march that has no ending, to a dream from which there is no waking, to a task that will consume all the hours of all our days." [19]

In another move to alleviate the shortage of priests, the cardinal in 1963 established the Pope John XXIII National Seminary for Delayed Vocations in Weston, Massachusetts, with twenty-three in the "freshman" class. He felt that older men might be attracted to the priesthood if they were not required to submit to seminary training suited to younger men. In his pamphlet on the Society of St. James, he explained the need: "Father Frank McGuiggan had been for years a well-known Shakespearean actor." After serving in World War I, he began his clerical studies in 1919 and was ordained in 1928, at the age of forty, "after a hard, challenging course at Boston College and St. John's Seminary. He died two years later . . . but who can completely tell the story of the grand work for God and the church in those two years? It is for men like Father McGuiggan that I proposed to establish this seminary."

In this unique institution, men who have given up worldly careers for a religious vocation wear civilian dress. Among men in the first class, ranging in age from twenty-seven to fifty-four, were a geologist, chemistry professor, school superintendent, three servicemen, three school teachers, a pharmacist, a psychiatric caseworker, four businessmen, a religious brother, a laboratory technician, and an attorney. When the cardinal ordained the first nine in St. Ignatius Church in Brookline early in May 1968, he told them: "You have rubbed shoulders with the world—you know the world and therefore are better at understanding it than we are. When we were ordained, most of us entered a world we did not understand." Later in the month, the cardinal ordained the other members of the first class.[20]

A month later, Cushing presided at the tenth anniversary departure ceremony and concelebrated mass of seven priest volunteers who joined the Society of St. James. During the service at historic St. Stephen's Church in the North End, which the cardinal had restored, he said the society at the time had twenty-four priests in Bolivia, twelve in Ecuador, and fifty-six in Peru. The seven clergymen, given missionary crosses during the ceremony, left for Peru to take a concentrated language course before being assigned to posts in Bolivia, Ecuador, and Peru.[21]

Thus, even in the midst of turmoil, Cardinal Cushing kept old programs going and launched new ones. Meanwhile, he braced himself against demands of the renewed church.

One issue that was not sufficiently aired at Vatican II was birth control, simply because Pope Paul had smothered an open discussion.[22] However, to study the problem, he did appoint a papal commission, which included physicians and married couples, as well as theologians. The commission gave Paul a majority recommendation that the church relax its rules about allowing only the rhythm method to control birth. When Paul ignored the recommendation and issued his encyclical *Humanae Vitae* in July 1968, millions of couples who, after learning that the papal commission was instructed to study birth control, were using pills, coils, diaphragms, or other devices, found themselves in a bind. So did Pope Paul, who was reaffirming the church's condemnation of the birth control pill, which dates from a 1958 statement by Pope Pius XII. The millions of Catholics, on learning that the statement was being reexamined in Rome, had expected the church to update its position. In 1963, the Catholic monthly *Jubilee* had published dozens of letters by priests and laymen urging a relaxation of the church's stand, and when the encyclical dashed their hopes, a Miami layman said, "What we really need is freedom to dissent from the Pope." A housewife coolly observed: "I'm not concerned with the infallibility of the Pope. What worries me is the infallibility of the pill."

Monsignor George A. Schlichte, rector of the Pope John XXIII National Seminary, and seven members of his faculty reflected Cardinal Cushing's views when they dissented from Paul's opinions: "The recent statement of Pope Paul," Schlichte said, "is more disappointing at a time when Roman Catholics are experiencing a new sense of Christian maturity. It reflects a view which, according to recent scholarship, is neither biblical, theological, nor truly historical. The pronouncement . . . is an expression of a minority view which is contrary to the consensus of the International Lay Congress in Rome, against the almost unanimous opinion of theologians, and at variance with the majority report of the papal commission on birth control."

Father Gregory Baum, a noted theologian, felt that because Pope Paul's encyclical is reformable and not infallible churchmen must tolerate dissent. Father John Mahoney, a professor of dogmatic theology, said the Pope did not speak infallibly on the subject. Therefore his statement is "fallible." He added that "a doubtful regulation such as this is not binding in conscience."

The unexpected ruling confirmed the suspicions of some that the Pontiff was vacillating between conservative and liberal positions. If Cushing took a more tolerant attitude than Pope Paul, it was understandable in view of the controversy in Massachusetts, where Irish Catholic solidarity for years had blocked every effort to repeal or amend an 1879 law forbidding the dissemination of birth control information. When the contraception issue came up, billboards in subways warned that birth control was against God's law. In Holyoke, Massachusetts, when Margaret Sanger was scheduled to speak in behalf of planned parenthood, Catholic leaders forced the First Congregational Church to withdraw permission to an organization known as the Mothers Health Council to use its church buildings for the meeting.[23]

In 1948, when his views were more narrow and conservative than they became later, Archbishop Cushing denounced what he called a conspiracy of "birth controllers, abortioners, and mercy killers." In that year, when the Planned Parenthood League put the issue on the ballot, former mayor Frederick W. Mansfield, acting as his legislative agent, opposed the measure at State House hearings. When Cushing criticized proponents for the money they spent in pushing the measure, a Planned Parent League spokesman countered: "How does the archdiocese maintain its tax-exempt status when tax laws deny such exemption to groups engaged in influencing legislation?"

Actually, the League of Catholic Women, whom Cushing encouraged to campaign against the referendum, spent sixty-nine thousand dollars on a drive run by its Committee in Opposition to Referendum, as compared to the fifty-one thousand dollars spent by the Planned Parent League. On the Sunday before election, Cushing ordered all parish priests to condemn the measure, and for the second time in six years it was soundly defeated. Except for Connecticut, the Bay State was the only one to oppose legally the dissemination of birth control information.

One Catholic who stood apart was Dr. John Rock, a world authority on fertility and birth control. He was a professor of clinical gynecology at Harvard Medical School and director of the first fertility clinic of its kind at the Free Hospital for Women in Brookline. In 1963, in a book *The Time Has Come* he described the first effective means of fertility control made possible by a new oral contraceptive. Just before the book was published, Archbishop Cushing in his *Pilot* column observed that church law required every Catholic writing on a subject pertaining to faith or morality to submit his manuscript to church authority for an imprimatur or statement by the local bishop that the contents were free from doctrinal or moral error. He said Dr. Rock's book bore no such imprimatur. "Therefore, the opinions on the morality of artificial birth control as presented . . . lack any official approval as authentic Catholic teaching." Cushing did not condemn the book, however, admitting that Rock had presented a detailed and graphic account of the history of the controversy and granting that some of his suggestions could contribute to domestic peace in a pluralistic society. The book, he said, contained several statements that were theologically incorrect and misleading.

In 1964, when another Catholic physician, Dr. Joe L. Dorsey, urged repeal of the Massachusetts law,[24] *Pilot* editor Lally admitted in a foreword that most people feel with him "that the time is ripe for reconsidering the question in the light of the claims of a plural society." Dr. Dorsey said the law was "an albatross around the neck of Catholics whenever religious liberty is brought up." [25]

Outside Massachusetts, Catholic opposition by the hierarchy was still strong. In 1959, a council of American bishops said "United States Catholics . . . will not support any public assistance, either at home or abroad, to promote artificial birth prevention." It became a national issue. At about the time Senator John Kennedy said that while he respected the moral doctrine of his church, as President he would do what seemed best for the American people in accordance with his oath of office if a recommendation for government aid came to his desk. In December 1962, he authorized the United States support for a U.N. proposal to provide birth control assistance to any country that requested it.

By 1964, American opinion on the subject had changed so drastically that both President Johnson and former President Eisenhower recommended programs of tax support. Eisenhower and Truman that year were co-chairmen of the sponsors' council of the World Planned Parenthood movement. In June 1965, Governor Nelson Rockefeller of New York signed a bill repealing his state's eighty-four-year-old statute against birth control. That same month the Supreme Court declared Connecticut's anti–birth control statute unconstitutional on the novel grounds that it invaded the right of privacy. In his State of the Union message in 1965, President Johnson said: "I will seek new ways to use our knowledge to help deal with the explosion in our world population and the growing scarcity in world resources." The National Catholic Welfare Conference answered through Monsignor John Knott, director of the Family Life Bureau: "Despite popular opinion . . . the attitude of the Catholic Church toward contraception is still one of condemnation as a moral evil. It has not changed." Later he said the federal government was supporting a "contraceptive, anti-life program."

He did not reflect Cardinal Cushing's opinion. When the Massachusetts legislature in 1966 passed and Governor Volpe signed a bill lifting the ban on birth control, the church, according to Paul Blanshard, did not "change a syllable of its moral teaching on that question, but, led by Cardinal Cushing, it faced the fact that Catholics could no longer force such moral teaching upon their non-Catholic fellow citizens."

The cardinal, meanwhile, had become less adamant in his opposition to birth control measures. In 1964 he said: "The church's idea is that birth control through artificial means is contrary to nature—contrary to natural law—but I am convinced that through more and more research, especially along the lines of the rhythm theory, they will come up with a nonartificial way of controlling births." [26]

Soon after his return from the third session of Vatican II, the cardinal addressed a Communion breakfast where he received a check for ten thousand dollars from the fishing and waterfront industries. He said the church had authorized a medical study of birth control: "We are hopeful of coming up with a foolproof natural birth control method, or else we will have to pass new laws at the next ecumenical council."

In 1965, the prelate, who was once so firmly against repealing the Massachusetts law, said he had changed his thinking since Vatican II had begun its study of family planning, assuring worried mothers seeking specific guidance that he hoped the problem would be resolved when Vatican II opened its fourth session. "My sympathy and love go out to those people who are having problems with large families and who are worried sick about the church's teaching," he said in a radio interview. "I'm hoping and praying that all these problems will be settled by the commission's report." [27] He said this on Haywood Vincent's show. When a telephoner asked whether Catholics who had gone against the church's teaching in using contraceptives were guilty of mortal sin, he said: "Only God knows that, my dear. I do not see where I have the obligation to impose my will on those who do not accept the faith as I do." [28] During an interview on another telephone-in radio show in Boston,[29] a woman with several children called to say she and her husband could not properly support them, yet he did not believe in birth control. After consoling her as best he could, Cushing hung up the telephone receiver and, forgetting that he was still on the air, turned to the moderator. "Why in hell doesn't she use the pill?" he asked.

One afternoon two circulation directors of Boston newspapers came to his residence to present him with the Newspaper Hall of Fame award, which goes to former newsboys who have achieved international repute.[30] When they asked why there had been no clerical rumbling in the archdiocese following Pope Paul's encyclical, he said he was happy to let sleeping dogs lie and suggested that the use of contraceptives was a matter of individual conscience. "Besides," he added, "you can't put a cop under every bed."

Many clergymen agree. The priest-editor of the Oakland, California, diocesan newspaper said it was ultimately a matter of the married couple's conscience.[31] Even Archbishop James P. Davis, one of the three Puerto Rican bishops who had advised their parishioners not to vote for Governor Luis Muñoz Marín because he advocated government-backed birth control, said: "In the final analysis, it comes down to a matter of private conscience." [32] That is the cardinal's position, one often privately expressed.

An exception was Patrick Cardinal O'Boyle of Washington, who

suspended dissident priests. When he mounted the pulpit in St. Matthew's Cathedral at a noon mass, he was reading a pastoral letter
urging the faithful to obey the encyclical when a third of the congregation walked out.[33] He went on to warn against "false prophets"
who said birth control is a matter for individual conscience, while
conceding that a few of his brother bishops in other lands seem to have
adopted the new morality.

O'Boyle underestimated the number, as *Time* noted: "The fact is
that almost every national Catholic episcopate to issue an interpretation of *Humanae Vitae* has modified, subtly or otherwise, the Pope's
decree that each and every marriage act must remain open to the
transmission of life." [34] The gist of the comment was that Catholic
couples who wish to use contraceptives may do so while remaining in
the church.

Pope Paul considers contraception a denial of God's natural law
that cannot be changed for practical reasons, even when population
explosions spell starvation. In his talk to the United Nations in 1965,
he asked nations to insure "that there is enough bread on the tables
of mankind" rather than "encourage an artificial birth control, which
would be irrational, in order to diminish the number of guests at the
banquet table of life."

"The Pope visits India, weeps for its poverty, and condemns the
only sensible plan to control its teeming population. . . . Somehow
our law was broad enough to permit nuns in the Congo to take the
pill lest they conceive the child of the savage who was threatening to
rape them," writes Father Kavanaugh.[35] General William Draper
testified in 1966: "The world is increasing its population 2 percent
and its food 1 percent. This means that the world is falling behind
1 percent a year—or, to put it another way—food production is falling behind minimum needs by thirty million more each year." [36]
Thus, if present trends continue, disaster lies just ahead. Ironically,
the encyclical will be most effective in such impoverished areas as Latin America, where results will be most damaging. "Elsewhere," John
A. T. Robinson, the Anglican bishop of Woolwich, wrote in *The
Critic*, "it will have little effect, except to debase the currency of
intellectual honesty." [37]

Professor Andre Hellegers, of Georgetown University's department
of obstetrics and gynecology, who served on the papal commission
originally formed by Pope John XXIII, criticizes the inept biology of
Humanae Vitae: "It says that intercourse must be always open to the

transmission of life, then it asks us to perfect a method—rhythm—that is closed to the transmission of life. It implies that when a woman is sterile, the marriage act is open to the transmission of life. That is not true." Dr. Thomas Hayes of the University of California, a biophysicist, makes a similar charge: "The Church has already approved tampering with the total act of reproduction in rhythm—it should be consistent: approve all banned methods of contraception or ban them all." [38]

Pope Paul feels that if he alters his stand on his two most conservative issues, his reaffirmation of celibacy for western priests and his rejection of artificial birth control, he may be asked to go further, possibly to approve abortion and remarriage after divorce. Even more pressing demands are being made on him. Certain Dutch theologians, for example, no longer regard all premarital sexual relations as mortal sins.

Humanae Vitae prompted some clergymen in England to ask their superiors a simple question: "How can we depose the Pope?" [39] Some think that Pope Paul, caught between a sword and the wall, may ultimately resign.

Pope Paul is also tortured with worry about the "underground church," which he asked Cardinal Cushing to investigate in the United States.

chapter twenty-five

THE CHURCH IN
FOMENT

IN HIS TELEVISION INTERVIEW with Cardinal Cushing in 1968, Harry Reasoner asked about the future of the church in America. "Is it bright, or in trouble?"

The prelate gave no definite answer. There were things that concerned him, he said. One was the so-called underground church. "They are against what they call the institutional church, but I don't know how you're going to run a church without people at the head of it. Otherwise, everyone is going to go his own way."

In the spring of 1968 in a talk to the League of Catholic Women [1] at the Statler Hilton in Boston, Cushing minimized the importance of the informal movement. "I have been hearing a good deal lately about . . . the underground church. What it describes is apparently not always clear even to those who use the term, but it suggests some kind of community of Christians who consider themselves distinct from the rest of us. . . . It seems to be the kind of exaggerated effort that every so often comes from people of good will, whose zeal outruns their sense of balance. I know of only one underground church, and it is one with a very holy history." He meant the catacombs, which stretch for miles under Rome.

Historically, he went on, the underground church has seldom been absent, "and in our own day its story has been written in blood in the cellars and prisons of eastern Europe and elsewhere." He called this underground church the product of persecution, suppression, and violence, "and it is always marked by spiritual courage, Christian suffering, and the martyrdom of the saints. The church is only underground by the powers of evil, when wickedness has its hour and darkness prevails. For the rest, the Christian has no need to hide himself, no need to run away, no need of cover."

Changes wrought by Vatican II were not abrupt, he told his audience. The council merely gave expression to elements that have been at work for generations. Thus, the church is not yielding to the demands of the contemporary world and is not retreating. "Catholic faith does not change." Society, however, he said, "is not static, and the Christian is not some kind of religious fossil that endures like a monument through time."

In a commencement address at Boston College High School in 1968, he said Pope John "would be whirling in his coffin if he reacted whenever his name is taken in vain today. Hardly a week passes that some atheist dialoguing on television with some theologian does not maneuver himself into the folds of the mantle of Pope John." He rebuked those who held that church authority "stems from individual conscience and the consent of all the people of God." The supreme power of the church, he said, stems from God alone.

Nevertheless, Michael Novak perceived "dramatic underground activity" in the church, which he considers not only another advance in the gradual liberalization of Catholicism but also as a challenge that is more basic. "The fundamental character of the . . . church is being challenged—or being bypassed." Novak concludes that the apparent aim of the underground church is "a humanism whose only distinctively Christian characteristics are a special attachment to Jesus Christ and a concern for the welfare of the church as a historical people." [2]

In the spring of 1968, 235 priests jarred the hierarchy with their militancy in a two-day Chicago conference. The newly formed National Federation of Priests Councils, which represented two-thirds of the sixty thousand priests in the United States, heard Father Kavanaugh say: "The name of the game is power. This is what the bishops will understand." [3] The Reverend Patrick O'Malley, whom the delegates elected president of the organization, which is designed to give priests a louder voice in shaping the policies of a changing church, added: "The bishop is no longer king. We don't have to ask permission to undertake our projects." [4] He told the conclave that their organization was in line with the collegiality adopted at Vatican II.

Cardinal Cushing did not refer to the Chicago conference, which had ended a few hours before he addressed twelve hundred persons at a charity dinner on the South Shore of Boston. "Some priests, nuns, and lay people apparently have no fear of God or man," he said. "Some of them should not have become priests or nuns in the first place. They didn't have vocations." [5] Modern youth who challenge everything, he continued, include "hippies" and "hoppies." He assured his audience that "underground or overground, the church will survive." It was in this speech that he revealed for the first time that the Vatican had ordered him to determine the extent to which the underground church was functioning in America.

In his sunset years, the cardinal often lashed out at rebellious priests, nuns, and laity who were becoming a disruptive force in the church.[6] He has warned repeatedly that further liberalization of the church will not be accomplished overnight.[7] "We are Americans, with typical American activist mentalities," he said in the spring of 1969. "Once a goal has been determined, its acquisition must be immediate." In the modern age of turbulence, he charged that the cause of Christian renewal is being undermined by a heresy of hate. He was irked by the suggestion that "each person should do his own thing." [8]

The cardinal is a reformer, not a revolutionary. "Cushing fits in with the new spirit," said William Storey, an associate professor of history at Duquesne University, "but I wonder if he realizes that the whole process must got a lot farther." A lot farther, in the opinion of some young priests, and a lot faster. Cushing is in no great hurry. He is not concerned with such superficial matters as whether women should be permitted not to wear hats in church or how often they should go to confession.

In the spring of 1969 he announced new ecumenical guidelines that gave Catholics the right to participate in services in other Christian churches, a significant advance over guidelines issued two years earlier. "We must continue, with imagination and vigor, to explore additional means for healing the wounds of religious division," he said. He urged Catholics to participate in ecumenical prayer services and to seek other opportunities "to work with their separated brothers for any common concern in which they can and should cooperate." In reference to "ecumenical marriages," Cushing's guidelines recommend that children be taught the traditions and beliefs of the non-Catholic parent and that the entire family attend each other's worship service. Catholics may attend Protestant services, but this does not fulfill their obligation to assist at mass. Attendance at Orthodox rites would, however, fulfill this obligation.[9] In a later announcement, Cushing said Catholics could fulfill the obligation by going to mass on Saturday instead of Sunday.

Despite these concessions, the cardinal shares many of the concerns of Pope Paul, who early in 1969 named an international theological commission to study the relationship between permissible dissent within the church and heresy.[10] The dean of the American hierarchy obviously opposes a breakdown in the basic disciplines of the church.

Years earlier, Cushing had welcomed to Boston Hans Kung, a Swiss theologian who was considered one of Europe's most profound Catholic scholars.[11] The cardinal wrote a preface to Kung's book, *Structure of the Church,* and sponsored the first United States speech of Father Kung, who wrote another book (*The Council, Reform and Reunion*), which grates on many cardinals.[12] Thus the evidence is that Cushing is a liberal, but not a radical.

In the late 1960s, the aging cardinal still retained his interest in community affairs. One issue in which he was involved was a lottery. Another was the marriage of Jacqueline Kennedy to Aristotle Onassis.

A state lottery was a problem Cushing inherited from Cardinal O'Connell. The issue had come into focus in 1935 when Governor Curley tried to push through a bill to establish a lottery. The bill passed the House of Representatives, but Boston newspapers and ministers attacked the measure. Even so, passage seemed certain. Then, according to Curley, on the eve of the final vote, Cardinal O'Connell warned that a lottery was a pure gambling device, which "encouraged wagering among the poor, who could least afford it." [13] O'Connell further charged that lotteries were a source of corruption and warned against any official endorsement of gambling, even though the state treasury was depleted. When the House convened the following day, sixty-eight legislators switched their votes to defeat the proposal.

"Such outspoken protests by church leaders are unusual," wrote Murray Levin.[14] "The Massachusetts Council of Churches (Protestant) has shown its influence by successfully opposing the legitimization of 'games of chance' and the repeal of laws forbidding activities on Sundays (the so-called Blue Laws.)" [15]

In 1958, despite the opposition of both Catholic and Protestant clergymen to a "Massachusetts sweepstakes," the overwhelming majority of citizens who voted on the issue favored it. On December 5 of that year, the Boston *Record-American* quoted Cardinal Cushing verbatim on his stand: "The lottery, as a form of large-scale gambling, is economically unsound, socially disintegrating, and morally dangerous." Later, Cushing drastically changed his thinking: "I am not against lotteries, raffles, or bingo games as long as they are not abused. Beano is played mostly by poor old ladies and men for a little recrea-

tion that will keep their minds active and their interests alive." [16]
Another time he told reporters: "If we can have lotteries in Ireland,
England, and other countries of Europe, why can't we have them in
the States?"

The chief advocate of a lottery in the commonwealth is his friend,
Francis Kelly of Dorchester, who served twice as attorney general of
Massachusetts and once as Lieutenant Governor, the only Democrat
ever to defeat Leverett Saltonstall in a political contest. Since the late
1940s, he has proposed a lottery to solve the tax problems. In the 1960
primary, when he ran for governor, the sweepstakes was the closest
thing to a real campaign issue.

Kelly proposed that tickets be sold during the year in state-chartered
banks and by treasurers of the 39 cities and 312 towns in the commonwealth, whereupon an opponent accused him of trying to make Boston
the Las Vegas of the East and of putting the commonwealth in the
crime business. Kelly countered that representatives of the state's largest and most powerful industry—illegal gambling—"continue year
after year to cause the defeat of our practical and popular sweepstakes
bill by cowardly circulating false propaganda claims that Cardinal
Cushing is greatly opposed to a Massachusetts sweepstakes drawing to
obtain new revenue for our state, cities, and towns." [17]

The Catholic clergy is not inalterably opposed to gambling. One
priest, observing that it was illegal for the man in a saloon to bet on a
horse, said: "Meanwhile, all of those bums who don't work can go to
the track and bet on nine races and it's perfectly legal. That's ridiculous." [18] Cardinal Cushing, who has said that if the state legalized
lotteries he would buy the first ticket, thanked Kelly for sending him
twenty-five lottery receipts purchased in New York. "It certainly would
be wonderful if I came through as a winner, because the greatest problems I have now are to finance our Catholic system of education." The
cardinal, as a result of his involvement in the "Biography of a Bookie
Joint" controversy, knew that bookies conduct the most profitable
business in the commonwealth, as the Massachusetts Crime Commission concluded after a four-year investigation. In another letter to
Kelly, Cushing wrote: "It is too bad that Massachusetts does not follow
the example of San Francisco. Thanks for the lottery tickets. If I ever
win, it will be the biggest ad for a lottery in Massachusetts." [19]

Since 1964, the cardinal in off-the-cuff remarks has been endorsing a
lottery. In a visit to the Soldiers Home in Chelsea that year he drew
the usual tittering with his running banter, but the loudest laugh

came when he told an old tad that he had paid thirty dollars for ten tickets on the New Hampshire sweepstakes. "If I win, I'll give it to this hospital and all these good men." [20]

Four years later, he publicly said: "It is my opinion that we will never have a new stadium unless we have a Massachusetts sweepstakes to pay for it." [21] Cushing was for a stadium as long as it was not built too near any of his institutions. In 1967, when Governor Volpe's study committee proposed a fifty-five-million-dollar stadium to be constructed near Regis College, the cardinal told seven hundred persons at a reception at the college that if the Weston stadium proposal reached the legislature, he would do all he could to block it. Rarely has he been so outspoken on a political issue.

When Kelly plumped for his favorite proposal again in 1969, he once more invoked the name of Cushing to buttress his stand, referring to other states and countries that conduct lotteries "honestly and regularly." He said New York, New Hampshire, Ireland, Israel, England, Italy, and sixty-three other countries were conducting legal and profitable lotteries. "Our state hypocritically collects taxes from all Massachusetts residents who win prizes in these lotteries. How inconsistent!"

The cardinal played an unpublicized role in a bill Kelly filed early in 1969 to remove a 1968 amendment to the Bookie Law that makes religious, fraternal, and charitable organizations who conduct games of chance guilty of a felony and punishable by a state's prison sentence up to three years or a three-thousand-dollar fine or both. Cushing considered the amendment outrageous.

At the 1968 reception at Tara, Cushing was talking to Lieutenant Governor Francis Sargent of Massachusetts when Kelly walked into the room. "Frank, come over here and get into the picture," Cushing said. After they posed for a photographer, the cardinal turned to Kelly. "What are those people down at the State House doing, Frank? Are they trying to make felons out of us with that stupid new law? Someone ought to file another bill to get rid of it."

"Did you hear what Cardinal Cushing just said, Frank?" Kelly said to Sargent when they were alone.

"I heard every word."

"Well, you expect to go farther in politics," Kelly said. "Why don't you file the bill he mentioned?"

"I think it would be better if you did," Sargent said. "You file it and I will speak on it."

As it turned out, Sargent's cousin, Attorney General Elliot Richardson of Massachusetts—later Undersecretary of State—filed the bill. Sargent, who did not appear at the hearing, later in the year vetoed a beano bill. Kelly then filed his own bill. He said at the hearing: "Churches, temples, fraternal, veteran, and charitable civic organizations for many, many years have been conducting pleasant games of chance honestly and without a scandal of any kind, with profits going to worthy causes. The ridiculous 1968 amendment which was quietly passed by the legislature without a roll-call now prevents decent citizens who would like to purchase a chance ticket of some kind . . . the opportunity to make such a purchase."

Cushing complained that the amendment put innocent persons who buy chance or raffle tickets in the same category as bookies, and he was disappointed when the legislature in 1968 refused to remove the amendment, knowing that this increased the bookies' monopoly on illegal gambling in the commonwealth. During the closing days of the 1969 legislature, however, when Sargent, who became governor when Volpe resigned to become Secretary of Transportation, he signed into law a bill to legalize gambling games and lotteries held by veterans' organizations, fraternal clubs, and religious groups. The bill specifically forbids beano, however, largely because Governor Sargent had earlier in the year vetoed the beano bill with such fanfare.

Meanwhile, the cardinal held firm in his endorsement of a sweepstakes. Early in 1969, when the Sisters of Charity in New York won one hundred thousand dollars in a New York sweepstakes, they donated the money toward a new gymnasium. Cushing thinks sweepstakes proceeds can be put to similarly good use to solve the financial problems of Massachusetts.

The legalized gambling issue was parochial compared to the marriage of Jacqueline Kennedy to Onassis, which had undreamed of repercussions.

Edward B. Fiske noted in *The New York Times* that public disagreements between high Roman Catholic officials are rare. "But then," he said, "Richard Cardinal Cushing of Boston is no ordinary high Roman Catholic official." [22]

When Jacqueline announced her intention of marrying the Greek multimillionaire, Monsignor Fausto Vallainc, the Vatican's chief press officer, expressed the church's official view that she had "knowingly violated the law of the church" and was therefore ineligible to receive the sacraments." [23] Then came a rumor that she would be excommunicated by the church. On October 23, 1968, the cardinal ridiculed the idea in a talk to the Boston Caritas Guild: "This idea of saying she's excommunicated, that she's a public sinner—what a lot of nonsense! Only God knows who is a sinner and who is not. Why can't she marry whomever she wants?"

The cardinal, who for months had known that Jacqueline planned to marry Onassis, told the guild that the Kennedy family and their friends had tried to get him to dissuade her from the match. Four days before the wedding, Jacqueline, escorted by a Secret Service agent, had secretly come to the cardinal's residence for a two-hour consultation that was highly emotional and personal. She was already committed to the marriage at the time. She said Onassis had visited Hyannis Port often during the preceding months to get acquainted with the children.

"I married her," the prelate told the Guild. "I baptized her children. She lost two more. I carried the lifeless body of Patrick Bouvier Kennedy in a little casket from a cemetery in Brookline in an automobile all the way to Newport so that the lifeless form could be buried alongside Jack Kennedy." [24] Their discussion was so private and confidential it was almost like a confessional, he said. "My lips are sealed." He berated all who had been "knocking her head off, as it were," adding that they were "so far from the truth that no one would believe me if I ever . . . revealed what I know." He said she had written him a letter that would be worth hundreds of thousands of dollars if he let any of the national magazines publish it. He burned the letter.[25]

A few hours after Cushing had defended her marriage to a divorcé, Onassis spoke to newsmen as he flew into Athens: "Cardinal Cushing is Mrs. Onassis' best spiritual friend. We called Cardinal Cushing on the phone." [26] They thanked him for his support.

After Cushing's talk to the Caritas Guild, Vatican sources announced that Jacqueline was "in an irregular position with the church, and the cardinal certainly must have advised her of this in his talk with her." The Vatican City magazine, *L'Osservatore della Domenica,* in a harsher appraisal condemned her again as a public sinner, adding that she had practically renounced her faith and, accordingly, was in a state of spiritual degradation.[27]

Cushing's defense of the bride brought him an avalanche of hate mail. He responded with a sentimental account of his relationship with the late President: "What the future status of Jacqueline's marriage in the Catholic Church [may be] is not for me to decide, but of one thing I am certain: When my dearest friend, John Fitzgerald Kennedy . . . asked me to take care of Jacqueline and the children if anything happened to him, I can salute him today in memory and say, 'Jack, I have fulfilled my promise.' " Cushing added that Kennedy sensed that something was going to happen to him.

Then the prelate admitted that the savage criticism was too much to take. "I've had it," he said, adding that he was going to resign at the end of the year, eighteen months before the target date of August 1970. Grousing that 98 per cent of the mail either vilified or reproved him, he reminded reporters that his own sister had married a Jew outside the church. In the turmoil he was badgered by telephone calls from newsmen. To escape them, he and Monsignor George Kerr went to Boston College's Alumni Field to see their alma mater blanked by Penn State. The day after his sit-down with Jacqueline, Cushing had gone to South Dakota to speak, and even there, he had been pestered by reporters, he said.

The cardinal was incensed because a person who had attended the meeting of the Caritas Guild had tape-recorded his informal remarks, then left without hearing him amplify his observations. "I was talking to a group of men who know what any high school kid knows—that she can marry anyone she pleases . . . but not in the Catholic Church. I didn't qualify it because I was there only for a few minutes. But I would have assumed that everybody would understand that. I guess I was wrong." [28]

In announcing his resignation, he said he had no wish to stay around Boston if, "after forty-seven years as a priest around here they don't understand me. . . . I don't know whether I can weather this because I've never been through anything like this. I need about two months to get the finances of the archdiocese in shape for my successor and then I'll go to Peru. I'll have to go somewhere. I couldn't stay here." Later, although the tide of mail turned in his favor, he said he would still resign. "I'll be in touch with the Pope and I'll explain the whole thing to him."

Seldom had he sounded so bitter. "I didn't know there was that much hatred in the world," he said, referring to the insulting letters and adverse publicity. "There are a lot of people who hate the Kennedys. They hated the grandfather, they hated the father, they hated the son, they hate the girls, and now they're picking on me."

Roman Catholic clergymen around the country were generally sympathetic toward the cardinal's decision to resign. Monsignor Francis Wade, editor of *Catholic Week*, summed up the thoughts of many: "It was not so much a canonical judgment by the cardinal as one made out of love and understanding for this woman," he wrote in defending Cushing's approval of the marriage. "I suppose he's a little tired, the same as Cardinal Léger of Canada, who went to Africa to work with the lepers," a Florida priest said. "When Cardinal Cushing said Mrs. Kennedy had the right to marry anyone, I believe he was right. It is up to her."

Bishop Anson Phelps Stokes, Jr., commented: "He is a man with a big heart who has touched many by his Christian humanity. It is not easy to be both sensitive to human needs and to administer a great institution . . . now, more than ever, we need that quality of heart which he showed."

The late Rabbi Joseph Shubow thought the prelate's resignation would deprive "our city, our commonwealth, and all America of the idol of the poor, the healer of the sick in body and soul, and the comforter of the bereaved and the source of strength of the disinherited and afflicted." Shubow was shocked by the "savagery, inhumanity, and vulgarity of the assault against a great prince of the Catholic Church and truly a prince of mankind."

Thousands of persons wrote letters to editors in defense of Cushing. "Those tradition-bound theologians," wrote one, "would do well to restrict the scope of their proclamations and arguments to areas more fitted to their talents than the question of who is, and who is not, a public sinner." [29] Another wrote: "His whole life has been dedicated . . . to people of every race, creed, and color. Now in the twilight of his illustrious career, he is being subjected to vicious and vile hate letters. . . . These hate-mongers would do well to examine their own conscience." Even Jimmy Durante was outraged. "A coupla days ago I spoke to da cardinal and it's a shame what dey done to his feelin's. He's da greatest man I ever met." [30]

One periodical, *Christianity Today*, took a different tack, observing that Mrs. Onassis had "publicly entered into a situation which the church regards as sinful. Other less prominent persons under the cardinal's authority apparently have not been granted the same dispensation he advocates for her." As cardinal of the church, the editor said, Cushing was morally obligated to support its teaching. "If he cannot do so, a resignation is in order." [31]

After a fortnight, the cardinal cooled off, especially because he knew

Pope Paul wanted him to remain in the archdiocese until he reached the retirement age. Cushing still thinks cardinals should retire at the age of seventy: "The burdens of the office are getting so complex you need younger bishops trained to meet present problems."

In his first public appearance (except for the football game) since announcing his retirement, Cushing dedicated St. Alphonsus Church on the North Shore, the last of eighty-seven new parishes he would create, he told four hundred clergymen and lay persons. After cementing the cornerstone, he parted the canopy that protected the gathering from a downpour. "Maybe I should be in Greece," he said, putting his hand over his mouth, as if he had spoken out of turn.

Early in the summer of 1969, Jacqueline Onassis and her two children slipped unobserved into the cardinal's residence, where they had luncheon. When John-John fired a roll at the cardinal, his eminence tossed it back, joining in a game of catch. When the guests left, the cardinal turned to Jacqueline.

"Come back soon, and next time bring Ari." He grinned. "And tell him to bring his checkbook with him." The cardinal was back in the groove.

And then—a few weeks later—came another tragedy in the star-crossed family.

"I came into politics in my brother's place," John F. Kennedy said. "If anything happens to me, Bobby will take my place, and if Bobby goes, we have Teddy coming along." [32] Senator Edward Kennedy, the fourth son of Joseph and Rose, was the lone survivor and political heir apparent of the clan after his three brothers died in sudden violence in the service of their country. Ted's sister had died in a plane crash, and he had had a close call in another plane disaster in which two persons died.

On July 18, six women who had helped Robert Kennedy in his 1968 presidential campaign and five male friends of Ted met for a cookout at a small cottage at Chappaquiddick, a sandy islet about 250 yards from Martha's Vineyard. The occasion was the forty-sixth Edgartown Yacht Club Regatta. Ted finished ninth in the first race that Friday afternoon. One of the six women who rooted for him was Mary Jo Kopechne, a slim, twenty-eight-year-old blonde who had been Robert Kennedy's secretary. The women had reservations in a motel several miles from the motor inn where the men were registered. A two-car ferry shuttles automobile traffic from Martha's Vineyard to Chappaquiddick between 7:30 A.M. and midnight.

According to Ted, Mary Jo and he left the party around 11:15 P.M. to catch the last ferry back to the Vineyard. Instead of taking the road leading to the ferry, he turned right onto a dirt road leading to a narrow wooden bridge without guard rails. His 1967 Oldsmobile plunged into the water after going eighteen feet over the humpback bridge.

In a television statement a week after the tragedy, he told thirty-five million watchers that he had no idea how he got out of the car, which had overturned in the tidal water. "I made immediate and repeated efforts to save Mary Jo by diving into the strong and murky current, but succeeded only in increasing my state of utter exhaustion and alarm." He admitted that his conduct and conversation during the following several hours, to the extent that he could remember them, made no sense. "I do not seek to escape responsibility for my actions by placing the blame either on physical or emotional trauma brought on by the accident or anything else. I regard as indefensible the fact that I did not report the accident to the police immediately."

His explanation raised more doubts than it dispelled, as *The New York Times* reported: "His emotion-charged address leaves us less than satisfied with his partial explanations for a gross failure of responsibility, and more than ever convinced that the concerned town, county, and state officials of Massachusetts have also failed in their duty thoroughly to investigate this case because of the political personality involved." [33] Ted's shallow defense brought international attention to the calamity.

While tongues wagged about the "Kennedy curse," tritely repeating that the Kennedy story had all the elements of a Greek tragedy, Ted hoped to be forgiven for his incomprehensible conduct. "I would understand full well," he told the television audience, "why some might think it right for me to resign. I ask you tonight, the people of Massachusetts, to think this through with me. In facing this decision, I seek your advice and opinion. In making it, I seek your prayers."

The court verdict was two months in jail, suspended. To avoid a trial, which, said *Life* magazine, "would become a lurid carnival," Ted pleaded guilty to the charge of leaving the scene of an accident.

For once Cushing, the hard-pressed spiritual adviser of the Kennedys, was at a loss for words. His longest statement to reporters on the accident was, "No comment." Meanwhile, after Ted's television statement, the *Pilot* ended its editorial on "Time of Tragedy" with words that did not ring with conviction: "What had to be said, has been said;

what answers are available, have been given. Our prayers should be grateful that it was not worse and hopeful that the days ahead will be better."

An inquest begun in Edgartown, Martha's Vineyard, on January 5, 1970, hoped to get answers to several questions: Where were Kennedy and Miss Kopechne going? Why did the accident go unreported for nine hours? Assuming that Kennedy was in a state of shock, why did not the two lawyer friends he summoned for help—Joseph Gargan and Paul Markham—call the police? Though it was only a slight possibility, there was a chance that Mary Jo's life might have been saved had there been an air bubble in the car.

How did Kennedy get back to Edgartown? If, as he said in his television statement, he swam from Chappaquiddick, almost drowning in the effort, why did Markham and Gargan let him swim out into the blackness with his back in a brace and in a state of shock? If he was in a state of shock, why was he able to walk down to the lobby of the hotel wearing dry clothes and ask the time at 2:24 A.M.? The person he asked said he seemed normal.

Why didn't he use the ferry to Edgartown? Although the service ends at midnight, a telephone call on the Chappaquiddick dock can summon it for any legitimate reason, provided the call for it is made known to the police department.

Did Kennedy make seventeen telephone calls in the several hours following the tragedy? Why did he wait six days to offer an explanation on television?

It is hard to imagine that the days ahead for Ted Kennedy, politically, at least, will be better, as the *Pilot* hopes. The tragedy, however, may enable him to escape the fate of his brothers. In any case, as Cardinal Cushing knows better than most persons, the Chappaquiddick incident was a sad climax in the Kennedy story.

chapter twenty-six

CHURCHMAN OF THE CENTURY

REPORTERS WHO CALLED THE cardinal's residence to get the prelate's reaction to the Chappaquiddick tragedy were told he was indisposed. During the past year, the sick, weary cardinal has been slowing down. Again, only in letters and in off-the-cuff remarks has he revealed his suffering. In a note written early in September 1968, he said: "I am short of breath as a result of the terrible weather we have had. It has increased my asthma and emphysema beyond anything I have experienced in the past."

A short time later he scribbled a footnote in another letter: "I was getting ready for mass when I fainted and hit the floor so hard my back aches, but I hope to be up and around in a few days." He made perhaps his most revealing admission in his informal chat with Howard Nelson after the mid-February radiocast in 1969. Noting that he was going on seventy-four, he said: "I can't eat. My emphysema is terrible. I'm like a dead man, like a statue. Unless I have oxygen, I can't breathe." Only his iron will kept him going, especially when broken ribs added to his suffering.

Early in the summer of 1969, the cardinal was a guest at the South Shore Charity Guild's seventeenth annual testimonial dinner at the Surf to benefit his charities. The voice was unmistakable, but the prelate sounded tired and uncommonly subdued. Guests noticed that he spoke quietly, without his usual wit, humor, and gusto. Yet he somehow stuck to his busy summer schedule.

On July 9, he spent a few hours with youngsters at Children's Vacation House at Sunset Point, Nantasket, a free summer camp for underprivileged children that had been founded by Cushing half a century before. "I enjoy doing all I can for the poor—especially the little ones," he told reporters, "and I'm really proud of this place. It has given free vacations to over twenty-five thousand children since 1919. It's a wonderful program and has always been nonsectarian." *

When the beige limousine pulled up, the children hopped up and down, shouting, "The cardinal is here—His Eminence is here!" After they serenaded him with their favorite song, "Hey, Look Me Over," the prelate slung a guitar over his shoulder and strummed it, accompanying the children in a rousing chorus of "Up, Up with People." Father Eugene McNamara, executive director of the Catholic Charitable Bureau, drew a laugh when he said: "He's another Elvis Presley."

"More like the old man of the mountain," Cushing said.

A Franciscan sister shook her head in admiration. "I don't know how he does so much for so many—I really don't."

The cardinal seemed sluggish on arrival, but his energy resurfaced as he toured the playground, even taking a turn on a swing with a child on his lap. During the celebration of the fiftieth anniversary of the camp, Secretary of State John Davoren handed the cardinal a check representing the proceeds of the Secretary of the Commonwealth Charity Ball.

Early in August, the cardinal seemed to be everywhere. He blessed the Gloucester fishing fleet, as in other years he had blessed the fleet in Pleasure Bay off South Boston, home of the "Cushing Armada." He took more than two thousand nuns of all faiths to Fenway Park to see the Red Sox play. "The religious habit is your ticket to a grandstand seat, sister," the invitation read. In the middle of the month he staged his sixth annual ecumenical football game, this time a contest between the Boston Patriots and the Atlanta Falcons at Boston College Stadium.

It was more of an effort to make the ecumenical rounds, but early in August the cardinal was the speaker at the centennial of the Concordia Lutheran Church in Manchester, Connecticut. "A few years ago," Cushing said in his sermon, "it would have been thought very strange indeed for a Catholic archbishop to be celebrating with you the diamond jubilee of your parish; but times have changed, and for the better, so that I can feel thoroughly at home in your midst today, and you are pleased to listen to my few words of Christian friendship and encouragement.

"We know that Lutherans were among the earliest settlers of this

---

* The summer camp program is supported by the Proparvulis Club, the Society of St. Vincent de Paul, and the Emmanuel House. The camp has two-week sessions for girls in July and a similar setup for boys in August.

country, long before the founding of the republic, and even though the names are no longer very meaningful for our generation, we can recall the towns of New England and New Sweden here on our eastern coast, where they first established themselves. As the west opened up to the pioneer and the settler, many went into the land of promise, and in their sturdy traditions turned the wilderness into a fertile farmland." Although many say God is dead, he told the congregation, "there are many signs, which, if we read them rightly, point to a new interest in the gospel and the words of revelation."

Cushing continued to press for his fifty-million-dollar drive, especially because the archdiocese, already facing a heavy debt, was feeling the effects of inflation. "Raising money, I'm telling you—it's a job. What are they going to do when I get out?" [1] The cardinal promised a million dollars for the poor in Roxbury. "I want to spend that money there," he told guests at a fund-raising dinner, "and I'm going to check all the bills to make sure it goes there."

He told the story of Tim, whose brother in Ireland had died and left him three million dollars. Fearing the shock might kill Tim, his wife asked their pastor to break the news gently. The priest came to Tim's bedside. "My dearest friend, compose yourself. Relax and don't be nervous. I have sad news, bad and good for you. Your brother John died."

"God rest his soul," Tim said. "He's better off. He has suffered with heart trouble and other ailments for years."

"Your brother John left you three million dollars. Quiet, now Tim, quiet. You mustn't get excited."

"God be praised. That's fine news. I'll put the money to good use."

"I was afraid you would drop dead," Tim's wife said. "But tell me —what will you ever do with three million dollars?"

Tim told her not to get excited. "I'll put away one million for the education of our children; another million I'll save for you and me in our old age. And the third million I'll give to the good padre who came here to break the sad news."

At this point, Cushing wrote in his *Pilot* column, the priest dropped dead.

"So, my dear friends," he went on, "the moral of the story is this. Be good to me. I need your help. But don't give me a million dollars, because if you do, I'll also drop dead, and I am not ready to render an account of my stewardship. By the way, when did you help me last?"

Cushing, who had spent over three hundred million dollars to develop the Boston see into one of the world's greatest, is having financial trouble with his parochial school system, but his hospital program is flourishing. In mid-summer of 1969 he turned the first spade of earth for an enlarged Carney Hospital that will take three years to complete at a cost of $11.5 million. His overall expansion program will be difficult to match, for he is the master builder in all church history.

Cardinal Cushing can retire in 1970 in the knowledge that he is largely responsible for the new climate of acceptance in a once frosty commonwealth, which in recent years elected an Italian Catholic (John Volpe) governor and a Negro (Edward Brooke) and an Irish Catholic (Edward Kennedy) United States senators. The Boston Irish were still a "downtrodden" majority when Cushing was born, and Boston was still the most class-bound city in the nation. Even after Irish Catholics got their chokehold on politics around the turn of the century, the Yankees denied them status. "It was almost as appropriate in those snobbish days to say that Boston was a part of Beacon Hill and the Back Bay," Curley writes in his autobiography, "as it was to say later, when the Irish assumed political control, that Boston was part of South Boston." [3] It was a far cry from 1849, when a Bostonian considered it "something of a sensation" to see an Irishman in South Boston.

In 1968, Abigail Adams Homans, the great-great-granddaughter of John and Abigail Adams, was thinking particularly of John F. Kennedy when she said: "It used to be that, generally speaking, we looked down upon the Irish, we thoroughbred Yankees. And now we're run by the Kennedys. They represent the aristocracy. The old Yankee families are gone, or we survive but don't count any longer." [4]

John F. Kennedy and Richard Cardinal Cushing are primarily responsible for the climate of acceptance, although Cushing himself prefers to be thought of as a catalyst—an instrument of change without being itself changed. He can retire in the knowledge that he is the strongest link between his church and the Protestant and Jewish community. More than that, he can retire in the knowledge that he has done more even than John F. Kennedy, not only for people of his own race and religion, but for people of all races and creeds everywhere. For no churchman has ever shown more charity and love for so many people. Although he denies that he is deeply religious, he is truly a saintly person who has no equal as a Christian if Christianity is love. Napoleon said he needed five million people to love him. Cushing has many more than that.

When the history of the twentieth century is written, Cushing, the most colorful, earthy, and outspoken prelate of his time, will be recorded as one of the great men of the era, and as the spiritual leader of two million Catholic Americans, he will be remembered as a simple, lovable priest who wished the world had only one eye so he could dry its tears. He was merely tethered in Boston, as Bishop Sheen noted. The pasturage of the churchman of the century is as wide and all-encompassing as the priesthood itself.

The cardinal celebrated his seventy-fourth birthday quietly at home, with none of the bustle and commotion of former birthday celebrations. A special mass in his honor was celebrated on Channel 7 in Boston from the Government Center studio chapel by Auxiliary Bishop Daniel A. Cronin, assisted by Monsignor James J. Scally of the Cathedral of the Holy Cross. Monsignor Scally said the cardinal had "traversed literally every inch of the archdiocese, bringing comfort, consolation, or encouragement to anyone in need of it." Bishop Cronin added that the cardinal had been able, "by means of the pen, words of encouragement, and financial assistance, to help throughout the world."

Following the mass, Channel 7 repeated a 1967 television documentary of the cardinal's life. In it, Bishop Stokes, Rabbi Shubow, Billy Graham, and other religious leaders lauded the cardinal as being "ecumenical long before it was the agenda of the Catholic Church." A nun said he was "father to more children than any father I ever knew," and Cushing himself, who during his entire ministry has preached friendship, love, and understanding, said: "What a wonderful treasure of beautiful thoughts are summed up in that word 'friend.'" There is also a wonderful treasure of thoughts summed up in the name "Cushing."

It was hard to follow Cardinal O'Connell onto the stage. It will be harder to follow the churchman of the century.

NOTES

CHAPTER ONE/*ORIGINS OF A "SOUTHIE"*

[1] For an account of this visit, see William R. Callahan, Boston *Globe,* August 29, 1953.

[2] *The Catholic Standard,* September 5, 1958. The genealogical information on the Cushing (Cushion) family comes from Peter Kilroy and Walter Mahon-Smith, editors of *The Catholic Standard,* who received it from James Fouhy, Richard Rice, and Canon Michael J. Hurley, all of Glanworth, and from the Reverend John O'Shea, C.C., Whitechurch, County Cork. From this it appears that James Cushion, the cardinal's grandfather, who came to Glanworth in 1848, was a Protestant. In a 1969 radiocast Cardinal Cushing told Howard Nelson that most of his relatives were Protestant. He was not, of course, thinking of his immediate relatives. James Cushion, the cardinal's grandfather, who was a convert, married Bridget Foley. Thomas Morrissey, according to James Fouhy (a publican in Glanworth), lived to be ninety-eight. Morrissey gave Fouhy the information on the cardinal's forebears.

[3] *Ibid.*

[4] John J. Toomey and Edward P. B. Ranking, *History of South Boston* (Boston, 1901), published by the authors.

[5] John H. Fenton, *Salt of the Earth: An Informal Portrait of Richard Cardinal Cushing* (New York: Coward-McCann, 1951).

[6] Francis Russell, *The Great Interlude* (New York: McGraw-Hill, 1964).

[7] John Gunther, *Inside U.S.A.* (New York: Harper & Row, 1947).

[8] William V. Shannon, *The American Irish: A Political and Social Portrait* (New York: Macmillan, 1966).

[9] *Ibid.*

[10] Russell.

[11] Oscar Handlin, *Boston's Immigrants: A Study in Acculturation* (Cambridge, Mass.: Harvard University Press, Belknap Press, 1959).

[12] *The Kennedys,* by the editors of *Life* (New York: Time-Life Books, 1968).

[13] Henry Greene, (B.A. thesis, Harvard University, 1963).

[14] *The Catholic Standard,* September 5, 1958.

[15] Interview with Canon Michael J. Hurley in Glanworth, April 11, 1968.

CHAPTER TWO/*THE HARD WAY*

[1] Archbishop Cushing was speaking informally at Blinstrub's Village on May 7, 1950.

[2] Joseph Dever, *Cushing of Boston: A Candid Portrait* (Boston: Bruce Humphries, 1965).

[3] *The World's Cardinal,* published by the Daughters of St. Paul (Boston, 1964).

[4] Dever.

[5] *Ibid.*

[6] Lucius Beebe, *Boston and the Boston Legend* (New York: Appleton-Century-Crofts, 1936).

[7] Donal O'Higgins, Boston *Herald-Traveler,* November 12, 1968.

[8] John H. Fenton, *Salt of the Earth: An Informal Portrait of Richard Cardinal Cushing* (New York: Coward-McCann, 1965).

[9] *Ibid.*

[10] *The World's Cardinal.*

[11] *Ibid.*

[12] *Ibid.*

[13] *Ibid.*

[14] *Ibid.*

[15] Dever.

[16] *Ibid.*

[17] Fenton.

[18] *Ibid.*

[19] Albert Duhamel, in his review of Fenton's biography in *The New York Times,* July 4, 1964.

[20] WBZ–TV interview with Arch MacDonald, June 30, 1964.

[21] Fenton.

[22] WBZ–TV interview with Arch MacDonald, June 30, 1964.

[23] Francis Russell, *The Great Interlude* (New York: McGraw-Hill, 1964).

[24] *The World's Cardinal.*

[25] Interview with Robert Heffernan of Scituate, Massachusetts, who grew up with Cushing in South Boston.

[26] *Ibid.*

CHAPTER THREE / *TWO ROADWAYS*

[1] Joseph Dever, *Cushing of Boston: A Candid Portrait* (Boston: Bruce Humphries, 1965).

[2] Lawrence H. Fuchs, *John F. Kennedy and American Catholicism* (New York: Meredith Press, 1967).

[3] George L. Croft and Edward G. McGrath, Boston *Sunday Globe,* November 23, 1958.

[4] Dever.

[5] Interview with Mrs. Maurice Brodie, Hull, Massachusetts, in June 1968.

[6] Croft and McGrath, Boston *Sunday Globe,* November 23, 1958.

[7] *The Catholic Standard,* October 8, 1959.

[8] *The World's Cardinal,* published by the Daughters of St. Paul (Boston, 1964).

[9] *Ibid.*

[10] John H. Fenton, *Salt of the Earth: An Informal Portrait of Richard Cardinal Cushing* (New York: Coward-McCann, 1965).

[11] *Catholic Digest,* April 1956.

[12] *Ibid.*

[13] Francis Russell, *The Great Interlude* (New York: McGraw-Hill, 1964).

[14] James Michael Curley, *I'd Do It Again: A Record of All My Uproarious Years* (Englewood Cliffs, N.J.: Prentice-Hall, 1957).

[15] Leonard S. Whelen of West Roxbury, Massachusetts, an instructor in the classics.

CHAPTER FOUR / *THE VINEYARD OF THE LORD*

[1] Joe McCarthy, *The Remarkable Kennedys* (New York: Dial Press, 1960).

[2] Boston *Telegram,* June 5, 1922. See *Harvard Alumni Bulletin,* April 7, 1969.

[3] William V. Shannon, *The American Irish: A Political and Social Portrait* (New York: Macmillan, 1966).

[4] John Gunther, *Inside U.S.A.* (New York: Harper & Row, 1947).

[5] John Henry Cutler: *Three Steps to the White House: The Colorful Life and Times of John F. ("Honey Fitz") Fitzgerald* (Indianapolis: Bobbs-Merrill, 1962).

[6] Joseph Dever, *Cushing of Boston: A Candid Portrait* (Boston: Bruce Humphries, 1965).

[7] George L. Croft and Edward G. McGrath, Boston *Sunday Globe,* November 23, 1958.

[8] Joseph F. Dinneen, *Collier's,* November 10, 1951.

[9] *The World's Cardinal,* published by the Daughters of St. Paul (Boston, 1964).

[10] *Ibid.*

[11] *Ibid.*

[12] Interview with the Reverend Alan Travers, First Baptist Church, Duxbury, Massachusetts, September 14, 1968.

[13] *The World's Cardinal.*

[14] *Ibid.*

[15] Dever.

[16] CBS–TV documentary with Harry Reasoner, May 14, 1968.

[17] *The World's Cardinal.*

[18] John H. Fenton, *Salt of the Earth: An Informal Portrait of Richard Cardinal Cushing* (New York: Coward-McCann, 1965).

CHAPTER FIVE/*HIDDEN YEARS*

[1] John H. Fenton, *Salt of the Earth: An Informal Portrait of Richard Cardinal Cushing* (New York: Coward-McCann, 1965).

[2] *The World's Cardinal*, published by the Daughters of St. Paul (Boston, 1964).

[3] *The Catholic Standard*, September, 1959.

[4] Joseph Dever, *Cushing of Boston: A Candid Portrait* (Boston: Bruce Humphries, 1965).

[5] Interview with the Reverend Francis Cloherty, Holy Name Church, Duxbury, Massachusetts, August 22, 1969.

[6] *The World's Cardinal*.

[7] *Ibid.*

[8] Joseph E. Dinneen, *Collier's,* November 10, 1951.

[9] Boston *Herald-Traveler,* June 18, 1969.

[10] "Where Is Father Hennessey?" a pamphlet written by Cushing.

[11] Thomas G. Duffy, *Let's Go* (London: Sheed & Ward, 1928).

[12] Details of Mother Kevin's dramatic life are portrayed in a missionary film, "More Than I Can," and more information is recorded in the congregation's magazine, *The Daystar*.

[13] Ray McPartlin, Boston *Globe,* wrote a series of sixteen articles on the life of Cushing soon after he became archbishop, September 29–October 14, 1944.

[14] John Larner, *Pilot,* June 28, 1964.

[15] *The World's Cardinal*.

[16] *Ibid.*

[17] Fenton.

[18] *The World's Cardinal*.

[19] *Ibid.*

[20] *Ibid.*

CHAPTER SIX/*BISHOP OF THE MISSIONS*

[1] Robert Gannon, S.J., *The Cardinal Spellman Story* (New York: Doubleday, 1962).

[2] John H. Fenton, *Salt of the Earth: An Informal Portrait of Richard Cardinal Cushing* (New York: Coward-McCann, 1965).

[3] Interview with Richard Condon, director of the St. Vincent de Paul Society, October 16, 1968.

[4] Joseph Dever, *Cushing of Boston: A Candid Portrait* (Boston: Bruce Humphries, 1965).

[5] Cushing in a ninety-minute talk in a Methodist church in Sudbury, Massachusetts, in January 1964.

[6] Gannon.

[7] *Ibid.*

[8] *The World's Cardinal,* published by the Daughters of St. Paul (Boston, 1964).

[9] *Ibid.*

[10] Fenton.

[11] *Ibid.*

[12] *The World's Cardinal.*

[13] *Ibid.*

[14] *Ibid.*

[15] *Ibid.*

[16] *Ibid.*

[17] *Ibid.*

[18] Fenton.

[19] *Ibid.*

[20] Boston *Herald-Traveler,* November 7, 1968.

[21] Fenton.

[22] Letter from Kilcullen to the author, December 9, 1968.

[23] Dorothy G. Wayman, *Cardinal O'Connell of Boston: A Biography of William Henry O'Connell* (New York: Farrar, Straus and Giroux, 1955).

[24] Fenton.

[25] Interview with Richard Condon, October 16, 1969.

[26] John Gunther, *Inside U.S.A.* (New York: Harper & Row, 1947).

[27] Joseph F. Dinneen, *Collier's,* November 10, 1951.

[28] *The World's Cardinal.*

[29] *Ibid.*

[30] Dinneen.

CHAPTER SEVEN / *GETTING THE HANDOUTS*

[1] John H. Fenton, *Salt of the Earth: An Informal Portrait of Richard Cardinal Cushing* (New York: Coward-McCann, 1965).

[2] *Ibid.*

[3] John Gunther, *Inside U.S.A.* (New York: Harper & Row, 1947).

[4] *The World's Cardinal,* published by the Daughters of St. Paul (Boston, 1964).

[5] *Ibid.*

[6] Boston *Globe,* January 18, 1946.

[7] *Pilot,* October 16, 1945.

[8] Boston *Record-American,* February 15, 1945.

[9] *The World's Cardinal.*

[10] Cushing told this story in an address to the twenty-sixth Diocesan Council of Catholic Women.

[11] "My Dear Children of God," *McCall's,* December 1966.

[12] CBS–TV documentary with Harry Reasoner, May 14, 1968.

[13] *Ibid.*

[14] *Ibid.*

[15] *Pilot,* May 27, 1954.

[16] "The Good Fight," *The Catholic Mirror,* published in the diocese of Springfield, Massachusetts.

[17] Joseph Dever, *Cushing of Boston: A Candid Portrait* (Boston: Bruce Humphries, 1965).

[18] Robert Gannon, S.J., *The Cardinal Spellman Story* (New York: Doubleday, 1962).

[19] *Pilot,* November 6, 1954.

[20] *Ibid.*

[21] *Time,* August 21, 1964.

[22] Helen Hayes, *On Reflection* (New York: M. Evans and Company, 1968).

CHAPTER EIGHT/*MASTER FINANCIER*

[1] *The World's Cardinal,* published by the Daughters of St. Paul (Boston, 1964).

[2] An address to students at Radcliffe College, April 9, 1964.

[3] John H. Fenton, *Salt of the Earth: An Informal Portrait of Richard Cardinal Cushing* (New York: Coward-McCann, 1965).

[4] Joseph Dever, *Cushing of Boston: A Candid Portrait* (Boston: Bruce Humphries, 1965).

[5] Talk to the congregation in a Methodist church in Sudbury, Massachusetts, January, 1964.

[6] Dever.

[7] *Ibid.*

[8] *Ibid.*

CHAPTER NINE/*DEFENDER OF THE FAITH*

[1] Lawrence H. Fuchs, *John F. Kennedy and American Catholicism* (New York: Meredith Press, 1967).

[2] Paul Blanshard, *American Freedom and Catholic Power* (Boston: Beacon Press, 1958).

[3] Boston newspapers gave the event full coverage.

[4] *The New York Times,* September 23, 1945.

[5] John H. Fenton, *Salt of the Earth: An Informal Portrait of Richard Cardinal Cushing* (New York: Coward-McCann, 1965).

[6] Boston *Herald,* June 5, 1950.

[7] Address in Cleveland to the mid-century convention of Newman clubs, June 1950.

[8] Fuchs.

[9] *Ibid.*

[10] The late Bishop Sheil addressed a conference of the United Automobile Workers Union on April 9, 1954.

[11] Fred W. Friendly, *Due to Circumstances Beyond Our Control* (New York: Vintage Books, 1968).

[12] *Library Journal,* Vol. 77. No. 19 (November 1, 1952), pp. 1845, 1846.

[13] Joseph Dever, *Cushing of Boston: A Candid Portrait* (Boston: Bruce Humphries, 1965).

[14] *Ibid.*

[15] Arthur Derounian, *Under Cover: My Four Years in the Nazi Underworld of America—The Amazing Revelation of How Axis Agents and Our Enemies Within Are Now Plotting to Destroy the United States* (New York: Dutton, 1943).

[16] *Ibid.*

[17] *Ibid.*

[18] John Gunther, *Inside U.S.A.* (New York: Harper & Row, 1947).

[19] *Time,* August 21, 1964.

[20] Blanshard.

[21] *Time,* August 24, 1964.

[22] Cushing amplified on this theme in various addresses and in his writings.

[23] *U.S. News and World Report,* December 23, 1955.

[24] *Ibid.*

CHAPTER TEN/*THE PILGRIM*

[1] Anthony Moore, *The Catholic Standard,* March 26, 1948.

[2] Archbishop Cushing provided the silver casket in which the body of Pope Pius X lay in St. Peter's Basilica prior to the official canonization on May 29, 1954. Signora Guiseppina Parolin, daughter of the sister of Saint Pius X, in a dispatch from Rome to the Boston *Globe,* spoke of Cushing as the one whom "my family must thank most for the early canonization of my dear uncle Guiseppe." Although she had never met the archbishop, she said she and her relatives were deeply grateful to him and the good people of Boston, "their favorite American city," who sent so many petitions to the Vatican in behalf of Pius X. Signora Parolin, who called Cushing "her favorite American," mentioned the silver casket he donated. (*Pilot,* June 5, 1954).

[3] *The World's Cardinal,* published by the Daughters of St. Paul (Boston, 1964).

4 Joseph Dever, *Cushing of Boston: A Candid Portrait* (Boston: Bruce Humphries, 1965).

5 Warren Carberg, Boston *Post,* September 24, 1949.

6 According to the last Dahill descendant in the vicinity, Kitty Tobin, whose father, Patrick Doyle, was a second cousin of Richard J. Cushing, nobody living in the environs of Ballyduff in 1968 knew Mary Dahill. The same was true when Cushing visited Cork. There is no account of Mary's baptism, no trace of her house. The vague recollections of the villagers of Ballyduff lead nowhere, but they ring with nostalgia: Michael Feeney, Garrymagoul, says Cardinal Cushing's mother lived in Cunningham's boreen (an unkept road) on the same side as Cunningham's house. He was definite about that but did not know if she was born there, and there is now no trace of the house. Paddy Murray and Michael Waters said she lived later near Tom Spillane's farmhouse. This is all the information Mrs. John (Kitty) Tobin could "rake up." The author interviewed her in Ballyduff and later received this information in a letter from her.

7 *The World's Cardinal.*

8 *Ibid.*

9 *Ibid.*

10 *Ibid.*

11 Letter from Cushing to Lord Mayor Sean McCarthy shown to the author during an interview in Cork, April 1968.

12 *Pilot,* November 6, 1954.

13 *Ibid.*

14 *Time,* November 8, 1968.

15 Interview with Canon Michael J. Hurley in Glanworth, April 1968.

16 Interview with the Reverend Matthew Sheehan at St. Colman's Seminary, Cork city, April 1968.

17 *The New York Times,* July 22, 1954.

CHAPTER ELEVEN/*PREACHING FROM THE HOUSETOPS*

1 John Gunther, *Inside U.S.A.* (New York: Harper & Row, 1947).

2 Lawrence H. Fuchs, *John F. Kennedy and American Catholicism* (New York: Meredith Press, 1967).

3 Gunther.

4 According to Pierce Robinson of Marshfield, Massachusetts, brother of the author of *The Cardinal,* the character was a composite of cardinals O'Connell and Spellman. Stephen Fermoyle was modeled on Cushing. The surname suggests Fermoy, just a few miles from Glanworth.

5 *Catholic Digest,* November 1955.

6 *Ibid.*

7 Harold Kaese, Boston *Globe,* January 30, 1969.

[8] John H. Fenton, *Salt of the Earth: An Informal Portrait of Richard Cardinal Cushing* (New York: Coward-McCann, 1965).

[9] *The New York Times,* January 9, 1959.

[10] *The New York Times,* June 12, 1959.

[11] Letter dated August 6, 1968, from Goddard Light of Rye, New York, president of the Rye Historical Society.

[12] Francis Russell, "The Last of the Bosses," *The Great Interlude* (New York: McGraw-Hill, 1964).

[13] *Ibid.*

[14] Leo Damore, *The Cape Cod Years of John Fitzgerald Kennedy* (Englewood Cliffs, N.J.: Prentice-Hall, 1967).

CHAPTER TWELVE / *THE RED HAT*

[1] Ray Jenkins, *London Observer,* July 21, 1963.

[2] *Reader's Digest,* August 1968.

[3] *The World's Cardinal,* published by the Daughters of St. Paul (Boston, 1964).

[4] Patrick McDonough, a member of the governor's council of Massachusetts.

[5] William Cardinal O'Connell, *Recollections of Seventy Years* (Boston: Houghton Mifflin, 1934).

[6] Richard Cardinal Cushing, *Call Me John: A Life of Pope John XXIII,* published by the Daughters of St. Paul (Boston, 1963).

[7] *Ibid.*

[8] *Ibid.*

[9] Jim Bishop, Boston *Record-American,* August 15, 1965.

[10] Cushing.

[11] Joseph Dever, *Cushing of Boston: A Candid Portrait* (Boston: Bruce Humphries, 1965).

[12] In the spring of 1969, Santa Susanna, for whom the American Roman Catholic Church in Rome was named, was one of nearly thirty saints dropped in a drastic revision of the liturgical calendar of the Roman Catholic Church. Another dropped was St. Christopher, patron of travelers and the figure in millions of St. Christopher medals, of which Cushing has given many to friends.

[13] The Boston *Traveler,* December 17, 1958.

[14] *Ibid.*

[15] A mozzetta is a short capelike garment; a biretta, a square-shaped red hat for everyday wear.

[16] Edwin O'Connor covered events for the Boston *Globe.*

[17] John Larner, *Pilot,* November 6, 1954.

[18] Boston *Herald-Traveler,* April 11, 1969.

[19] Jeremiah V. Murphy, Boston *Globe,* April 11, 1969.

CHAPTER THIRTEEN / *A NEW KIND OF PRINCE*

[1] John Cogley, *The Commonweal*, November 16, 1951.

[2] James Kavanaugh, *A Modern Priest Looks at His Outdated Church* (New York: Trident Press, 1967).

[3] Reverend George J. Hafner, "Don't Call Me Father," *The Saturday Evening Post*, June 29, 1968. Hafner was suspended by his bishop for establishing an unauthorized experimental parish in New Jersey.

[4] Lawrence H. Fuchs, *John F. Kennedy and American Catholicism* (New York: Meredith Press, 1967).

[5] CBS–TV documentary with Harry Reasoner, May 14, 1968.

[6] Boston *Sunday Globe*, June 28, 1964.

[7] *Irish Sunday Press*, September 11, 1949.

[8] Interview with Richard Condon, October 16, 1968.

[9] Lawrence Stone, Nantasket, Hull, Massachusetts.

[10] Peter Braestrup, "What the Press Has Done to Boston and Vice Versa," *Harper's*, Vol. 221 (October 1960).

[11] Murray Levin, *The Alienated Voter: Politics in Boston* (New York: Holt, Rinehart and Winston, 1960).

[12] *The Catholic Standard*, April 24, 1959.

[13] *The World's Cardinal*, published by the Daughters of St. Paul (Boston, 1964).

[14] *The Catholic Standard*, May 1, 1959.

[15] John H. Fenton, *Salt of the Earth: An Informal Portrait of Richard Cardinal Cushing* (New York: Coward-McCann, 1965).

[16] *The New York Times*, January 1, 1959.

[17] *Ibid.*, August 13, 1959.

[18] *Ibid.*, August 16, 1959.

[19] *Ibid.*, November 23, 1959.

[20] *Ibid.*, October 12, 1959. For a more detailed account see *The Catholic Standard*, October 23, 1959.

[21] *The New York Times*, October 12, 1959.

[22] *The World's Cardinal*.

[23] *Ibid.*

[24] John Murphy, a photographer with the Boston *Record-American*.

[25] *The World's Cardinal*.

[26] *The Catholic Standard*, May 20, 1960.

[27] *Ibid.*

CHAPTER FOURTEEN / *THE KEY SHOP*

[1] Boston *Herald*, August 24, 1961.

[2] Louis M. Lyons, "Boston: Study in Inertia," *Our Fair City*, Robert Sharon Allen, ed. (New York: Vanguard Press, 1947).

[3] Fred W. Friendly, *Due to Circumstances Beyond Our Control* (New York: Vintage Books, 1968).

[4] *Ibid.*

[5] *Ibid.*

[6] Marya Mannes, "Just Looking," *The Reporter,* January 4, 1962.

[7] Station WEEI, Boston, with Paul Benzaquin.

[8] Boston *Globe,* June 11, 1964.

[9] Friendly.

[10] Joseph M. DeMambro, in a letter from Cardinal Cushing, 1964.

CHAPTER FIFTEEN/*LATIN AMERICA*

[1] "The Missionary Society of St. James the Apostle."

[2] *Ibid.*

[3] Joseph Dever, *Cushing of Boston: A Candid Portrait* (Boston: Bruce Humphries, 1965).

[4] Cushing said this in January 1962 in connection with the Bay of Pigs captives.

[5] Dever.

[6] Robert Gannon, S.J., *The Cardinal Spellman Story* (New York: Doubleday, 1962).

[7] *Ibid.*

[8] Cushing's pamphlet was published by the Daughters of St. Paul, Boston, Massachusetts.

[9] Reported in many American newspapers on August 29, 1960. Also in *The Catholic Standard,* Dublin, Ireland.

[10] Archbishop Romulo Carboni, apostolic nuncio to Peru, and Archbishop Juan Landozurro, of Lima.

[11] August 29, 1960.

[12] Boston *Herald,* August 2, 1964.

[13] Richard Cardinal Cushing, "Saving Souls in Latin America" (Boston: Daughters of St. Paul).

[14] *Time,* August 21, 1964.

[15] Richard J. Connolly covered the trip for the Boston *Globe.*

[16] The Reverend R. W. Nickerson, Lisbon, New York, in *Time,* Letters to the Editor, September 4, 1964.

[17] Terry Storms, La Place, Louisiana, *Time,* September 4, 1964.

[18] *America,* January 21, 1965.

[19] *Time,* February 14, 1969.

[20] A moderately progressive periodical published weekly at Notre Dame, Indiana, by the Congregation of Holy Cross.

[21] Quoted in Evelyn Lincoln, *Kennedy and Johnson* (New York: Holt, Rinehart and Winston, 1968).

[22] Dever.

CHAPTER SIXTEEN/*"WHAT'S THE WORD FROM LAKE STREET"*

1 William V. Shannon, "Massachusetts, Prisoner of the Past," *Our Sovereign State*, Robert S. Allen, ed. (New York: Vanguard Press, 1949).

2 Joseph F. Dinneen, *Collier's*, November 10, 1951.

3 James Michael Curley, *I'd Do It Again! The Story of All My Uproarious Years* (Englewood Cliffs, N.J.: Prentice-Hall, 1957).

4 Murray B. Levin with George Blackwood, *The Compleat Politician: Political Strategy in Massachusetts* (Indianapolis: Bobbs-Merrill, 1962).

5 Shannon.

6 Katherine Loughlin, "Boston's Political Morals," *The Commonweal*, Vol. 43 (March 15, 1946).

7 *The New York Times*, September 2, 1945.

8 Joseph Dever, *Cushing of Boston: A Candid Portrait* (Boston: Bruce Humphries, 1965).

9 Boston *Globe*, August 5, 1949.

10 *The New York Times*, October 4, 1946.

11 Boston *Globe*, January 29, 1957.

CHAPTER SEVENTEEN/*CUSHING AND THE KENNEDYS*

1 John Gunther, *Inside U.S.A.* (New York: Harper & Row, 1947).

2 John Henry Cutler, *Three Steps to the White House: The Colorful Life and Times of John F. ("Honey Fitz") Fitzgerald* (Indianapolis: Bobbs-Merrill, 1962).

3 James Michael Curley, *I'd Do It Again! The Story of All My Uproarious Years* (Englewood Cliffs, N.J.: Prentice-Hall, 1957).

4 Edgar Litt, "Political Cynicism and Political Futility," *The Journal of Politics*, Vol. 25 (May 1963), pp. 312–23.

5 William H. A. Carr, *JFK: A Complete Biography, 1917–1963* (New York: Lancer Books, 1963).

6 *Ibid.*

7 William J. Duncliffe, *The Life and Times of Joseph P. Kennedy* (New York: Macfadden-Bartell, 1965).

8 *Ibid.*

9 *The Fruitful Bough*, privately printed in 1965 by Halliday Lithograph, West Hanover, Massachusetts.

10 Joe McCarthy, *The Remarkable Kennedys* (New York: Dial Press, 1960).

11 *Ibid.*

12 Carr.

13 *Ibid.*

14 McCarthy.

[15] Ralph DeToledano, *R.F.K.: The Man Who Would Be President* (New York: Putnam, 1967).

[16] CBS–TV documentary with Harry Reasoner, May 14, 1968.

[17] Francis J. Lally, *The Catholic Church in a Changing America* (Boston: Little, Brown, 1962).

[18] Victor Lasky, *J.F.K.: The Man and the Myth* (New York: Macmillan, 1963).

[19] Arthur Schlesinger, Jr., *A Thousand Days* (Boston: Houghton Mifflin, 1965).

[20] *Look,* December 10, 1968.

[21] Lally.

[22] *Look,* March 3, 1959.

[23] James MacGregor Burns, *John Kennedy: A Political Profile* (New York: Harcourt, Brace & World, 1960).

[24] Theodore C. Sorensen, *Kennedy* (New York: Harper & Row, 1965).

[25] *Ibid.*

[26] Evelyn Lincoln, *Kennedy & Johnson* (New York: Holt, Rinehart and Winston, 1968).

[27] Lawrence H. Fuchs, *John F. Kennedy and American Catholicism* (New York: Meredith Press, 1967).

[28] *Ibid.*

[29] *Ibid.*

[30] *Look,* March 3, 1959.

[31] McCarthy.

[32] *Ibid.*

[33] Carr.

[34] Fuchs.

[35] John H. Fenton, *Salt of the Earth: An Informal Portrait of Richard Cardinal Cushing* (New York: Coward-McCann, 1965).

[36] Interview with John B. Hynes, June 3, 1969.

[37] Lally.

[38] WBZ–TV interview with Arch MacDonald, 1964.

[39] Bela Kornitzer, *Look,* November 19, 1964.

[40] Edgar Litt, *The Political Cultures of Massachusetts* (Cambridge, Mass.: M.I.T. Press, 1965).

[41] McCarthy.

[42] Carr.

[43] Earl Mazo and Stephen Hess, *Nixon: A Political Portrait* (New York: Harper & Row, 1967).

[44] Fenton.

[45] CBS–TV documentary with Harry Reasoner, May 14, 1968.

[46] *Ibid.*

[47] *Ave Maria,* July 22, 1961.

48 Richard J. Whalen, *The Founding Father* (New York: New American Library, 1964).
49 Duncliffe.
50 *Ibid.*
51 In St. Patrick's Cathedral, New York City, with the then Senator's brother Bobby and Jacqueline's sister Lee as godparents. See Evelyn Lincoln, *My Twelve Years with JFK* (New York: McKay, 1965).
52 *Time,* January 19, 1962.
53 Anthony Clifford, *America,* September 8, 1962. Anthony Clifford is the pen name of Edward Anthony Connell, an observer of the Massachusetts political scene.
54 Whalen.
55 Litt.
56 Whalen.
57 Litt.
58 *Ibid.*
59 *Time,* September 28, 1962.
60 Whalen.
61 William Manchester, *The Death of a President* (New York: Harper & Row, 1968).
62 Lincoln, *My Twelve Years with Kennedy.*
63 Pierre Salinger, *With Kennedy* (New York: Doubleday, 1966).
64 Jim Bishop, *The Day Kennedy Was Shot* (New York: Funk & Wagnalls, 1968).
65 *Look,* November 19, 1964.
66 *Ibid.*
67 Manchester.

CHAPTER EIGHTEEN/*A TIME OF GRIEF*

1 William Manchester, *The Death of a President* (New York: Harper & Row, 1967).
2 Jim Bishop, *The Day Kennedy Was Shot* (New York: Funk & Wagnalls, 1968).
3 Manchester.
4 Bishop.
5 John H. Fenton, *Salt of the Earth: An Informal Portrait of Richard Cardinal Cushing* (New York: Coward-McCann, 1965).
6 Manchester.
7 *Ibid.*
8 *Ibid.*
9 *Ibid.*

[10] *Ibid.*

[11] *Ibid.*

[12] Bela Kornitzer, *Look,* November 17, 1964.

[13] Murray Kempton, writing in *The New Republic.*

[14] Kornitzer.

[15] Theodore H. White, *The Making of the President 1964* (New York: Atheneum, 1965).

[16] Manchester.

[17] *Ibid.*

[18] *Ibid.*

[19] Mrs. Jack E. Penhollow, Des Moines, Iowa, in a letter to the editor, *Look,* February 11, 1964.

[20] Manchester.

[21] *Ibid.*

[22] White.

[23] Kornitzer.

[24] William J. Duncliffe, *The Life and Times of Joseph P. Kennedy* (New York: Macfadden-Bartell, 1965).

[25] Fenton.

[26] Boston *Globe,* August 5, 1964.

[27] George Collins, Boston *Globe,* March 16, 1967.

[28] Arlene Grimes, Boston *Herald,* June 6, 1968.

[29] Fenton.

[30] Kornitzer.

[31] *The Fruitful Bough,* privately printed in 1965 by Halliday Lithograph, West Hanover, Massachusetts.

[32] Fenton.

[33] Robert Hassett, Boston *Herald,* January 20, 1964.

[34] Fred Brady, Boston *Traveler,* January 20, 1964.

[35] Fenton.

[36] Letter to the author from Dr. C. Gordon Brownsville, Brewster, Massachusetts, 1968.

[37] *The World's Cardinal,* published by the Daughters of St. Paul (Boston, 1964).

[38] Joseph Dever, *Cushing of Boston: A Candid Portrait* (Boston: Bruce Humphries, 1965).

[39] Boston *Globe,* June 21, 1964.

[40] *Ibid.,* June 20, 1964.

[41] *Ibid.,* June 23, 1964.

[42] Ralph De Toledano, *RFK: The Man Who Would Be President* (New York: Putnam, 1967).

[43] *Ibid.*

[44] Boston *Globe,* March 16, 1967.

[45] Cushing said this on January 27, 1967.

[46] Boston *Herald,* March 17, 1967.

[47] Article by Cushing in *This Week,* January 26, 1969.

[48] Editorial, *Washington Post,* June 9, 1969.

[49] *Look,* November 26, 1969.

[50] *Ibid.*

[51] Bob Creamer and Frank Falacci, Boston *Herald-Traveler,* June 6, 1968.

[52] Jim Bishop said this on "The Merv Griffin Show."

[53] Arlene Grimes, *Boston Herald,* June 6, 1968.

[54] *Ibid.*

[55] *Look,* November 26, 1968.

[56] Arlene Grimes, Boston *Herald,* June 6, 1968.

[57] *Ibid.*

[58] Ted Lewis, New York *Daily News,* June 6, 1968.

[59] William H. Honan, *The New York Times Magazine,* February 23, 1969.

[60] *This Week,* January 26, 1969.

CHAPTER NINETEEN/*A SECOND REFORMATION*

[1] John H. Fenton, *Salt of the Earth: An Informal Portrait of Richard Cardinal Cushing* (New York: Coward-McCann, 1965).

[2] *Ibid.*

[3] Talk to students at Radcliffe College, April 9, 1964.

[4] *Paul Blanshard on Vatican II* (Boston: Beacon Press, 1966).

[5] Fenton.

[6] For other rules, see Paul Blanshard, *American Freedom and Catholic Power* (Boston: Beacon Press, 1958).

[7] Boston *Globe,* November 16, 1968.

[8] The Reverend Dr. Edwin P. Booth, minister emeritus.

[9] Fenton.

[10] Joseph Dever, *Cushing of Boston: A Candid Portrait* (Boston: Bruce Humphries, 1965).

[11] Boston *Globe,* April 20, 1959.

[12] Edgar Litt, *The Political Cultures of Massachusetts* (Cambridge, Mass.: M.I.T. Press, 1965).

[13] *The World's Cardinal,* published by the Daughters of St. Paul (Boston, 1964).

[14] *Ibid.*

[15] Lawrence H. Fuchs, *John F. Kennedy and American Catholicism* (New York: Meredith Press, 1967).

[16] *Time,* August 2, 1964.

[17] Cardinal O'Connell took part in only one of three elections for which he was eligible.

[18] Ray Jenkins, *London Observer,* July 21, 1969.

[19] *Ibid.*

[20] *Ibid.*

[21] *Ibid.*

[22] *Pilot,* November 6, 1965.

[23] Interview with Joseph M. DeMambro, August 3, 1969.

[24] Jenkins.

[25] *Ibid.*

[26] William J. Duncliffe, Boston *Record-American,* June 21, 1963.

[27] Fenton.

[28] *America,* September 1963.

[29] Talk at the Methodist church in Sudbury, January 1964.

[30] *Paul Blanshard on Vatican II* (Boston: Beacon Press, 1966).

[31] Father Walter M. Abbott, reported in *The Christian Century,* June 24, 1963.

[32] *U.S. News and World Report,* June 24, 1963.

[33] Dever.

[34] "The Revolution in the Roman Catholic Church," *Reader's Digest,* August 1968.

[35] *Ibid.*

[36] "Letter from Vatican City," which appeared in two issues of the magazine (December 29, 1962, and January 9, 1965).

[37] Trude B. Feldman, correspondent for *The Jewish Press,* a New York weekly.

[38] Boston *Record-American,* December 6, 1964.

[39] *Time,* August 21, 1964.

[40] *Reader's Digest,* August 1968.

[41] *The New York Times,* July 4, 1965.

[42] James Kavanaugh, *A Modern Priest Looks at His Outdated Church* (New York: Trident Press, 1967).

[43] James Finn in a review of *Exploding Church: From Catholicism to catholicism,* by Frederick Franck (New York: Delacorte Press, 1968).

[44] Mrs. R. E. Voght, Birmingham, Michigan, in "Letters," *Look,* February 11, 1964.

[45] *The Crusader,* quoted in the *Reader's Digest.*

[46] Joan Sweeney, Boston *Sunday Herald,* April 7, 1968.

[47] *Time,* August 21, 1964.

[48] *Time,* July 12, 1968.

[49] *Time,* August 21, 1964.

[50] *Ibid.*

[51] *Ibid.*

[52] Michael Novak, *Saturday Evening Post,* December 28, 1968, and January 11, 1969.

[53] Clarence W. Hall, author of *Adventurers for God,* excerpted in the *Reader's Digest,* August 1968.

[54] Boston *Traveler,* April 3, 1967.

55 Boston *Record-American,* April 26, 1964.
56 Letter from Cardinal Cushing to Joseph DeMambro, 1964.
57 Boston *Record-American,* June 1, 1964.

CHAPTER TWENTY/*MAKING THE ROUNDS WITH CUSHING*

1 *Pilot,* June 16, 1962.
2 *Time,* August 21, 1964.
3 *The World's Cardinal,* published by the Daughters of St. Paul (Boston, 1964).
4 Sent to Ralph Tedeschi in 1968.
5 CBS–TV documentary with Harry Reasoner, May 14, 1968.
6 John H. Fenton, *Salt of the Earth: An Informal Portrait of Richard Cardinal Cushing* (New York: Coward-McCann, 1951).
7 *Ibid.*
8 Joseph Dever, *Cushing of Boston: A Candid Portrait* (Boston: Bruce Humphries, 1965).

CHAPTER TWENTY-ONE/*IN THE EYE OF A HURRICANE*

1 WBZ–TV interview with Arch MacDonald, June 30, 1964.
2 Robert Gannon, S.J., *The Cardinal Spellman Story* (New York: Doubleday, 1962).
3 *Good Housekeeping,* May 1966.
4 Boston *Traveler,* March 30, 1968.
5 Boston *Herald,* May 12, 1964.
6 At the Suenens lecture.
7 *This Week,* September 22, 1969.
8 *Reader's Digest,* August 1968.
9 Boston *Sunday Herald-Traveler,* January 5, 1969.
10 John H. Fenton, *Salt of the Earth: An Informal Portrait of Richard Cardinal Cushing* (New York: Coward-McCann, 1965).
11 *Ibid.*
12 Joseph Dever, *Cushing of Boston: A Candid Portrait* (Boston: Bruce Humphries, 1965).

CHAPTER TWENTY-TWO/*LAST LOOK AT IRELAND*

1 Speech Cushing gave in Ireland when he blessed a new chapel and novitiate wing for the Franciscan Missionaries of Mary at Loughglynn, Roscommon. Quoted in *The Catholic Standard,* August 20, 1965.
2 Boston *Record-American,* July 3, 1965.

[3] Note from Cushing to Francis Kelly.
[4] Interview with Francis Kelly.
[5] WBZ–TV interview with Arch MacDonald, June 30, 1964.
[6] *Ibid.*
[7] Joseph Dever, *Cushing of Boston: A Candid Portrait* (Boston: Bruce Humphries, 1965).
[8] Joseph M. DeMambro.
[9] Boston *Herald,* August 5, 1965.
[10] *The Catholic Standard,* August 20, 1965.
[11] Boston *Record-American,* March 26, 1968.
[12] *The Catholic Standard,* August 21, 1965.
[13] *Ibid.*
[14] Boston *Record-American,* August 19, 1965.
[15] *Ibid.*
[16] *The Catholic Standard,* August 27, 1965.
[17] "Faithful Is Ireland," *Catholic Digest,* March 1946.
[18] Boston *Record-American,* August 19, 1965.
[19] Boston *Globe,* October 27, 1965.
[20] *The New York Times,* October 5, 1965.
[21] *Ibid.*
[22] *Ibid.*

CHAPTER TWENTY-THREE / *SHADY SIDE OF THE HILL*

[1] Boston *Record-American,* November 10, 1967.
[2] The phrase is from *Time.*
[3] Speech in Topsfield, Massachusetts, August 7, 1968.
[4] Anthony Athanas, owner of Pier Four, sponsored the dinner on December 13, 1965.
[5] Boston *Herald,* May 26, 1966.
[6] Cushing was speaking at St. John the Evangelist Church in Hopkinton. See Boston *Record-American,* October 16, 1966.
[7] Boston *Herald,* July 19, 1967.
[8] Boston *Record-American,* November 17, 1967.
[9] *Ibid.*
[10] Boston *Herald,* May 5, 1968.
[11] An enlarged Blinstrub's Village was built on a South Boston site overlooking Malibu Beach in the fall of 1969. Thanks to Cushing, again, an array of topflight entertainers performed at the "inaugural."
[12] Lawrence H. Fuchs, *John F. Kennedy and American Catholicism,* New York: Meredith Press, 1967).
[13] Boston *Record-American,* April 10, 1968.

14 Boston *Globe,* April 10, 1968.
15 Boston *Sunday Globe,* December 28, 1968.

CHAPTER TWENTY-FOUR/*MORE PRIESTS AND FEWER BABIES?*

1 CBS–TV documentary with Harry Reasoner, May 14, 1968.
2 *Time,* May 10, 1969.
3 The Reverend George J. Hafner, "Don't Call Me Father," in "Speaking Out," *Saturday Evening Post,* June 29, 1968.
4 *Ibid.*
5 Published by Trident Press, New York, in 1967.
6 Quoted in *Look,* June 29, 1968.
7 *Time,* February 23, 1968.
8 *Time,* July 10, 1964.
9 WBZ–TV interview with Arch MacDonald, June 30, 1964.
10 At Jimmy's Harborside Restaurant, Boston.
11 Joseph Dever, *Cushing of Boston: A Candid Portrait* (Boston, Bruce Humphries, 1965).
12 *Time,* May 10, 1968.
13 James Kavanaugh, *A Modern Priest Looks At His Outdated Church* (New York: Trident Press, 1967).
14 According to Edward Marciniak, executive director of the Chicago Commission on Human Relations.
15 *Newsweek,* April 18, 1966.
16 *Ibid.*
17 *The Christian Century,* April 13, 1966.
18 *Time,* April 15, 1966.
19 Boston *Herald-Traveler,* April 9, 1968.
20 Boston *Sunday Globe,* May 12, 1968.
21 Boston *Globe,* June 24, 1968.
22 Gregory Baum, O.S.A., in *The Commonweal.*
23 Lawrence H. Fuchs, *John F. Kennedy and American Catholicism* (New York: Meredith Press, 1967).
24 In *The New England Journal of Medicine.*
25 *Ibid.*
26 WBZ–TV interview with Arch MacDonald, June 20, 1964.
27 *The New York Times,* June 24, 1965.
28 *Ibid.*
29 Paul Benzaquin's talk show.
30 Lester Zwick of the Boston *Record-American* and Frederick O'Neal of the Boston *Globe.* Interview with Zwick.
31 *Look,* December 10, 1966.

[32] *Ibid.*

[33] *Ibid.*

[34] *Time,* October 4, 1968.

[35] James Kavanaugh, *A Modern Priest Looks at His Outdated Church* (New York: Trident Press, 1967).

[36] *Congressional Record,* May 3, 1966, p. 9128.

[37] Patrick O'Keene, Boston *Sunday Herald-Traveler,* September 1, 1969.

[38] *Ibid.*

[39] *Ibid.*

CHAPTER TWENTY-FIVE/*THE CHURCH IN FOMENT*

[1] At the thirty-second diocesan congress of the league.

[2] Michael Novak, "The Underground Church," *Saturday Evening Post,* December 28, 1968.

[3] *Time,* May 21, 1968.

[4] *Ibid.*

[5] Boston *Globe,* May 23, 1968.

[6] *Ibid.*

[7] Boston *Globe,* April 21, 1969. Cushing addressed more than a thousand members of the Roman Catholic Archdiocesan Central Council of the Society of St. Vincent de Paul at its twentieth annual Communion breakfast at the Statler Hilton Hotel.

[8] Boston *Globe,* April 21, 1969.

[9] Boston *Globe,* May 11, 1969.

[10] *Time,* May 9, 1969.

[11] *Ibid.*

[12] *Time,* August 21, 1964.

[13] James Michael Curley, *I'd Do It Again! A Record of All My Uproarious Years* (Englewood Cliffs, N.J.: Prentice-Hall, 1957).

[14] Murray B. Levin, *The Compleat Politician: Political Strategy in Massachusetts* (Indianapolis: Bobbs-Merrill, 1962). Written in collaboration with George Blackwood.

[15] *Ibid.*

[16] Boston *Globe,* June 14, 1967.

[17] Boston *Globe,* July 1, 1969.

[18] *Ibid.*

[19] The cardinal wrote to Kelly in 1968.

[20] Boston *Herald,* March 31, 1964.

[21] Boston *Herald,* January 2, 1968.

[22] *The New York Times,* October 27, 1968.

[23] *Time,* November 1, 1969.

[24] Boston *Globe,* October 24, 1968.

25 *Ibid.*

26 Boston *Globe,* October 25, 1968.

27 Boston *Globe,* November 7, 1969.

28 Boston *Globe,* October 25, 1968.

29 *Time,* November 15, 1968.

30Boston *Herald-Traveler,* November 7, 1968.

31 *Christianity Today,* November 22, 1968.

32 *Time,* August 1, 1969.

33 *The New York Times,* August 3, 1969.

CHAPTER TWENTY-SIX/*CHURCHMAN OF THE CENTURY*

1 "Howard Nelson Show," in a taped conversation that was not heard by the radio audience, February 16, 1969.

2 *Pilot,* August 2, 1969.

3 James Michael Curley, *I'd Do It Again! A Record of All My Uproarious Years* (Englewood Cliffs, N.J.: Prentice-Hall, 1957).

4 Abigail Adams Homans, *Town & Country,* March 1968.

INDEX